Judging Faith, Punishing Sin
Inquisitions and Consistories in the Early Modern World

Judging Faith, Punishing Sin breaks new ground by offering the first comparative treatment of Catholic inquisitions and Calvinist consistories, offering scholars a new framework for analysing religious reform and social discipline in the great Christian age of reformation. Global in scope, both institutions played critical roles in prosecuting deviance, implementing religious uniformity, and promoting moral discipline in the social upheaval of the Reformation. Rooted in local archives and addressing specific themes, the essays survey the state of scholarship and chart directions for future inquiry and, taken as a whole, demonstrate the unique convergence of penitential practice, legal innovation, church authority, and state power, and how these forces transformed Christianity. Bringing together leading scholars across four continents, this volume is an invaluable contribution to our understanding of religion in the early modern world. University students and scholars alike will appreciate its clear introduction to scholarly debates and cutting edge scholarship.

Charles H. Parker is a Professor of History at St Louis University, Missouri.

Gretchen Starr-LeBeau is an Associate Professor in the Department of Religion at Principia College, Illinois.

Judging Faith, Punishing Sin

Inquisitions and Consistories in the Early Modern World

Edited by

CHARLES H. PARKER

Saint Louis University

GRETCHEN STARR-LEBEAU

Principia College

CAMBRIDGE
UNIVERSITY PRESS

CAMBRIDGE
UNIVERSITY PRESS

University Printing House, Cambridge CB2 8BS, United Kingdom

One Liberty Plaza, 20th Floor, New York, NY 10006, USA

477 Williamstown Road, Port Melbourne, VIC 3207, Australia

314-321, 3rd Floor, Plot 3, Splendor Forum, Jasola District Centre, New Delhi - 110025, India

79 Anson Road, #06-04/06, Singapore 079906

Cambridge University Press is part of the University of Cambridge.

It furthers the University's mission by disseminating knowledge in the pursuit of education, learning and research at the highest international levels of excellence.

www.cambridge.org
Information on this title: www.cambridge.org/9781316505861

First published 2017
First paperback edition 2020

A catalogue record for this publication is available from the British Library

Library of Congress Cataloging in Publication data
NAMES: Parker, Charles H., 1958– editor. | Starr-LeBeau, Gretchen D., editor.
TITLE: Judging faith, punishing sin : inquisitions and consistories in the early modern world / edited by Charles H. Parker, Saint Louis University; Gretchen Starr-LeBeau, Principia College.
DESCRIPTION: 1 [edition]. | New York : Cambridge University Press, 2016. | Includes bibliographical references.
IDENTIFIERS: LCCN 2016022435 | ISBN 9781107140240 (Hardback)
SUBJECTS: LCSH: Ecclesiastical courts–History–16th century. | Ecclesiastical courts–History–17th century. | Ecclesiastical courts–History–18th century. | Catholic Church–Discipline. | Protestant churches–Discipline.
CLASSIFICATION: LCC KB1580 .J83 2016 | DDC 262.9–dc23 LC Record available at https://lccn.loc.gov/2016022435

ISBN 978-1-107-14024-0 Hardback
ISBN 978-1-316-50586-1 Paperback

Contents

List of Maps		*page* ix
List of Tables		xi
List of Contributors		xiii
Acknowledgments		xv
	Introduction	1
	Charles H. Parker and Gretchen Starr-LeBeau	

PART I INSTITUTIONAL CONTEXTS AND OPERATIONS

SECTION A	Local Contexts and Regional Variations	15
1	Consistories	15
	Raymond A. Mentzer	
2	Inquisitions	28
	Christopher F. Black	
SECTION B	Tribunals and Jurisdictions	40
3	Consistories	40
	Margo Todd	
4	Inquisitions	52
	Gretchen Starr-LeBeau and Kimberly Lynn	
5	Consistories and Civil Authorities	66
	Sara Beam	
6	Episcopal Courts in Iberia, Italy, and Latin America	77
	Edward Behrend-Martínez	
7	Church Courts in England	89
	Martin Ingram	

SECTION C Judges and Shepherds   104

8 Consistories   104
   William Naphy

9 Inquisitions   116
   Kimberly Lynn

SECTION D Inquisition and Consistory Records   128

10 Consistories   128
    Christian Grosse, translated by Charles H. Parker

11 Inquisitions   140
    Kim Siebenhüner, translated by Heidi Bek

PART II CONSISTORIES AND INQUISITIONS IN ACTION

SECTION E Programs of Moral and Religious Reform   155

12 Consistories   155
    Philippe Chareyre, translated by Charles H. Parker

13 Inquisitions   167
    Doris Moreno Martínez, translated by Gretchen Starr-LeBeau

SECTION F Victims as Actors   180

14 Consistories   180
    Timothy Fehler

15 Inquisitions   193
    Lu Ann Homza

SECTION G Negotiating Penance   204

16 Consistories   204
    Karen E. Spierling

17 Inquisitions   215
    John F. Chuchiak IV

SECTION H Gender on Trial: Attitudes toward Femininity
and Masculinity   229

18 Consistories   229
    Jeffrey Watt

19 Inquisitions   240
    Allyson M. Poska

PART III ECCLESIASTICAL DISCIPLINE'S EXPANDING
REACH AND DECLINE

SECTION I   Disciplinary Institutions in the Atlantic World   253

20 Consistories   253
    Mark Meuwese

21 Inquisitions   266
    Allyson M. Poska

SECTION J   Disciplinary Institutions in an Asian
Environment   279

22 Consistories   279
    Hendrik E. Niemeijer

23 Inquisitions   292
    Bruno Feitler

SECTION K   The Endgame: The Decline of Institutional
Correction   306

24 Consistories   306
    Joke Spaans

25 Inquisitions   317
    James E. Wadsworth

Conclusion: Reformations of Penance and Scholarly Renascences
    of Disciplinary Institutions   331
    E. William Monter

Bibliography   341
Index   377

Maps

1 Inquisition Tribunals in Iberia   *page* xvii
2 Inquisition Tribunals in Italy   xviii
3 Locations of Reformed Consistories in Europe   xix
4 Inquisitions and Consistories in the Early Modern World   xx

Tables

12.1 Distribution of Discipline Cases before the Nîmes
   Consistory   *page* 163
22.1 Ethnic Identity of the Censured in Batavia   286

Contributors

SARA BEAM is Associate Professor of History at the University of Victoria

EDWARD BEHREND-MARTÍNEZ is Professor of History at Appalachian State University

CHRISTOPHER F. BLACK is Professor Emeritus in Italian History and currently an Honorary Professorial Research Fellow at the University of Glasgow

PHILIPPE CHAREYRE is Professor of History at the Université de Pau et des Pays de l'Adour

JOHN F. CHUCHIAK IV is Professor of History at Missouri State University

TIMOTHY FEHLER is Professor of History at Furman University

BRUNO FEITLER is Professor of History at the Universidade Federal de São Paulo (UNIFESP)

CHRISTIAN GROSSE is Professor of History and Anthropology of Modern Christianity at the Université de Lausanne

LU ANN HOMZA is Professor of History and Dean for Educational Policy at William and Mary

MARTIN INGRAM is an Emeritus Fellow in History at Brasenose College, University of Oxford

KIMBERLY LYNN is Associate Professor in the Department of Liberal Studies at Western Washington University

RAYMOND A. MENTZER is Professor of Religious Studies and the Daniel J. Krumm Family Chair in Reformation Studies at the University of Iowa

MARK MEUWESE is Professor of History at the University of Winnipeg

E. WILLIAM MONTER is Professor of History Emeritus at Northwestern University

DORIS MORENO MARTÍNEZ is Professor of History at the Universitat Autònoma de Barcelona

WILLIAM NAPHY is Chair in History at the University of Aberdeen

HENDRIK E. NIEMEIJER is Research Director of the Centre for Indonesian Maritime Culture, History and Global Interactions at the Universitas Diponegoro, Semarang, Indonesia

CHARLES H. PARKER is Professor of History and the Eugene A. Hotfelder Professor in the Humanities at Saint Louis University

ALLYSON M. POSKA is Professor of History and Director of Women's and Gender Studies at the University of Mary Washington

KIM SIEBENHÜNER is SNF Forderprofessorin at the Historisches Institut der Universität Bern

JOKE SPAANS is Lecturer at the Universiteit Utrecht

KAREN E. SPIERLING is Associate Professor of History at Denison University

GRETCHEN STARR-LEBEAU is Associate Professor of Religion at Principia College

MARGO TODD is the Walter H. Annenberg Professor of History at the University of Pennsylvania

JAMES E. WADSWORTH is Professor of History at Stonehill College

JEFFREY WATT is Professor of History at the University of Mississippi

Acknowledgments

This volume is a tribute to many talented people of goodwill who not only made publication possible but also made the final version much better than it otherwise would have been. It is an honor to have worked with them and a pleasure to express our appreciation here. The intellectual quality of the volume rests on the outstanding work of the twenty-six contributors. They collaborated readily to make the volume as integrated as possible, completed drafts and revisions in good time (usually anyway), and endured space constraints and protracted periods of waiting with patience and grace. Many offered timely advice, and all lent us their support. Kimberly Lynn and Allyson Poska stepped up on short notice when two authors had to step away from the project, for which we are especially grateful. Special thanks to Ray Mentzer, Jeff Watt, and Bill Monter who gave translation assistance on the essays of Christian Grosse, Philippe Chareyre, and Kim Siebenhüner. We feel privileged to work in partnership with such fine historians.

Cambridge University Press has gained our deep respect and gratitude for taking on this project. Lew Bateman, senior acquisitions editor, recognized the value of a comparative study of religious discipline right away and encouraged us to make connections and think comprehensively. We are grateful for his support, wisdom, and guidance throughout the ups and downs of the review and publication processes. Several of his editorial assistants provided much useful practical help with manuscripts, agreements, and forms. We thank three anonymous reviewers who made a wide range of suggestions and criticisms that significantly enhanced the quality of the volume.

Our respective departments and colleagues at the University of Kentucky, then Principia College, and Saint Louis University provided consistent moral, intellectual, and financial support for which we are deeply grateful. We especially appreciate financial support for indexing the volume provided by Principia College and Saint Louis University. Many thanks also to Philip Koski, a PhD student at Saint Louis University, who assisted with editing during 2013–14; Dick Gilbreath in the Department of Geography at Kentucky, who produced the maps; and Susan Larson, who provided advice on the translation of Doris Moreno Martínez's essay.

Several contributors wished to make specific acknowledgments. Sara Beam thanks the Institut d'Études Avancées de Paris and the European Union Research Institutes for Advanced Study Fellowship program for their support in completing this project. Conversations with Graeme Murdock and Christian Grosse as well as the editorial suggestions of Marjorie Garson were also invaluable. Gretchen Starr-LeBeau thanks the American Philosophical Society for a sabbatical fellowship that provided time to work on this project in general and to write Chapter 4 in particular. Christian Grosse acknowledges support from the Swiss National Fund for Scientific Research and financed by the Faculty of Theology and Religious Studies at the University of Lausanne. He also thanks Noémie Poget, Amélie Isoz, and Salomon Rizzo. Willam Naphy thanks Lucas Kriner, doctoral student at St. Andrews University, for sharing statistical data on weekly attendance at Geneva consistory meetings. Edward Behrend-Martinez thanks Michael Behrent, Craig Caldwell, Scott Jessee, Ralph Lentz, Lucinda McCray, and Jason White – all of the European History writing group of Appalachian State University – for reading drafts of his chapter and providing valuable feedback. The supporting research for Bruno Feitler's chapter was funded by CNPq (Conselho Nacional de Desenvolvimento Científico e Tecnológico) and FAPESP (Fundação de Amparo à Pesquisa do Estado de São Paulo).

A number of the papers were presented in an early form at the Sixteenth Century Studies Conference in Cincinnati, Ohio, in October 2012. We all benefited considerably from the perceptive comments and questions raised by the various audiences.

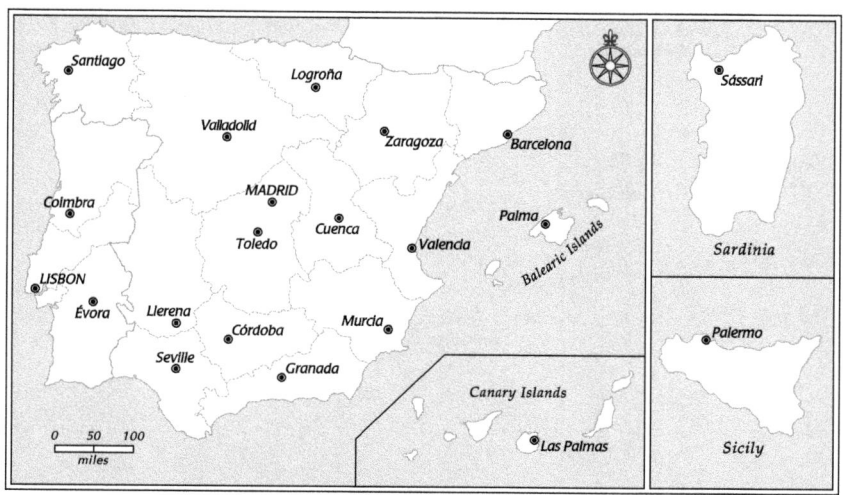

MAP 1 Inquisition Tribunals in Iberia, map by Richard Gilbreath

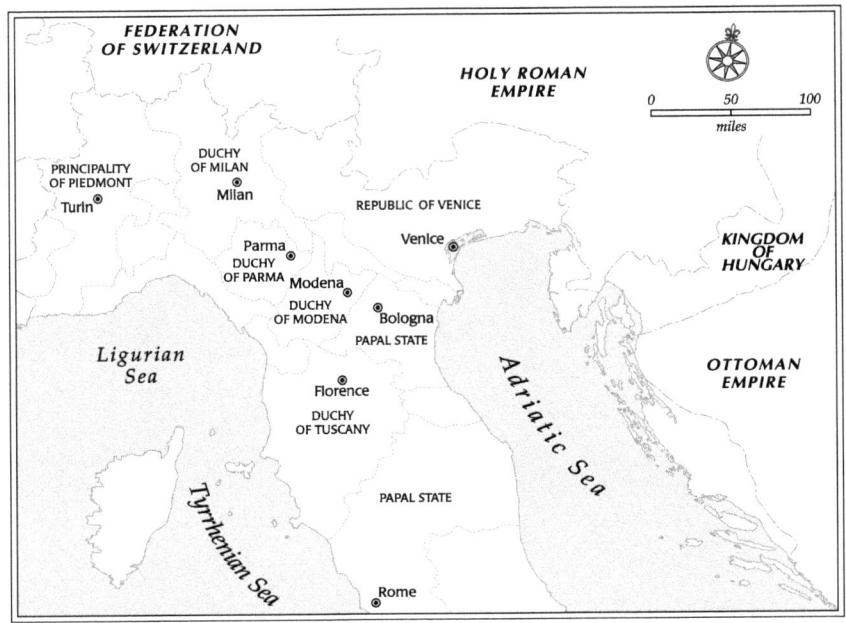

FEDERATION
OF SWITZERLAND

HOLY ROMAN
EMPIRE

0   50   100

miles

DUCHY
OF MILAN

PRINCIPALITY
OF PIEDMONT   Milan

Turin

REPUBLIC OF VENICE

KINGDOM
OF
HUNGARY

Venice

Parma
DUCHY
OF PARMA   Modena

DUCHY
OF MODENA   Bologna

PAPAL STATE

Ligurian
Sea

OTTOMAN
EMPIRE

Adriatic Sea

Florence
DUCHY
OF TUSCANY

Tyrrhenian Sea

PAPAL STATE

Rome

MAP 2 Inquisition Tribunals in Italy, map by Richard Gilbreath

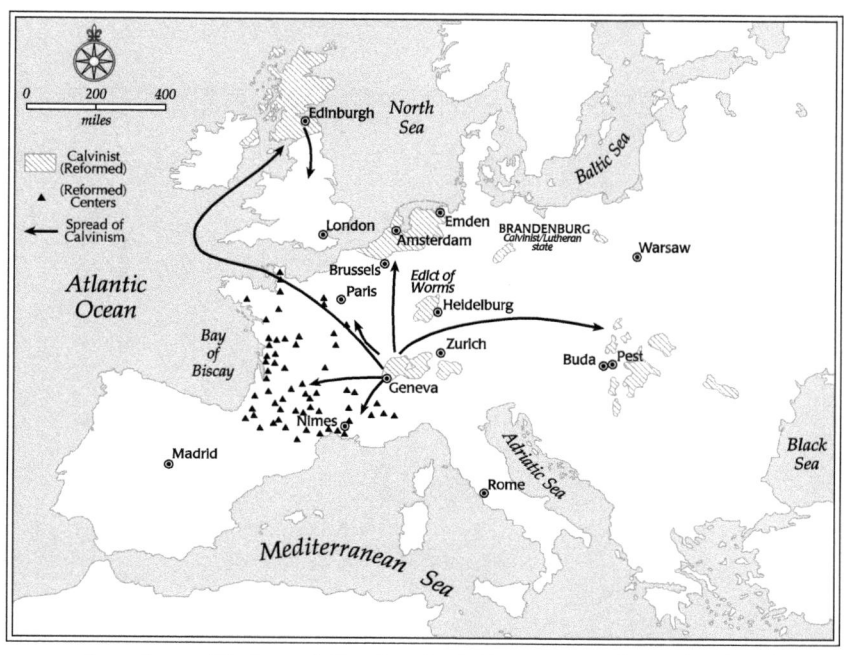

MAP 3 Locations of Reformed Consistories in Europe, map by Richard Gilbreath

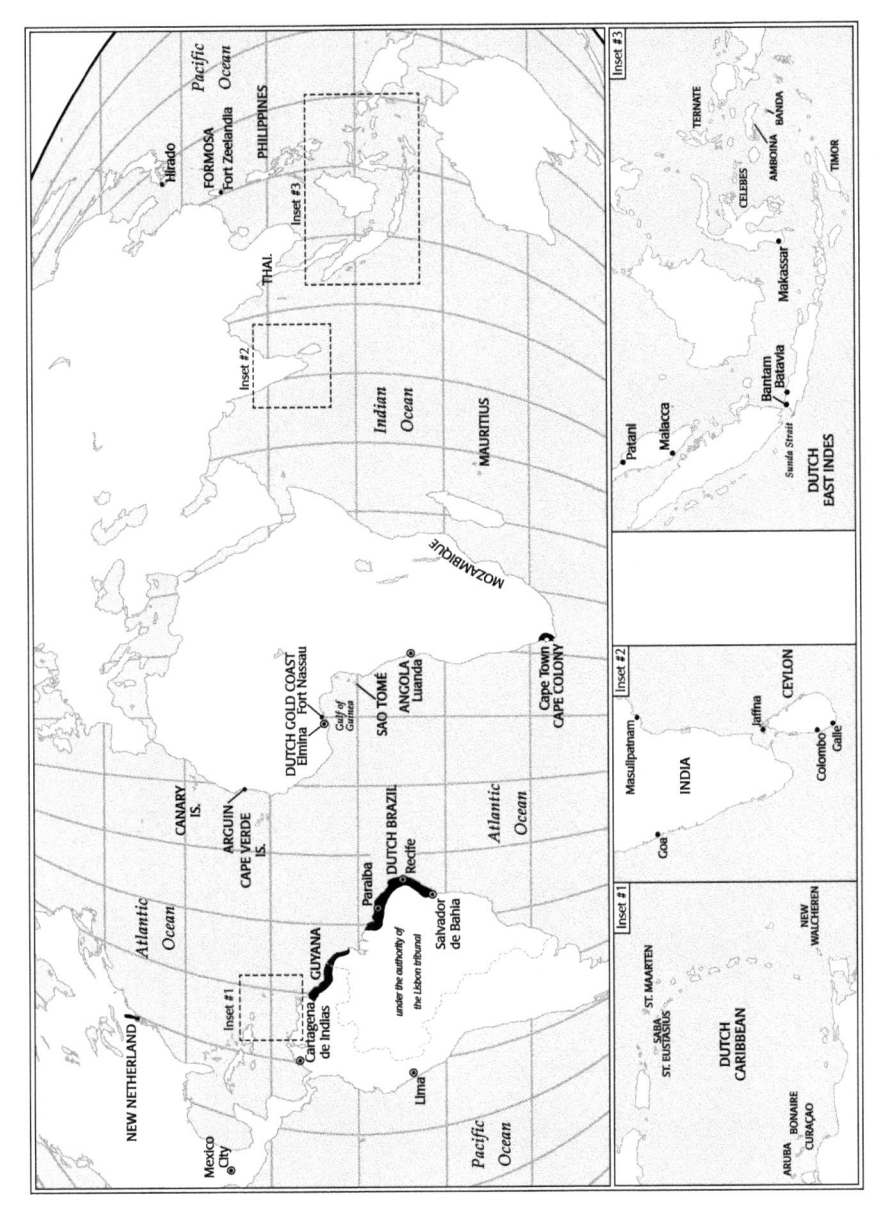

MAP 4 Inquisitions and Consistories in the Early Modern World, map by Richard Gilbreath

Introduction

Charles H. Parker and Gretchen Starr-LeBeau

Judgment and punishment loomed over early modern men and women. Of course, for Christians, there was the Final Judgment that awaited at the end of time, when the dead would rise from their graves and Christ would separate the saved from the damned. But Christians also knew that they could face a more immediate, present judgment from the ecclesiastical tribunals that regulated their parishes and congregations. Indeed, many thousands of men and women across many disparate lands stood before ecclesiastical tribunals in the early modern period as a result of accusations of heretical beliefs or moral transgressions. All faced judgment; countless suffered punishments ranging from rebuke and public humiliation, to banishment or whipping, up to and including in some cases death.

These widespread disciplinary campaigns not only addressed individual misdeeds; they also infused a sharpened sense of Christian identity into Catholic and Protestant churches in an era marked by intense religious strife. Across western Christendom's *longue durée*, the early modern period stands out as the paramount age of reforming and restructuring, emerging out of long-standing theological debates over authority, persistent criticisms of the clerical hierarchy, periodic demands for biblical authenticity, and intermittent preoccupations with idolaters, heretics, and Jews. The hardening of religious boundaries gave rise to an emphasis on discipline in both Catholic and Protestant dominions enacted through established penitential protocols for reconciliation and consolation. Confession and penitence bound together surveillance operations, ecclesiastical and civil courts, parishes, and sacraments. Consequently, religious discipline, performed through the processes of confession and penitence, formed a hallmark of early modern Christianity.

While hundreds of various disciplinary courts dotted the confessional map of Europe, two institutions central to implementing the programs of religious reformation were Catholic Inquisitions and Reformed Protestant (Calvinist) consistories. Originating as a means to extinguish heresy in the 1200s, Inquisitions became permanent tribunals in the fifteenth and sixteenth centuries in Spanish, Portuguese, and Italian territories with authority to try cases of suspected heresy. This volume focuses on early modern Inquisitions, rather than other Catholic disciplinary institutions such as ecclesiastical courts or state courts, for their distinctive linkage of ecclesiastical authority, state power, legal mechanisms, and theological oversight and moral discipline. Consistories also had a long history before the sixteenth century. In medieval Catholic usage, a consistory designated a conclave of clerics and referred specifically to formal gatherings of the College of Cardinals in Rome. With the advent of the Reformation, some German Protestant church districts reformed their courts and referred to them as consistories. In the Reformed tradition, the Genevan church under the direction of John Calvin developed the consistory as a board of pastors and lay elders who governed the congregation and prosecuted those charged with various moral infractions. Calvin's notion of the disciplinary function and organizational structure for the consistory took root in Reformed and some Lutheran churches, spreading from Poland and Lithuania in the east to France and across the Atlantic to the west, from Scotland in the north to Switzerland in the south, and to many points in between. Attention to consistories in this volume focuses on their functions in disciplining Calvinist communities as a point of comparison with the amending activity of Catholic Inquisitions. By limiting the volume to Calvinist consistories, rather than expanding to include other kinds of Protestant discipline, we have sharpened our comparative institutional focus with Inquisitions.

Since the 1970s, a large number of international scholars have revolutionized the study of both Catholic Inquisitions and Calvinist consistories. This agenda brought many scholars together in working especially on the Spanish Inquisition, but also on the Portuguese and Italian Inquisitions, following in the latter case in the pioneering footsteps of Carlo Ginzburg in the 1960s. This generation of scholars introduced quantitative, anthropological, social, and political approaches to the study of Inquisitions. For consistories, students of Robert Kingdon mined the records of the Genevan consistory, but scholars interested in the local reception of

Calvinism also focused on archival sources across Reformed territories to reconstruct the patterns and practices of discipline.

Interestingly, historical scholarship on Inquisitions and consistories has followed parallel trajectories, though with little intersection or cross-fertilization. The initial trend in research on both institutions from the 1960s to the 1980s concentrated on statistical analyses of records. Studies in various regions described how the various tribunals functioned, traced the ebb and flow of investigations for particular accusations over time, and called attention to the limitations of their authority in society. Inquisition scholars took the particularly rich administrative resources of the *Suprema* – the governing council of the Inquisition in Spain – and analyzed the summaries of 44,000 cases for patterns in accusations and sentencing, finally giving scholars a sense of the scale on which the Spanish Inquisition operated. The quantification of cases over extended periods of time – sometimes over hundreds of years – also gave scholars confidence to make big claims about the role of Calvinist religious discipline in the inexorable "civilizing process" described by the sociologist Norbert Elias.

Heinz Schilling maintained, for example, that Calvinist discipline contributed substantially to "the making of the modern mind."[1] In the last ten to fifteen years, scholarship on Inquisitions and consistories has given attention to the dynamics of local religious practices from different angles. Historians working on Calvinist and Catholic regions have supplemented inquisitorial or consistorial records with municipal and ecclesiastical archives to historicize religious practice and discipline in local social and cultural contexts. For example, studies have unpacked the cultural meanings of excommunication; reconstructed the hopes and fears of refugees and minorities; explored the intersections of gender, power, and authority; illustrated the changing discourse about the nature of religious practice in an age preoccupied with the presence of witches and devils; and illustrated the encounters between Christian clerics and indigenous peoples around the world.

For all the rich insight yielded by these lines of inquiry, scholarship on Catholic and Calvinist programs of discipline has remained in two divergent and self-contained fields of research and discourse. Language differences and nationalist alignments in European scholarship certainly have inhibited integrated, transregional, and cross-denominational perspectives. Academic societies, symposia, and conferences also have divided along these religious and national fault lines. Even more surprising, however, is the lack of internal comparative work among these institutions. Scholars working on Inquisitions have tended to focus their research on just one of the main tribunals – Spanish, Portuguese, or Italian – or even one tribunal within those Inquisitions, such as Toledo, Evora, or Venice. National and urban boundaries equally constrain studies of consistories. In part, this may be due to the abundance of records available to scholars of these institutions, as well as the linguistic challenges of working in several jurisdictions.

Despite the similarities in the historiographies of consistories and Inquisitions, there has been little effort to study them in juxtaposition to one another. A perception of incommensurability between Inquisitions and consistories most likely has formed a primary obstacle to comparative analysis. And there were important differences. Inquisition courts functioned as state courts authorized by the Papacy (or in the case of the Roman Inquisition, operated by the Papacy with some degree of local cooperation); they were staffed by a vast number of judges, canon lawyers, and clerical and lay functionaries; they had the right to use torture; and they possessed the authority to relax the accused over to the secular arm for execution. Conversely, consistories operated as the governing board of local Reformed churches and did not serve as independent courts. Furthermore, pastors, who shouldered manifold ministerial responsibilities, and unpaid elders, who held down full-time jobs, constituted the personnel of consistories. They could not torture or imprison anyone of their own volition – though they might work closely with state powers who could. Thus consistories did not possess the resources, the institutional structures, or the broad legal and punitive powers that Inquisitions wielded. While it is important to remain mindful of these disparities, overestimating differences or discounting the possibilities for comparisons also deprive historians of opportunities for identifying cross-confessional patterns in religious discipline.

Contemporaries often equated the two institutions. Protestant opponents of Calvinist discipline regularly classified consistories as new forms of Inquisition. One such detractor, Johannes Uytenbogaert, charged that the Reformed Church order in the Netherlands resembled a Genevan-styled Inquisition because it compelled pastors and elders to "go into the homes of their members and see what books they have."[2] Uytenbogaert was by no means original; he was simply parroting well-known analogies made by Protestants since the formation of the Genevan consistory. A range of writers who championed freedom of conscience and toleration equated consistories with Inquisitions and Calvinist discipline with the revival of "papal tyranny" throughout the early modern period. These polemics highlight the symbolic import and coercive force of these self-consciously reforming Catholic and Protestant organizations. The critics' denunciations also allude to the common legal and ecclesiastical heritage of Inquisitions and consistories so evident to people in the sixteenth and seventeenth centuries.

Both institutions, as well as episcopal and civil courts, belonged to the intersection of law, religious authority, and secular power emerging from the rediscovery of Roman law in the High Middle Ages. Adapted from Roman law, inquisitorial procedure and episcopal visitations indisputably shaped the Inquisitions of the early modern period. Calvin might have justified his ecclesiology from the New Testament, but he found models for church governance and discipline from canon law, medieval episcopal courts, and his own training in law. In many respects, consistories in Reformed lands took on the quotidian responsibilities of Catholic (diocesan) ecclesiastical courts, adjudicating disputes and punishing public and private moral transgressions. Yet the extraordinary religious and cultural program of transforming Catholic communities into Calvinist ones bred an urgency and determination that likened consistories to Inquisitions, especially from 1550 to 1650, the most severe period of confessional conflict.

Similarly, almost all Inquisitions and consistories depended on state power in some form to carry out their work; each lost its capacity to discipline when states withdrew their support in the eighteenth century. Furthermore, the apparent distinctions in the ability to punish may not have been as stark as it appears at first glance. In some cases, such as Scotland, consistories' authority to punish verged on the prerogatives exercised by inquisitors. Even in Geneva, where the consistory did not seem to have much coercive power, close connections between criminal courts and the consistory – and the presence of individuals who served both institutions simultaneously – resulted in a more punitive corporal punishment from consistories and their allies than scholars previously grasped. Thus the combination of functional similarities and structural distinctions among Inquisitions and consistories invite a comparative approach. But merely juxtaposing these two institutions and their impact on surrounding societies, while fascinating, is not our ultimate goal. Rather, our aim with this volume is to raise, and begin to answer, two related questions. First, we want to point the way to a sustained comparative analysis of these two institutions, one that provides insights into these bodies specifically as institutional entities with a significant, albeit controversial, impact on the places where they functioned. Second, we contend that a close study of these institutions suggests broader, cross-confessional patterns in disciplinary practice in Catholic and Protestant communities in Europe and overseas.

Judging Faith, Punishing Sin represents an initial step in meeting these ambitious goals by attempting to introduce a cross-confessional approach to the study of penitential conventions in the early modern period. The essays in this volume examine the multifaceted dimensions of Catholic Inquisitions and Reformed consistories in comparative perspective. Rooted in local archives and addressing specific themes, the essays survey the state of scholarship and chart directions for future inquiry. Since scholarship on both Inquisitions and consistories also suffer from a dearth of intracomparative study, this volume suggests fruitful lines of exploration within each field of research. These comparisons isolate thematic aspects of inquisitional and consistorial enterprises and contextualize them in their distinct settings to connect local actions to the large-scale patterns of religious discipline that historians refer to generally as confessionalization. Developed by Schilling and Wolfgang Reinhard in the 1980s, the thesis maintains that confessional identity in Europe grew out of a cooperative program of social discipline by territorial (or national) states and churches in the Reformation. This volume does not aim to critique the theory per se, but to promote and add nuance to the comparative study of discipline and religious identity.

In taking on a topic of this immense scope, it has been necessary to make several decisions about coverage and focus. One choice was to give exclusive attention to Inquisitions and Reformed consistories from among all the diverse disciplinary bodies within Europe in order to bring analytical clarity to the common and divergent programs, experiences, strategies, and influences relevant to them. Certainly, Lutheran, Jesuit, Anabaptist, and Jansenist forms – to name a few – also merit comparative study, and we believe these essays point out directions for future research into cross-confessional discipline and religious identity. A second choice was to privilege thematic analysis over territorial coverage. Each author in this volume brings a particular analytical expertise that is vital for a comparative study. Yet this particular orientation also means that certain areas receive substantial attention, including Iberia, Italy, Switzerland, France, the Netherlands, England, and Scotland, at the expense of other regions, such as Eastern Europe, Scandinavia, the Baltic, and Ireland. We are convinced that the analytical focus of these essays will generate fresh lines of inquiry relevant to all of early modern Europe and its colonies. A third choice was to keep the volume a manageable size by severely limiting the endnotes. We thank our contributors for their forbearance with the challenges that this posed.

The volume threads together three themes. Part I, "Institutional Contexts and Operations," establishes the bureaucratic framework of early modern Inquisitions and consistories, and highlights key research being done as part of what might be called a "new institutional history." Specifically, it signals a growing recognition of the importance of individuals – be they elders, inquisitors, pastors, judges, lawyers, notaries, or other functionaries – as active creators of these institutions both in their commonalities and in their local particulars. This process of construction as presented here has several elements, from the broad regional variations that also reveal common practices, to the functioning of these tribunals as only two among many competing (and sometimes cooperating) courts and jurisdictions, to the central place of lay and clerical bureaucrats in fashioning these institutions in text and in praxis. These essays collectively chart a path for future scholars to tease out these processes in a systematically comparative way. Raymond A. Mentzer (Chapter 1) and Christopher F. Black (Chapter 2) launch the volume by setting forth the origins, spread, and regional variations of consistories and Inquisitions, respectively. The operation of both organizations depended on local circumstance and personnel, though they both also networked widely across Catholic and Protestant worlds. Furthermore, their intracomparative approach – bringing together scholarly insights on Iberian and Italian Inquisitions, and consistories from across Reformed Europe, respectively – provides an object lesson for scholars on the critical importance of a multilingual, multiterritorial approach to studying Inquisitions and consistories. Together, they build on the insights of Francisco Bethencourt and point the way forward to an approach that reveals the distinctive variation in these apparently monolithic entities.

The legal bases for prosecuting misbelief and misconduct, as Gretchen Starr-LeBeau, Kimberly Lynn, and Margo Todd demonstrate, were far more enunciated for Inquisitions than for consistories. Starr-LeBeau and Lynn (Chapter 4) make clear that inquisitors followed a well-established body of canon and civil law – in which many trained – that had a standardizing influence on practice. Yet Todd (Chapter 3) establishes that Scottish sessions, and consistories throughout Europe, borrowed heavily from ecclesiastical and civil courts in their pursuit of peace and orderliness. Though consistories absorbed more local and lay culture, they adapted the judicial forms that were embedded and even exemplified in inquisitorial tribunals. The three chapters by Sara Beam (Chapter 5),

Edward Behrend-Martínez (Chapter 6), and Martin Ingram (Chapter 7) delineate the ecclesiastical and secular counterparts to Inquisitions and consistories calling attention to the vast archipelago of episcopal and civil courts in the early modern period. Considering diocesan courts in Iberia, Italy, and Latin America, Behrend-Martínez underscores the sporadic and extraordinary nature of investigative work that waxed and waned with fluctuating anxieties about heresy and Judaizing. Though it was a consistent public presence, the Genevan consistory, according to Sara Beam, bore close resemblance to an Inquisition, as elders and pastors cooperated closely with secular courts to crack down on crime and uphold godly society. Bereft of both early modern institutions, England retained an episcopal court system, yet one can discern their methods of proceeding in Martin Ingram's treatment of the English ecclesiastical court structure. It is through his clear examination of the episcopal courts that a medieval heritage common to Inquisitions and consistories emerges most vividly.

Chapters 8 and 9 turn attention to the underappreciated role of individuals in fashioning these tribunals, their actions, and their self-presentation and documentation in written sources. William Naphy and Kimberly Lynn remind us that complex matrices of personal relationships, familial alliances, and corporate allegiances underlay these institutions. Indeed, their contributions caution against the church-state binaries that run through most historical narratives. These judicial tribunals were staffed with idiosyncratic individuals who came to a variety of different conclusions even as they conducted their business in the interest of the common good. Christian Grosse (Chapter 10) and Kim Siebenhüner (Chapter 11) address the parallel challenges that sources from these institutions pose and propose strategies for how scholars might interpret the institutions in ways that contemporaries understood them. Both authors insist that what for historians is the classic problem of factuality in the documented record actually stems from the gap between the logic of courts and the experiences of individuals brought before the tribunals. And both provide a clear indication of the functional similarities of these institutions as legal tribunals, and demonstrate the insights that legal history can contribute to understanding the records generated by these bodies.

Part II, "Consistories and Inquisitions in Action," takes up new scholarly understandings of the messy interactions among church officers, civil authorities, the accused, and those who turned them in. In so doing, this part points out a critical need for scholars to reexamine the individual interactions that built these institutions in practice. Philippe Chareyre (Chapter 12) and Doris Moreno Martínez (Chapter 13) showcase the use of space and spectacle within the programs of moral reform. These chapters highlight key interpretive strategies through which commonalities between Inquisitions and consistories come into focus. Catholic and Calvinist officers both employed what Bartolomé Bennassar memorably described in an essay on the Spanish Inquisition as a "pedagogy of fear"; both also employed exemplary punishment and surveillance over and manipulation of public space to refashion Christian society. Shifting focus to the accused, Timothy Fehler and Lu Ann Homza in Chapters 14 and 15 explore the strategies of men and women within the grip of disciplinary institutions. Fehler provides ample evidence that defendants before consistories, with the possible exception of Scotland and Geneva, had a wide range of options at their disposal between the extremes of complete submission and outright defiance. The legal environment and harsher penalties of early modern Inquisitions both circumscribed defendants and provided a mechanism of defense, as Homza demonstrates. Those brought before both consistories and Inquisitions, these authors make clear, were not helpless victims but often active and even defiant in their self-defense. In Chapters 16 and 17, Karen E. Spierling and John F. Chuchiak IV move from tactics of the accused to Inquisitions and consistories as a site of negotiation – among inquisitors, pastors, elders; between disciplinary officials and secular officials; and between disciplinary officials and those they attempted to discipline. Spierling offers a glimpse into the constantly changing social and political landscape for pastors and elders as they had to broker a place in society with municipalities and found it necessary to bargain with and among church members. Chuchiak, by contrast, emphasizes negotiations among inquisitors, defendants, and theological consultants as all parties stretched legal requirements variously for the advantage or disadvantage of the accused. In Chapters 18 and 19, Jeffrey Watt and Allyson M. Poska utilize the lens of gender to scrutinize the agency of the accused. These chapters use distinct approaches to emphasize the fundamentally gendered nature of religious discipline, and the patriarchal assumptions that undergirded the rulings of these profoundly masculine institutions. Poska notes the gendering of heresy accusations, and the sexual humiliation of female defendants in particular, while also emphasizing women's use of gender expectations in crafting a defense. Watt by contrast marshals quantitative evidence to show that consistories pursued male miscreants more than women. Watt states that most women accepted the disciplined social and domestic order, as patriarchal as it was, even though this order meant that wives had to return to abusive husbands.

Part III, "Ecclesiastical Discipline's Expanding Reach and Decline," traces these disciplinary institutions across space and time. Empire building pushed Christianity to the "ends of the earth," and wherever missionaries dared to convert, inquisitors, pastors, and elders attempted to police. The new environments for western Christianity created enormous cultural difficulties for Catholic and Protestant officers as Mark Meuwese (Chapter 20), Allyson M. Poska (Chapter 21), Hendrik E. Niemeijer (Chapter 22), and Bruno Feitler (Chapter 23) demonstrate. In the Americas, Poska and Meuwese note that on the surface, the scope and function of the two institutions could hardly be more dissimilar. The Reformed presence in North America was peripheral and consistories looked inward to the pastoral needs of European settlers and personnel of the Dutch West India Company. By contrast, by the end of the sixteenth century, inquisitorial tribunals were occupying a central place in colonial centers in Central and South America, promoting moral reform and ferreting out Judaizers. Yet neither institution confronted the challenge of indigenous beliefs. Native peoples were not tried in Inquisition courts, but rather through extraordinary tribunals that functioned like Inquisitions but were technically distinct, and consistories focused only on those within the confessional community. In contrast to the Americas, consistories and Inquisitions in Asia functioned in a more parallel fashion, though the latter operated on a much smaller scale. Hendrik E. Niemeijer relates the success of Calvinist proselytizing in the East Indies, which aligned with the political ambitions of the Dutch East India Company. Discipline in the colonial setting served to impose a Christian order and morality in public space. Inquisitions in Goa, Feitler recounts, also supported the imperial priorities of the Portuguese. There, Inquisitions even exerted policing powers over indigenous non-Christians, a particular feature of the overseas Portuguese Inquisition.

These four chapters bring a renewed appreciation for institutional religious discipline as a unique trait of early modern Christianity and its support of European empires. One wonders from these chapters how the sustained interactions among church officers with indigenous societies affected attitudes about moral discipline in Europe. Furthermore, these chapters point out the important work that still needs to be done in combing through the scattered documentation on colonial institutions of religious discipline. That work could help piece together a broader comparative picture of these institutions, shine a spotlight on the role of race in these tribunals' activities, and integrate our understanding of colonial tribunals into the twinned narratives of Inquisitions and consistories on the one hand, and early modern empires on the other.

The ecclesiastical machinery for prosecuting misbelief and misbehavior underwent significant transformation in the eighteenth century. Joke Spaans (Chapter 24) and James E. Wadsworth (Chapter 25) conclude this part by accounting for the fundamental changes to these disciplinary regimes. The traditional narrative credits Enlightenment rationalism with curtailing the most extreme forms of religious intolerance in European societies. Wadsworth and Spaans both counter that these changes had little to do with rational thought, but resulted largely from the shifting jurisdictional grounds between civil authorities and ecclesiastical tribunals. Spanish and Portuguese governments transferred greater prerogatives to civil officers, just as church domains in Reformed Protestant polities fell increasingly in the realm of secular law enforcement. Both Catholic and Protestant clergy appealed to individual consciences to instill moral self-discipline in their flocks; both regarded liberalism as the primary threat to true religion and order. Both essays identify the need for further study into the altered relations between church and state, the advent of an industrial economy, and the expansion of intellectual culture, all of which seem to foster an emphasis on the conscience as the locus of religious discipline.

It is fitting that one of the only historians to work extensively on both Inquisitions and consistories, E. William Monter, concludes the volume by highlighting the cross-confessional concern with penance in the early modern period. As Monter ably notes, both Calvinists and Catholics identified some sins as grave enough to merit creating an extensive network whereby sins and sinners were sought out and sinners identified and publicly shamed. In effect, secular and sacred authorities worked together to allocate significant resources toward the project of effective penance, contrition, and reformation. For all their differences, consistories and Inquisitions shared this common motive-force. Monter rightly notes that the scholarship on these two institutions most identified with early modern religious discipline have taken different trajectories, which has obscured an investigation of parallels. It is also possible that Inquisitions, as more instantiated institutions, received earlier attention per se, while research on consistories emerged more organically from broader studies of Reformed communities. But those historiographical trajectories, however distinct, are coming together in a cross-confessional study of religious discipline that weaves together the insights of multiple strands of research to provide new understandings of the parts and the whole.

Early modern religious discipline stood at the nexus of profound changes in political life, legal practice, and western Christian theology and praxis. The Reformation hardened religious boundaries and demanded doctrinal and moral compliance to its creeds. While both Catholics and Calvinists initiated parallel programs of social discipline, Inquisitions and consistories also exacerbated religious differences by punishing theological and intellectual dissent. Consequently, these efforts contributed to a sharpened demand for creedal conformity, yet perpetuated fragmentation in western Christianity, setting it on a new course for modernity.

Notes

1 Heinz Schilling, *Civic Calvinism in Northwestern Germany and the Netherlands, Sixteenth to the Nineteenth Centuries* (Kirksville, MO, 1991), 40.
2 Johannes Uytenbogaert, *Kerckelijcke Historie, vervatende verscheyden ghedenckwaerdige saken, in de Christenheyt voor- gevallen. Van het jaer vier hondert af, tot in het jaer sesthien-hondert ende negenthien. Voornamelijck in dese Geunieerde provintien* (Rotterdam, 1647), 152.

PART I

INSTITUTIONAL CONTEXTS AND OPERATIONS

Section A

Local Contexts and Regional Variations

I

Consistories

Raymond A. Mentzer

The consistory is likely the most distinctive and recognizable, and surely the most controversial, of the ecclesiastical institutions associated with John Calvin and the Reformed tradition. As such, it has been the subject of considerable study. Historians have invariably placed heavy emphasis on the Genevan model for understanding consistorial structure and endeavor. They have not always taken equally careful note of the ways in which beyond Geneva it was molded and adapted to differing national needs and aspirations. As Calvin's reform movement spread, communities in France, the Netherlands, Scotland, parts of the Holy Roman Empire, and Hungary established churches and consistories in keeping with their understanding of the biblical prescriptions that he enunciated and instituted. Still, the consistory differed in composition, competence, and function from one territorial church to another. Indeed, slight variations sometimes existed from one local church to another within a single kingdom. At the same time, scholars have long characterized the consistory as a highly coercive instrument. According to this viewpoint, the consistory was an exacting church tribunal for the punishment of a broad range of misconduct that the reformers dubbed sinful and, to a lesser extent, the eradication of erroneous belief. This appraisal is decidedly severe.

Investigation of the consistory in the wider European context has led to the emergence of fresh interpretative perspectives on these matters. In France, for example, the consistory was an ecclesiastical council whose responsibilities broadened beyond morals control to include ecclesiastical administration, management of financial affairs, and assistance to the poor. More generally, a revisionist generation of historians has emphasized the consistory's pastoral role in settling disputes and counseling married couples alongside its more spectacular punitive activities. Robert M. Kingdon, who until his death in December 2010 was the undisputed expert on the Genevan consistory, proposed an amended view of the consistory and its objectives in a posthumously published collection of essays. While far from discounting the importance of disciplinary activities, he underscored the pastoral efforts of the Genevan consistory. It sought to strengthen the family and marriage, pacify an admittedly raucous society, and advance complex rituals of reconciliation. This assessment is all the more remarkable as it comes from a scholar who as late as 1996 maintained that the Genevan consistory was an institution "for controlling as closely as possible Christian behavior." Perhaps the fullest articulation of this newer understanding of the consistory comes from Scott Manetsch in his 2013 study of the Genevan pastorate. The ministers of Geneva seated in the consistory were "spiritual shepherds." They sought to change "inward attitude[s] of the heart," "protect the weakest, poorest and most vulnerable members" of society, "root out social and economic injustice," "reconcile estranged spouses," and settle arguments among neighbors. Consistorial discipline, Manetsch concludes, became a vigorous form of pastoral care.[1]

What then was the Reformed consistory? How ought it to be best understood? What did it seek to accomplish? Who were its members? How did it operate? Not surprisingly, the answers to these fundamental questions vary over time and space.

When John Calvin first arrived at Geneva in August 1536, Guillaume Farel, then principal pastor, immediately persuaded him to help in the reform of the church there. Yet within two years, the municipal magistrates wearied of their strident approach and forced the pair to leave. Calvin went to Strasbourg where Martin Bucer, that city's reformer, placed him in charge of the French refugee church. Bucer's experience in establishing a church and implementing ecclesiastical discipline proved crucial to Calvin's thinking. Meanwhile, by 1540 the Genevan authorities decided to invite Calvin to return and lead their church. Following a protracted period of negotiation, Calvin reentered Geneva on September 13, 1541. Among the conditions he demanded was a free hand to organize the church. Calvin began by drafting, in cooperation with municipal authorities, a basic constitution for the renewed church; it was founded on the Biblical model as he understood it. The result was the *Ecclesiastical Ordinances*. Promulgated by the Genevan General Council on November

20, 1541, they created four ecclesiastical offices or ministries – pastor, doctor (or teacher), elder, and deacon – along with a consistory, which had responsibility for the establishment and maintenance of moral discipline and ecclesiastical order.

The *Ecclesiastical Ordinances* were an explicit statement of the structure of the Christian church. The municipal legislation opened with a precise summary.

Firstly, there are four official orders which our Lord instituted for the government of His Church, namely: pastors; secondly, doctors; thirdly, elders ... and, fourthly, deacons. If then we wish to have the Church well-ordered and maintained in its entirety, we must observe this form of government.

The *Ordinances* proceeded to explain in detail the duties of each of the four offices or ministries. The pastors were to "proclaim the Word of God ... administer the sacraments, and ... exercise fraternal discipline together with the elders." The members of the second office – that of doctor or teacher – were to "instruct the faithful in sound doctrine." In reality, the doctors trained future pastors in educational institutions such as the Academy of Geneva. The elders, according to the Genevan *Ordinances*, had the special albeit controversial duty to "watch over the life of each person, to admonish in a friendly manner those ... at fault ... [and] ... to administer fraternal discipline." Fourth, the deacons cared for the needs of the poor and other members of the congregation who were in distress. The final section of the *Ordinances* explained that the consistory, namely the pastors and elders, was to gather each Thursday "to see whether there is any disorder in the Church and to consult together concerning remedies." The text also provided specific guidance regarding those faults over which the consistory had jurisdiction and suggested appropriate corrective measures. Specific mention was made of criticism of "received doctrine" and failure to attend sermon services or participate in the Lord's Supper. As for remedy, the *Ordinances* proposed private rebuke and, for more serious matters, public admonition. Finally, the most egregious offenders were to be excluded from the Supper and reported to the magistrate. In all of this, the pastors and elders were reminded that the purpose of discipline was "to bring sinners back to our Lord."[2]

Calvin famously characterized discipline as the sinews of the church, and in his *Harmony of the Gospels* offered an explicit scriptural warrant for its exercise by the consistory.[3] The key Biblical text was Matthew 18:15–17 in which Jesus instructed his followers:

If your brother sins against you, go and tell him his fault, between you and him alone ... if he does not listen, take one or two others along with you ... if he refuses to listen to them, tell it to the church; and if he refuses to listen even to the church, let him be to you as a Gentile and a tax collector.

Calvin argued that because the Christian church did not exist when Jesus uttered the pivotal words "tell it to the church," he must have meant some Jewish institution, most likely the Sanhedrin, a tribunal composed of both priests and laymen. The Reformed consistory, also made up of clergy and laypersons, was in turn the appropriate sort of subsequent Christian ecclesiastical body for the implementation of church discipline.

The consistory of Geneva proved a malleable model for Reformed churches throughout Europe. While certain of its features were specific to the circumstances of Geneva, as the Reformed movement spread various aspects were adjusted to meet local settings and constraints. The consistory in France, kirk-session in Scotland, and presbytery in Germany, the Netherlands, and Hungary unquestionably replicated the institution initially fashioned by Calvin. Yet each of these arrangements evidenced a particular character in conforming to the special cultural and ecclesiastical modalities, political and social conditions of the national territory in which it was located. The consistory during the Reformation era was far from a rigid construction; it could be organized and operate in a variety of ways.

The political constitution of Geneva, an independent city-state, inevitably affected arrangements for its church and consistory. The circumstances meant a close cooperative relationship between ecclesiastical and political authorities, which was not always possible in other parts of Europe. All of the city's pastors and twelve lay elders sat on the Genevan consistory. Although the elders were not ordained, they functioned as crucial members of the ministry. They served an annual term and were selected from the membership of the Genevan municipal councils: two from the Small Council, four from the Council of Sixty, and six from the Council of Two Hundred. These elders, men who were also elected city councillors, were in the majority and, as such, they wielded considerable power in the ambitious endeavor to monitor closely people's moral conduct and religious beliefs. As William Naphy points out in Chapter 8, the Genevan consistory was effectively a permanent committee of the municipal government.

Beyond the pastors and elders, the consistory employed a secretary to maintain an abbreviated written record of its deliberations and a summoner to notify individuals who were requested to appear before the body.

Deacons did not participate in the meetings, as was frequently the case for Reformed churches in other parts of Europe. Deacons everywhere were given responsibility for assisting the indigent. At Geneva, they had charge over the direction of the Hospital-General. This institution had been established by municipal authorities in 1535, the year prior to Calvin's arrival. In designating the hospital administrators as deacons, Calvin incorporated a preexisting institutional arrangement into his ecclesiastical structure. But the deacons did not sit on the Genevan consistory and had no role in its deliberations. Similarly, the doctors were not members of the consistory, although several of the doctors, Calvin and Beza for example, were also pastors and would have participated by virtue of this latter capacity. Finally, the office of doctor was rarely included in the structure of Reformed churches outside Geneva.

Morals reform, often taken to be the primary function of the Genevan consistory, meant the promotion of virtue as well as the suppression of vice. On the level of religious matters properly speaking, the consistory chastised individuals for such faults as absence from church services and catechism lessons, Sabbath breach, polluting contacts with "popery," irregularities surrounding marriage, blasphemous utterances, and resort to sorcery and magic. Failings of a more behavioral nature included verbal disputes and physical quarrels, abusive and scandalous language, sexual misconduct, dancing, games and other frivolous activities, excesses of food and drink, and participation in charivaris, masquerades, and carnival. In light of these activities, an older interpretative model viewed consistorial discipline as an intimidating and intrusive control mechanism for the repression of unlicensed sociability and the imposition of an emerging bourgeois morality. Others have challenged this understanding. Kingdon maintains that the consistory at Geneva functioned as a court to correct sinners, but was also a compulsory counseling service to settle "disputes between family members, neighbors and business partners."[4] Though mindful of the larger campaign to suppress immoral conduct, proponents of this reading emphasize the consistory's role in pacifying a disputatious society, above all settling people's seemingly innumerable squabbles and promoting the amicable resolution of conflict between spouses and within households.

If the consistory of Geneva functioned primarily as a morals tribunal or, in less harsh language, an obligatory counseling service, outside Geneva it often acted as the executive institution for the local church with charge over administrative and financial affairs, social welfare programs, and morals reform. Thus, the consistory within the Reformed Churches of France was primarily an ecclesiastical council whose composition and responsibilities diverged in significant ways from that which Calvin and the Genevan political authorities envisioned. It had, to be sure, much in common with its counterpart at Geneva, but there were significant differences.

The French equivalent of Geneva's *Ecclesiastical Ordinances* was the *Discipline of the Reformed Churches of France*, first drafted by the national synod meeting at Paris in 1559. The *Discipline* laid out the various regulations and practices governing the organization of the church. It prescribed the manner for administering baptism and celebrating the Lord's Supper; described institutional structures such as the consistory, colloquy, and synod; defined the duties of pastors, elders, and deacons; and explained the financial administration of the church. The *Discipline* also enumerated a variety of moral shortcomings and offered explicit direction to ecclesiastical officials for dealing with these problems and punishing offenders. Subsequent national synods continually updated these regulations.

The principal difficulty with which Reformed ecclesiastical authorities in France had to wrestle was that they were a religious minority, frequently persecuted and at best grudgingly tolerated. Unlike Geneva, where the magistrates encouraged, nurtured, and guided the Reformation project, the French monarchical state generally opposed the religious transformations embodied in Protestantism. The crown and other political authorities considered the French Reformed Churches a threat, which had to be contained if not eradicated. Except for certain communities where the municipal councillors or local nobles were sympathetic to the Reformed movement, governmental backing was wholly absent. The lack of cooperation and mutual support between church and state resulted in a consistorial organization different from that of Geneva. French Protestants, while wholly admiring of the ecclesiastical arrangements established by Calvin, needed to modify and adapt the system to the particular circumstances of their kingdom.

The foundation of the French system was the local church and its consistory. The system vested substantial authority and considerable autonomy with the local community, while maintaining an elaborate hierarchy of colloquies, provincial synods, and national synods. Thorny issues, whose solution defied the local church, were forwarded to the colloquies and provincial synods, and if beyond resolution by these bodies or if they seemed of broad significance, the matters passed to the national synod, which had the option of integrating its decision into the national *Discipline*. Still, the key to the French consistorial-synodal system was the local community of faith. According to the *Discipline*,

In each church there will be a consistory composed of individuals, notably the pastors and elders, who will conduct its proceedings. The pastors will preside over this company.[5]

The passage draws attention to an immediate adjustment to the Genevan model. In France, a pastor rather than an elder presided over the consistory's meetings. A memorandum composed by the Church of Nîmes in the 1580s, roughly twenty years after the establishment of its church and consistory, offers additional clarification. In churches such as that of Nîmes and in the Netherlands where there were several pastors, they presided "in turn." Other churches followed a similar procedure.

The French national *Discipline*'s explanation of the place and responsibilities of deacons makes clear other divergences from Genevan practice.

As for the deacons, seeing that the churches, given the needs of the times, have until now successfully utilized them in the administration of the Church ... [they] will normally be present ... in the consistory.[6]

The deacons, who did not participate in deliberations of the Genevan consistory, were an integral part of the French meetings. Yet the stature and authority of the deacons varied widely in France. At Nîmes, for instance, deacons appear to have been prominent members of the community. Elsewhere, their prestige never matched that of pastors and elders. French churches typically had six or eight, ten or twelve elders, but far fewer deacons. Even a large church such as that of Nîmes maintained a ratio of no more than one deacon for every two elders. Smaller communities had only one or two; others had none. Even the prominent Church of Castres had sixteen elders, but no deacons. There, the elders assumed responsibility for what was normally the deacons' task of providing assistance to the poor.[7] Altogether, the number and nature of officials serving on the consistory varied considerably from one church to another in France.

The distinctive character of the French Reformed churches is perhaps nowhere more evident than in the exercise of excommunication, which barred an individual from participation in the sacraments, notably the Lord's Supper. The absence of a helpful working relationship between church and state meant that the French consistories had considerable independence in applying this grave ecclesiastical penalty. The consistories excommunicated as they saw fit and could only be challenged by the colloquies and synods. In many imperial German and Swiss city-states, by way of contrast, the secular magistrate retained strict control over excommunication. It was a complicated matter with significant political, civic, and social ramifications. Geneva, where the consistory, largely at Calvin's insistence, had the right to excommunicate, was unusual. Yet we must remember that the Genevan elders also held political office, and thus the magistracy retained a strong voice in the process.

The French consistories were far less constrained in their employ of excommunication, but the situation had its drawbacks. The Reformed churches of France did not need permission from political authorities to exclude men and women from the sacraments. Without the backing of the state, however, the effect was diminished. Ecclesiastical authorities found it difficult to limit social and economic contacts between excommunicates and other members of the congregation. The consistory, moreover, was unable to restrict the legal rights of excommunicates. It could not, for instance, prevent them from pursuing civil or criminal suits in the court system as had been the case under medieval arrangements. Protestant church leaders in France had extensive discretion regarding excommunication, but the effects were attenuated.

While acknowledging the directives contained in the national *Discipline*, some local French churches, particularly during the early years of the Reformation, drafted their own disciplines. These church orders occasionally displayed adaptations that responded to local demands for specific guidance in the conduct of church affairs. Thus, the *Police de l'Église réformée de Bayeux*, composed in 1563, begins with a long and detailed explanation of the "the four orders of those who have public responsibilities." It then clarifies the role of pastors, "ministers of the Holy Gospel"; of elders, who with the ministers watch over morals; of deacons, who "care for the poor"; and finally (and exceptionally), of the teachers "who instruct the young as much in the rudiments of the faith as in language." Other articles of the Bayeux *Police* discuss the sacraments, ecclesiastical censure, marriage, visiting the sick, and burial of the dead. Another example is the *Discipline de l'Église de Saint-Lô*, also written in 1563. It differs from the national *Discipline* of 1559 in several respects. Among the most novel aspects is the stipulation that "only the ministers and elders watch over and investigate scandals within the church." The deacons, who in most French Reformed churches participated in the gatherings of the consistory, were explicitly excluded. The *Discipline* of Saint-Lô is also unusual because it appears to be the only one for France to designate the office of magistrate as one of the four ministries. The magistrate was the "protector of peace and public tranquility."[8] Finally, the text of the *Mémoire de l'ordre qu'on tient au consistoire de*

Nîmes dealt with similar questions of organization and function, but in a more succinct manner. This difference may reflect the fact that the *Mémoire* was written twenty years later, during the 1580s, after a series of successive national synods had resolved many of the initial problems. As noted earlier, the Nîmes *Mémoire* established the order by which the pastors presided over the consistory meetings, described the duties of each member of the consistory, outlined the processes for the collection and distribution of funds for the poor, and explained the procedures for the monthly visits to the municipal school by one of the pastors and two deacons.[9] Altogether, these three local disciplines satisfied the needs of the provincial churches that composed them, while maintaining conformity with the overall directives contained in the national *Discipline*.

The developments described for France were by no means exceptional. The church in Scotland, to take another example, also possessed an elaborate national discipline. John Knox and a group of ministers drafted the *First Book of Discipline* already in 1560–1. Yet this initial *Discipline* was neither precise nor systematic. It, for instance, planned the establishment of ten superintendents to replace the bishops. This particular proposal, however, never found favor and yielded to emphasis on the local kirk and session (the Scots equivalent to the Genevan consistory). Eventually in 1578, the General Assembly – as the national synod was termed in Scotland – adopted the far more elaborate *Second Book of Discipline*. It initiated a scheme that in due course included the General Assembly, provincial synod, presbytery, and kirk-session. The Scottish churches adopted the near-universal consistorial model – Geneva being the notable exception – of having ministers, elders, and deacons serve on the session. They also followed the standard understanding that pastors and elders had primary responsibility for the exercise of discipline, while deacons saw to financial matters and cared for the poor.

In the Netherlands a national consistorial-synodal system was never fully realized. A Dutch synod meeting at Emden in 1571 approved a church order. These Emden Articles, though endorsed three years later by the provincial Synod of Dordrecht, were not implemented due to deep-seated opposition. In keeping with the region's long tradition of decentralization, the seven provinces of the Dutch Republic closely guarded their ecclesiastical and political rights. Thus, discipline was chiefly the concern of the local churches, albeit under the watchful eye of the classis (the Dutch equivalent of the colloquy or presbytery) and the provincial synod. Dutch consistories exercised broad powers to discipline congregants, administer poor relief, appoint pastors, and organize church services. Their membership included pastors, elders, and deacons, though deacons typically met separately from the ministers and elders, except for small congregations. On the other hand, membership in the Dutch Reformed Church, despite its status as a state church, was voluntary. Only those willing to submit to discipline were considered full members and thereby eligible to participate in the Lord's Supper, even if they attended sermon service regularly. The situation obviously diminished the ability of the consistory to "reform" Dutch society.

Within the Empire, there were but a few Reformed princely states. The most prominent were the Palatinate and Nassau, where political leaders established consistories, although they functioned under close governmental supervision. Consistorial discipline in Hungary and Transylvania also reflected the particulars of the region's political configuration and cultural traditions. Developments in the different regions proceeded at varying speed. Churches in western Hungary organized presbyteries (or consistories) in the early seventeenth century. Lay elders, the cornerstone of the Reformed disciplinary project, worked closely with ministers to implement Christian discipline and assure proper worship. In eastern Hungary and Transylvania problems arose. The clergy became deeply divided over the need to establish consistories, and by mid-century, civil authorities feared that the consistorial structure undermined established ecclesiastical and political authority.

Almost nowhere did the introduction of consistorial polity go unchallenged, albeit in different ways and from different quarters. Individual sinners were sometimes extremely irked, as was one unhappy Genevan who complained in the mid-1550s that "the devil and the consistory never sleep."[10] In France, the theologian Jean Morély, while not rejecting the right of pastors and elders to administer the church, argued that the congregation, by which he meant adult males who had publicly confessed their faith, should have the right to decide doctrinal and disciplinary matters. Perhaps the fiercest debates were those that raged between civil and religious authorities over who had the right to excommunicate. The issue erupted forcefully at Geneva in 1555. The struggle had been simmering for nearly a decade. A group composed mostly of members of the city's leading families coalesced around the figure of Ami Perrin.

They objected to the influx of foreign refugees, the dominance of French pastors, and the strict discipline imposed by the consistory. When discontent turned into violent clashes in the streets, the Perrinist party was crushed. Among other things, the triumph of Calvin and his supporters gave the church complete control over ecclesiastical discipline and confirmed the consistory's right of excommunication, unlike the situation at Strasbourg, Basel, Berne, and Zurich, where the state reserved control over excommunication. Opposition elsewhere was less combative. At Leiden in the Netherlands, relations between the Reformed consistory and the Leiden magistracy were generally respectful, if occasionally strained. The issues were straightforward. Who would control the public church and, for example, the appointment of elders? How much power would the consistory have over its own membership? Similarly, in Hungary ecclesiastical leaders and political authorities became mired in arguments over authority in church governance.

On the other hand, support for the consistorial system was not lacking. At Geneva, members of some established families as well as newly arrived religious refugees seem to have welcomed the moral purity established by the consistory. In France and the Netherlands, women, who typically had few options for redress of grievance through civil justice, viewed the consistory as an accessible and legitimate forum to right wrongs and restore honor. Servant women believing they were mistreated by the employers readily appealed to the consistory. Other women, when called unflattering names by neighbors, appeared before the consistory to seek restoration of injured pride and tarnished reputation. Church discipline was the guarantee of their good name.

How ultimately should the consistory be viewed, particularly in comparison to the Inquisition? To begin, consistorial systems tended to be fairly decentralized. The watchword in France and the Netherlands, for instance, was that "No church shall exercise primacy or power over another."[11] Consistorial power was exerted at the local level by local authorities. Colloquies and provincial synods had oversight to the extent that they occasionally ruled on appeals from the decisions of local consistories. In those places where the national synod met regularly, it updated the procedures set out in the national church discipline. Given the local emphasis, it ought not to surprise that consistories, unlike the Inquisition, had no extensive or firmly established procedural rules apart from the general guidelines voiced in the various church orders. The consistory was only one element discussed in these disciplines, which never provided the sort of detailed and thorough direction contained in Inquisitorial manuals. Still, in some few churches, Nîmes for instance, where elders had legal training, they occasionally if unofficially invoked legal language and practices.

Another key aspect of the Reformed consistory was the substantial role assigned to the laity. Although the consistory was an ecclesiastical institution, it had a significant measure of lay involvement. Election as elder or deacon to serve an annual term on the consistory allowed laymen, typically individuals prominent within the community, to have a conspicuous and considerable function within the church. They were, as much as the pastors, responsible for the formidable yet delicate task of implementing a religious and moral transformation within their community. This opportunity, at once attractive and demanding, simply did not exist in the medieval or early modern Catholic Church.

Pastors and elders seated in the consistory tended to fasten onto public misconduct and were decidedly less concerned with secret sin. They made an important distinction between "public" and "private" sin. Consistories were not much interested in private "vices" such as masturbation or homosexuality, and never engaged in the probing, often lengthy interrogations that were the hallmark of the Inquisition. There was little interest in building a composite portrait of the offender and his or her life and inquiring into the interior mental universe of the sinner. In fact, relatively few cases of erroneous belief came to consistorial attention. Rather, the focus was on public scandal, a concern embodied in the principle, frequently expressed by consistories everywhere, that public sin demanded public atonement. The penalties applied by the consistory also differed in significant ways from Inquisitorial justice. Consistories did not imprison or impose capital punishment, though they typically cooperated with the state. Thus, sinners whose activities appeared to be criminal would have been turned over to civil authorities for a completely separate trial under the auspices of criminal justice. The most notorious consistorial punishments were public shaming and excommunication. Even so, private tongue-lashings were more common.

In the end, consistories across Europe flowed from a clear Genevan model, though modifications occurred regarding membership, the presiding officials, and the institution's relationship to the state. If scholars have come to understand that the consistory was far from a monolithic institution, they have also begun to reevaluate its core enterprise, stressing a pastoral as well as punitive purpose. Altogether, the consistory did more than impose discipline and chastise miscreants. It also provided counsel and fostered virtue, seeking to redirect sinners to the path of godliness through repentance and reform.

Notes

1 Robert M. Kingdon, "Consistory," in *The Oxford Encyclopedia of the Reformation*, ed. Hans J. Hillerbrand (New York, 1996), 1:416; Scott M. Manetsch,

Calvin's Company of Pastors: Pastoral Care and the Emerging Reformed Church, 1536–1609 (Oxford, 2013), 214–20.

2 For the complete text: "Ordonnances ecclésiastiques," in *Registres de la Compagnie des Pasteurs de Genève, 1546–1553*, ed. Robert M. Kingdon and Jean-François Bergier (Geneva, 1964), 1:1–13.

3 John Calvin, *Harmonium Evangelica*, in *Calvini Opera*, vol. 45, col. 514–15.

4 Robert M. Kingdon, *Adultery and Divorce in Calvin's Geneva* (Cambridge, MA, 1995), 4.

5 Isaac d'Huisseau, *La Discipline des Eglises réformées de France ou l'ordre par lequel elles sont conduites et gouvernées* (Geneva, 1666), 84.

6 d'Huisseau, *Discipline*, 84–5.

7 Janine Garrisson, *Protestants du Midi, 1559–1598* (Toulouse, 1980), 100; Archives Nationales, TT 234, dossier 6. Registre de consistoire de Bédarieux; and TT 269, dossier 25, Registre du consistoire de St. Gervais. Archives Départementales du Tarn, I 1, I 2, I 3, Registres du consistoire de Castres.

8 Michel Reulos, "Police et discipline de l'Église de Saint-Lô (1563)," appended to "Les débuts des Communautés réformées dans l'actuel département de la Manche (Cotetin et Avranchin)," in *Réforme et Contre-réforme en Normandie*, special issue of *Revue duDépartement de la Manche* 24 (1982, fascicules 93–94–95), 36, 48–9, 50.

9 Archives Départementales du Gard, 42 J 28, fol. 372–5.

10 Manetsch, *Calvin's Company of Pastors*, 190.

11 d'Huisseau, *Discipline*, 117; Alastair Duke, "The Ambivalent Face of Calvinism in the Netherlands," in *International Calvinism, 1541–1715*, ed. Menna Prestwich (Oxford, 1985), 121–2.

2

Inquisitions

Christopher F. Black

Reference is often made to "The Inquisition," whether in a medieval or modern context, as if a single entity or institution, perceptions of which tend to be based on often distorted views of the Spanish Inquisition founded in 1478. This is misleading and myth bound. A legal procedure of "inquiry" (*inquisitio*) evolved from Roman law, and through adaptations by the medieval Church became the hallmark of the various early modern institutions called Inquisitions, and is still part of many secular legal systems. It is the alternative to the accuser versus accused adversarial system, and involves a magistrate figure who organizes an inquiry following an allegation or evidence of a crime, formulates accusations, and also conducts any subsequent trial. Many variations developed in the way the main ecclesiastical magistrate/inquisitor was assisted and how he conducted the inquiry and trial. "Early Modern Inquisitions" start with the creation of a permanent Inquisition in Spain from 1478. This chapter points to some variations between and within three major Inquisitions that developed thereafter. To facilitate comparative analysis, and implying a degree of commonality or unity, what will be indicated here are the diversity and variations in the centrally structured Inquisitions of Spain, Portugal, and Rome, and also variations within them. While the Spanish and Portuguese Inquisitions were subject to royal rulers, the Roman Inquisition, though under a papal monarchy, outside the Papal State had to negotiate with different princes and republics. In all cases the center's relationships with dependent tribunals were affected by local political and social relations, by variable jurisdictional challenges as notably from bishops. Also the staffing of tribunals was not uniform, while the personalities, competence, and rigor of inquisitors created different effects – harsh or more emollient. The inquisitors' targets and victims can also be seen to differ, with the Iberian tribunals having much greater concern with Jewish and Muslim converts than did the Italian ones. This last factor has impacted the historical reputations of the early modern Inquisitions.

"The Inquisition" has had a bad press through the centuries, with the various versions all tarred with a black brush based on the worst excesses by some Spanish tribunals at the outset, especially against Judaizers. A Black Legend of Inquisition cruelty and tyranny was fostered by Philip II's internal enemies, as well as external Protestants. Powerful hostile writings by, for example, Antonio del Corro (alias Reginaldus Montanus, a Spanish Protestant) in 1567, the Spanish convert to Anglicanism James Salgado (*The Slaughter House, or a brief description of the Spanish Inquisition*, 1682), Philipp van Limborch (*Historia Inquisitionis*, 1692), or Voltaire's writings in the eighteenth century fed the historians' and polemicists' attacks, further fueled by information on the cruelties of the Goa tribunal. Nineteenth-century scholars benefited from access to some archives for Spain, such as Juan Antonio Llorente, a former inquisitor, then later the American Henry Charles Lea, whose extensive research work remains valuable. From his Protestant perspective he still saw the Spanish Inquisition as almost totally evil, but his documentation helped others develop a more nuanced understanding of variations in inquisitorial behavior over time and place.

The historiography over the last century has still concentrated more on Spain and its dependencies than Portugal or the Roman Inquisition, and strong debates continue over the extent to which the Inquisition damaged Spanish culture and inhibited modernization. Francisco Bethencourt has been the one scholar to attempt a global comparative study. While Iberian harshness against alleged Judaizers and *moriscos* is still stressed, inquisitors (under all three Inquisitions) are seen as more skeptical about witchcraft accusations than magistrates were in many Protestant and other Catholic states. This partly connects with recent emphases, as by John Tedeschi (and followed by me), that once fully established, the Inquisitions were strong on due legal processes and aimed at the salvation of souls and repentance rather than determining condign punishment. Recent historians downplay the extent of torture and death sentences under Inquisitions in comparison with secular courts in these countries or in other states. Henry Kamen has increasingly pointed to limitations of inquisitorial control in Spain, to geographical variations, and to less inquisitorial responsibility than is often alleged for supposed Spanish cultural and scientific backwardness.

For Italy, modern archival scholarship has largely concentrated on certain cities (notably Venice, whose rich archival material became available in the nineteenth century) or on the handling of certain issues, such as magic and superstition, the Jews and Judaizers, book censorship, or on trials of major accused such as Cardinal Giovanni Morone, Pietro Carnesecchi, Giordano Bruno, and Galileo. But Andrea Del Col, Adriano Prosperi, and I have now attempted fuller coverage of the workings of the Inquisition at center and periphery and of the diversity of targets and aims. I have been teasingly accused of not being condemnatory enough of Roman Inquisition behavior and overdoing revisionism. But my context was comparative: the Roman version judged as less harsh and more carefully legalistic than the Iberian one, or Italian and other European secular courts.

The medieval ecclesiastical inquisitions effectively started with Pope Gregory IX's commission in 1231 to the Dominicans (an Order founded in 1220) to examine perceived heretics in southern France and northern Italy, notably those designated as Cathars. Inquisitors were empowered beyond those of ordinary bishops to deal with a local heresy and generally ceased when that problem was eradicated. This was not a permanent institution or centrally controlled network. In 1478, Pope Sixtus IV, however, responded to a request from King Ferdinand and Queen Isabella, the "Catholic Monarchs" of Castile and Aragon in Spain, to have a permanent Inquisition, primarily to inquire into the extent to which Jews who had converted to Christianity (voluntarily or under pressure) remained good Christians without reversion to Judaism. While authorized by the papacy, this Inquisition was essentially a department of state with henceforth very limited papal control – which Sixtus soon regretted. The second major early modern Inquisition was started in 1536, in Portugal, again largely under monarchical control.

Finally in 1542, Paul III's bull *Licet ab initio* launched a centralized and permanent papal Inquisition, later known as the Roman Inquisition or the Holy Office. Prior to this, local and medieval Inquisitions had been active in various parts of north-central Italy trying to curb supporters of new heresies or unorthodoxies, whether influenced by Luther, Zwingli, Bucer, Melanchthon, and others from the north, or Italian followers of the Spaniard Juan Valdés (who had fled Spain to Naples), or independent groups who had been rethinking the teachings of St. Paul and St. Augustine even before Luther, as in Venice. The 1542 refoundation was largely promoted by Cardinal Gian Pietro Carafa (later Paul IV), who – while an advocate of church reform in behavior – was very conservative theologically, was worried by the ineffectiveness of local inquisitorial action, and argued for the need for centralized control from Rome. Formerly a diplomat in Spain, he judged a centralized Inquisition as efficacious. The Roman Inquisition was presided over by the pope, with a select commission of cardinals organizing a network of tribunals and major trials in Rome. Eventually a larger Congregation of the Holy Office was formed, with a solid bureaucracy.

Given Italy's political divisions, inquisitorial organization was more complex than in Iberia. The Roman Inquisition covered the Papal States and other states in north-central Italy (except the Republic of Lucca, which developed its own anti-heresy body). It did not extend throughout Catholic Europe. The Spanish monarchs had created tribunals for Sicily (from 1478) and Sardinia (from 1492), and these remained. When Spanish control over the Kingdom of Naples was agreed in 1559 by the Treaty of Cateau-Cambrésis (concluding the Italian Wars from 1494), Philip II sought Spanish Inquisition control there. The Papacy, as feudal superior for the Kingdom, refused. The King as effective ruler banned the open operation of tribunals under the Roman Congregation. In practice, medieval-style episcopal Inquisitions operated in the Kingdom, with commissioners and other Rome-appointed officials interposing in various ways. Malta (ruled by the Knights Hospitallers of St. John from 1530) from 1561 and Avignon came to have tribunals under Roman supervision.

All three Inquisitions developed local tribunals across their territorial areas in fits and starts through the late fifteenth and sixteenth centuries. By 1600 the Roman Inquisition had about forty full tribunals under its control, with a few more added by the 1630s. The effective Spanish tribunals by then numbered about fourteen (but Madrid did not have its own till 1659 with Toledo being the controlling tribunal); by the end of the seventeenth century twenty-one tribunals may have been operative across the empire. The Spanish colonial tribunals were in the Canaries by 1507, Mexico and Lima by 1570, and Cartagena by 1610. Portugal eventually settled on three mainland tribunals (Lisbon 1539, Evora 1536, and Coimbra finally established from 1565) and one in Goa from 1560, but no permanent one in Brazil, which was controlled from Lisbon. The union of the Spanish and Portuguese crowns from 1580 to 1640 (when the Portuguese started to rebel) brought some central monarchical control, but a degree of difference and autonomy remained, especially in the remoter colonial worlds. As Doris Moreno Martínez notes in Chapter 13, the Inquisition's impact was significantly less in Catalonia than in Castile.

In Iberia the Inquisitions were essentially departments of state, maintaining a distance from the papacy and archbishops. The kings could use the Inquisition tribunals for their own political purposes and as a way of getting at opponents. However, the central Spanish organizing body, the *Suprema*, and local inquisitors were not entirely dominated by the crown, and there were conflicts and tensions. Philip II struggled to resist inquisitorial attempts to investigate the holdings of the royal library at the Escorial for prohibited books. Viceroys exercised significant power and influence over tribunals in the Americas.

Rome's control over tribunals and inquisitors in Italy was variable. Firstly negotiations had to be made with other states how tribunals should operate and with what involvement from lay representatives. In the Venetian Republic after considerable initial reluctance the state agreed to a Venetian tribunal that would be led by three churchmen – the patriarch, the inquisitor, and the papal nuncio – to be joined by three patrician assistants (*Assistenti*, or *Savii sopra eresia* – wisemen concerning heresy). This was a sort of diarchy. The patriarch was usually a Venetian, and effectively a choice of the Venetian Senate to be approved by the Pope. It is difficult to ascertain the extent of the assistants' involvement during trials, or behind the scenes and off the record. The nuncio played a significant role, and was often more important in major cases than the inquisitor, especially over decisions about sending an accused to Rome, or consulting the pope or Congregation over sentencing. Lay representatives were also involved in the other tribunals' activities on the mainland and parts of Dalmatian coast within the Venetian Republic, at least in consideration of certain charges, torture, and sentencing, if not through full investigative processes (*processi*). (The word *processo* is often translated as "trial," which can be misleading given its implication in English of a full proceeding leading to a verdict. The Italian word can cover stages from recorded denunciation or self-denunciation, questioning of witnesses and accused, formal accusation, interrogations, defense, sentence, and punishment. Many *processi* never came to a full trial and verdict.) The nuncio in Piedmont also played a significant role alongside the inquisitor. In Tuscany, where the Medici Grand Dukes generally favored the papacy, inquisitors may have had a fuller personal control of trial procedures. In Lombardy inquisitors had to weave their way between pressures from both Spanish governors and powerful archbishops such as Carlo Borromeo. Borromeo was an ardent campaigner against witchcraft and sorcery, but lost several struggles against local inquisitors and Inquisition cardinals in Rome who took a more skeptical and emollient line against witchcraft denunciations.

The interaction between the center and periphery in Italy has become easier to study since the opening of the Holy Office archive, as much correspondence has survived and Congregation registers give a fuller idea of what instructions were sent out, and what issues were considered by the Congregations. Local inquisitors were expected to consult over torture and sentencing for the more serious offenses, but evidently this was not always done. In the now famous case of the Friulian miller Menocchio Scandella, Carlo Ginzburg originally thought that his death sentence after his second trial followed a Rome decision; however, Andrea Del Col has shown that the decision was made locally by an inquisitor and a lay official, with Rome being informed later. In practice, consultation varied between tribunals, with the Friuli tribunals having less contact and consultation with Rome than Siena or Modena in sampled periods of the sixteenth and seventeenth centuries. Michele Seghizzi, inquisitor in Cremona and Milan in the early seventeenth century, "bombarded" the Congregation with questions, forcing that body to clarify jurisprudential issues. Published documentation has shown for the sixteenth century that Inquisition cardinals often corresponded with archbishops in Naples and other churchmen in the Viceroyalty, despite Spanish wishes to keep inquisitors at bay. In the Roman Inquisition, the amount of documentation sent to Rome from the local inquisitor varied. As my study of a Modena inquisitor's relations with Rome indicates, in some cases Rome wanted a full transcript of a process or investigation, so the cardinals could advise on torture, punishment, or amelioration of a sentence. Otherwise they asked for a digest or select aspects of evidence.[1] In Spain, the *Suprema* expected to have a digest of each case, the survival of which in large numbers has been a boon to historians. Historians of the Roman Inquisition have no such summary database, though they do have some rich deposits of full case processes, as in Venice, Udine, Modena, Bologna, Siena, and Rome.

In the Catholic worlds, the Inquisitions had rivals in controlling the faithful, their fundamental beliefs and religious morality, and not exclusive domination. In Protestant areas it could be simpler when consistories were the primary investigative body, even if punishments were the responsibility of others. The bishop-inquisitor relationships and controls over the faithful or deviants varied geographically and in time. As already indicated, Neapolitan archbishops and bishops continued to behave in an inquisitorial way. Similarly bishops played the inquisitorial role in Central and South America until the establishment of formal Inquisition tribunals in Mexico, Lima, and Cartagena. In Sicily, inquisitors often were also simultaneously bishops, but bishops who were not inquisitors could vigorously challenge inquisitors over jurisdictional controls. This also happened in Sardinia, where bishops might appeal for papal support against the Spanish *Suprema*. An inquisitor's career could be completed by appointment as bishop, notably in Portugal where over a quarter of the bishops from 1536 to 1613 were former Inquisition officials, as Kimberly Lynn discusses in more detail in Chapter 9.

The composition and manning of local tribunals differed considerably. We have already noted the Venetian configuration; there the inquisitor might take information on his own with a notary, but no formal Inquisition or trial would be staffed only by them. However, in other Italian tribunals the inquisitor could serve singly as both accuser and judge. In contrast a Spanish tribunal would more likely involve two or three inquisitors and a prosecutor (*fiscal*). Inquisitor General Torquemada in 1498 wanted a jurist and theologian, or two jurists, as inquisitors. The notary played a crucial role, recording the formal process, but also taking prior testimony, making copies of all or part (for the defense, or to inform bishops, congregations, lay representatives). He might have to turn evidence written in local dialects into more formal Italian, Spanish, or Portuguese, and in Italy often recorded questions in Latin. The formulaic answers of some accused, especially in putting themselves at the court's mercy, suggest that a notary may have coached the accused. A tribunal could employ a whole range of other participants at the center and through its district: messengers, policing officials, extra notaries, scribes, and sometimes translators. The inquisitor might have as assistant a junior Dominican (*converso*) beside him, as in Ancona or Modena. A prosecutor (*fiscale*) might be employed, but he was not necessarily a permanent employee in Italy, though his equivalent in Spain probably was. Vicars general and vicars covered the province or district, again with their notaries and assistants. These vicars might be from religious orders, or be lay clergy, even parish priests. More scandalous inquisitorial behavior, illegal or irregular, seems to have come from such local vicars, less trained in inquisitorial jurisprudence, and more susceptible to local paranoia over witchcraft for example.

Whether the inquisitorial process was led by one or more inquisitors, conducting investigations, hearing witnesses, confronting the accused, bringing formal charges, and hearing defenses, they were likely in more serious cases to seek other advice and consult. As already indicated, consultations could take place with the distant Congregations in Rome, the *Suprema* in Madrid, or the *Conselho Geral* in Lisbon, with bishops or episcopal vicars, and with lay representatives. Additionally larger tribunals had consultants, theologians, and jurists, formed into local congregations; other inquisitors took opinions on a more *ad hoc* basis. If the matter was controversial or ambiguous, reference to the Holy Office in Rome could lead to further consultations there. Where local cases involved dubious literature, decisions about censorship would not be just the inquisitor's, but also based on opinions from outside assessors. During a trial, as over cases of devilish "possession," or superstitious causes of illness or death, the inquisitor would consult physicians, healers, or exorcists. However, in Italy at least, the value of exorcists was contentious with some practitioners seen by the Inquisition as fraudulent.

Besides the personal consultations, inquisitors, in judging the accused, increasingly had manuals, manuscript then printed, to guide them on due process in pursuing cases, to question, torture, classify offenses and degrees of heretical offending, and so allocate suitable punishments. Some common ground existed between the medieval and early modern advice and between the Iberian and Italian arenas, when the medieval manual of Nicholas Eymeric (d.1399), *Directorium Inquisitorum* (initially 1376 manuscript, first printed 1520), was widely used then updated by Francisco Peña, a Spaniard who served also in Rome, in editions from 1578. Many other guides, local and international, circulated. Prospero Farinacci's evolving five-volume work, *Tractatus de haeresi* (1581 to 1614), was the contribution of a leading jurist, a layman most of his life, incorporating wide jurisprudential approaches. For Italy, Eliseo Masini produced the more user-friendly vernacular guide, *Sacro Arsenale* (editions from 1621 to 1730), based on experience as inquisitor in Ancona and Genoa. Kimberly Lynn in Chapter 9 discusses guides and libraries in more detail.

Thus in the main Inquisition areas inquisitors did not rule alone or arbitrarily, but under guidance, written and oral. Deviations from the true faith were thus judged collectively and with due consideration. Manuals stressed that reconciliation should be sought, errors corrected, and education offered, more than seeking to mete out condign punishment. As Nicholas Davidson agrees, the intention was to save souls, converting the guilty.[2] Tribunals were, controversially, backed by "familiars" (*familiari*), privileged hangers-on designed to boost the image of the inquisitor and Inquisitions generally. Though potentially eyes and ears to assist tracking offenders, there is little evidence to show they really helped, at least in Italy.

In parts of Italy the "spontaneous appearance" system led to what some of us see as plea bargaining when people wanted to reconcile themselves with the Catholic Church, having been Protestant, Orthodox, Jewish, or Muslim – whether through birth, voluntary conversion, or compulsion. Italians who had backed Calvinists in the French Religious Wars sought reintegration into Tuscany or the Venetian Republic. Other cases derived from the interactions between the Ottoman Empire, the Venetian Republic, Spain, and Malta: the enslaved, soldiers changing sides, or various ethnic and religious persons in the Balkans unhappy with Ottoman rule seeking relief or income in the Venetian Empire or Spain. Sometimes encouraged by Jesuits or Capuchins, they approached Inquisition tribunals for reconciliation through penancing. Notaries and translators seemingly assisted a plea-bargaining process, after assurances that, say, while overtly Muslim, the supplicant was always Catholic at heart. Much has recently been revealed through studies of the Venetian border fortress of Palmanova using Udine archival material.

The remits of the Inquisitions were different from, and narrower than, those of consistories. Consistories were more interested in morality and social order than Inquisitions, which at least in earlier stages were more focused on theological heresies. Inquisitions did take on some wider issues of immoral and unchristian behavior by stretching definitions of heresy, such as sexual offenses that betrayed the sacrament of marriage. But morality, social conflict, violence, and misbehavior (prime concerns for consistories) were in the Catholic countries the target for others: parish priests, religious orders, or confraternities. Parish clergy were meant to check on the seriously immoral, unfaithful, and faithless at least through the mandatory annual confession and communion, with theoretically an official record of the unreconciled in the *status animarum* (state-of-souls) registers, which should have gone to the bishop. Preaching missions, notably by Jesuits and Capuchins, aimed to bring peace to neighborhoods, and reconcile family members. Some confraternities, such as the Nome di Dio (Name of God), similarly embarked on local peacemaking and curbing of blasphemy to save offenders from being arraigned by, or denounced to, the inquisitors. Christian Doctrine confraternities aimed to instruct adults found ignorant, as well as children, in the basics of the faith.[3]

The Iberian and Roman Inquisitions started with different major targets, with differing concepts of "heresy," but showed some convergence from the later sixteenth century in shifting issues of superstition, morality, and good Christian conduct. In Spain, then Portugal, the initial concerns were with Judaizers or *conversos*, converted Jews who allegedly reverted to Judaic practices, and *moriscos*, converted Muslims likewise seen as backsliders. From the 1520s fears developed then about Lutherans and Erasmians (with some confusion over the differences between them). Also targeted were *alumbrados*, advocates of a form of mysticism, seen as contaminated by Jewish beliefs and even Sufism. In Italy the post-1542 Roman Inquisition focused on followers of northern Protestants (generally designated "Lutheran"), a range of evangelicals, and Valdesians. In the kingdom of Naples, followers of an old heresy, the Waldensians, who linked themselves with Calvinists, became the victims of a brutal campaign from state and church. By the late 1560s the major threats to Catholic orthodoxy were essentially curbed, symbolized at the intellectual and high theology level by the final trial and execution in 1567 of the Florentine noble, Pietro Carnesecchi, a leading Valdesian. Also disparate groups of urban reformers were dispersed, condemned, or won over, as in Venice, Lucca, Mantua, and Bologna.

While major heretical propositions would continue to surface at elite or artisan levels, the Roman inquisitors turned, as some statistics can show, to issues such as magical arts, heretical and lesser blasphemy, abuse of sacraments, priestly solicitation in the confessional, and reading and possessing prohibited books. Spanish and Portuguese tribunals followed similar trends, though they could revert to pursuing Judaizers and *moriscos*, as in the 1620s–40s. Witchcraft accusations could surface in secular and episcopal courts as well as before the Inquisitions. In all Inquisitions, skepticism about sorcery accusations or pacts with the devil largely prevailed, panics were rare, dismissals frequent, and punishments generally lighter. The Sicilian tribunal consistently pursued Muslims and *moriscos* from the 1550s to 1650s. There bigamy was part of their remit, as in Galicia or Mexico, but not for the Venetian, Friulian, or Maltese tribunals, for example. Though numerically less significant, cases of "false sanctity" among women, advocacy of silent or mental prayer (by both sexes), and new versions of mysticism deeply worried inquisitors in Italy and Iberia, while new *alumbrados* were pursued in New Spain – partly because all undermined clerical authority and male control. The colonial Spanish and Portuguese tribunals in the Americas or West Africa had to confront ancient local cults, with possibly a greater syncretism of Christian and pagan beliefs (and Hindu and Muslim in Goa) than in the Old World. They also hunted down crypto-Jews escaping European persecution and/or seeking fortunes in the Americas. Proportionately they seem more preoccupied with book importation and censorship, from early days seeking to ensure Protestant books got nowhere near New Spain, Peru, the Azores, or Goa.

A major contrast between the Inquisitions came in their public display of punishments and reconciliations – notably in the *auto de fe*. These were more prominent and policy driven in Iberia, the colonies, and Sicily, than in mainland Italy. As Kamen argues, they were imposed in the mid-sixteenth century as major spectacles to demonstrate Inquisition power, and then attracted an intrigued public, as Doris Moreno Martínez notes in Chapter 13.[4] In Italy, these displays had a short period of promotion in the 1550s and 1560s with Pius V, an enthusiast for their publicity value. Successive popes saw them as possibly counterproductive and alienating. Italians did not burn Judaizers. Spain and Portugal persisted with *autos*, and Sicilians remained enthusiasts in the eighteenth century after the Habsburgs lost control, though the percentage of victims burned may have declined. The Roman Inquisition did persist with some very public executions of major individual heretics; historically the most notorious was that of Giordano Bruno, burned at the stake in Campo dei Fiori, Rome in 1600.

The execution rates for those denounced and convicted, as far as they can be assessed, were in reality low, and lower than myths usually attribute for all early modern Inquisitions. The worst period for casualties was probably in Spain in the period to the 1530s. Most punishing, with 6 percent execution rate in 1536–1767, was Portugal (and with Goa the most brutal tribunal). Spain then had about a 3 percent execution rate, with possibly over 4 percent in the early seventeenth century. For Italy (where overall figures are harder to estimate), the range runs from 1.6 percent to 2.4 percent, though the Roman Inquisition's outpost in Avignon had an execution rate of over 4 percent (with Protestants filling the highest category). The people with most to fear were those who might be denounced as Judaizers in Iberia and the colonies; Protestant foreigners arriving there in ports were disproportionately vulnerable, as in Sicily. Witch-hunts produced few executions and nowhere near the casualties that occurred in parts of Germany, Switzerland, or Scotland. In terms of fearing denunciation and pressure to self-denounce, but not facing dire punishments, Iberians were probably worse off than Italians. But apparently Catholics in Inquisition areas were less likely to appear before Inquisitions or episcopal courts than Calvinists in key cities and towns would face consistories or kirk sessions. Consistories seem more intrusive and pro-active than Inquisitions into social and moral conducts, with shaming, lecturing, and short-term excommunication as the likely punishments, not imprisonment, whipping, or worse.

This discussion has emphasized diversity between and within the inquisitorial systems, as affected by state organizations, local politics, and the degree of challenges from episcopal jurisdictions. In facing targets all Inquisitions spent less time on high theological heresy and focused more on improving good Catholic behavior, moral conduct, and eliminating superstitions. The Iberian Inquisitions faced real or imaginary problems of Judaizers and *moriscos* far more than the Roman Inquisition, and they had issues of converts from "paganism" and indigenous rites in the colonial worlds. This partly explains the greater brutality of those Inquisitions in reality and historical reputation. Future historians could well pay more attention to variations occasioned by local political and social conditions and the attitudes or enthusiasms of individual inquisitors.

Notes

1 Christopher F. Black, "The Trials and Tribulations of a Local Roman Inquisitor: Giacomo Tinti in Modena, 1626–1647," online, *Giornale di Storia* 12 (2012): www.giornaledistoria.net. See also Christopher F. Black, The Italian Inquisition (New Haven and London, 2009), esp. 81–82, 115–117.
2 Nicholas D. Davidson, "The Inquisition," in *The Ashgate Companion to the Counter-Reformation*, ed. Alexandra Bamji, Geert H. Janssen, and Mary Laven (Burlington, VT, 2013), 99.
3 Christopher F. Black, *Church, Religion and Society in Early Modern Italy* (New York, 2004) esp. 94, 119–29, and 134; and idem, *Italian Confraternities in the Sixteenth Century* (Cambridge, 1989).
4 Henry Kamen, *The Spanish Inquisition: An Historical Revision* (London, 1997), 205.

Section B

Tribunals and Jurisdictions

3

Consistories

Margo Todd

When Reformed consistory courts were established at the parish level, they used many of the procedural and bureaucratic structures of earlier ecclesiastical tribunals, but they also looked for their models to contemporary civil courts. In particular, they emulated the composition and practices of town bailies or aldermanic courts, as one would expect, given the urban settings of first-generation Calvinism. In national Reformations like Scotland's, these town models would be used from the second generation in rural settings as well. Reformed consistories thus departed from traditional church tribunals, whether Catholic or non-Calvinist Protestant, though the law they were executing was ecclesiastical.

They did so in ways that underline the centrality of the local laity in their operations. Most obviously, with the notable exception of Geneva, those sitting in judgment were nearly all unsalaried lay elders; the parish minister (or ministers, in large towns) was the only exception, and occasionally parish courts did sit and render judgment even in the minister's absence. Lay domination went further, however. Investigative mechanisms, evidentiary rules, the prohibition of advocacy, and explicit admission of women's testimony (a contested issue) all point to the important role played by laypeople in their operations. All participants in a case were local; the neighbors were both accused and judges, prisoners and bailies, and deponents for both parties in adjudicated disputes. Given the small size of early modern towns, by and large everybody sitting in the consistory chamber knew each other.

The laicism and localism of consistory courts matter, in two ways. First, they help explain their notoriously rigorous prosecution of people whose sins threatened the community's well-being, and their particular harshness during times of plague or famine, when toleration of sin was presumed to be the source of divine judgment. At the same time, they make more comprehensible the courts' frequent resort to admonition in lieu of penalty, "gentle" chiding of the young, and suspension of punishment "in hopes of further amendment." Offenders were treated as individuals – their families were not punished, and their property was not sequestered lest their heirs suffer for sins not their own and their children become financially dependent on the town. Fines were imposed on a sliding scale – evidence of the judges' awareness of their neighbors' circumstances. In the British Isles, torture was not used (except in a minority of witchcraft charges), and following the traditional practice of ecclesiastical courts, the secular arm carried out corporal punishment when ordered. The courts' concern was with what contemporaries called "good neighborhood" – the maintenance of peace and orderliness at the local level in a society too often beset by violence and hardship. Their personnel were part of the community – men who ate and drank, celebrated and mourned with their neighbors and who very much wanted the approval as well as the respect of their fellows.

Detailed exploration of this phenomenon is made possible by the survival of both session minutes and burgh court and guild records for the Scottish burgh of Perth in the century following the 1560 Reformation. Perth, one of Scotland's "four great burghs" and early on a notably "forward" Protestant town, provides the case study, but a glance at data from other Scottish, Dutch, Genevan, eastern European, and Huguenot congregations sustains the argument. Scotland's was the most extreme of the Calvinist Reformations. Scots Reformers went beyond their continental counterparts by abolishing even Christmas and Easter from the liturgical calendar, and some sessions met and enforced sermon attendance four times a week. But Scotland possessed the only nationally established Reformed church government and may be taken to represent the ideal of the Calvinist judicial Reformation.

PERSONNEL

Lay elders dominated Scottish sessions numerically: in general, from a dozen to twenty men served at any given time, together with any the minister or the minister of the parish. Perth, a town of about 6,000 in the

1570s, had only one minister until 1595, but twelve laymen served on its session for most of its sixteenth-century history, rising to fourteen when two "landwart" suburban elders were added in 1592, and to eighteen or nineteen by the end of the century.[1] Those who sat in judgment over their neighbors in this town were selected from a surprisingly broad swath of urban society. From 1577, the date of Perth's earliest surviving session book, through 1590 eighty-one men served as elders. After its initial founding, the session was a self-replicating group (though congregational veto was possible); nevertheless, in some years there was an almost complete turnover of the elders at the annual fall election. Nor were these men all members of the merchant oligarchy: of that eighty-one, about equal numbers were merchants and craftsmen (thirty-eight and thirty-four, respectively), an additional five were notaries (one of these was also a schoolmaster), one was a local landed gentleman. (Three are of unknown occupation.)[2] Further research is necessary to determine how usual this social breadth was, but the numerical imbalance between laymen and clergy was quite typical not only of Scots sessions but also of Huguenot, Dutch, and Hungarian consistories. Ironically Geneva was the one great exception: there a dozen elders sat with the whole Company of Pastors, which ranged from nine to nineteen ministers. Ministers also sat in the Utrecht consistory in greater numbers than in Perth, though they were not a majority – six, with eight elders; in Delft eight elders sat with four ministers; and in Emden four elders met with the pastors. But in Nîmes nine or ten elders joined the pastor, a balance typical for Huguenot churches. The French Walloon church near Frankfort had a session of two pastors and six elders, and in areas of Hungary and Transylvania where "parish presbyteries" were established, the proportions were much like Scotland's: in Kiskomárom, in western Hungary, the minister met with fourteen to sixteen elders. Deacons generally did not meet with the consistories unless the business of the day was poor relief. A salaried notary served as clerk.

Perth's elders, quite typically, preferred to meet with the minister present, but in his absence, they carried on with the business of the court, even in quite serious disciplinary matters. For seven months in 1584 Perth's minister was in exile, and the session met as usual, even in a case of alleged rape and "notorious" or capital adultery.[3] This is not to say that ministers were not exceptionally important judges: they may have comprised a numerical minority, but they wielded considerable authority. Still, when decisions were divided and votes had to be taken, the minister cast only one and could be overruled. Lay judges, already the norm in other urban tribunals (council, bailies, and guild courts), had obviously transferred readily to the new Reformed ecclesiastical court. In Zurich, and even in Geneva, where the Company of Pastors could outnumber elders on the consistory, lay control of discipline was manifested by a periodic and highly contested magisterial control of excommunication, and by the requirement that the council rather than the consistory judge and pronounce sentence on ecclesiastical offenders meriting criminal punishment – both rare phenomena in Reformed Europe.

Perth's sixteenth-century session met to address disciplinary and administrative problems about once a week – the norm in other Scots burghs and in continental consistories as well.[4] But Perth's session was an unusually zealous one: by 1597 there would be two discipline days weekly (Monday and Thursday), with a third meeting added on Tuesdays in 1598 for hospital business. In 1621 the elders added a regular Friday discipline meeting. Elders also attended presbytery meetings on Wednesdays, so that the office was an onerous burden on men with businesses to run.[5] Fines levied for absence from meetings and lapses in punctuality suggest that some elders bore it grudgingly.[6] Just as in Huguenot and Dutch settings, however, only rarely did anyone try to decline the office, which clearly carried considerable power and status along with obligation. It is worth noting that in Scotland those absentees' fines, like the more substantial penalties paid by offenders, went not to the court or its personnel, but to the poor box: there was no financial incentive for judges to serve.

JURISDICTION

The law that guided the tribunal was much the same as the canon law of pre-Reformation archdeacons' courts: sexual offenses, blasphemy, Sabbath breach, slander and quarrelling, and heresy were the main concerns in Scotland, with occasional charges of witchcraft or charming. In Huguenot courts, dancing was a new target (not a Scottish worry, for reasons that are unclear), as were confessionally mixed marriages. The Geneva consistory innovated by prosecuting those who continued to have their children baptized with the names of local saints instead of using only biblical names, as the pastors insisted. The only new offenses in Scotland, however, were observing traditional festivities and ceremonies, and visiting ancient sacred sites like holy wells, presumably for "superstitious" rather than merely festive purposes.

The lay elders who sat in judgment on their neighbors knew their charges well, in part because the jurisdiction of the consistory was parochial, not (as in pre-Reformation Britain) regional, with a single archidiaconal court, for instance, drawing cases from more than 150 parishes. This remained the sorry state of the Calvinist realm across Scotland's southern border, where bishops, archdeacons and their tribunals were retained, to the despair of puritans, and not incidentally, where offenders' fines were paid to the court's officers rather than to the parish poor.

For more effective oversight of behavior and belief, the Scottish parish was divided into "quarters" (or "districts," as they were called in continental Reformed settings) with an elder or two in charge of each, assigned to visit families regularly (at a minimum, before each communion) to quiz them on their catechism, ensure that family religious exercises were maintained, and investigate rumors of sinful behavior. As suburbs grew beyond the town walls, new districts were added, along with more elders. Again, this was typical of consistorial systems on the continent: Nîmes, for instance, defined eight "districts" inside its walls, one or two outside, with an elder assigned to each. Geneva's 1541 *Ordinances* likewise assigned elders to each of the city's neighborhoods and the 1561 revision required annual visitations of all households in each quarter annually before the Easter communion. The point to remember here is that with small jurisdictions and these highly structured oversight schemes, judges and accused were part of the same lay community.

LAY PROSECUTION

Initiation and prosecution of a case likewise reflected the centrality of the laity in the consistory's operations. Charges were generally brought by one of five groups – elders on visitation, offended neighbors, masters or mistresses of naughty servants (required by law to report them), burgh officers concerned with disorder, or sinners themselves seeking the comfort of confession (or aware that a pregnancy was a dead giveaway of sexual sin). Occasionally a kirk officer would present an offender, but this was not usual: the officer's primary responsibility was to pursue the contumacious – those who had been summoned but failed to appear. There was no systematic clerical investigation; even in cases of suspected popery or heresy, pairs of elders were generally assigned to visit and reason with suspects.

Elders' visitations could be either scheduled (as before each communion) or surprise (as on Sundays when during sermon time elders were sent to prowl their quarters' homes and alehouses to seize Sabbath-breakers).[7] Some cases doubtless stopped short at this point. A Utrecht elder who kept a visitation journal recorded hearing confessions, admonishing offenders to reform, and settling quarrels in people's homes so that all sins need not be brought to the consistory. This surely happened often enough that we see in consistory records only the tip of the iceberg.

Occasionally the town watch or bailies referred a case to the elders. George Makchanse and Elspet Cudbert, for instance, were during a communion service in 1585 "both apprehended in naked bed together in filthy fornication" by the Perth watchmen – for which they were condemned by the session and turned over to the bailies to be carted backwards through the town and put in irons.[8]

Many more cases, however, were brought because of "common bruit" or widespread rumor of misbehavior. Thus "diverse bruits arisen upon her by the neighbors dwelling about her" brought Effie Tully to the session's attention in 1587, her [adulterous] behavior "greatly cried out against by the whole honest and godly neighbors as most filthy."[9] In such examples lies an important indicator of why so invasive a system of moral and doctrinal discipline managed to establish itself in Scotland: it had strong support from laity in the community (at least the "honest and godly" ones), so much so that many people were willing in effect to serve as police and officers of the court. Scotland is clearly representative on this point: in Languedoc, for instance, women's gossip networks were a staple of the consistories' efforts to ferret out sin, the godly women of the community routinely using the courts for their own purposes. In the Netherlands, women's participation in disciplinary efforts is now understood as a lure to their membership in Reformed churches. Here the common ground with inquisitorial courts is evident: ecclesiastical tribunals could be made to serve popular interests, as Gretchen Starr-LeBeau and Kimberly Lynn show for Spain. Doubtless some of those reporting their less circumspect neighbors to the courts were mere busybodies, or were working out grudges or wreaking vengeance on enemies. In Perth, Margaret Donaldson insisted that those who charged her with harlotry in 1583 were simply envious of her relationship with the Earl of Errol.[10] But others were doubtless seeking orderliness in the community, or were convinced by the preachers' insistence that such disasters as floods, famines, and pest were divine visitations on a community that tolerated sin in its midst. Perhaps the most eloquent testimony to lay support for discipline comes from the numerous instances of sinners reporting themselves to the session for offenses that could not otherwise have been discovered – as, for instance, the married couple in Aberdeen who confessed sexual intercourse during a fasting season.[11]

Once a case was initiated, the accused were summoned by the kirk officer. If they failed to appear at the appointed time, they would receive two more warnings and then could be fined for contumacy. Repeated contumacy could result in gaoling, with the town magistrates responsible to seize the recalcitrant. By 1581, the Perth elders were sufficiently annoyed by offenders' failure to appear that they adopted an "Act of disobedient persons" mandating immediate gaoling of anyone "being warned and not compearing."[12] The bailies nearly always carried out the session's orders with alacrity. In the court, no representation was permitted: women as well as men appeared on their own behalf.

A person charged and guilty was best advised to confess the offense; lying about it at first and admitting it later often produced a greater penalty. One who insisted on innocence was constrained to prove it, though evidentiary rules differed from those of modern courts. In 1577, the Perth elders told a man who denied fathering an illegitimate child that he must swear an oath to that effect. Such oaths were generally held as proof – testimony to the seriousness with which contemporaries took swearing. John Swenton, the accused, was given a week to consider whether he would swear, and as the elders probably expected, at his next appearance he declined to give his oath. This they construed as tantamount to an admission of guilt, and indeed he confessed his sin at his next appearance.[13] A woman's oath bore as much weight as a man's: it was the oath of Swenton's partner that convinced the elders to investigate his paternity in the first place. A few weeks into the case, her charge that he had "made a faithful promise of marriage to her before the begetting of the last bairn" was also referred "simply to her oath"; she swore, and her word was accepted. There were hierarchies of oaths, left over from medieval practice. Taking one's "great oath" or swearing "the holy evangels touched" (putting one's hand on the Bible, as Swenton did in response to his partner's second oath) was most convincing. An oath taken in circumstances where lying was thought impossible was likewise beyond doubt, as in the case of a woman in labor identifying her child's father, or when the oath was taken in the physical presence ("in the face") of the contesting party – *prima facie* evidence of truth-telling.[14] When the elders were unconvinced by the pleas or testimony they had heard, they often summoned witnesses to depone the truth of a matter. Again it is noteworthy that the testimony of women was taken as lawful and reliable, a stance which the elders quite self-consciously debated in a

1582 case of notorious adultery, concluding "with one voice that famous women [women of good reputation] ought to bear witness in any matter that comes before them and their testimony received."[15] Huguenot, Dutch, and Genevan consistories also received testimony from women as a matter of course, though some expressed distrust; still, half of the people appearing before the Geneva consistory as plaintiffs, defendants, and witnesses were women.

In particularly troubling and uncertain cases, the elders sought detective services. In 1585, when a woman suspected of fornication claimed to have spent the night in Kintolloch with a female friend, the minister asked one of the burgesses through that village to ask the friend whether the Perth woman was really there; the burgess reporting that there was no such woman in Kintolloch, the elders' doubts were resolved.[16] The Scots session's arm was long, but even in a realm where Protestantism was not the state religion, Reformed consistories followed suit: the Nîmes elders wrote to their counterparts in Orange in 1580, for instance, to track down an errant fiancé. Even in more mundane cases, regular communication between parishes allowed the elders to investigate suspicious circumstances: couples who claimed that their marriage banns had been proclaimed in another parish, for instance, had to produce a testimonial to that effect from the clerk or reader of that kirk. This document was then scrutinized by the session, always aware of the black market that had grown up in forged testimonials.[17]

When all the evidence was in place, the session decided on an action. In most cases, decisions seem to have been consensual, so that the "haill elders" could act as one; sometimes, however, a division was recorded, either with the statement that "the most part" of the elders judged, or with a list of dissenting voters. The majority ruled.

PENALTIES

Penalties for those convicted by the session ranged widely, from "gentle admonition" to excommunication, banishment, and execution. The more drastic were extremely rare: the point of the disciplinary tribunal, as the chapters by Raymond Mentzer and Philippe Chareyre note, was not to punish, but to bring sinners to repentance and amendment of behavior. Statutory penalties (like execution for notorious adultery, or huge financial penalties for sabbath breach or engaging in banned festivities) were generally ameliorated, sometimes with explanation in the register. The elders considered such factors as youth or "simpleness of mind," visible sorrow for sin (tears being the best indicator), and poverty.[18] Fines were imposed on a sliding scale, though it must be noted that the wealthy could in some circumstances buy their way out of gaoling or corporal punishment.[19] And most strikingly, Catholicism was nearly always addressed not with penalties, but with long and painstaking efforts at persuasion.

For sins requiring more than mere admonition, the usual sentence was either a fine or public humiliation – in Scotland, sitting on an elevated "seat of repentance" in the kirk in the face of the congregation for a prescribed number of Sundays, in sackcloth and barefoot for more serious sins, followed by public confession of the sin and ritualized reception back into the congregation. Only during plague seasons could this sentence be commuted to a money payment. To ensure compliance, convicted persons were often required to secure a "cautioner" or surety who was liable to a hefty fee if the sinner either failed to perform repentance or pay a fine, or relapsed after repentance. Cautioners were (and remain) a staple of Scots law; here we have an example of the elders adopting an already familiar legal mechanism to enforce the new Protestant discipline. Cautioners were in effect a combination of probation officers and bail bondsmen. They were generally men of substance, though well-off women served as well.[20] Their fines, like others, went to the kirk's poor box.

The session adopted and adapted contemporary bureaucratic as well as legal conventions to facilitate efficient administration of prescribed penalties. One of these was simply the keeping of minutes – written records of acts and obligations by which people could be held to their promises. Perth's clerks even developed a system of coded marginal annotation for quick reference in order better to track compliance with required public repentance or payment of fines.[21] Those who would understand the pervasiveness and efficiency of Reformed discipline would do well to attend to bureaucratic convention, not just theology and preaching. Inquisitions did not corner the market on careful record keeping.

For the most serious sins, corporal punishment required the cooperation of the magistrates, since ecclesiastical courts after as before the Reformation were supposed not to have power over life or limb. In a Scottish town, only the bailies could legally have corporal punishment implemented. In practice, partly because of the personnel overlap between the magistracy and the session, the clerk generally records that the session assigned recalcitrant offenders to ward (gaol), crosshead (two hours pilloried in irons at the market cross), dunking, carting (being paraded on a dung cart through the town), banishment, and even execution, fully confident that the bailies would comply. Contrast this with Geneva, where cases liable to corporal punishment were remanded to the council for judgment, or Utrecht, where in 1628 the burgomaster told the consistory that it was impossible for the magistrates to control sabbath profanation. A sentence to the crosshead was prescribed for the most audacious sinners, like Barbara Brown of Perth, who flaunted her illicit relationship with Thomas Smyth on the very Sundays when she was sitting on the stool of repentance.[22]

The most serious spiritual penalty was excommunication, pronounced by the minister in the name of the congregation. What is striking from the minutes is how seldom it was imposed. Perth in the sixteenth century averaged an excommunication every two or three years – a striking contrast to Geneva's 9,256 from 1542 to 1609. Again, the mother church proves the exception to the rule. The Scots elders seem to have taken seriously the instructions in the *First Book of Discipline*, whose authors regarded excommunication as a last resort for only the most recalcitrant and impenitent offenders. They first visited and reasoned with sinners to persuade them of their errors, "travailing" to elicit confession and repentance, so that they "excommunicate *not* those whom God absolves."[23] If these efforts failed, ministers pronounced the sentence, but in the name of the whole congregation – the practice of exiled Huguenot and Dutch congregations in London in the 1560s as well, articulated by the Polish reformer John à Lasco in the order that he produced for the stranger churches, the *Forma ac ratio* (1550).[24] There were exceptions: in Geneva the consistory struggled to wrest control of excommunication from the magistrates, and the Dutch and French exile churches in Elizabethan England found their power of excommunication *de facto* taken by the diocesan bishop, though otherwise their consistories functioned in the usual reformed manner. But these exceptions occurred in unusual circumstances and serve to prove the rule. When James VI restored episcopal authority in Scotland, the bishops served as rubber stamps to session and presbytery pronouncements of excommunication – at least until the 1630s, and then their efforts to usurp English-style episcopal power brought on civil war. The kirk ruled itself, and disciplined whom it would.

Things could be even worse for Scottish sinners who failed to repent, or whose offenses were very serious. The worst of the lot could be banished from the community (the bailies' authority again underpinning that of the session), or put to the horn (outlawed), or even executed. In Scotland as everywhere in Europe, prostitutes were particularly subject to banishment, as when Christen MacGregor was expelled in 1582 "in respect of the great abuse of her body."[25] Horning meant that no one, including kin, could feed or shelter the offender; indeed, one "put to the horn" could be captured on sight and brought to the local magistrate for execution, since by statute law (as the horning proclamation for adulterers iterated) "all notorious and manifest committers of adultery shall be punished with all rigor unto the death, as well the man as the woman," and their goods escheat to the crown.[26]

In practice, the execution of sinners was a rarity, occurring in early modern Perth only once. In 1585, Helen Watson and David Gray, both married to other people, were apprehended in David's bedchamber by the town watchmen, who brought them to the session. The elders questioned both offenders and witnesses, discovered that their relationship had been going on for some time, and then took the unusual course of turning the couple over to the bailies for inquest. Very shortly thereafter, the unfortunate pair was hanged – the sole instance in this burgh of adulterers being executed.[27] But context matters: since the fall of 1584, plague and a concomitant famine had been raging in Perth. The session made quite clear its presumption of the close relationship between pest and adultery in its supplication to the bailies for an inquest: they sought "justice according to God's law and the laws of this country lest that otherwise being long winking at their wickedness, God of his justice plague both us and you with the rest of this city, as miserable experience has begun to teach us."[28] The record does not indicate whether Watson and Gray were penitent, or whether anybody cared. In the midst of a natural disaster understood as divine judgment for the toleration of sin, the need of the community to identify and eliminate the source of plague overcame the commitment of the kirk to securing repentance, amendment of life, and re-integration of sinners into the community of the faithful. It is no accident that the only reports we have of shaving and ducking fornicators also occur in this plague season.[29] Reformed discipline amid the crisis of epidemic disease gave way to sheer terror and primitive recourse to scapegoats.

Even at the worst of times, though, it was the laity who sustained the system – reporting sin, offering testimony, sitting in judgment as elders, urging gentleness where appropriate, investigating claims, and enforcing penalties. The successful establishment of the Reformed parochial judiciary happened because laypeople in the parishes seized upon it, negotiated its terms for their own purposes, and cooperated actively in implementing its objectives in their communities.

Notes

1 National Records of Scotland, Edinburgh [hereafter, NRS] ms CH2/521/2, fos. 66v, 85v, 107v, 133v, 160r.
2 *The Perth Kirk Session Books, 1577–90*, ed. Margo Todd (Cambridge, 2012), [hereafter, *PKSB*], 461–83.
3 *PKSB*, 283–91.
4 *PKSB*, 31–2 *et passim*.
5 *PKSB*, 31–2.
6 *PKSB*, 102, 168, 179, 231, and 276.
7 *PKSB*, 311, 351, 431, 452.
8 *PKSB*, 325–6.
9 *PKSB*, 47, 374.
10 *PKSB*, 267.
11 NRS ms CH2/448/2, f. 267.
12 *PKSB*, 190–1.
13 *PKSB*, 69–72.
14 *PSKB*, 80.
15 *PKSB*, 238 for the 1582 "Act of witnesses."
16 *PKSB*, 294.
17 *PKSB*, 372.
18 *PKSB*, 90 and 445.
19 *PKSB*, 336; NRS mss CH2/521/6, pp. 199, 202, 211, 237; CH2/521/7, pp. 330–6.
20 *PKSB*, 78, 93, 98, and 133–4.
21 *PKSB*, 6, 65.
22 *PKSB*, 314.
23 *First Book of Discipline*, ed. James Cameron (Edinburgh, 1972), 168–9.
24 *PKSB*, 122, 163, 269, 304–6, 317, 350.
25 *PKSB*, 243.
26 NRS-WRH ms JC 26/Box 2 (Justiciary Court processes), December 22, 1588.
27 *PKSB*, 294–5.
28 *PKSB*, 295.
29 PKSB, 310, 314.

4

Inquisitions

Gretchen Starr-LeBeau and Kimberly Lynn

Early modern Inquisitions were first and foremost judicial tribunals. They operated within the bounds of Roman law as rediscovered and revised in legal practices of the medieval and early modern periods, in a manner not radically different from other judicial tribunals of the day. They adopted and adapted prosecution protocols, evidentiary standards, and the use of judicial violence – that is, interrogative torture – to secure the confessions that were so important to a successful prosecution. As such, they were far more elaborate institutions than consistories were; Inquisitions operated using trained and specialized personnel, internationally disseminated manuals, and a global reach, even if inquisitorial activities varied markedly over time and individual tribunals manifested significant regional differences and did not consistently cooperate with each other in prosecutions. Indeed, in stark contrast to consistories, early modern Inquisitions were notable not for their localism, but for the international standards (and sometimes personnel) on which they relied. Early modern Inquisition courts were the sites of key intersections in society – between secular and sacred authority, and between clergy and laity – that may have increased tensions but also gave early modern Inquisitions much of their power.

INQUISITION AS A LEGAL PRACTICE

As scholars have long since demonstrated, Inquisitions brought together the power of the nascent state and the power of religious authority within the fabric of a legal structure that wove together and strengthened those powers. Inquisitorial procedure as developed in the twelfth and thirteenth centuries for use broadly in both secular courts and ecclesiastical cases (including but not limited to heresy) allowed for one's character or reputation – one's *fama* – to serve as accusation. This was a key innovation, because heresy prosecutions did not have a conventional victim or aggrieved party or evidence of a tangible crime. Moreover, heresy was likened to the crime of treason. This pivotal legal development opened up new kinds of penalties for heretics, such as the confiscation of goods as well as infamy and civil disabilities for them and their descendants.

The inquiry (*inquisitio*) carried out variously by clerics or jurists was intended to produce evidence that a crime had been committed and by whom. The same clerics or jurists who investigated the crime then stood in judgment of the accused perpetrator. Those investigations could require extensive questioning of many people, sometimes including the use of torture. It was, in short, a kind of questioning that was complex, invasive, and labor-intensive. To be effective, it required not only the power of the church, which had a long-standing set of ecclesiastical courts and experience in overseeing legal procedures, but also the coercive power of the state. And in fact it was often the state, rather than local authorities, who benefited from this interaction. Local officials in numerous places resisted the imposition of early modern Inquisitions. The nascent Spanish state found it to be a useful weapon, not only in bringing rebellious subjects to heel but also in taming fractious regional nobles. A particularly well-known example is the resistance of Aragonese elites to the Spanish Inquisition – cast as a Castilian incursion – in its first decades. Naples and Venice were each known for their efforts to preserve local control of inquisitorial activities. Secular officials often encouraged the prosecution of heresy for their own purposes and provided support at key moments in the process. Heresy was also in most realms a crime against the state as well, and could be prosecuted as such. Perhaps most obviously, secular political powers undergirded the authority of inquisitorial tribunals by carrying out their executions.

This conjoining of secular and clerical power was inherent in the construction of investigative procedure in the Middle Ages, but it became particularly marked in the early modern period. The three major early modern inquisitorial tribunals – those of Spain, Portugal, and Rome – all used ecclesiastical court structures as an arm of a state authority. The Spanish and Portuguese Inquisitions were state offices under the authority of their respective crowns. The Roman Inquisition was a more complex institution with a variety of mixed jurisdictions, but Thomas Mayer has argued persuasively that the Sacred Congregation of the Holy Office, as it was officially known, was an office of the Papal States – what Mayer describes as a bureaucracy and incipient absolutist state – even as it extended its jurisdiction into independent states in northern Italy such as Venice and Tuscany. But political support did not mean that religious motives were absent or simulated. "Righteous correction" and rebuking sinners were themselves righteous works with a long history, and Christine Caldwell Ames has demonstrated that a confirmed belief by clerics about the grave danger to society of heresy drove medieval inquisitorial practices. Early modern political theory likewise charged secular rulers with responsibility for the spiritual welfare of their realms. And early modern inquisitors advanced precisely these arguments. One Inquisition manual, circulated among both Spanish and Italian inquisitors, maintained that heretics should be punished more harshly than murderers because they killed not bodies but souls. Theorists of Inquisition described heretics as wolves and foxes hiding among the sheep, heresy as contagious and a force of corruption in society, and Inquisitions as evoking earlier practices described in biblical texts, as well as the punishment of false belief among the pagan ancient Greeks and Romans.[1]

Early modern Inquisitions were powerful tribunals, not only because of their linkage between secular and clerical authority but also because they existed at the nexus of lay and clerical interests. Certainly, there was much resistance to the establishment and institutional growth of Inquisitions on the part of some clergy and laity. But Inquisitions required the participation and support of laypeople to function as tribunals. Though many were brought unwillingly before the inquisitors, either as the accused or as witnesses, others seem to have made use of early modern Inquisitions to resolve grievances and settle scores (though note that not all "spontaneous" confessions were spontaneous, as Kim Siebenhüner discusses in Chapter 11). In this way, too, we see the continuity between Inquisition courts and other courts of the premodern period, as exemplified by Daniel Smail's discussion of the participation of locals in the legal culture of Marseille in the later Middle Ages. This changed over time, of course. In the early years of the Spanish Inquisition, many individuals saw heresy accusations and the Holy Office as a mechanism through which to punish a hated neighbor or business rival, and evidence of this appears in other tribunals as well. But there are some indications that voluntary participation in the legal actions of early modern Inquisitions declined as the dangers of coming before Inquisitions became more apparent. In any case, from the late fifteenth until well into the eighteenth century, there are ample traces of the legal savvy exhibited by a wide variety of early modern people when they confronted Inquisition tribunals.

JURISDICTION

The jurisdiction of early modern Inquisitions was subject to ongoing contestation. It was carved out of existing judicial bodies, but also emerged from evolving inquisitorial procedure and the notion of *fama* as an accusatory force. The crimes pursued changed over time and from place to place, and authorities both collaborated with and competed with one another to pursue heresy, since it was a crime in secular legal codes as well as ecclesiastical ones. Indeed, the position of heresy as a secular and religious crime meant that procedures and jurisdictions could move back and forth between the two kinds of tribunals. Witchcraft prosecutions were sometimes pursued in inquisitorial, ecclesiastical, and secular courts, and theorists debated that matter. Unlike in Spanish and Italian tribunals, the Portuguese Inquisition left a wide variety of issues to the regular ecclesiastical courts and maintained a more acute focus on Judaizing cases. Spanish Inquisition courts pursued sodomy charges, while their Roman counterparts did not. And sometimes it was advantageous for a defendant to be transferred to the Inquisition's jurisdiction. And there were other kinds of conflicts with secular authorities. The Spanish Inquisition, for example, claimed jurisdiction over the civil and criminal cases of its officials and lay affiliates (a kind of extension of the canon law claim to exclusive jurisdiction over clerics); these cases were often disputed by secular authorities.

There was jurisdictional jockeying within the institutions as well. The Spanish *Suprema* reviewed the activities of the district tribunals and urged consultation in capital cases and other serious matters, and Rome sought, especially across the later sixteenth century, to extend its hold over Italian tribunals. And the relationship between the Inquisitions was not absolutely clear. Because of his status as archbishop of Toledo, the famous sixteenth-century Spanish Inquisition trial of Bartolomé Carranza was revoked to Rome, despite significant resistance from the king. There is evidence that a few on trial before the Spanish Inquisition's tribunal in Sicily fled to Rome to present their cases there instead. There was great confusion over how inquisitors should evaluate the relative authority of the various indices of prohibited books, and there is new evidence of occasional collaboration between Spanish and Portuguese tribunals.

Fama was an issue for both consistories and Inquisitions, but inquisitors focused as much on intentions as on acts, which was not the case for consistories. And, across the sixteenth century, in the midst of heated debates among clerics about pastoral care and the correction of error, Inquisitions extended their claim to investigate so-called secret heresies, moving even further into the jurisdiction of confessors. In that arena and others, inquisitors sometimes clashed with bishops (who possessed ordinary jurisdiction over heresy), even though there was also extensive cooperation among them and many bishops had formerly been inquisitors. When the Spanish Inquisition founded its first tribunals in the Americas, it excluded jurisdiction over the indigenous population; the bishops, instead, were entrusted with pursuing heresy, error, or "idolatry" among those populations. In Italian tribunals, the bishop or his representative was frequently a participant in trials, and delegates of the bishop (referred to as ordinaries) often sat in Spanish tribunals, especially when voting about torture or capital sentences.

PROCEDURES

Inquisitorial procedures for the most part echoed those of other tribunals developed from Roman law, particularly after the initial phase of trials. While medieval Inquisitions occasionally relaxed the rules of evidence, used inappropriate witnesses, or restricted access to defense counsel, this was not generally the norm with early modern tribunals, which were staffed with trained jurists. Francisco Bethencourt has noted that inquisitors in Italy tended to be theologians rather than canon lawyers, but Mayer notes that even in the Roman Inquisition much of the staff were trained in law.[2] While staff varied between secular and inquisitorial courts, therefore, the trial procedures had notable similarities, even given the variation in secular law across early modern Europe and in European colonies. Moreover, personnel often had experience in more than one kind of court, and there was extensive borrowing back and forth between civil and canon legal theory. Francisco Peña's career is suggestive of the potential complexities. Of Aragonese origin, trained in theology and civil and canon law, he spent his career mainly in Rome, served on the Rota (the papal appellate court) and became its dean at the turn of the seventeenth century. He also consulted with the Roman Inquisition (as well as on Gregory XIII's massive project to reissue the code of canon law), theorized on legal topics including editing and reissuing several earlier Inquisition manuals, all while opining on other major controversies of the day and acting as a kind of unofficial Spanish ambassador at the papal court.

Scholars have debated how distinctive early modern Inquisitions' legal processes were relative to other early modern tribunals. An excellent example of this is the question of access to defense counsel. By the sixteenth century, inquisitors' manuals like Peña's popular new edition of Nicolau Eymeric's fourteenth-century tract stipulated the presence of a defense attorney, but it is not clear how consistently these rules were followed or how much latitude such counsels might have. Edward Peters, for example, takes severe restrictions faced by defense counsels as a given, while Henry Ansgar Kelly has argued vociferously that defendants had access to a variety of legal protections. Part of this disagreement may stem from regional differences in the practices of various tribunals and changing practices over time. Thomas Mayer, for example, argues that there were no defense counsels per se in the Roman Inquisition. In Spain, by contrast, defense counsels were a customary part of every trial.

Of course, the mere presence of a defense attorney did not guarantee a strong defense for the accused. Laziness, venality, and the subordinate status of defense attorneys relative to other members of the tribunal could all conspire against a strong defense. It is also important to note that inquisitorial procedure rested on a presumption of guilt; the burden lay with the accused to prove innocence. Mencia de Almeida's son wrote to the Spanish inquisitors handling his mother's case to request that they provide his mother with a defense attorney with a record of providing a strong defense for their clients.[3] On the other hand, even defendants without counsel could receive effective advice if educated family members in effect litigated their case in correspondence with the tribunal. Giovanni Battista de Freschi Olivi wrote frequent, extensive letters to the Venetian inquisitors, urging them to act mercifully in his mother's case and advising them on details of her history – essentially acting as an unofficial defense attorney.[4] And such appeals could even involve transatlantic travel, as in the case of Isabel de Ovalle y Pizarro, who arrived at the royal court in Spain from Peru in 1642 and successfully appealed to the *Suprema* and the Inquisitor General to bring her father's trial by the Lima tribunal to a conclusion.[5] In other instances, relatives sought to smuggle legal strategies and critical information into inquisitorial jails to aid the accused. In these cases we see not only another side of the interactions of laity and inquisitors but also what we might call the portability of legal knowledge in the early modern world, since an understanding of secular courts could assist one in interacting with inquisitorial tribunals as well.

Inquisitorial rules of evidence and the treatment of witnesses show the extent and limitations of distinctive inquisitorial procedure. Following the precepts of Roman law, confession, referred to as the "queen of proofs," was the preferred form of proof; absent that, the coincident testimony of two witnesses was required for any charge, and hearsay evidence was insufficient on its own to convict. Furthermore, the rules about standards for witnesses applied in early modern Inquisition courts as well. This meant that if a defendant could prove that a witness testified out of ill-will, his or her testimony would be stricken from the record.

Yet such rules protecting defendants were made more difficult by one of the most notable innovations in procedures among early modern Inquisition courts: the secrecy of witnesses. The defendant could know the substance of the testimony against him or her, but not the names of those who testified for the prosecution.[6] While there were medieval precedents for this, and early modern secular courts experimented with this idea as well, withholding the names of prosecution witnesses was one of the distinctive hallmarks of inquisitorial procedure. Scholars of the Spanish Inquisition have traditionally assigned this practice to Isabel, the Catholic Monarch. She feared that Judaizers would attempt to wreak revenge on their accusers if their identities were known, so the story goes. But whatever its origins, the results were significant. The defense was compromised in its ability to function, and for the relatively small number of defendants who attempted to discredit witnesses as malicious (a process known in the Spanish Inquisition as *tachas*) the process became a struggle to name as many potentially negative witnesses as possible in order to try to guess their accuser. Two other Spanish Inquisition defense strategies were calling character witnesses to vouch for the defendant (*abonos*) or summoning witnesses who would refute particular elements of the charges (*indirectas*). Early modern Inquisition courts also introduced another innovation to the detriment of the accused; they sometimes placed spies in cells to gain more information about the defendant and his or her wrongdoing, as John Chuchiak notes in Chapter 17.

Inquisitorial procedure in general, and the innovations of early modern Inquisition tribunals in particular, were all designed to help inquisitors determine the intentions as well as the acts of the accused and so to try to ascertain whether the misdeed was an accidental misstep, or a self-conscious attempt to contravene the church. But intentions were and are notoriously difficult to determine, as inquisitors were well aware. Ultimately, the best guide to an individual's intentions was considered to be a genuine statement of intention by that individual, but he or she was unlikely to speak in such a coercive environment. This conundrum sometimes led inquisitors to turn to one of their most important procedural tools: torture.

TORTURE

The most infamous of all inquisitorial procedures was torture. It remains a prominent theme in popular representations of Inquisitions and a source of debate for scholars. Acknowledging that Inquisition practice reflected the prevalence of torture in early modern judicial bodies generally, and that early modern Inquisitions were not the unrelieved chambers of horrors imagined by polemicists, in no way mitigates the coercive threat and real anguish caused by this practice. Torture was seen as an essential tool in compelling the confessions that were so important legally and soteriologically. Even though torture was rare in Inquisition trials, it was inseparable from the functioning of the court and laypeople's understanding of it. Torture helped inquisitors acquire the confessions needed to convict heretics. And fear of the Holy Office, in part because of its use of torture, helped drive coerced lay participation.

For the most part, the decision to put a defendant to torture was carefully regulated by inquisitors – both in legal theory and in practice – because jurists understood that someone who was tortured might say what they thought the interrogator wanted to hear, rather than reveal the truth. Inquisitors were concerned about the problem of false confessions (they also prosecuted on charges of false witness). There were some exceptions to the general rule of regulating torture – Mexico, for example, where inquisitorial practices seem to have been more arbitrary than elsewhere – but they were not common. Inquisitors generally resorted to torture in cases where there was a significant discrepancy between the statements of innocence by the accused and the significant evidence against them, or in cases where there was ambiguity about the guilt of the accused due to an absence of witnesses (as, for example, in witchcraft accusations). In theory, there had to be substantial yet partial proof to vote to torture the accused. Defendants who had lied to inquisitors in the past were not considered reliable witnesses and might be tortured to ensure that their statements could be trusted – though of course torture itself made testimony less reliable, as inquisitors well knew. Torture was also reserved for cases of particular concern or import to the Holy Office, since traditionally legal scholars argued that torture could only be used in a case where the penalty was death or mutilation.

In practice, there was some flexibility in these rules, so that even though the three major Inquisition tribunals all referred to the same strictures, it seems that Italian tribunals were more sparing in using torture than Iberian tribunals. It is not clear if there was a distinction in the use of torture between Spain and Portugal, though the Portuguese tribunal was harsher to its defendants in most respects. Judaizers were tortured more often in Iberia than in Venice, for example. And impressionistic evidence suggests that elites were tortured less often than others, again in keeping with traditional jurisprudence that argued that the nobility were exempt from torture. In rare instances defendants who were tortured in contradistinction to the standards of procedural norms – such as by local officials, without the permission or even prior knowledge of inquisitors – could protest or sue, as Lu Ann Homza's ongoing work on the Basque witchcraft trials has demonstrated. For both religious and legal reasons inquisitors preferred the accused to confess; torture was the last, most drastic means available to inquisitors to achieve that goal. Therefore, torture was used to gain confessions, not to cross-examine witnesses or as punishment, as was the case in early modern Muscovy.

The process by which torture was administered was tightly structured, too. Once there were supervisory boards established for early modern Inquisitions – the *Suprema* in Spain, the General Council (*Conselho Geral*) in Portugal, the Sacred Congregation in Rome – torture was supposed to be (and usually was) approved by them, even though there are instances of the *Suprema*, for example, reprimanding tribunals for proceeding independently or irregularly. Inquisitors might consider such factors as the age and health of the accused, and the importance of a confession to the case.

Once the decision had been made to torture a defendant, inquisitors initiated a procedure designed to guarantee the reliability of testimony gained by torture. Much of this was intended to utilize the psychological force of torture without resorting to torturing the defendant physically. Each torture session required the presence of an inquisitor; a prosecutor; a bailiff; a notary to record testimony precisely, including cries, screams, and sometimes even facial expressions; and a doctor, who was present to confirm that the defendant could sustain more torture. The doctors observed but did not intervene. And even despite the presence of doctors and the existence of a codified procedure, there were exceptional tragic cases like that of Mencía de Luna, who died in Lima in 1635 after she fainted during torture.[7] The defendant's counsel was not present. The defendant was led to the door of the torture chamber and admonished to reveal all he or she knew. If the defendant chose not to speak, the procession entered the torture chamber where the defendant was shown the torture instruments and told to confess once again. If the defendant refused again, the functionaries of the Inquisitions would strip her or him down and lash her or him tightly to the torture instrument. This was in equal parts humiliating and painful. Only then, if the defendant still had not confessed, would the inquisitors begin the torture session. In fact, these preliminary admonitions to speak were often effective. Many individuals confessed at one of these junctures.

Further strictures guided inquisitors after torture had begun. In theory, a person could be tortured only one time. Torture was uncommon and almost always confined to one session, but there were occasions when torture was "suspended" so that it could continue in a later session. Furthermore, statements made under torture had to be ratified at least twenty-four hours later, when the defendant was not threatened with torture. In this way inquisitors hoped to confirm the legitimacy of what they had learned through physical and psychological coercion. To modern-day ears, it sounds bizarre that anyone believed that defendants – quite likely still in pain – would fail to corroborate their testimony. And yet, several defendants seem to have done just that. Juana González confessed in 1485 to reciting a number of Jewish prayers and denying Christian theological concepts when tied to a torture instrument designed to simulate drowning. Yet when asked to confirm her testimony made under torture, she affirmed the validity of the prayers, but retracted her denial of the virginity of Mary. And as Juana's case shows, defendants were capable of explaining to inquisitors in an apparently plausible manner why some testimony was reliable and some was not.[8] Of course, denying statements made under torture also increased the risk of being tortured again because even a false statement made under torture was circumstantial evidence that could be used against one. Several forms of torture were in use in early modern inquisitorial and secular tribunals – though none, it should be noted, were employed by consistories. The Spanish Inquisition seems to have used three methods: simulated drowning (*toca*), the rack (*potro*), and the strappado (*garrucha*).

PENALTIES

The penalties meted out by early modern Inquisitions ranged widely, depending on the accusation, the tribunal, the inquisitor, and the individuals involved in the case. In Iberia and Iberian colonies, decisions on appropriate punishment were usually made locally, following established guidelines, as Bruno Feitler details in Goa for example in Chapter 23. In at least some cases in the various tribunals of the Roman Inquisition there was consultation with Rome, as Christopher Black explains in Chapter 2. Yet however penalties were determined, this phase of the tribunals' activities also demonstrated the close connections between sacred and secular authority that characterized early modern Inquisitions.

Some accusations that came before early modern Inquisitions were considered lesser offenses and carried lighter punishments. Furthermore, prosecutors were successful if they made a persuasive argument, assembling the evidence according to the rules of humanist discourse in a way that plausibly demonstrated the validity of the accusation. If a prosecutor was not entirely successful in this, a case could be ruled "partially proven," with a lesser penalty assigned. Outside of Iberia (under the Roman Sacred Congregation, for example) clergy might suffer lighter punishment. Such lighter penalties might involve swearing an oath not to repeat the offense or engaging in penitential devotions for a set period of time. In almost all the tribunals (except Venice and in some cases Goa), the penalty for any offense always included the seizure of all the defendant's property. Some of this property was used to pay for the defendant's upkeep during the course of the trial; the remainder went to support the activities of the tribunal.

More serious cases, fully proven, merited more serious penalties. These included (in addition to the customary seizure of goods) imprisonment, whipping, forced service on the galleys, exile, or execution, either by garroting or by the pyre. Imprisonment was in many ways the least onerous of these punishments. Early modern Inquisitions' jails were primarily for those whose trials were ongoing, not for holding convicted prisoners. In many cases, defendants sentenced to imprisonment were placed under house arrest, as was the case with Galileo. In addition, imprisonment was almost considered a spiritual quarantine rather than a punishment per se. Sentences given as "perpetual incarceration" were frequently commuted within a few years. Imprisonment, in short, was a relatively uncommon sentence, and one often associated with ambiguous or unpersuasive prosecutions. Punishment by whipping, in contrast, was a more straightforward penalty assigned to straightforward cases. Sentences generally specified between fifty and three hundred lashes – a punishment apparently more lightly administered than the floggings meted out in the eighteenth and nineteenth centuries. Forced service in the galleys for a period of between two and eight years might at the longer end have been a death sentence, though some men survived it. Inquisitors sometimes expressed their dissatisfaction with the customary sentences and the lack of penitential jails, arguing that there was not a sufficient institutional framework for spiritual rehabilitation of those they had convicted, and that punishments like galley service tended only to make people more irreligious. Exile, while apparently less grave, could be devastating. In a society where communal bonds were vital to maintaining an often precarious existence, isolation from family and friends was dangerous and debilitating. The Inquisitions' victims were without resources and forced to relocate several leagues from home depending on the terms of the sentence. Cities at this time generally restricted immigration, and citizenship requirements were high. A man or woman sentenced to exile would most likely be reduced to a fragile existence at the margins of society.

The most serious – and infamous – penalty meted out by inquisitors was execution. The Spanish Inquisition's peculiar term for a capital sentence – relaxation to the secular arm – reflected once again the close link between inquisitorial authorities and the state. Images of heretics perishing in flames as ghastly inquisitors leered over them are memorialized in paintings and popular culture alike. Of course, executions were on average quite rare in early modern Inquisition tribunals, with a few periods of frequent executions interspersed with years with few if any death sentences. After the 1530s, the total execution rate for early modern Inquisitions has been estimated as less than 6 percent, with the Portuguese tribunal at the upper end. In this as in most matters regarding early modern Inquisitions, there was significant regional variation; early decades of trials against Judaizers were particularly lethal, for example. And *autos de fe*, the ceremonies of reconciliation and execution occasionally staged by inquisitors and described by Doris Moreno Martínez in Chapter 13, occurred only in Iberia and Iberian colonies; the Roman Inquisition did not stage them. Generally speaking, whether or not there was an *auto de fe*, repentant victims were mercifully strangled or beheaded before being burned at the stake, while unrepentant defendants were spared no indignity or suffering and were burned alive.

Executions were also a final site of the intersection between secular and religious authority in the operation of early modern Inquisitions. Technically, Inquisitions did not issue death sentences and did not execute anyone; rather, they handed those they deemed unrepentant or relapsed heretics over to the secular authorities for execution. Everyone understood this to be a death sentence issued by the Inquisition. Yet this critical power given to inquisitors – and not available to consistories – required close cooperation with secular authorities to be effective. Indeed, clergy were forbidden by canon law from attending executions, let alone participating in them.

Once again, secular authorities' own concern with heresy and their willingness to make common cause with inquisitors strengthened Inquisitions just as Inquisitions in turn strengthened the state. Secular authorities were not mere participants in the ritual drama of executions crafted by inquisitors; as Bethencourt has noted, they were given the latitude to stage those executions as they wished. Civil authorities constructed a variety of ghoulish execution sites, from a simple bonfire, to huts in which the condemned were imprisoned and then immolated, to the plaster statues in which victims were sealed and burned to death in fifteenth-century Seville. The Roman Inquisition also issued death sentences, carried out by the various states under which the tribunal operated. These states generally used the same methods and the same location for Inquisition victims as they used to execute all other criminals – another sign of the continuity between secular and sacred justice. Unrepentant heretics were burned alive; those who confessed at the last minute were executed then burned. The consistency in form between criminal and inquisitorial executions in territories under the Roman Inquisition extended even to Venice, which to the dismay of inquisitors drowned its criminals in the lagoon at night, with no public ceremony whatsoever.

Examining early modern Inquisitions as judicial tribunals can serve to demystify the institutions, even as it highlights the particularities of their operations. Unlike consistories, Inquisitions were legal tribunals with an international corpus of manuals, rulings, and trained jurists from which to draw. Though they experienced significant local variation in operations, they were not in any meaningful sense local institutions in the way that consistories were. They were also, self-evidently, not lay institutions, even though they did have some lay personnel. Rather, they served as an important point of intersection between the laity and the clergy, sometimes to the benefit of both. But in their close cooperation with secular authorities, and the mutual strengthening that emerged from that close but sometimes rocky relationship, we can see surprising similarities to the interaction of consistories and secular authorities described by Sara Beam in Chapter 5.

Notes

1 Diego de Simancas, *Enchiridion Iudicum Violatae Religionis* (Venice, 1569), 11.
2 Francisco Bethencourt, *The Inquisition: A Global History, 1478–1834* (Cambridge, 2009): 92; Thomas Mayer, *The Roman Inquisition: A Papal Bureaucracy and its Laws in the Age of Galileo* (Philadelphia, 2013), 14–19.
3 Archivo Histórico Nacional, Inquisition section, legajo 132, expediente 16.
4 Brian Pullan, *The Jews of Europe and the Inquisition of Venice, 1550–1670* (London and New York, 1997 [original publication date 1983]): 282–7.
5 Kimberly Lynn, *Between Court and Confessional: The Politics of Spanish Inquisitors* (Cambridge, 2013), 272–3.
6 But note that secrecy was forbidden in Portuguese trials until 1547.
7 Irene Silverblatt, *Modern Inquisitions: Peru and the Colonial Origins of the Civilized World* (Durham, NC, 2004), 38–40.
8 Gretchen Starr-LeBeau, *In the Shadow of the Virgin: Inquisitors, Friars, and Conversos in Guadalupe, Spain* (Princeton, 2003), 274.

5

Consistories and Civil Authorities

Sara Beam

The key difference between early modern Inquisitions and consistories was structural: Inquisitions were judicial courts under the (at least nominal) authority of the papacy, empowered to torture and to issue death sentences against unrepentant recidivists. In contrast, Reformed consistories, with the notable exception of the Scottish kirks, did not have the authority to imprison or to punish sinners' bodies. This difference between Inquisitions and consistories has sometimes been attributed to a Protestant hesitation to punish sin with pain. But an examination of how consistories interacted with other courts, notably the secular criminal courts to which they often referred sinners, reveals more similarities than differences between Catholic and Protestant strategies. In order to understand the lived experience of godly discipline in early modern Reformed communities, it is essential to recognize the extent of the collaboration between ecclesiastical courts and their civil counterparts.

Much recent scholarship has stressed the differences between the aims of consistories (to reform the sinner and reconcile him/her with God) and those of criminal courts (to punish the criminal), and this tendency has sometimes led to assessments of godly discipline based on a consideration of consistory records alone. Other historians have qualified this distinction, emphasizing that criminal courts were also religiously motivated: like the consistories, they too were Christian institutions whose ultimate aim was to promote a godly society. In Geneva, certainly the wording of criminal sentences frequently alluded to Scripture and professed the aim to enact God's justice. Civil courts throughout western Europe sought not only to punish but to reform, imposing penalties such as imprisonment in houses of correction or a humiliating public apology. In order to understand both the distinctive roles that criminal courts and consistories played and the goals that they shared, we need to look in more detail at how these institutions worked together and how that collaboration changed through time: that is, we need to examine the records of the civil courts in juxtaposition with those of consistories. As the chapters by Raymond Mentzer and William Naphy indicate, the consistory in Geneva often worked in tandem with the Small Council, a body of twenty-five elected magistrates that was responsible for running the city and for judging crime. Elsewhere, consistories were often frustrated with the unwillingness of civil authorities to prosecute sin with vigor.

From its inception, the Genevan consistory was very active: by the 1560s as many as one adult in twelve residing in the city was summoned before the pastors and elders every year. Most defendants confessed their sins and were corrected, reprimanded, and then repented. Those who did not could be temporarily prohibited from taking communion, a sanction frequently imposed by the consistory between 1555 and the mid-1570s. In addition, at almost every weekly meeting, the consistory also referred individual sinners to the Small Council, with the explicit aim that the consistory's spiritual sanctions be supplemented with a criminal sentence. In the 1550s, at least 43 percent of all criminal cases overseen by the Small Council were initiated by consistorial referrals. The Genevan consistory did not have the authority to pronounce a criminal sentence against a sinner; its referral instead offered advice and drew the Small Council's attention to the possibility that a crime had been committed. As the sole body responsible for prosecuting crime, the Small Council was then free to dismiss the case entirely, to conduct a preliminary interrogation and let the matter drop, or to carry out a thorough trial. A full-fledged criminal investigation might include amassing the testimony of witnesses and physical evidence, interrogating the defendant with torture should he or she refuse to confess, and imposing a criminal sentence.

Since both the consistory and the Small Council shared some personnel, procedures, and standards of proof, including a heavy reliance on witnesses' testimony and defendants' confessions, the Small Council often followed up on the consistory's referrals and judged the sinner according to both criminal and spiritual criteria. Criminal sentences often made explicit reference to individuals' moral failings and violation of divine law: when in 1562 Nicolas Burmod was tried, tortured, flogged, and ultimately banished from Geneva for having committed several thefts, the Small Council's final sentence noted that his acts "contravened God and his saints' commandments [thereby] meriting serious corporal punishment."[1] Thus even when they were judging public-order crimes such as theft and murder, the Small Council magistrates were also engaged in godly discipline. Indeed, the Small Council sometimes referred criminals back to the consistory for further moral instruction.[2] Judging faith and punishing sin were two sides of the same coin at the height of the Genevan Reformation; the consistory and the Small Council spun a tight web of godly discipline whose aim was to create a harmonious community before God. Like Catholics, Protestants spun this web using both spiritual sanctions and, at times, physical pain.

Sexual offenses illustrate the symbiotic relationship between the consistory and the Small Council at the height of the Reformation. The consistory was the tribunal of first instance for most marital difficulties and sexual irregularities (with the exception of sodomy). By the 1550s, judging sexual misconduct had become one of the its central functions: breaking of marriage promises, desertion, fornication/adultery, wife-beating, divorce, and other marital troubles comprised 217 of the 390 cases investigated by the consistory in 1552. It is important to note that in almost 50 percent of these cases, the consistory did not consider the spiritual sanction to be sufficient, and, as a result, sent the case on to the Small Council. If the individuals confessed their guilt, the Small Council was usually quick to act: after a four-day trial in 1561, Louis Decrouz and widow Bartholomee Dorsieres, accused of living as man and wife, were both sentenced to six days in prison, fined fifty *escus*, and ordered to "beg pardon of God and of justice," a sentence that combined punitive elements with efforts at reintegration into the Christian community.[3] Unmarried men and women suspected of having multiple partners were treated more harshly. Etienne Falquet, brought to the attention of the Small Council for being engaged to three different women, was charged with bigamy and sentenced to "beg pardon on his knees, carry a burning torch around the city and to be banished."[4] Accusations of bigamy against men were relatively rare, but unmarried women suspected of having multiple sexual partners were often banished for the crime of *paillardise* (fornication) and were occasionally tortured beforehand.[5]

The harshest criminal punishments issued for sexual infractions were reserved for adulterers, whose sins were often uncovered through a referral from the consistory. Although the punishment for most adulterers in Geneva was banishment, the Small Council occasionally imposed the death penalty.[6] Jacques Rivit, a cobbler and bourgeois of Geneva, was found guilty in 1564 of having committed "the damnable and detestable crimes of incest and adultery" with the sister of his first wife and also to having committed fraud by approving her betrothal to his servant while he continued to have sex with her; as a result, he was decapitated.[7] Similarly, in 1570 a peasant woman named Clauda Mermod was convicted of having abandoned her husband back in her home village to come to Geneva, where she had sex with a married man from Lausanne. Whereas her lover was only banished, Clauda, who confessed her crime without torture, was drowned.[8] By choosing to refer such cases to the Small Council rather than seeking to resolve the matter with repentance and reconciliation, the Genevan consistory was effectively consigning these sinners to flogging, banishment, and death. These referrals make it clear that Protestants were comfortable punishing sin with corporal punishment, at least during the sixteenth century.

The consistory and the Small Council also worked closely together to punish the sin/crime of blasphemy. This was an ambiguous and varied infraction that could range from speaking God's name in anger to making statements that challenged the basic theological tenets of the Christian faith. In Protestant cities comparable to Geneva, such as Zurich or Bern, church courts usually only dealt with minor blasphemy. In Geneva, by contrast, the consistory was the court of first instance for most offences against God. Its investigation of blasphemy accusations was exceedingly thorough: numerous witnesses would be called in, and sometimes the utterance of a single curse would be considered over the course of several meetings. Claude Dancet, a Genevan cobbler, was accused of blasphemy in 1550. Although at first he denied it, a few consistorial sessions later he was eventually forced to admit his guilt after several witnesses testified against him.[9] Common blasphemous statements included "death of God" or "blood of God," though sometimes individuals were more creative: the butcher Nicolas Borsatti, was summoned before the pastors and elders for having said, while gesturing toward the genitals of a horse, "see here, this is how God pisses through his member."[10] Like many Genevan blasphemers, Borsatti was a repeat offender and had also been accused of wife-beating, petty fraud, public drunkenness, and failure to attend church over a number of years.[11] The pastors and elders seemed to deal with men such as Dancet and Borsatti with resigned patience, trying to correct their behavior; clearly, what they wanted to do was educate and reform. Only after several violations and a demonstrated lack of repentance (when Borsatti was asked to repent for his cursing by kissing the ground, he refused and replied that "he would kiss shit") did the consistory refer such men to the Small Council, which often sentenced them to a few days in prison or to carrying a burning torch while making amends.[12]

In another example, Claude Vulliermoz was chained to the prison walls by the Small Council and induced to confess that he had asserted that he would rather hear a dog bark than hear Calvin preach; having fulfilled his sentence of begging the magistrates' pardon, Vulliermoz was returned to the consistory for further instruction.[13] In short, the consistory and the Small Council cooperated to regulate blasphemy as they did sexual offenses, each contributing in different ways to the correction and punishment of the recalcitrant individual.

Perhaps the most notorious case of blasphemy is that of Michael Servetus, the freethinking humanist who arrived in Geneva hoping for tolerance but who was instead executed as a heretic by the Small Council in 1553. Servetus was unusual, however, not only in his radical anti-Trinitarian theology but also in the severity of the punishment imposed on him. The Small Council did not often go so far as to execute the religiously heterodox. Nevertheless, cases of blasphemy referred by the consistory to the Small Council did sometimes result in corporal punishment and banishment, even for men of relatively high status.

Whereas in Protestant Zurich civil authorities punished most blasphemers of high social standing with fines, in Geneva even well-established citizens were subject to corporal punishment. Jacques Chapelaz, a Genevan citizen whose status granted him full political rights to vote and to hold civic office, admitted in 1561 to having said that he had swallowed the devil and to having threatened the individuals who reported him to the authorities with violence. The Small Council's investigations also revealed that Chapelaz was a recidivist who seven years earlier had been imprisoned for swearing. As a result, the Small Council condemned Chapelaz to have his tongue pierced with a hot iron.[14] Two years later, Pierre Jaccon, also a citizen and a master pin maker, admitted to having committed blasphemy and to having strayed from the true faith. In 1562, during the first civil war in France, Jaccon was working in Lyon during which time he attended Catholic mass, denounced a Reformed co-worker causing him to lose his job, wore the Catholic colors in the city streets, and even predicted that the Catholics would win the war (which turned out to be true but was blasphemous because it expressed doubt in God's divine plan). For his apostasy, Jaccon was whipped, branded on the forehead, and banished from the city on pain of death.[15] During the four years between 1560 and 1563, at least sixteen men were sentenced to corporal punishment or banishment for committing blasphemy, an average of four individuals each year.[16] These punishments would have been a powerful signal not only of how little religious diversity the authorities were willing to tolerate but also of how severely one could be punished for offenses originally identified by the consistory.

It would, however, distort the lived reality of godly discipline to suggest that morals regulation was entirely a top-down affair with little community support. Although the very existence of consistorial discipline demonstrates that spiritual heterodoxy and everyday concupiscence were commonplace in Reformation Geneva, it is unlikely that the courts would have been able to investigate and punish sin unless a core group of community members supported those goals. As Margo Todd and Jeffrey Watt affirm in their chapters, many investigations undertaken by the consistory were initiated by neighbors. In criminal trials, the testimony offered by multiple witnesses was often internally consistent, which suggests that witnesses had reached a consensus about the offender's behavior before going to the authorities. Petramande, wife of Jean François Morel, found herself accused of adultery as a result of this kind of process. In 1567, the consistory chastised Petramande several times for talking and socializing with two men before the pastors and elders referred the matter to the Small Council. In its referral, the consistory helpfully included a list of potential witnesses whom the criminal court might contact for information. In total, eight men, several of them respectable bourgeois and citizens, as well as three women, testified that the accused men often loitered in or near Petramande's home when her husband was away. Though none of the witnesses had seen anything untoward occur, the consistency of their reports was deemed evidence enough to justify interrogations – with and without torture – of Petramande and of the two accused men. Ultimately, none of them confessed: despite their denials, the two men were banished whereas Petramande was released.[17] For a number of decades, Genevan society as a whole was engaged in a search for moral purity that involved a significant portion of the community: accusers, witnesses, pastors, elders, judges, and sinners all had important roles to play in godly discipline.

During the height of the Reformation, sins such as blasphemy and adultery resulted in stiff punitive sentences, imposed by the Small Council after a referral from the consistory. Men and women of all ranks of life were tortured, banished, and sometimes executed for these crimes. As a result, Genevan residents during the 1550s and 1560s probably experienced far higher levels of fear that they would be punished for a wide range of sins than did most Spanish residents during the height of the Inquisition. Unlike godly discipline in the Dutch Republic, whose impact on most residents was relatively limited, in Geneva close collaboration between the consistory and the Small Council resulted in morals regulation that impacted a wide swath of Geneva's population.

This symbiotic relationship between the consistory and the Small Council did not, however, last long. The magistrates, who between the 1540s and the 1560s for the most part supported the idea that recalcitrant sinners all of social classes deserved corporal punishment, soon began to have doubts. As early as the mid-1570s, the Small Council began to complain that the consistory's frequent recourse to suspension from communion was counterproductive and took steps to reassert its authority over excommunication; in response, the pastors began to complain that the Small Council was no longer prosecuting sins such as blasphemy and fornication with sufficient diligence. Indeed, the Small Council became demonstrably less willing to force male members of the urban elite to obey consistorial discipline. By the end of the sixteenth century, when members of the various elected city councils refused to present themselves before the consistory when summoned, the Small Council did little to back up the pastors' authority.

As a result, by 1600 criminal punishments for both blasphemy and sexual offenses changed significantly: specifically, they became less violent. Whereas the consistory continued to exclude sexual sinners from communion during the seventeenth century, the Small Council gradually abandoned torturing, flogging and banishing sexual sinners in favor of fines.[18] Blasphemers were also treated more charitably: the last individual executed for blasphemy in Geneva was Nicolas Antoine, a pastor who converted to Judaism and ran through the city streets proclaiming his spiritual revelation in 1632; Antoine was burned at the stake, a decision taken by the Small Council with the backing of most pastors. His trial was, however, highly exceptional. Seventeenth-century Genevan society had not abandoned godly discipline, but the Small Council became increasingly reluctant to employ corporal punishment against sinners; even outright apostates were usually corrected and reincorporated into the community.[19] The widespread conviction that violent purging could produce a purified godly community was beginning to wane.

Reformed pastors in communities outside of Geneva and Scotland were less successful in convincing civil authorities to support their moral reform agenda. This was not for lack of trying. In rural Hungary, where godly discipline was sometimes resisted by the nobility, archdeacons repeatedly urged local clergy to work more closely with village councils. The hope was that these councils would reinforce the presbytery's shaming sanctions with corporal punishment and fines. Some villages did threaten to punish swearing with the stocks and tongue slitting, but Reformed archdeacons were not satisfied that the law was being vigorously applied. In France, tensions between La Rochelle's town council and its consistory also limited the effectiveness of godly discipline. There rowdy groups of law clerks known as the Basoche continued to be active and to mock the consistory's efforts to suppress traditional carnival culture for decades after the establishment of the Reformed faith.

Consistories also had trouble obtaining the cooperation of civil courts in communities where several religions and/or cultural traditions existed within the body politic. Even in the Dutch Republic, where the Reformed faith was the established church, some local magistrates and many lay folk were unwilling to conform to the moral strictures advocated by the most fervent Reformed clergy. In many Dutch cities, urban magistrates' primary aim was instead to maintain the peace in religiously heterodox communities where Catholics, Mennonites, and various mainstream Protestant groups lived in relative harmony together. Outside of Europe, imposing consistorial discipline was even more difficult. Hendrik Niemeijer's chapter shows that in the Dutch colonies, where the Reformed faith competed with Catholicism and other religious traditions for the souls of local, enslaved, and mixed-race populations, the consistory was even less able to impose moral regulation upon the entire population.

There were, to be sure, some small, somewhat isolated and semi-autonomous communities, such as Montauban and Nîmes in France during the Wars of Religion and the English colonies of New England during the mid-seventeenth century, that were as successful as Geneva in imposing godly discipline. In Montauban, the consistory and the city council were run by more or less the same set of families, and this overlap made it possible for them to impose rigorous moral control, defending their tiny Reformed "island" against the surrounding flood of Catholicism. In Massachusetts and Connecticut, lay-dominated church congregations functioned similarly to consistories in that they censured sinners but had no authority over corporal punishment; Puritan congregations judged matters as diverse as absence from church to sexual sin to personal conflicts between congregants. In difficult cases, individual churches were quick to refer individuals to the county court, which was able and often willing to fine and imprison them. It is important to note that these local campaigns to achieve moral purity, often undertaken with urgency due to a perceived military and/or religious threat posed by nearby Catholics or native American communities, rarely persisted in an intense form for more than fifty years. Like Geneva, these communities were characterized by relatively high levels of religious, social, and economic homogeneity and a tight integration of ecclesiastical and civil elites.

The only large polity that was able to establish a relatively long-lasting collaboration between civil authorities and consistories was Scotland, where the Reformed church became the sole legitimate faith. There, as in tiny Geneva, a remarkable convergence of civil and ecclesiastical law enabled a rigorous regime of godly discipline. At the local level, the kirk session judged moral and religious misdemeanors with a consistency that had a profound effect on the daily lives of lowland residents. Their ability to do so was strongly influenced by the support of lay elites, civil courts, and the presbyteries. In seventeenth-century Stirling, it was not uncommon for the kirk session to refer difficult cases of adultery, suspected witchcraft, and blasphemy to a wide variety of courts, including the regional presbytery, the sheriff court, the burgh court, and the High Court of Judiciary. Yet, as in Geneva, Scottish kirks became increasingly hesitant to prosecute members of the social and political elite after the 1590s, probably in order to ensure their continued support for disciplining the rest of the community. Analyzing the impact of the kirk on Scottish society is impossible without acknowledging its imbrications in a complex web of disciplinary institutions, whose collective aim to reform Scottish society remained remarkably focused for most of the early modern period.

If the records of consistories and civil courts are worth examining side by side for communities where they collaborated well together, they are equally so even when this relationship was less symbiotic. Analyzing how different institutions pursued moral regulation clarifies that godly discipline in early modern Europe inadvertently led to the emergence of a clearer distinction between private sin and public crime by the eighteenth century. Throughout the early modern period, civil authorities continued to render judgment on what we would call sin. They oversaw such matters as marriage, luxury consumption, and poor relief – framing them within a Christian conception of right living – and in fact came to have the ultimate authority over these matters. But if we compare the functioning of ecclesiastical and civil tribunals over long periods of time we can see the process by which some offenses came to be treated less as sins than as crimes; that is, came to be desacralized. In early modern Rotterdam and Delft, both consistories and city authorities both were responsible for judging extramarital sex, but over time they evolved different penal approaches that in turn redefined the moral and social role of sexuality. Consistories tended to handle cases of adultery within the Reformed church, and were hesitant to shame the church community by referring such cases to the criminal court. On the other hand, consistories judged and publicly humiliated young couples who began to have sex before marriage. Civil courts were more lenient when faced with a young couple who had made informal marriage vows but had also consummated the relationship before the wedding. Because civil courts were primarily interested in promoting financially stable family units, magistrates were willing to turn a blind eye to the infraction as long as the couple promised to marry soon afterwards. By the middle of the seventeenth century, these distinctions hardened, and civil authorities became increasingly concerned with regulating the economic implications of illicit sexual relations: establishing child support for children born out of wedlock or condemning bigamous men because they could not afford to support two families. Possibly the fact that consistories handled the moral ramifications of fornication freed civil authorities over time to focus on financial implications, and in doing so led to the gradual desacralization of fornication as an offense.

Another advantage of the comparative study of civil and ecclesiastical courts is the light it throws on infrajustice or subjustice, the many informal means by which individuals regulated personal conflicts. Going to court was often a negotiating tactic among early modern individuals, families, and communities in conflict. The accusers' aim was not always formal punishment of the defendant: initiating a court case often sparked informal negotiations between hostile parties that resulted in a private settlement of differences. Current research suggests that individuals chose courts that were the least expensive and most likely to resolve conflicts quickly, but also that revenge against an opponent could involve initiating multiple suits in different jurisdictions. In Geneva, where consistorial justice was free, individuals might have been more likely to frame their conflict in terms that the consistory would recognize than to pursue the matter before civil authorities where costs could be punishing. In eighteenth-century Lausanne, Jeanne Elizabeth Champrenaux came before the consistory complaining that another woman had slanderously accused her of being pregnant. Medical examination revealed that Jeanne Elizabeth was in fact not with child, but the investigation also unearthed that the quarrel between the women originated in other questions, specifically disapproval over a proposed marriage between Jeanne Elizabeth and the nephew of her slanderer. From the perspective of plaintiffs, bringing the consistory's attention to a conflict or a sin was but one of many tactics that they could use to achieve their aims. The fact that many individuals continued to turn to the consistory throughout the early modern period demonstrates that community members believed it capable of resolving conflicts effectively, but also suggests that clear-cut distinctions between judging sin and crime did not necessarily exist in the minds of plaintiffs and possibly of judges as well.

More so than Inquisitions, early modern consistories were profoundly local institutions whose ability to effect godly discipline was defined by their particular relationship with civil authorities and the willing participation of local residents. In Geneva, where such collaboration existed during the height of the Reformation, the consistory spearheaded a rigorous regime of moral regulation across the city. Yet, like the Spanish Inquisition, the initial enthusiasm for punishing sin with corporal sanctions waned within a matter of decades. Consistories in most communities could not count on civil authorities to share their priorities. As a result, most consistories focused on shame and humiliation rather than pain in order to impose discipline on the faithful.

Notes

1 Archives d'État de Genève (AEG) Procès criminel série 2 (PC2) 1254.
2 AEG Procès criminel série 1 (PC1) 1717; AEG PC1 1230.
3 AEG PC1 958.
4 AEG PC1 880. See also AEG PC2 1233; AEG PC1 973.
5 AEG PC1 1076; AEG PC1 1434.
6 AEG PC1 346; AEG PC2 750; AEG PC1 914; AEG PC1 915.
7 AEG PC1 1220.
8 AEG PC1 1594.
9 AEG PC1 815; *Registres du Consistoire*, vol. 5, 9-11, 17.
10 Ibid., 59.
11 Ibid., 59, 86, 94, and 176–7; *Registres du Consistoire*, vol. 2, 298.
12 AEG PC1 699; AEG PC1 657; AEG PC1 908.
13 AEG PC1 626; AEG PC1 568.
14 AEG PC1 995.
15 AEG PC1 1092.
16 AEG PC1 917; AEG PC1 955; AEG PC1 995.
17 AEG PC1 1394.
18 AEG PC1 2665; AEG PC1 2958; AEGPC1 2991.
19 See AEG PC1 2512; AEG PC1 2595; AEG PC1 3407; AEG Registres du conseil de la ville 149, f. 232.

6

Episcopal Courts in Iberia, Italy, and Latin America

Edward Behrend-Martínez

Despite the persistent and perhaps misleading focus of researchers on inquisitorial and criminal courts, from the late Middle Ages through the sixteenth century the most organized and persistent juridical presence in western Europe was the Catholic Church's network of diocesan courts.[1] Church courts were central judicial institutions in the everyday lives of early modern Italians, Iberians, and Iberoamericans. Furthermore, not only were church courts pervasive, but they could be quite adaptable to local concerns. This judicial system resulted from bishops' roles as the most important organized bureaucratic and religious authorities throughout the European Middle Ages. In Spain alone there were forty episcopal courts by 1600, and ten in Portugal. These episcopal courts had provided the only institutional Christian cohesion that existed before the early modern period in western Europe. Many of their powers had increased appreciably with the reforms of Innocent III (r. 1198–1216) and the growth of church finances and power until the late fifteenth century. The Catholic Church and its canonists also pioneered the modern introduction and integration of Roman law into Europe. As a result, their significance was equal to the better-studied inquisitorial tribunals or secular criminal courts.

In order to understand the use and scope of ecclesiastical courts in Iberia, Latin America, and Italy, it is important to study the Catholic Church as an early modern state unto itself, complete with ideology, bureaucracy, law, and courts. Although this vast state came into conflict with the growing power of monarchs and other authorities throughout the early modern period, its legal jurisdiction and apparatuses continued to function more or less independently. Episcopal courts, and the educated personnel who worked in them, provided a legal system available to everyone – clerics and laymen – through networks of parishes, parish priests, monasteries, and other clergy. Until the mid-sixteenth century, secular courts were mere shadows of the church's vast array of ordinary church courts whether measured by organization, finances, legal codification, or personnel. Yet historians know much more about secular and Inquisition courts, and their growth and legal codification, than they know about ordinary church courts. The reasons for this are likely teleological; it is difficult to ignore the trend toward royal centralization and the triumph of secular justice over ordinary ecclesiastical courts by the end of the eighteenth century. Furthermore, the bewildering array of parochial and episcopal archives, many still uncatalogued, that reside in regional centers or small towns make research difficult.

The Catholic Church provided all dioceses with a general and more or less uniform legal code from which local bishops, vicar generals, and lawyers could settle disputes. The canon law the church developed during the High Middle Ages was based on Roman law (especially as expounded by Justinian) that the papacy had elaborated over the centuries. Then in the twelfth century, important jurists such as Peter Lombard, Gratian, Hugoccio, and then Innocent III reconciled church law, Catholic belief, and everyday religious practices during the High Middle Ages. Because of the weight of its authority and its ancient tradition, church law gives the impression of being inflexible and dogmatic. Yet, during the early modern period at least, three factors mitigated canon law's legalism: First, local synodal constitutions and decrees shaped canon law to suit local purposes. Second, judges' interpretations of canon law and verdicts could be ad hoc and even creative. Third, the sheer bulk of canon law provided various interpretations for jurists to employ.

Synods played a crucial role in the local use of canon law. Synodal decrees amended ecclesiastical law, and so changed it to fit local and colonial circumstances. Displaying the energy of late medieval society, most dioceses began regularly convening synods – councils of religious leaders of a diocese – to deal with diocesan business and to confront local problems. Synods grew in regularity in the sixteenth century, especially after the Council of Trent, and in early modern colonies Iberians continued the practice of holding synods in their new dioceses abroad. From synods in the Old World and the New, there emerged constitutions and decrees that dealt with local realities and religious practice; although based on earlier synods in older dioceses, synodal constitutions invariably addressed problems peculiar to local regions and bishoprics, as Richard

Trexler found for Italy: "When the bishops and town counselors wrote their laws, they reckoned with using a host of legal instruments to modify them to immediate needs."[2] So aside from the canon law that formed the basis of all diocesan law, there existed a local legal corpus that dealt with regional issues and problems. One might expect that the Tridentine decrees of 1563 would have challenged local diocesan customs and rules; undoubtedly this occurred on occasion. However, Trent did much more to invigorate local diocesan courts rather than curtail their authority.

Yet the bishops' courts remained crucial to many people through the eighteenth century, at least in the Catholic areas of Europe, for several reasons. First, if one were in the market for litigation, church courts were relatively cheap. They were as accessible, often, as one's local parish or even monastery; an initial complaint could be vetted by a confessor or monk, and from one of these local church parishes or monasteries a complaint could easily be directed to the diocesan court. Second, the church courts dealt with personal issues that secular officials usually could not: primarily marital, romantic, and spiritual disputes. For instance, the greatest single complaint related to interpersonal disputes in most dioceses was a broken marriage promise. These cases involved one party accusing another of having broken a verbal promise to marry and usually trying to marry a third party. These cases not only show how people's quotidian concerns brought them to the church court but also the relatively inexpensive litigation that the court offered; in Spain, for instance, the bulk of such cases were brought by small farmers (*labradores*) and artisans. If a litigant could demonstrate poverty, they would be defended *pro bono* and pay less in court fees.

A crucial variable regarding the business of these courts was the bishop and whoever he placed in the position of vicar general and fiscal general. It is clear that activist bishops increased court business by prosecuting offenses they were particularly interested in eradicating. The bishop's court in Cuenca heard twenty-two cases of long-term extramarital affairs in a campaign it waged between 1590 and 1600; most of those cases were actually prosecuted in one year, from the fall of 1591 to the fall of 1592.

Economically, of course, the church was a powerful and far-reaching institution, so the church courts necessarily dealt with an array of financial and property questions that affected anyone connected to it, its personnel, land, and buildings. Throughout Italy, Iberia, and the New World, parish churches, cathedrals, and episcopal landholdings were an enormous component of the economy. Clerics necessarily controlled all business that occurred on their holdings. This was the case, for instance, with one of Cordoba's slaughterhouses, which happened to belong to the Cordoban cathedral. The town council of Cordoba, which wished to tax and regulate local markets, litigated in the church court in 1504 to move the slaughterhouse, but to no avail; the church kept control of the meat market, and presumably its taxes as well.

And since the early modern church in Iberia and Italy had such large property holdings, most people were affected by its interests. These church institutions did not only take in money, but could loan it as well: in Lima the convents of Santa Catalina, Santa Teresa, and Santa Clara provided ten-year annuities to local elite families at a fixed rate of interest. The church courts also handled all problems arising from special donations to its institutions. So when a citizen from Cuenca wanted to establish a diocesan charity to fund dowries for future generations of women in his family, it was the church court that registered and administered the fund's implementation.[3] Church courts also handled problems arising from the distribution of church offices and benefices, most of which guaranteed some fortunate cleric a perpetual annuity. The bulk of the church courts' business dealt with such mundane, yet often important, financial and property issues.

Church courts also handled criminal cases. As is well known, any crime, with the exception of those reserved for the Inquisition, that involved a cleric or anyone who could claim they fell under the jurisdiction of the church, could be tried in its courts. This amounted to 4–5 percent of the population during the sixteenth century. In fact, like the secular and inquisitorial courts, many dioceses had their own jails to hold offenders awaiting trial. The Florentine archbishop commonly tried fifteenth-century clerics for everything from drunkenness, fornication, performing mass while excommunicated, to attending theatrical performances; sex crimes like concubinage and fornication were, by far, the most common complaint. As in Spain, Italian church courts also dealt with accusations of sodomy, though these were quite rare. Infanticide and abortion cases appeared occasionally in church courts, especially if these unwanted children had resulted from the adventures of promiscuous clerics. Unlike Spain, in early sixteenth century Fiesole, Italy, the diocesan court was the main jurisdiction for investigation of infanticide: Richard Trexler found the court investigated 281 cases between 1500 and 1540 alone.[4]

Church courts dealt with a wide variety of disciplinary issues regarding clerics, or anyone on church property, as several criminal cases from the diocese of Calahorra (northern Spain) attest. The bishop's court in that diocese had to prosecute a priest in 1674 for refusing to bless a new mother until she gave him a rooster.[5] And in 1743 the church court prosecuted a surgeon for stealing a woman's corpse so he could practice dissecting it in the local church; the woman's surviving husband had, understandably, become enraged.[6] As in Italy, however, clerical crimes could often be quite serious, involving sex and violence, as when Dr. Juan Francisco Roldan was tried for beating two teenage girls in 1706.[7] In 1695 the court – with the special participation of its bishop – prosecuted a philandering Basque priest Antonio de Garayzabal for impregnating three of his parishioners.[8] He confessed, and the court charged him the litigation costs and made him swear not to persist in his womanizing. The court prosecuted him two years later for fathering another child. Again, Garayzabal confessed, paid court costs and promised not to relapse.

The courts maintained an array of personnel whose number depended on the wealth and relative business of the diocese. Typically, though, several notaries, procurators, a bailiff, a prosecuting attorney (fiscal general), and the head ecclesiastical judge (vicar general) were its usual officials. They worked out of the courts' offices. Sometimes the court would be attached to the episcopal palace, other times the diocesan cathedral, or even separately, in the most populous city in the diocese. In the diocese of Calahorra and La Calzada, for instance, the court did not reside in either of the bishopric's cathedral towns, but instead worked out of Logroño, the largest city of the diocese. The court maintained business hours, though, again, these varied depending on the season and what was on the court's docket. Rather, he oversaw the appointment of the vicar general who did.

Other officials who usually worked with the courts were officials of first instance, such as the inspector generals (*visitadores*) of the diocese whose job involved traveling to inspect parishes and communities in the name of the bishop. They could initiate criminal cases against clerics and laity alike and then forward their cases to the diocesan court. Local vicars, archpriests, and even parish priests occasionally took on roles as judges of first instance, listening to marital disputes, exposing crimes, and issuing orders. This occurred, for example, when a vicar of Bilbao, Diego de Unzaga, tried Beti de Venitt for adultery and other crimes in 1698, such as eating meat during Lent and consorting with English Protestants.[9] Still, after Tridentine reforms, such local authority was supposed to be limited; vicars were not supposed to preside over local trials themselves in any official capacity. Whether local priests, vicars, and even monks actually had judicial authority or not, they occasionally acted as if they did, ordering laymen to do this or that based on the authority of their office alone. Abbeys and other monastic institutions had occasionally carved out jurisdictions of their own independent of their local diocese. The abbot of the Cluniac monastery Santa María de la Real, for instance, tried one case of annulment due to sexual impotence independently of the diocesan court, though the institution still fell within the jurisdiction of the diocese of Calahorra and La Calzada.[10] Convents could also wield quasi-independent justice within their walls, as Gene Brucker describes in Florence. This was especially important when abbesses and confessors needed to protect the reputations of convents while disciplining sexually promiscuous nuns.[11]

In order to do its work in remote locations, the diocesan court often deputized local clerics as provisional judges (*juezes de commission* in Spain). These provisional judges then hired notaries to make inquiries and take testimonies, which were then sent to the vicar general. It should be noted that church courts in Spain regularly took testimonies from women, especially in cases involving marital or family disputes, and lawyers never attacked the authority of a woman's testimony based simply on the fact that she was a woman. The court also employed other professionals as needed: translators, doctors, midwives, and surgeons. If litigants were not satisfied with the vicar general's verdict at the diocesan level they had two options. First, they could attempt to remove the case to another jurisdiction. This was usually possible only if one of the litigants had a residence and/or a history in an alternate diocese. This happened in the 1678 case of Don Antonio Francisco de Idiaquez Velez Yqueziara, who tried, to no avail, to move the annulment case he was losing against his wife from the diocese of Calahorra y La Calzada, to the diocese of Pamplona, and then to the diocese of Madrid.[12]

A second option was appealing the case from the lower diocesan court to the archbishop's court. There were only thirteen such archdiocesan courts in Iberia – Burgos, Granada, Zaragoza, Toledo, Santiago de Compostela, Seville, Valencia, Tarragona, Lisbon, Evora, and Braga. Once the case was adjudicated there, it could be further appealed to the Papacy or papal nuncio himself, who usually resided in Madrid. Any time a case moved to a new court, the entire case up to that point had to be transcribed and sent to the new court where it would form the basis for the case there. Such transcription copying, of course, cost more money. So, unlike in the courts of first instance, appeals depended on the deep financial pockets of the litigants, even though initial litigation may have started cheaply. Any case that was appealed would drag on for years, run to hundreds of pages, include travel and lodging expenses, and naturally cost a great deal. Because of the time and expense, the litigant who could afford to continue litigating could often win the suit or force his or her opponent into settling out of court. There were many ploys to extend litigation, including putting off court dates by feigning illness, usually with doctors' notes, preparing a second or third set of questionnaires that required more witness interviews and testimonies, and simply ignoring court orders.

These usually undocumented outcomes bring up one of the features of early modern Spanish litigation that has often perturbed historians: the high number of trials without a verdict. A large percentage of litigation ended before a verdict could be given. Initially historians of Spanish litigation saw this as evidence that Spain's courts were inefficient, costly, or indifferent. More recently scholars have pointed out that beginning a court case itself was a formidable step that may have often prompted an extrajudicial resolution of the dispute. Our modern judicial system often presents state-sponsored verdicts as the desired outcome of all litigation. However, early modern litigants may have used the initiation of a case as a way to prompt a resolution of a dispute out of court. Bringing defendants to court and/or sequestering their goods and assets were already punitive steps that were often enough to force someone to compromise outside of court. The punitive effects of the process of litigation are clear in the criminal case against the parents of Antonia Pereira in the Galician town of Parderrubias in 1748. Antonia had had an affair, resulting in an unwanted pregnancy, with a local cleric.[13] Even though the local secular court took months prosecuting the case, the real punishment of the father, mother, and older sister was the time they spent in prison. This imprisonment deprived the family of working the fields, causing them to lose a whole season's crops.

One can come to some admittedly imprecise measure of the wealth, time, and personnel wielded by various Spanish courts by the relative weight and length of the cases they adjudicated. If we look at a typical municipal criminal case and compare it to a church court case, we find that the secular criminal trials are abbreviated, with few witness testimonies and rather swift justice, with decisions being made in a matter of days or weeks. Ecclesiastical justice worked much more slowly, even in criminal cases. Initial testimonies were taken, and once the charge was accepted, an interrogatory questionnaire was written up, which was used to collect another round of testimonies. A rebuttal interrogatory questionnaire could then be created by the defense, and submitted, spawning more testimonies. It was not uncommon for such cases to last several months and often over a year. The wheels of ordinary ecclesiastical justice were slow; those of Inquisitions were often the slowest, but produced the most elaborated and polished judicial documents of all these court systems. Reading Inquisition trials one appreciates the skills of the Holy Office's notaries when compared to those of the church court, and especially when compared to the hand of secular court notaries.

This brings up the relationship between the ordinary church court and Inquisitions, for which Spain provides one example. By the early to mid-sixteenth century the Spanish Inquisition had stopped its peripatetic habits and settled into permanent offices in key towns and cities. In the diocese of Calahorra and La Calzada, it at first resided in Calahorra, but, as with everyone else in that diocese including the bishop, the inquisitors preferred Logroño, where they eventually relocated. In Cuenca, the Inquisition inhabited the city's most prominent structures. One expects, then, that diocesan courts and Inquisition tribunals resided in close proximity in several cities throughout the peninsula. However, it is important to recognize that even during its high point in the sixteenth century, the Inquisition's business was sporadic; it depended on finding and eliminating outbreaks of heresy, and once the threat of that particular heresy was eliminated, its work slackened. Its operations were necessarily secret. In character, then, it functioned very differently from the ordinary ecclesiastical courts, which were public and constant. Church courts had to deal with the steady stream of daily business: marital cases, benefices, financial litigation, etc. It was not uncommon for the two systems to share some personnel and institutional space, however. Some regular church personnel likely worked piecemeal for the Inquisition when they were needed. This was especially true of the office of *comisario*, the ecclesiastical field advisor to Iberian Holy Office. *Comisarios* were usually high-ranking clerics who the Inquisition brought in for professional advice. Their status and financial support benefited from association with the Inquisition. In several marital cases in the diocese of Calahorra and La Calzada, for instance, clerics connected with the Inquisition often used it as part of their title when appearing before the court. In part because the two institutions shared personnel, jurisdictional lines between the church courts and the Inquisition were well understood.

Church courts were more traditional than the Inquisition in that they were concerned with actions rather than beliefs. Their investigations focused on what people did and the sins they committed rather than heretical beliefs and thoughts. As with their schedule and the nature of their litigation, church courts were much more ordinary courts than inquisitorial ones, and church courts resorted to much more ordinary punishments. They fined those convicted and then admonished them to live a better life.

The church's jurisdiction vis-à-vis secular courts was not as clearly defined as its relationship vis-à-vis the Inquisition. Although all courts understood the general areas of demarcation between royal and ecclesiastical justice, evidence of jurisdictional disputes dated from the High Middle Ages and continued through the early modern period. In extraordinary instances royal courts could take control of an ecclesiastical case through a procedure called *via por fuerza*. Such conflicts might have resulted from the fact that these courts did not share personnel. Several different types of cases might fall into one or the other system for several reasons. First, one or more of those involved in the litigation may have been a cleric. So a criminal case that may have begun in a secular criminal court could be claimed by ecclesiastical jurisdiction and brought before a church court. In such a case often the entire secular trial would be transcribed and sent to the church court, and they would then take control. Since some crimes and legal issues overlapped the competency of each court, cases sometimes brought them into conflict. Marriage and separation was one of these, since the division of the property of a couple would usually be handled in a secular court, while the decision as to whether or not a couple could separate had to be handled by a church court. Certain crimes, such as witchcraft, could be and were litigated in various courts – secular, inquisitorial, and ecclesiastical. Through comparisons, several historians have generally concluded that church courts and Inquisition courts in Iberia were more deliberative, pragmatic, and skeptical than secular courts were, especially regarding witchcraft.

Ecclesiastical courts were more concentrated, powerful, and widespread in Italy than in other parts of Europe. They had also developed earlier and remained more robust than Italy's urban courts throughout the High Middle Ages. This was attributable not only to the papal presence but also to the crucial role that legal theorists and popes such as Alexander III (r. 1159–81) and Innocent III had in developing canon law, legal practices, and the study and implementation of Roman law. Not only was ecclesiastical jurisdiction naturally most developed where the pope was the temporal authority, as in the Papal States, but the dynamic ecclesiastical court system provided a rich array of positions allowing ambitious clerics to advance their careers and accrue wealth. David Herlihy and Christiane Klapisch-Zuber, for instance, estimated that there were up to 4,500 clerics employed in Florence and its *contado* alone.[14] It was not a coincidence that in Italy urban courts became the most highly developed in Europe; the sophistication of Italy's church courts directly influenced the development of its urban court systems. Rather, Italy had been well served by a vibrant judicial network – ecclesiastical, secular, and inquisitorial – since the High Middle Ages. This was bolstered by the presence of Europe's preeminent law school at the University of Bologna. Yet, even with the proximity of Rome, and the common practice of delegating cases to Rome, provincial dioceses were able to retain some of their own character and prerogatives.

In Latin America, bishops' courts were theoretically even more powerful than in Europe for several reasons. First, the few bishops based in Santo Domingo, New Spain, and Peru had expanded powers as representatives of Spanish religious authority. The Spanish Crown naturally used them to check the power of local colonial elites as well as the regular clergy. Both regular and secular New World clergy had the most contact with – and power over – indigenous Catholic converts. And the New World bishops sat at the pinnacle of the church's power there. It fell to the bishops, monks, and priests – not to the Inquisition, which from 1541 was prohibited from prosecuting Native Americans – to monitor and correct indigenous religious and social rituals and practices. On the ground, far from the oversight of any other authorities, Catholic clergy wielded an enormous power. *Visitador general* Ambrosío Martínez in San Juan de Huaylla, Peru, 1608, for example, proceeded *ex officio* against a widow and her lover.[15]

Ecclesiastical courts exerted even more power over newly converted indigenous peoples than over Europeans. This authority, along with a critique of it, is evident in Guaman Poma de Ayala's treatise against the church. One of his seventeenth century work's purposes was to expose the overreaching powers of Catholic bishops into the lives of indigenous Peruvians. On the other hand, as with all colonial governance in the Americas, the vast distances, lack of personnel, and limited resources available to officials provided a counter weight to the actual power that bishops wielded. Bishoprics themselves were much more vast and populated in the Americas than the bishoprics of Iberia. Whereas the fifty or so dioceses of Iberia each only covered a couple thousand square miles, the dozen bishoprics of colonial America might easily be ten times the size. Actual litigation in these American courts was also rarer for colonial citizens, and was most often relegated to the colonial metropolises like Santo Domingo, Lima, and Mexico City. This urban character of colonial litigation also meant that the majority of litigants came from the Empire's *criollo* elite. So, on balance, the greater authority that church courts might have had in the Americas was limited by the New World's geographic and cultural distances and limited personnel.

Historians are trained to look for change over time. Perhaps because of this focus on change, it is difficult to describe, or easy to overlook, the perdurability of an institution like the Catholic Church and its courts. Yet, even though its power waxed and waned between 1500 and 1800, the persistence of the church's jurisdiction, its bureaucracy, and courts during the early modern period in Iberia, Italy, and Latin America is difficult to deny. Part of the reason ecclesiastical courts formed such an important part of early modern life was their specific focus on questions of family life, on the religious, and on its vast property holdings. But another reason was the church's ability to adapt to change with the growth of Empire and population, the growth of slavery, and the growth of the power of the state. Church courts exist, of course, to this day. And if they still wield some kind of power in the twenty-first century, it stands to reason that they were anything but defunct in the eighteenth. Indeed, it could be argued that one of the reasons current sexual scandals in the Catholic Church exist is due to its understanding that it still holds a jurisdiction separate from secular law.

Notes

1 The archives referenced in this essay are Archivo Catedralicio y Diocesano de Calahorra (ACDC), Archivo Diocesano de Cuenca, Curia Episcopal (ADCE), Archivo Historico Provincial de Logroño (AHPL), Arquivo do Reino de Galicia (ARG), and the Archivo Arzobispal de Lima (AAL).

2 Richard C. Trexler, *Synodal Law in Florence and Fiesole, 1306–1518* (Rome, 1971), 172.

3 On dowry endowments see ADCE, Episcopal Legajos 847-2082-B, 850/2132, 856/2213. For examples of litigation against clerics for failing to say masses for the dead, see ADCE, Legajo 947-B/4097.

4 An example of such cases in Spain is an abortion charge from Treviño in 1705 (ACDC Legajo 674/55) and an infanticide case from 748/23 from 1666.

5 ACDC, Legajo 27/109/33, 1674.

6 ACDC Legajo 23/25-21, Treviño, 1743

7 ACDC Legajo 27/197/19, 1706.

8 ACDC Legajo 27/323/32, 1695, Helorrio.

9 ACDC, Legajo 288/28, Bilbao, August 28,1698, Local Vicar Diego de Unzaga vs. Beti de Venitt.

10 AHPL, Lejo J 965/3.

11 Gene A. Brucker, "Ecclesiastical Courts in Fifteenth-Century Florence and Fiesole," *Mediaeval Studies* 53 (1991), 229–57, esp. 239–40.
12 ACDC, Legajo 27/345/31
13 ARG Legajo 5923, num. 57.
14 David Herlihy and Christiane Klapisch-Zuber, *Les Toscans et leurs familles: Une étude du Catasto florentin de 1427* (Paris, 1978), 156.
15 *AAL*, Causas Criminales de Matrimonio, Legajo 1, Expediente 3. Huayllac, Testimony by Ambrosio Martinez, Jan. 15, 1608.

7

Church Courts in England

Martin Ingram

"Discipline" was among the watchwords of Catholic and Protestant Reformations alike as these movements unfolded in the sixteenth and seventeenth centuries. Among the most striking of the many new forms of personal and communal action generated by this wake-up call was a remodeling of judicial and quasi-judicial institutions for inculcating Christian beliefs, encouraging and, if necessary, enforcing strict religious observance, and raising standards of personal morality by education, persuasion, punishment, or penance.

England took its own exceptional course. At the beginning of the sixteenth century its ecclesiastical courts were sophisticated and for the most part very serviceable institutions. This was perhaps the fundamental reason why they survived the complex developments of the English Reformation, albeit with important changes in organization and purpose and in an altered relationship with the English crown. They were none-theless the object of a variety of further reform initiatives, designed to bring them in line with new Protestant understandings of church discip-line. If these had been carried through to their conclusion, the courts would have been profoundly altered. In the event the failure of such efforts led to the denunciation of the courts by the more extreme "puritan" or "godly" proponents of further reformation as scandalous symptoms of a church "but halfly reformed." While their vituperative criticisms were effectively brushed aside in late Elizabethan and Jacobean England, they were not wholly silenced and contributed to the climate of opinion that led to the temporary abolition of the courts during the Civil Wars and Interregnum. The revival of the courts after the Restoration and their persistence into the mid-nineteenth century may be seen as yet more signs of their resilience, though the story in this later period is essentially one of decline.

ENGLISH CHURCH COURTS AROUND 1500

The courts were "top down" institutions organized on the basis of the two ecclesiastical provinces (Canterbury and York); dioceses (twenty-one of them before the Reformation, including the four Welsh sees and the three dioceses in the northern province); and archdeaconries (of which there were two or more in all but the smallest dioceses). Individual bishops were the linchpin of the system. Some of them exercised jurisdiction personally in their own courts of audience and all on occasion acted directly to address what they regarded as serious threats to religion and morals. Around 1500 the most important targets of such action were Lollard heretics, even though they were few in number and very patchily distributed. Proceedings against them were generally designed to secure their abjuration and reintegration into the orthodox Christian community. But they were subject to imprisonment and a variety of penances, while a statute of 1401 empowered bishops to hand over relapsed or obdurate heretics to the secular powers to be executed by burning. Plainly this was an extremely powerful weapon in the ecclesiastical armory. In the years before the Reformation it was claimed, perhaps tendentiously, that the bishops were effectively able to silence any criticism of the church by threatening to prosecute complainants as heretics. Such fears were part of the context of the furor aroused by the imprisonment and supposed murder of the London merchant Richard Hunne in 1514.

The activities of the ordinary episcopal (usually referred to as consistory) courts, and the lesser courts held in the name of archdeacons and bishops' commissaries, were far more mundane. Much of their business was party-and-party litigation, including disputes over testamentary matters, tithe, defamation, and matrimony. Suits for the enforcement of disputed marriage contracts were much more numerous than those for separation or annulment, and to the twenty-first-century eye are striking for offering women as well as men an opportunity to seek redress. Till the late fifteenth century the courts also heard many debt suits in the guise of prosecutions for "breach of faith," but this area of jurisdiction withered rapidly in the face of challenges from the royal courts. In the early sixteenth century the church's handling of defamation was also barred in cases where the matter at issue was a crime – theft or murder, for example – cognizable in the secular courts. These changes may in retrospect look like efforts to confine the church courts more obviously to the spiritual and ecclesiastical sphere, but are perhaps more plausibly seen as turf wars between jurisdictions that mostly worked in harmony but at the margins fought tenaciously for a share of lucrative business.

The church courts also exercised a very extensive disciplinary jurisdiction in matters of faith and morals. In England these "ex officio" proceedings were highly summary – in contrast to the prolonged stages of "instance" or party-and-party suits – and this made it feasible to bring prosecutions in large numbers. Yet in practice their scope was limited. Many matters of personal morality and religious observance were dealt with in the private forum of the confessional, or were simply regulated by social expectations and community pressure. While the church courts mounted occasional prosecutions for matters as diverse as selling wares on Sundays and holy days and witchcraft or sorcery, they focused their attention mainly on sexual transgressions, notably adultery and fornication, and irregularities involving marriage – for example, unlawful separation, bigamy, or unduly postponing the church wedding after a marriage contract made in the presence of family and neighbors. Even though these were highly personal matters, proceedings tended to be formal, even bureaucratic in tone, conducted as they were by trained professionals. Increasingly the positions of scribe and registrar were filled by laymen, while the judges were clerical lawyers.

THE IMPACT OF THE REFORMATION

Amid the tumultuous changes from 1529 to 1553, it would not have been surprising if the church courts had themselves suffered major alteration. Among the possibilities was the complete dismantling of the spiritual jurisdiction in its existing form and the transfer of most of its business to the secular courts. But such a wholesale shift posed practical problems. More basically, it was hardly likely that Henry VIII, having extended royal control over the church and about to subdivide several large dioceses to create new ones, would favor the church courts' immediate dismemberment. Another approach was to reform the courts and the existing body of canon law, a project that commenced under Henry VIII but acquired added meaning and greater urgency amid the self-consciously Protestant policies of Edward VI's reign. As it eventually emerged in 1553, the *Reformatio legum ecclesiasticarum*, hammered out by a commission of clergy and laymen headed by Archbishop Thomas Cranmer, made far-reaching proposals. Among other things it boldly addressed current debates among continental and English Protestant divines about the need for harsher punishments for adultery, for changes in the divorce laws to enable the innocent party to remarry in certain cases, and for measures to render invalid the marriages of young people contracted without parental consent. Many Protestant states had indeed already altered their laws to bring them more clearly in line with what they supposed was the word of God. But in England such proposals remained highly controversial. For these and other reasons the *Reformatio legum* was doomed from its inception. An attempt to revive it in the parliament of 1571 was likewise to fail. Meanwhile the church courts in their existing form trundled on. The patchily surviving evidence suggests that amid the corrosive uncertainties of the 1530s and 1540s the courts in many areas faltered and their business dwindled. Yet in Gloucester diocese under Edward VI the redoubtable Bishop John Hooper was able to galvanize his consistory court into an effective agent of Reformation.

THE ENGLISH INQUISITION?

The courts proved equally apt to serve the turn of Queen Mary's determination to restore Roman Catholicism, playing an important part in the project not only of restoring the material fabric of Catholic worship but also of pastoral renewal. Afforced by royal commissions, the courts also proved effective in the process of eliminating Protestants and others who refused to conform. Previously the burning of heretics had occurred as an occasional exemplary measure in a situation where orthodoxy embraced the overwhelming majority of the population. In Mary's reign, in contrast, the scale of punitive activity was far greater. The incineration of nearly three hundred people and the legal harassment of countless others reveal the capacity of the English church courts to serve as an effective means of guarding the faith.

When Elizabeth came to the throne and re-established a Protestant settlement, it was tacitly accepted that similar savage methods should not be used against Catholics. On the other hand, the crown did need a powerful instrument to enforce its religious policy. The matter became more urgent with the unfolding of political events, including the Northern Rising (1569) and the Papal Bull of Excommunication (1570) – especially as the queen remained unmarried and the succession was uncertain. Increasingly the government presented "recusants" who rejected the Protestant settlement as disloyal and seditious, and a battery of penal statutes was gradually assembled against both the Catholic lay population and the Jesuits and other missionaries who infiltrated from continental seminaries from 1574. Additional weapons were developed in the form of the courts of High Commission, based in London, York, and Durham and augmented in the southern province by local commissions in individual dioceses. Backed by royal authority, these bodies exercised powers of arrest, imprisonment, and fine that were denied the ordinary church courts.

In the 1580s and 1590s the High Commission courts were also mobilized against Puritans, but especially against a developing group of Presbyterians, who proposed the abolition of bishops and the existing church courts and their replacement by locally based consistories of ministers and lay elders on the Calvinist model. *A fortiori* the small minority of radical separatists, who rejected the state church as hopelessly corrupt, were also targeted. Puritan protests against the High Commission, backed by some common lawyers and at least tacitly supported by a wider circle of sympathetic laymen, centered on the use of the oath *ex officio*, by which suspects might be forced to incriminate themselves. Supporters of the Puritan victims of the High Commission claimed bitterly that it was "a Court of Inquisition more than Spanish, to sift and ransack by oath the most secret thoughts and consciences of all men."[1] But in light of the Armada, subsequent threats of Spanish invasion, and the dreadful example of religious war in France and the Netherlands, the government had little difficulty in tarring Presbyterians and separatists with the brush of extremism. The accession of James VI of Scotland renewed the hopes of godly activists, but few of their aims were realized in the 1604 Hampton Court Conference. In the bitter aftermath, James and his bishops used the ecclesiastical courts to enforce a subscription policy that effectively coerced the majority of more moderate Puritans into public conformity while isolating obdurate extremists. Some ninety ministers were deprived of their livings. Reinforced as they were by the High Commission, the English church courts proved effective weapons in the enforcement of ecclesiastical policy at the highest level.

VISITATIONS

Puritan criticisms predated the bitter disputes of the period 1589–1605. But earlier they were directed not at the ecclesiastical courts as dangerous agents of authoritarian government, but at their supposed corruption, inefficiency and – as relics of the popish past – fundamental unsuitability as instruments of Protestant discipline. Famously John Field and Thomas Wilcox's *Admonition to the Parliament* of 1572 denounced them as "the filthy quagmire, and poisoned plash of all the abominations that do infect the whole realm." This diatribe, expressing the views of the more extreme of the church's critics, is misleading in two ways: first, in presenting a grossly exaggerated picture of the weaknesses of the courts; and secondly, in obscuring the fact that in the first two decades of Elizabeth's reign the more moderate among the godly cooperated with the ecclesiastical establishment – indeed at this stage the two categories overlapped – in seeking ways to modify the existing courts to meet the needs of Protestant evangelism.[2]

The most enduring of the measures was successful precisely because it built on well-established procedures. For generations bishops and archdeacons, in person or through their officials, had conducted visitations, tours of inspection that enabled ecclesiastical judges to confront directly parish clergy and local churchwardens and elicit from them information about what was amiss – whether defects in church fabric or liturgical equipment, ministerial failures, lapses in religious observances, or moral failings on the part of parishioners. But before the Reformation the frequency and thoroughness of such visitations varied greatly. The liturgical and doctrinal changes of the Reformation years demanded a more consistent approach to ensure local compliance – a goal that could hardly be accomplished overnight, given that the shift from Catholic to Protestant worship demanded major physical changes and heavy expenditures, and on the other hand was premised on a profound reorientation of religious understanding and behavior on the part of ordinary parishioners.

To meet these challenges, visitations became much more systematic. Bishops increasingly issued printed "articles of inquiry" listing matters on which information was required, and on which locally elected officers (churchwardens) were examined on oath. The parish-by-parish responses to these articles generated – in addition to much information concerning church fabric and furnishings – large numbers of prosecutions for a variety of clerical faults and, in the case of the laity, such matters as absence from church, failing to receive the holy communion, not learning the catechism, tippling in service time, working on Sundays or holy days, and dancing or playing games in the church or churchyard or at unlawful times. The large numbers of cases concerning religious observance, alongside the marital matters and sexual transgressions that had traditionally dominated disciplinary proceedings, gave a permanent tilt to the agendas facing ecclesiastical judges and administrators in the period of the "long Reformation."

EXPERIMENTS IN CONGREGATIONAL DISCIPLINE

Another initiative of the time was less enduring. There are signs that early in Elizabeth's reign the authorities planned to give the system a stronger congregational focus – consistent with a vision of reformed Protestant discipline – reserving the energies of the courts to deal with notorious and intractable cases. The point of reference was the disciplinary model found in St Matthew's gospel. Thus the canons of 1571 prescribed:

> If any offend their brethren, either by manifest adultery or whoredom or incest or drunkenness or much swearing or bawdry or usury or any other uncleanness and wickedness of life, let the churchwardens warn them brotherly and friendly, to amend. Which, except they do, they shall personally show them to the parson, vicar, or curate, that they may be warned more sharply and vehemently of them, and if they continue so still, let them be driven from the holy communion till they be reformed.

It was only if such local admonition was unsuccessful that they should be punished by the church courts. But the growth of the Presbyterian movement from the 1570s, and the government's eventual discovery that in some areas "classes" and consistories were actually in the process of formation at the grassroots, made this congregational approach seem far too dangerous. The change is manifest in the canons of 1604. Instead of the emphasis on charitable admonition preceding denunciation to court, there is the terse instruction that churchwardens and their assistants shall at the next opportunity "faithfully present all ... offenders [to the ecclesiastical court] to the intent that they, and every of them, may be punished by the severity of the laws." Hierarchy was reasserted, perhaps at the cost of making the courts seem more remote.[3]

THE REFORMATION OF PENANCE

Another area of debate was the practice of penance. Before the Reformation, penitents had characteristically been ordered to go barefoot and bare-legged, clad only in a shirt (men) or a smock (women) and carrying a lighted wax candle. They had had to walk before the procession at the parish church on a Sunday or major feast, kneel during the Mass, and present the candle to the priest or before the principal image in the church. In theory the severity of penance could be increased by whipping, but by the early sixteenth century this had become rare. Only slightly more common was penance performed in the marketplace of the nearest town, to publicize the event and increase the shame and ignominy experienced by the penitent. In practice, indeed, penance in whatever form had often been commuted into a money payment.

English Reformation thinking on penance moved in several directions. One was increased severity. Some judges favored greater use of market-place penances. The trend began in Edwardian times and was continued in a Catholic context under Mary, while in the early part of Elizabeth's reign the practice became somewhat more widespread. Reform proposals in the convocation of 1563 reflect demands for even greater harshness. A "general note of matters to be moved by the clergy" reflected that "some think banishment and perpetual prison to be meet for adulterers," and itself proposed that "adulterers and fornicators may be punished by strait imprisonment and open shame if the offender be vile and stubborn."[4]

Punishments of this sort were indeed inflicted by the courts of High Commission. But their use by the ordinary church courts raised difficult jurisdictional issues. In any case, such severe penalties might be thought to smack too much of retribution, whereas the ethos of ecclesiastical discipline had always been medicinal, designed to reform the sinner. Yet clearly some changes were essential. Beginning in the reign of Edward VI, the traditional rituals, associated with Catholic understandings of the doctrine of atonement, were replaced with practices consistent with Protestant doctrine. Features such as going bareheaded and barefooted continued. Penitential dress was modified to make the wearing of a white sheet the standard garb. Penitents could no longer walk in procession, since such rituals had been abolished. Instead they were often ordered to begin their penance standing in the church porch, then to move into the body of the church and remain there in full view during the service. The candle they had formerly carried was replaced by a white rod – an occasional feature of pre-Reformation penances and now adapted to Protestant use – to symbolize submission to wholesome discipline. The most striking innovation was that penitents could no longer get away with simply performing ritual actions. They now had to declare their sins openly and candidly in open church, begging God (and sometimes their neighbors) for forgiveness, and finally leading the congregation in prayer. Often the occasion was enhanced by the preaching of an edifying sermon, or the reading of a homily, on whoredom, adultery, or another appropriate theme.

Basic to all these initiatives was a powerful determination that reformed penance should bring sinners to true repentance. In some areas in the early decades of Elizabeth's reign this aim was pursued with remarkable vigor – a process usually involving close liaison between the courts and the community, now conceived of as "the congregation," and the local minister. Commonly judges insisted that penitents should not be restored to full participation in church services until they showed clear "tokens of repentance," such as the shedding of tears. To achieve this end, some particularly dramatic and memorable penances were occasionally devised, including the use of sackcloth and ashes – reminiscent of practice in Scottish kirk sessions – and even prostration. But such imaginative efforts were comparatively short-lived, and from the later part of Elizabeth's reign into the early seventeenth century, the vigor of the penitential regime again diminished and penance tended to become a routine matter. Partly this was simply the result of bureaucratic inertia and the tendency of zealous regimes to lose their edge as time goes on, a process reinforced by administrative developments. It is observable that, whereas in the early Elizabethan period bishops and archdeacons themselves sometimes presided over the courts, in later times these functions were almost wholly given over to subordinates, mostly laymen professionally trained in civil law. In any case, as more and more cases were brought into the courts, there was simply not enough time to deal with them on an individual basis. To be sure, there was great diversity from jurisdiction to jurisdiction, and in the reign of Elizabeth, in particular, the details of the penances awarded varied enormously. But as time passed, marketplace penances became less common, as did the award of multiple penances. By the early seventeenth century it was standard practice for penitents, usually dressed in a white sheet and carrying a white wand, but rarely now required to go barefoot or bare-legged, simply to make confession in church on a single Sunday.

The actual performance of penance also became less common. Many poorer offenders never came to court at all and were simply excommunicated. Routine use of this sanction was one of the major criticisms of the late Elizabethan and early Stuart church courts; while the problem of contumacy was not as severe or as damaging to the courts as historians used to suppose, it was undoubtedly a weakness. Wealthier people escaped in a different way. It is hardly surprising that, in a society in which "credit" was increasingly highly valued, anyone with a reputation to lose was anxious to avoid the humiliation of public penance. But the traditional means of doing so, by commuting penance into a money payment, had become highly controversial. Elizabeth's reign witnessed fierce debates on the subject, many of the "godly" arguing that it defeated the whole object and demanding that the practice should be abolished. But the rigorists lost the battle, more conservative members of the Church hierarchy insisting that it was not necessarily in the interests of public order to expose leading citizens to shame and humiliation. In the decades around 1600, probably only a small proportion of penitents were able to avail themselves of this concession, but there was laxity of practice in some areas, and the fact that commutation was available at all inevitably blunted the edge of pastoral zeal and moral reformation.

RELATIONS WITH THE SECULAR COURTS

Although the church courts had avoided wholesale dismantlement in the 1530s, the issue of the boundary between the spiritual and secular juris-dictions remained sensitive throughout the sixteenth century. Defendants in party-and-party suits who believed that the matter at issue rightly belonged to the secular jurisdiction could apply for a writ of prohibition. While it is doubtful if this resulted in significant encroachment on the scope of the church courts' business (as opposed to its effect in individual cases), it did prevent any extension. More complex was the relationship between the ecclesiastical and secular courts in the punishment of sin. The Presbyterian threat made the crown hostile to any attempts to mingle lay and ecclesiastical powers in local courts; hence Puritan experiments along these lines at Northampton and Bury St Edmunds were promptly sup-pressed. More generally, the crown was wary when borough and city courts, acting on the basis of their charters or simply local custom, attempted to exercise jurisdiction over sexual offenders, since this could be interpreted as encroachment on the spiritual jurisdiction. Only when the claims of urban courts were well founded and based on long-established practice – as in major towns like Leicester and Colchester, provincial capitals such as Norwich and Exeter, and above all in the city of London – were they readily allowed.

On the other hand, the secular courts, usually by means of parliamen-tary statutes, either appropriated elements of ecclesiastical court business or developed a parallel jurisdiction. The Acts of Uniformity of 1552 and 1559 made absence from church punishable by the secular as well as the ecclesiastical courts, while (as noted earlier) the later sixteenth and early seventeenth centuries witnessed a string of statutes directed against Catholic recusants. Statutes of 1563 and 1604 made witchcraft – con-ceived in terms of harm to persons or property carried out by magical means – primarily a secular crime. Already in 1534 "buggery committed with mankind or beast" had been made a felony – though in fact the pre-Reformation church courts had rarely molested people for offenses of this nature, while prosecutions under the new act were relatively few. Bigamy and drunkenness were among other offenses that eventually became subject to secular penalty. The parliaments of Elizabeth, James, and Charles I also witnessed a long series of bills aiming to enact harsher measures against adultery, fornication, and bastardy. But the only substantive achievements were two measures concerning poor bastard children. An act of 1576 gave justices of the peace discretionary power to examine the circumstances of the birth of an illegitimate child who had been left at the charge of the parish or was likely to become chargeable, to make an order for maintenance and to punish the parents. A supplementary act of 1610 provided that the mothers of such children should be sent to a house of correction for one year. There were wide variations in the way these measures were enforced locally, and overall only a small proportion of bastardy cases were dealt with in this way. Neither act affected the rights of the church courts, which (as will be seen in the next section) continued to handle numerous cases of sexual transgression.

COURTS, CLERGY, AND COMMUNITIES IN JACOBEAN ENGLAND

In contrast to the convulsions of the Tudor period, the reign of James I was characterized by relative calm based in a reasonably favorable symbiosis of courts, clergy, and communities. In many ways the courts could be seen as performing a useful social service. Population had been rising steeply since the early years of Elizabeth's reign; in combination with other social and economic changes, this had, by the turn of the century, led to growing problems of poverty. One symptom was an increase in illegitimacy, a threat to parish finances, since poor children and their parents were likely to burden the poor rates. Hence the church courts' prosecution of unmarried mothers and others who engaged in premarital sex, as also of individuals who "harbored" bastard-bearers, was widely supported by rate-paying householders of middling substance in town and country – especially as it was precisely from these groups that churchwardens and sidemen, the crucial points of linkage between the courts and the parishes, were usually drawn. If these sinners could be put to penance, it made an example and sent a strong message. But from a practical point of view excommunication was as good or better, since it usually meant that the culprit had fled and relieved the parish of a possible financial burden.

It had long been the practice to turn a blind eye to courting couples who started sexual relations before the wedding; as a result, "bridal pregnancy" was commonplace. But from the 1590s and increasingly in the early seventeenth century, the courts started to prosecute people for this kind of antenuptial incontinence – though never as assiduously as cases of clear-cut fornication and with much regional and local variation. More generally, these harsh times made marriage itself an increasingly sensitive issue. Again local interests lent support to the church's efforts to ensure that weddings were conducted with due publicity (the reading of banns on three successive Sundays, or at least the issue of a valid license) and with the consent of parents and the wider community. As the regulations concerning marriage were tightened up and better enforced, so suits over disputed marriage contracts or "spousals" became redundant and declined sharply in number. On the other hand, defamation cases increased, as sexual reputation became more and more integral to the status of the middling sort, to an extent of men but of women above all.

Respectability as much as religion explains local support for other aspects of the church courts' work. In Jacobean England, Protestant sectaries were a negligible presence, while Catholic recusants, though numerous in the northwest and some smaller areas, were elsewhere a tiny and embattled minority. England had by now developed a strong Protestant identity. At the parish level, church attendance and participation in the sacraments, whatever their meaning in terms of individual piety, were important markers of status and belonging. It was taken for granted that the church courts should chivvy defaulters, take action against those who labored in the fields or opened shop windows on Sundays and holy days, and punish more sharply any who misbehaved in the church or churchyard. To be sure, individual churchwardens were not equally conscientious in "presenting" neighbors for their lapses, while the courts themselves were not altogether consistent in their efforts. But a basic level of compliance and co-operation was almost universal. Parishioners also used the courts to complain of non-resident or otherwise negligent or scandalous ministers. But the English ministry was by now earning a reputation as "*stupor mundi*," and such cases were quite few in most areas.

The "godly" ministers who had survived the purge of 1604–1605 had mostly learned circumspection and were willing to compromise by, for example, wearing the surplice on occasion. They found alternative means of expressing their zeal. In alliance with churchwardens and local magistrates, some of them spearheaded moral campaigns, which in particular parishes multiplied prosecutions of drunkards, sabbath-breakers, and the like. But high-pressure initiatives of this sort were hard to sustain, not least because they aroused opposition from less zealous parishioners, and if the Puritan presence in a community was weak, they might never make much headway. Skirmishing between the godly and their fellow parishioners occasionally degenerated into protracted feuds marked by spates of prosecutions initiated by both sides, often involving the secular courts as well as the church. Ecclesiastical judges did not necessarily side either with the precisians or with their detractors, but generally tried to administer the law impartially and restore peace to the parish.

CRISIS AND COLLAPSE

The equilibrium of the Jacobean church was always precarious. Impending trouble was signaled in 1618 by James I's publication throughout England of the Declaration of Sports, originally issued the previous year in Lancashire, where the zeal of a minority of godly Protestant ministers was sharpened by widespread recusancy and crypto-Catholicism. In pronouncing that it was lawful for the common people to indulge in dancing and many other traditional pastimes on Sunday after evening prayer (albeit on the understanding that they had diligently attended church beforehand), this royal proclamation stirred up profound issues of sabbatarian doctrine, set a gleeful populace at odds with godly clergy in numerous communities, and put a severe strain on the consciences of both clerical and lay Puritans. Moreover, the questions of public order raised by the Book of Sports were undoubtedly of wider concern. Ecclesiastical court books throughout England bear witness to an explosion of local conflicts that spluttered on into the 1620s, while trouble was renewed when Charles I reissued the Book of Sports in 1633.

Meanwhile the ceremonialist policies of the so-called "Arminian" group of churchmen, ascendant from the late 1620s, were causing disquiet far beyond the ranks of Puritans. All these changes helped make the courts vulnerable. It has been claimed that after the Reformation the English church courts "resembled a house shifted from its foundations by heavy bombing."[5] This image fails to do justice to the success with which the courts were successfully restabilized in the reigns of Elizabeth and James I. But the criticisms of the courts generated by common lawyers during the early Reformation years and later by Puritan activists – that they were not merely inefficient, corrupt, and tyrannical but also bureaucratic and hence fundamentally unsuitable as instruments of Protestant pastoral discipline – did have an effect. The charges may be thought of either as a corrosive agent that gradually ate away at the courts' credibility, or as a time bomb that might sooner or later be activated with explosive force. Perhaps the latter image is more apt. Fatally associated with unpopular aspects of Charles I's personal rule and the focus of considerable resentment in the 1630s, the courts collapsed suddenly amid the crisis of 1640–1642.

THE CHURCH COURTS IN THE LONG EIGHTEENTH CENTURY

It is testament to the resilience of these institutions that this was not the end. Save for a brief revival under James II the High Commission had gone forever, but following the restoration of Charles II in 1660 the rest of the network of ecclesiastical courts was reestablished and in the later seventeenth century their jurisdiction in matters of defamation, matrimony, tithe, probate, and administration was successfully revived. Indeed the courts continued to be active throughout the eighteenth century; it was only in the mid-nineteenth that most of their jurisdiction was dismantled. Still, the later seventeenth century may be regarded as the watershed, especially for the disciplinary side of the courts' activities. Here they faced increasing difficulties, because the existence of significant numbers of Protestant dissenters – a legacy of the Civil Wars and Interregnum period and unsuccessful efforts at comprehension – inevitably undermined the moral and practical authority of the courts. Institutions that were, on the one hand, dependent on spiritual sanctions and yet, on the other, highly formal and legalistic in their approach and methods were unlikely to win back converts. In the event the Toleration Act of 1689, as it was interpreted locally, destroyed the legal basis for the church courts' enforcement of religious and moral discipline. Though the courts remained a potent force in some areas well into the Georgian period, in most parts of England their impact dwindled rapidly amid the massive philosophical, social, and economic changes of the Enlightenment and of the emergent industrial revolution.

Notes

1 Ethan H. Shagan, "The English Inquisition: Constitutional Conflict and Ecclesiastical Law in the 1590s," *Historical Journal* 47 (2004), 549.
2 *Puritan Manifestoes: a Study of the Origin of the Puritan Revolt*, 2nd ed, ed. W. H. Frere and C. E. Douglas (London, 1954), 32.

3 *The Anglican Canons, 1529–1947*, ed. Gerald Bray Church of England Record Society 6, (Woodbridge, 1998), 193, 195, 409, but cf. 387.

4 Bray ed., *Anglican Canons*, 736.

5 Ralph Houlbrooke, "The Decline of Ecclesiastical Jurisdiction under the Tudors," in *Continuity and Change: Personnel and Administration of the Church in England, 1500–1642*, ed. Rosemary O'Day and Felicity Heal (Leicester, 1976), 257.

Section C

Judges and Shepherds

8

Consistories

William Naphy

The ecclesiastical courts that developed in the Reformed tradition (whether called consistories or sessions) along with Catholic Inquisitions are fascinating institutions for historians interested in the development of social control in early modern society. Nevertheless, scholarship has tended to focus on the institutional dimensions of Inquisitions and consistories with little attention given to the individuals who made them work. In an attempt to sketch out new directions for the study of consistories, this essay will focus on lay representation in Geneva, comparing it with the extremely limited information available on other Reformed consistories in the historiography. The importance of the Genevan institution in the Reformed world has meant that John Calvin's consistory has been extensively studied. However, these studies suggest, as with the wider study of Reformed church courts, that there is a need for general studies of the men who served alongside the more famous clerics such as Calvin and, later, Theodore Beza. This essay will attempt to bring the laymen on the consistory to the fore, serving to remind us that elders were an integral part of a living community who held a position often as important as that of magistrates. Also, just as magistrates are examined to understand how complex webs of status, family, and wealth made politics work, elders on consistories also need to be seen as individuals equally entangled in the multifaceted relationships that held early modern society together.

This essay will build on the essay by Sara Beam in the previous chapter, focusing on Geneva to demonstrate the significant overlap between elders and the ruling magistracy. It will also show the need to extend the study of the men comprising these bodies outside of Geneva to determine normative practices. The few studies that have focused on the elders as individuals suggest that the roles of magistrates and elders intersected extensively, but at this point it is difficult to draw general conclusions about the laymen of Reformed consistories. If subsequent research in Reformed territories reveals a similar pattern, it would indicate that the standard trope that the church, often "personified" as the consistory, typically struggled with the state or magistracy is problematic. The Genevan case underscores that this reading of church *versus* state was almost impossible in the city where the Reformed tradition was founded, and serves as a call for detailed study of lay elders elsewhere to ascertain the extent of church-state overlap via magisterial service on consistories.

There is a rich and lively historiography of Reformed church courts, which for the most part examines the work of the consistories as institutional bodies with little comment on the men (lay or clerical) who comprised the institution. Thus, Jeffrey Watt discusses the consistories of Geneva, Valangin, and Neuchâtel with reference to how they worked as institutions and how they were structured. Karen Spierling has a detailed and absorbing analysis of how individuals, especially servants, were examined before the consistory. In a similar fashion, Philip Rieder discusses the consistory as an institution critical to social control and to the inculcation of Reformed values in relation to healing practices. What unites these excellent studies is their treatment of the consistory as an institution almost with a life and will of its own. In this approach, the consistory *does* something or *admonishes* someone. This is accurate, but at the same time such a singular perspective omits the fact that the individuals comprising this institution and their individuality play into how they *do* something collectively.

Other studies outside Geneva take a similar tack. In discussing French consistories, for example, Raymond Mentzer has noted the distinct ways in which they were constructed, constituted by ministers (usually one or two), elders (more numerous), and also deacons. Yet in Geneva, the consistory consisted of the entire Company of Pastors and twelve elders, each of whom qualified because they were an elected magistrate. However, one learns little of the Frenchmen who *comprised* the consistories. Studies of other Reformed consistories likewise focus on the work of the consistory rather than its membership. Even in much older studies where membership was extremely limited (as with the Lutheran consistory in Brandenburg-Prussia) with only four to five men, the focus is on the work of the body rather than the men and the extent to which understanding something about them and their background might influence the evaluation of the institution's activities and decisions.

However, it would be wrong to conclude that all studies of consistories focus entirely on the institution's activities. Some do make passing references to individual lay members (interestingly, most studies name clerical members) but this is often in the specific context of the noted elder being convoked before the consistory and admonished. In other words, we tend to learn about elders when they were in trouble with their consistory. For example, Jan Engelszoon, Walish Pieterszoon, and Huijch Arienssen came before their consistory in Delft for a dispute involving Anabaptism. Elders John de l'Escluse and Henry May were called before their English Separatist church in Amsterdam because of a personal dispute. Cornelius Knijff is noted because his son was in trouble and the deacon Tini Caesarius and Hendrik Heusch are discussed in passing since they were suspected of embezzling church funds. John McCallum's work on Fife also comments on the moral failings of elders: Henry and James Johnstone were dismissed as elders about the same time Henry was charged with manslaughter; Robert Orrok, elder in Burntistland, was accused of fornication, violence and drunkenness and even his relative, the Laird of Orrock, was not able to stop his dismissal from the session. Robert Thompson slandered the ministers and elders of his own session when they had the temerity to admonish him for his scandalous relationship with a woman whose husband was at sea. In addition, one finds a regular litany of remonstrations with elders for Sabbath-breaking and not taking communion. Occasionally, we learn of individual elders when they were asked to undertake a specific task. Thus, the burgermaster-elder Harweijer was asked to lead the response to Arminianism in Kampen.

There are, though, exceptions where individual elders and their characteristics are analyzed. Margo Todd discusses many leading elders in her excellent study of the early Kirk in Scotland, though as often as not the elders are noted for their bad behavior. Darryl Ogier's work on Guernsey is almost polar opposite from the norm in that he discusses elders (e.g., Pierre Ollivier and Thomas Robert) but simply refers to the cleric as "the minister." Judith Pollmann's study of Arnoldus Buchelius is another example in which a close study of a single elder sheds considerable light, via his diaries noting consistory discussions and decisions, on how a consistory as an institution actually functioned as an amalgam of real, live individuals very much governed and influenced by their own status, wealth, relationships and presuppositions especially with regard to the reputation of their peers, relations and neighbors.

A couple of studies hint at the possibility of wider analyses of elders as a group of individuals. William Abbott notes that elders tended to be the "better sort" (prosperous farmers and successful merchants), while Mentzer includes a brief discussion of the professions and social status of elders at Nîmes suggesting that a basic statistical analysis might be possible and deepen discussions about the behavior of the consistory as a body. Alan Tulchin undertook such an analysis of the elders in Nîmes. He shows, for example, unlike the situation in Scotland (see Margo Todd's essay in Chapter 3), Nîmes' elders did not serve in judicial roles or on the city council. Nevertheless, while there is some very good analysis of the occupational background of the early eldership, there is not an extended study over time or a focus on individuals rather than eldership as a group. What is clear is that as a group, the elders were largely from the rung just below the top social level and, in that sense, were similar to Geneva where only one syndic and two senators on the consistory were from the top elite. However, the elders in Nîmes were not magistrates and this seems to have been a deliberate choice, whereas constitutionally all elders in Geneva had to be magistrates.

McCallum's careful analysis of elders in Fife detailed their engagement with issues coming before the session and their vocational background. He noted that some elders were quite casual in their attendance while others were "serious" elders. Five elders accounted for half the elders attending while "occasional" elders were considerably less frequent at the sessions (nineteen of twenty-eight elders attended ten or fewer of the fifty-seven possible meetings of the Anstruther kirk session in 1601). He analyzed the socio-economic and professional composition of four kirk sessions (Burntisland in 1602 and 1640; Kircaldy, 1619; and, Dysart, 1623) discovering that skippers were the largest contingent (seven) with merchants (two) and one maltman rounding out lay participation in the session. The failure to record professions or occupations for most might suggest that this was of little interest for contemporaries especially whereas sociopolitical status was more frequently noted. All town-dwelling elders on these sessions were noted as burgesses (equivalent to Genevan's native or naturalized citizen, *citoyen/bourgeois*) and three as bailies (equivalent to Geneva's syndics).

Indeed, McCallum's meticulous study of the elders highlights the power of the bailies in controlling the work of the sessions. Burntisland's records suggest that there were always at least three bailies on the session and that they rotated membership among their number on an annual basis producing a large number of "occasional" elders but ensuring most of the town council had experience on the session. In 1608, fourteen of fifteen session laymen (elders/deacons) were magistrates (or, put another way, 75% of the town council sat on the session). In 1623, fourteen of twenty-one of the laymen were magistrates. In the same year, in Dysart 65% of the burgh's magistrates sat on the session comprising 44% (seventeen of thirty-nine) of the session's lay membership. Earlier in 1589, twelve of the town's councillors of St Andrews and two (of the four) bailies were on the session along with the Dean of Guild. Without this careful analysis we would not realize how much the lay membership of the sessions of Fife were in fact, an extension of the town council.

The focus, then, in understanding these laymen is to remember just how many were magistrates, thus intimately combining church and state in their own persons. Consequently, as vital as consistories were in the processes of social control and establishing Protestant cultures, the membership of these institutions needs further study not least to uncover what sort of people were largely setting the agenda, alongside their clerical colleagues, in the creation of a Reformed godly society. Also, the prominence of magistrates might suggest that the consistories may have been less dominated by clergy than one might otherwise suspect. The implications of neglecting lay personnel in Reformed church courts are profound. It potentially skews historical perspective by casting these institutions as wholly ecclesiastical, speaking with the voices of the ministers who are usually noted and discussed in the historiography. One tends to assume, therefore, that Reformed consistories are church courts with the emphasis on "church" and overlook their role as "courts" in which lay personnel might well play a significant role.

The importance of lay personnel in the development of the Genevan consistory emerges from its origins. One of the first acts undertaken by Calvin on his return to Geneva from exile in Strasbourg in 1541 was to begin to stabilize the church's precarious position. Key to his efforts in fostering constancy was the establishment of a well-ordered consistory to oversee morals and religion in the city and, most importantly, to ensure that only those spiritually fit would receive communion. Such a court, common in German Protestant lands, was not novel; indeed the establishment of a consistory had been debated in Geneva. However, the Senate's records show that after discussion the decision 'sus l'erection du Consistoyre' was postponed until a later date.[1] This was accomplished when the new institution met for the first time on December 6, 1541.

However, the constitution of the institution's membership over the next two decades suggests that, in practical terms, there were three consistories. The first consistory, which existed from 1541 to about 1546, was marked by a high turnover in personnel and corresponded with a period of transition in the Company of Pastors. By 1546, this earlier consistory was largely replaced by a new body comprised of a group of high-quality French refugee ministers and new elders. This "second" consistory sat until the years immediately after the triumph of Calvin and his political supporters in 1555. During the immediate aftermath of this triumph, a new body of elders came onto the consistory as most of those who had served for the previous decade demitted office often to assume high political office in the city-state republic.

During the period 1556–1558, the institution itself underwent changes. The consistory gained the right to examine people under oath, in effect becoming a court before which lying now constituted the criminal offense of perjury. In addition, the consistory finally gained the absolute right to pronounce the ban of excommunication. Thus, institutionally a "third" consistory had come into being. Critical moments in the history of the state produced profound changes to the consistory. These changes substantially altered the lay personnel of the consistory, which had an impact on the institution and its ability to work successfully. The evolution of the institutional nature of the consistory is only understandable if the focus is on the laymen who matriculated rather than the ministers who remained largely constant after the mid-1540s. By examining these laymen in some detail both as groups and as individuals, one can get a greater sense of their ability to affect a Reformed consistory.

The first thing to note is the general volatility of membership on the consistory. In part, though, it must be remembered that the constitutional arrangement whereby the consistory's elders were a subcommittee of the city's three political councils created shifts in membership as syndics could not serve consecutive terms and the number of senators from a given family were limited. In that sense, the eldership had much in common with the changing pattern McCallum noted in Fife. Senior politicians served for a short period and often attended fairly irregularly, while the more "serious" (and perhaps eventually "professional") elders drawn from the Council of Two Hundred were a much more stable and more active (i.e., attended more often) group of elders. In general, the statistics (which rely on the excellent doctoral research of Lucas Kriner for access to which I am most grateful) for the first decade (spanning the "first" into the "second" consistories) are fascinating. There were nineteen ministers who attended sessions during 1542–1552 with each minister attending, on average, 99 sessions of a possible 408 (24%) while the forty-seven magistrate elders averaged 63 sessions each (15%).

This pattern, however, is misleading as some ministers and magistrates were extremely conscientious even when there were no apparent penalties for failing to attend. Eight ministers and ten elders attended over 100 sessions in the period.[2] It is worth noting that while eight of nineteen ministers (42%) were "above average" in attendance only fifteen of forty-seven elders (32%) were. This highlights the importance of "serious" magistrates – a core of magistrates who maintained the city government's presence on the consistory in this first decade. This dynamic highlights three important points. These eight ministers and ten elders would have come to know each other extremely well, having worked together on a weekly basis. Secondly, the phenomenal level of attendance by Calvin (76%) serves to remind us how conscientiously he took his role as a minister and pastor of the people of Geneva. Finally, there can be little doubt considering the level of attendance by these ten elders that lay members of the consistory were equally diligent in the exercise of their office.

In addition to the frequency of attendance at individual, weekly meetings of the consistory, it has also been possible to consider the length of service of individual magistrate-elders. Over the period 1542–1558, forty-seven separate magistrates served on the consistory as elders (not counting those who served as officers and secretaries). However, ten of these elders served for more than five years each during the years of the "second" consistory (c. 1546–1555). Guillaume Chiccand (noted above for his frequent attendance) served as an elder for thirteen years: 1546–1558; eleven years as an "ordinary" elder; one year, 1557, representing the Senate; and one year, 1558, as presiding syndic. Interestingly, his service as a "senior" magistrate-elder (1557–1558) was after Calvin's opponents were routed. Pierre Britillion (again, frequently at sessions) also served for thirteen years: 1544–1556 (entirely as an "ordinary" elder; when he left service in 1556 he was approximately 87 years old, dying in 1569 aged 100). Jean Chappuis (again a regular presence at the weekly sessions) served for ten years: 1546–1555 (once, 1553, representing the Senate); Mermet Blandin did also (second only to Calvin in his devotion to the weekly meetings): 1543–1552 (though he failed to complete his final full year as he died in the post). Pierre d'Orsières, Jehanton Genod, and François Servand all served eight years and all were among the group of ten elders who attended most frequently. Two elders served for seven years each: Jean-Philibert Donzel and Thivent Matellin. Finally, Michel

Morel (the ninth of ten elders noted above for their regular attendance) served for six years: 1543, 1546–1548, 1550 – all as a senatorial elder; and 1551 as presiding syndic. He was the closest the ruling senate ever seems to have come to having developed a "professional" elder who was also a long-serving senior magistrate (as senator and syndic). His conscientious weekly attendance and long service to the consistory was cut short by his death in 1552.

What is clear from this rather extensive recitation of numerical data is how much the consistory depended on a handful of elders not just for continuity of service over the years but also for the week-to-week running of the sessions. Their institutional memory and command of precedence in dealing with those convoked must have been extensive and echoes Kimberly Lynn's findings about the "substantial local knowledge" acquired by long-serving inquisitors. However, elders' "training" was almost nonexistent. Unlike Inquisitions, as Lynn notes, Reformed elders rarely had specific legal training; on the other hand, the ministers on the consistories were well-trained in theology. These ten men contrast sharply with the other thirty-seven elders. Of the latter, thirteen served only for one year and another thirteen only for two years; eight elders served for three years each and three served for four years. In a very real sense, then, one can suggest that at least twenty-six elders (serving one to two years only) never really settled into the post. However, nine of these "less committed" elder-politicians were clearly "occasional" because of the city's institutional structuring of the eldership. They only served as presiding syndics or senatorial representatives, emphasizing the extent to which Morel was anomalous as a long-serving, frequently attending and senior political representative on the consistory. Moreover, this discussion of the ten "serious" elders gives some idea of just how stable and effective the eldership was in the period of the "second consistory." Nine of the ten elders who attended most regularly in the period 1542–1552 and nine of the ten elders who served the longest number of years in the period 1542–1558 were clustered in the period c. 1546–1555.

While professions are notoriously difficult to identify for individuals in the early modern period (as Mentzer noted in his study of Nîmes), we do have information on twenty-three of the fifty-nine elders (39%) who served in the period 1542–1558. Two occupational backgrounds are particularly noteworthy. Five politician-elders were apothecaries (Aubert, Beney, Pensabin, Gervais, Du Pan).[3] Despite the prominence of their profession, no apothecary was a long-serving elder. Four further elders came from Catholic clerical backgrounds: Bernard, Fontannaz, Vellut,

Symond (also called Picard).[4] Other occupational backgrounds were: notary (Migerand, Tissot, Morel); miller (Vulliet, Chautemps, called Pitiod); draper (Des Arts, Chappuis, called Olivier); coppersmith (Delestra, Porral); hatter (Somaretaz,); cutler (Blandin); pursemaker (Britillion); and innkeeper (Verna).[5] Three of the ten longest-serving, best-attending elders came from the less socially prominent professions of cutler, pursemaker and draper – only Morel, a notary, was from a prominent profession. This contrasts with William Abbot's observation that elders tended to be of the "better sort."[6]

Just as certain professions were well represented in the consistory's membership, a number of family and extended family groups also played a role in the institution. Some had limited impact; Hudriod du Molard and his nephew, Jean, were both elders but seem never to have developed their consistorial roles into springboards to greater political power. In some cases, what appears to be a similar, limited familial role expands when wider relations are considered. Amédée Chasteauneuf and his brother, François were elders as was their stepfather, Pierre d'Orsières, and their brother-in-law, Domaine d'Arlod. Perhaps the most extensive, close familial group on the consistory were the Chiccand brothers (Antoine, Guillaume and Claude). Their uncle, Guillaume Vellut, was also an elder. Jean, their nephew, married the daughter of Michel Varro who, although not an elder, was married to the niece of Pierre d'Orsières, which means that, in the person of Varro, the Chasteauneufs and Chiccands were linked.[7] However, the most interesting familial group to serve on the consistory involved the large number of elders who were connected with François Favre, his daughter (Françoise) and her husband, Ami Perrin – Calvin's greatest opponents. Pierre Bonna (his brother, Jean-Philibert was also an elder), Pierre Tissot and Louis Bernard were all brothers-in-law to Françoise who, as senators, defended her before the consistory and Senate in 1547.[8] The elder Jaques-Nicolas Vulliet was also her brother-in-law.[9] Jean de la Maisonneuve, also an elder, married François Favre's niece. His father, Baudichon and uncle, Claude, were elders and Claude's son married the daughter of the elder Dominique Dentand.[10] Thus, the women of the Favre family linked no fewer than nine elders. Familial interconnections and professional associations demonstrate the complex webs of interaction that encased the elders of the Genevan consistory.

The men who served as elders also figured prominently in the city's poor relief system. As Philippe Chareyre's chapter points out, most French Protestant consistories included deacons as well as elders and ministers. Geneva did not in practice technically have "deacons" regardless of the assumptions in the *Ecclesiastical Ordinances*. Instead, Geneva had a magisterially controlled public welfare system operate through the *Hospital General* under the guidance of the *hospitaller* and his assistants, the *procurures*. In the period 1543–1558, three of the five *hospitallers* were elders (Fontannaz, Jessé, Collonda); two (L. Bernard, G. Chiccand) had been *hospitallers* before 1543 and one elder (Somareta) would be *hospitaller* after 1558. Although few elders ever served as *hospitallers*, the office was dominated by magistrates who also served as elders at some point in their lives. The situation among the *procurures* was similar. Of those who were assistants in 1543–1558 fully 50% also served as elders. Indeed, fully 36% of all elders in the period had served as *procurures*. It is interesting to speculate about the extent to which the heavy representation of magistrates connected with the city's poor relief system on the consistory was conscious and, perhaps, even intentional. The elders were co-optively elected by their fellow citizens who may well have seen a closer connection between the poor relief of the *hospital* and the social work, especially relating to interpersonal and domestic disputes, of the consistory than normally assumed. It may also have played a part in the ease with which deacons became an integral part of French consistories – the Genevan model in the minds of contemporaries may have been actually, if not obviously, connected closely with poor relief.

Because of the quality of sources in Geneva, it is possible to study individual elders in an effort to understand more deeply Geneva's consistory as an institution of the civic polity of Geneva. This approach has largely not been a feature of the historiography on consistories for two important reasons. First, the necessary ancillary sources (especially, notarial records) often do not survive. Second, the historiography still tends to focus on the consistories as ecclesiastical bodies (despite the numerical importance of elders in the Reformed world outside Geneva), and thus the individuals who warrant study are the ministers. Nevertheless, the quantity of sources in Reformed Scotland and the Netherlands suggest detailed studies of the elders can be undertaken there. Tulchin's work on the wider composition of the Reformed movement using notarial records proves that it is possible to study the lives, careers, and interconnections among lay members not only as a group (as McCallum elsewhere and Todd, in this volume, have done) but as individuals as well. Current work assumes that the extended biographies of clergy are essential for understanding them in their historical context. A similar assumption is needed about lay elders. Chris Langley's close study of the way the laity underpinned and maintained Scotland's Calvinist national Kirk in the 1640s and 1650s demonstrates not just the importance of the laity as individuals but also the need to study them as such and to incorporate the results into discussions of the Reformed movement.

Thus, while intriguing as an ecclesiastical institution, the Genevan consistory is much better understood as a collection of men – indeed politicians – working together with Geneva's clergy to create a godly society in the city. As we have seen, however, not all politician-elders were the same nor was the collection of men forming the institution static over time. The early years of the consistory were fairly chaotic with considerable alteration among elders as well as the Company of Pastors. By the mid-1540s, however, a group of elders began to cohere who would not just serve for many years but, as Lucas Kriner has discovered, would form the regular body of elders attending the consistory week-in, week-out. The elders were drawn from a diverse range of professions and although certain familial groups clearly had extensive involvement with the consistory no single group in any way dominated. Indeed, the single most striking characteristic of the men as a whole was the extent to which so many of them were also involved in the city's welfare system. These men, as Chiccand and Britillion suggest (and their examples could be replicated across the board), were not spotless in character, but many of them were extremely hardworking and dedicated not just to the consistory but also, as we have seen, to the wider welfare needs of the city. Thus, it is perhaps worth remembering that when an average Genevan or a poor religious refugee was called before the consistory, the elders represented not only a panel of powerful politicians deputed from the city's three councils, but the individual convoked also stood before a considerable number of men who had in their power the purse-strings of the city's poor-relief system. It can hardly be surprising that the consistory as an expression of the collective will of these politician-elders was able to command such authority.

Notes

1 AEG (Archives d'État de Genève), RC (Registres du Conseil), (volume) 35, fol. 207 (May 17, 1541).
2 Ministerial attendance: Calvin (309; 76%); Poupin (243; 59%); Des Gallars (204; 50%); Dagnion (191; 47%), Chauvet (189; 46%); Cop (186; 45%); Ferron (109; 27%); and, Fabri (101; 25% making him an 'average' minister in attendance). Likewise, ten elders attended more than 100 sessions each: Blandin (274; 67%); Morel (263; 64%); Britillion (221; 54%); D'Orsières (207; 51%); Jean du

Molard (207; 51%); Guillaume Chiccand (204; 50%); Jean Chappuis (163; 40%); Genod (138; 34%); Servand (120; 29%); and, Donzel (107; 26%).

3 AEG, RC 64, fol. 64 (22 Apr 1569); AEG, PC (Procès criminels, série) 1: 362 (February 14, March 11, 1542), (February 14, March 11, 1542); *Registers of the Consistory of Geneva in the Time of Calvin, Volume 1: 1542–1544*, ed. Robert M. Kingdon, Thomas A. Lambert and Isabella M. Watt (Grand Rapids, 2000), 87 n. 361, 182 n. 49.

4 Robert M. Kingdon, Thomas A. Lambert and Isabella Watts eds., *Registers of the Consistory of Geneva in the Time of Calvin, Volume 1: 1542–1544* (Grand Rapids, 2000), Kingdon, *Consistory*, 277 n. 355, 38 n. 159, 10 n. 32; *Registres du consistoire de Genève au temps du Calvin*, ed. Thomas A. Lambert, Isabella M. Watt and Wallace McDonald (Geneva, 2001), 2: 39–40 n. 8.

5 Kingdon, *Consistory*, 4, n. 6, 38 n. 158, 46 n. 193, 189 n. 80, n. 81, 331 n. 66, 417 n. 345; Amédée Roget, *Histoire du Peuple de Genève depuis la Réforme jusqu'à l'Escalade* (Geneva, 1870–7), 5: 36, n. 1; *Registres*, 2: 39 n. 2, 85 n. 284, 97 n. 345, 226 n. 667, 337 n. 1325.

6 William M. Abbott, "Ruling Eldership in Civil War England, the Scottish Kirk, and Early New England: A Comparative Study of Secular and Spiritual Aspects," *Church History* 75 1 (2006): 61–62.

7 *Notices généalogiques sur les familles genevoises, depuis les premiers temps, jusqu'à nos jours*, ed. Jacques-Augustin Galiffe, et al. 7 vols. (Geneva, 1829–95): 1, part 1, 311–12, 490–5; 1, part 2, 136–7.

8 *Registres*, 3: 146–47 and n. 909.

9 Galiffe, *Notices*, 1, part 2, 613.

10 Galiffe, *Notices*, 1, part 1, 385–94.

9

Inquisitions

Kimberly Lynn

There is no shortage of images of inquisitors. They remain fixtures of humorous parody and of our language of critique. In the entry for "Inquisition" in his *Philosophical Dictionary*, published in 1764, Voltaire skewered – among other things – an account of the Inquisition's history by Luis de Páramo (who had been a Spanish inquisitor) published in Madrid in 1598. Voltaire opined that "All men resemble Louis de Paramo when they are fanatics." And continued: "This Paramo was a plain man, very exact in his dates, who omitted no interesting fact and scrupulously calculated the number of human victims immolated by the Holy Office throughout the world."[1] Earlier in the volume, he had already condemned fanaticism, in its own entry, defining the fanatic as "the man who supports his madness with murder," that is, "such as judges who condemn to death those who have committed no other crime than failing to think like them; and these judges are all the more guilty, all the more deserving of the execration of mankind," he elaborated, because they were supposedly reasonable men.[2]

Polemic against inquisitors and Inquisitions was not, of course, Voltaire's invention. There was substantial dissent against the early modern Catholic Inquisitions from the process of their respective foundations onward; lasting images of inquisitors were generated in those conflicts and crystallized in Enlightenment critique. Voltaire alone has been calculated to have used the term "Inquisition" more than 400 times in more than seventy different works over more than fifty years. Inquisitors, by extension, became – and remain – symbols at the ready, invoked when combating religious fanaticism, censorship, excessive prosecutorial zeal, as well as torture and other inhumane uses of state power. Often envisioned as monks, they have also been used to symbolize the departure of Christian institutions from apostolic ideals. Like in Voltaire's use of Páramo, such critiques drew upon the writings of early modern inquisitors. Yet the image of the inquisitor has eclipsed the diversity of individual early modern inquisitors and their activities. And in so doing, I would argue, it has inhibited the ability to make sense of how Inquisitions functioned within early modern societies and to see inquisitors as part of the same social fabric as their contemporaries.

In 1968, the scholar Julio Caro Baroja pointed out the nearly complete neglect of the study of Spanish inquisitors. He noted the habit of writing about an "Inquisition without inquisitors," that is, about an institution whose human dimensions had been too little explored. Nearly fifty years later, it is still not uncommon to depict inquisitors as faceless and interchangeable. Individual inquisitors – especially below the level of Inquisitors General – remain relatively understudied; this is likely due, in part, to an understandable instinct to correct historical injustice, to give voices to the persecuted rather than further attention to the persecutors. Yet the best microhistories of trials have carefully researched the inquisitorial officials involved. And there is now renewed emphasis on charting inquisitors' thought and careers. Drawing on such work, this essay explores what characterized the people who held office as inquisitors, that is, as the judges in early modern Inquisition tribunals.

PERSONNEL

It is not even so simple to say who judged sin and heresy when the question is confined to the three early modern Inquisitions. The Spanish, Portuguese, and Roman Inquisitions – founded or reorganized in 1478, 1536, and 1542, respectively – each had an array of personnel, as is explained in more detail in Sections A and B. In a study first published in 1995, Francisco Bethencourt made a pioneering comparison of inquisitors and officials across the three institutions, which current research continues to refine. There were Inquisitors General and royal councilors of Inquisition in the Spanish and Portuguese monarchies (distinct even when their crowns were unified). By the later seventeenth century, there were twenty-one Spanish inquisitorial districts and four Portuguese tribunals (one in Goa, three in Portugal, Lisbon's with jurisdiction over the Portuguese Atlantic). Popes presided over a Roman Congregation of the Inquisition; under that, forty-seven tribunal foundations of varying kind have been counted in the Italian peninsula, more in the north.

Subordinate to the inquisitors (the judges), Spanish Inquisition district tribunals had a prosecutor (*fiscal*), who could be quite influential; additional lawyers, notaries and secretaries; accounting staff; a medical doctor; and a prison staff with a warden and his associates. The inquisitors, or at least the most senior, were often housed in the tribunal building. Theological and legal consultants were called to weigh the cases and to censor books. Sometimes a representative of the bishop participated. Away from the tribunal seat, there were commissaries who acted as the inquisitors' delegates with a limited set of powers. And there were familiars, the lay officials. The Spanish royal council (the *Suprema*) maintained a comparable staff, between 1555 and 1565 listing annual salaries for the Inquisitor General, four to seven councilors, two to three secretaries, a *fiscal*, a reporter who prepared information for the council (*relator*), a constable, a medical doctor, a nuncio, two porters, and an official who was both the receiver and accountant.[3] The Portuguese tribunals were similarly organized, with an important additional post of deputy, who functioned as a consultant and was in essence an apprentice inquisitor being prepared for promotion. Among the cardinals of the Roman Congregation of Inquisition were a secretary and a deputy; additional to the cardinals were a commissary, assessor, fiscal proctor, and notary, along with theological and legal consultants, and amplified by more notaries, assistants, secretaries, scribes, and a summarizer of proceedings. Earlier sixteenth-century Italian district inquisitors were materially dependent on their monasteries or local bishops; by century's end, papal incomes facilitated greater autonomy. And jurisdictional muddles continued. Perhaps the best studied Italian tribunal, Venice's Inquisition, by the later sixteenth century, comprised three ecclesiastics – inquisitor, nuncio, and patriarch (the last a nod to the episcopal faculty of ordinary inquisitor) or their representatives – and three representatives of civil authority, lay advisors from the Venetian aristocracy, aided by a fairly typical staff. In the kingdom of Naples, the episcopate managed to maintain significant control over Inquisitions, pushing back against Roman authority (repulsing attempts to found a tribunal of the Spanish Inquisition there).

INQUISITORS – SPANISH, PORTUGUESE, ROMAN

Medieval inquisitors were most commonly mendicant friars. By the mid-thirteenth century, a collective inquisitorial identity was already coalescing, drawing on inquisitors' manuals and self-depictions, and the canonization of a martyred inquisitor, Peter of Verona. Although they sometimes strategically invoked their medieval predecessors, early modern inquisitors were much more varied in terms of professional formation. District inquisitors investigated cases of heresy and passed judgment on the accused, and were also, to greater or lesser extent, administrators in charge of the tribunal staff and buildings, if any. Councilors of Inquisition and cardinals of the Congregation took part in appointing officials and sent directives to the districts; they were essentially elite courtiers and members of an appellate court. There is not sufficient evidence to estimate the total number of inquisitors appointed between the late fifteenth and early nineteenth centuries (when the early modern Inquisitions were suppressed). Spanish Inquisition tribunals generally had three inquisitors, but vacancies were common; illness, other temporary commissions, and inspections of the district also removed inquisitors from tribunal business. The staffing of the districts was quite variable: 73 different inquisitors appointed to Sicily from 1487 to 1712, 61 to Toledo from 1483 to 1620, 50 to Santiago de Compostela from 1560 to 1700, 134 to Valencia from 1481 to 1818, 16 to Mexico from 1571 to 1642, and 9 to Lima from 1569 to 1627.[4]

The broad outlines of the origins of Spanish inquisitors have been established. Often from the lower nobility or gentry, most often Castilians, they were embedded in social and political networks as both clients and patrons; they often had family connections to other royal or ecclesiastical officials, and very often to other Inquisition associates. The genealogical investigations for admission to inquisitorial office were not systematically required until the 1570s. After the early sixteenth century, the judges had degrees overwhelmingly in canon law (or both civil and canon law) – only very rarely in theology – most often from the universities of Salamanca or Valladolid; they were by and large secular clerics and jurists. This marked a significant departure from the late fifteenth century, when most had been Dominicans. Later, Jesuits had a small presence, but the general preference for jurist-clerics remained. Theologians were called as consultants, but not to perform the central judicial work. One guideline held that inquisitors – given the gravity of their work – should have reached the age of 40. Younger men were sometimes appointed, and other rulings offered 30 as the minimum age. Usually inquisitors had significant prior experience of some kind, such as posts in cathedral chapters, universities, or civil law courts, or had worked up through the inquisitorial ranks (from lesser attorneys to prosecutors to inquisitors as well as from lesser to more important district tribunals). Predictably, the *Suprema's* councilors tended to be better connected and more accomplished than their provincial counterparts, and the Inquisitors General another level above that.

There were 376 appointments to the *Suprema* between 1488 and 1819 and forty-six Inquisitors General who took office from 1483 to 1818. In the era often identified as the Spanish Inquisition's apex (circa 1541–1664) about two-thirds of the 158 appointees to the council had previous inquisitorial experience (91 as inquisitors, 13 of other kinds); this pattern intensified markedly after 1566 (from 1541 to 1566 only 6 of 23 had inquisitorial experience). Several were married laymen. All eight Inquisitor General nominees between 1539 and 1596 were members of the *Suprema*, though most had not previously served in a regional tribunal. In the first half of the seventeenth century, the council's profile remained roughly the same, with the notable addition of theologians, members of the higher nobility, and Dominican friars who had held high office in their order. Seats on the *Suprema* were ideally stepping-stones to the episcopate and presidencies of royal councils.

Portuguese inquisitors had similar characteristics. They most frequently had degrees in canon law from the University of Coimbra. The three inquisitors of each tribunal, like the commissaries, were ecclesiastics required to demonstrate their purity of blood. The tribunal in Goa was distinct in that its inquisitors (and commissaries) tended to be regular clergy; the Jesuits had even spurred the foundation of that tribunal. There were 149 appointments to the royal council of the Portuguese Inquisition from 1536 to 1821, and there was an even stronger pattern of promoting within the ranks than in Spain; 120 of the councilors had prior Inquisition experience. They often held posts on other royal councils and moved from the council to episcopal careers. The office of Inquisitor General was marked by its first effective occupant (technically the second), the Cardinal-Infante Henrique, the king's brother, who held office from 1539 to 1578, significantly shaping the institution and its first generations of officials. And later incumbents were also members of the royal family or highest nobility.

In the Italian tribunals, a different career formation was dominant. Inquisitors were theologians by training, stipulated to also have knowledge of canon law, and they were regular clergy, a mixture of Franciscans and Dominicans. In the institutional consolidation that occurred between 1540 and 1570, the Dominicans took control of many jurisdictions from the Franciscans and came to dominate the inquisitorial ranks under papal direction. Yet there remained important exceptions; the inquisitors in the Grand Duchy of Tuscany were Conventual Franciscans, while the inquisitors of Malta were usually secular clerics and simultaneously the papal nuncios. One study of nearly 100 Dominican inquisitors active in northern Italy between 1474 and 1527 has argued for continuities between their career patterns and those of later inquisitors. They had often exercised other responsibilities in the orders, and had sometimes also taught in monastic schools or universities. At its foundation in 1542, the Congregation of the Inquisition initially comprised six cardinals, elevated to thirteen by century's end, although attendance was variable in practice. A new study of its personnel between roughly 1590 and 1640 charts how – in the important era following Sixtus V's 1588 reorganization of the congregations – the Roman Inquisition developed a professional staff and the characteristics of its cardinal members were conditioned by papal priorities. While the Congregation's commissary was always a Dominican educated as a theologian, there was a significant presence of two kinds of theological consultants. And the Roman Inquisition was very much marked by legal training: the cardinals were often trained in both canon and civil law, jurists abounded among the professional staff, and there were ties to the Rota (the papal appellate court) both through the presence of its dean as a consultant and in the career trajectories of a few Inquisition figures.

As evidenced by William Naphy's Chapter 8 in this volume, there are some parallels in the scholarship on the judges of early modern consistories and Inquisitions. In each case, scholarly focus is turning increasingly toward examining the role of individual officials in driving judicial action, casting new light on bodies that have often been approached more from the perspective of institutional history or studied to reveal the histories of the prosecuted and persecuted. As in the case of inquisitors, it is becoming clear that family ties, educational and professional formations, and experience in other kinds of political and religious activity shaped the actions and priorities of consistory authorities, whether clerics or lay elders, and that a fuller account of the development of consistory judicial practices and social dynamics must attend further to those authorities as individuals. There are some striking parallels to inquisitors' trajectories in the careers of sixteenth-century consistory members. Both were deeply tied to other contemporary institutions and frequently held multiple offices involved in the work of governing as well as in the administration of charity, and their official charge was also seen as intertwined with pastoral duties. Perhaps the greatest divergences lay in the inquisitors' overwhelming tendency to be members of the Catholic clergy that consistory elders and clerics had so deliberately rejected; moreover, even as many Inquisition officials and affiliates were married laymen, its judges were so only in exceptional cases. They diverged also in the acquisition of office, in becoming judges by royal, papal, or conciliar appointment versus more localized election. The consistories seem also to have had more diversity in the backgrounds of elders who served as judges, still often local elites, yet from a range of trades and occupations, contrary to most inquisitors' more standard education in either law or theology. One last fault line between these early modern judicial classes that strikes me as significant is that of mobility; while some inquisitors stayed in one or two regions across their professional lives, many ranged widely, often appointed deliberately to places far from their kin. If both Inquisitions and consistories aimed to tie individual places and their inhabitants to more universally held ideals, in its judges' functions and origins, a consistory was seemingly a more locally based institution, by design.

RE-ENVISIONING INQUISITORS

To chart such patterns still does not close the question of who the inquisitors were. Attending to individual inquisitors' career trajectories, working habits, mobility, social networks, and intellectual activities, scholars are increasingly showing how those attributes of judges' lives permeated the courtroom and how they contributed to shaping their institutions, even as the judges were, in turn, shaped by the practices and priorities of their office. The remainder of this essay proposes some ways to see how inquisitors – and, by extension, inquisitorial actions – were woven into the social fabric of the early modern world. The judges of early modern Catholic Inquisitions were all men. They were also almost all clerics. Their official lives were thus shaped by their membership in the clerical class of society, by the mandate to offer pastoral care, and by the vehement debates about how the clergy should live that marked the early modern Catholic world both before and after the Council of Trent. Variously trained in law or theology, they needed some acquaintance with both disciplines. In their capacity as judges, they could encounter a wide range of witnesses and accused heretics, from elite courtiers and princes of the Church to impoverished rural peasants, men and women, lay and religious.

An awareness of the range of participants in heresy trials and range of figures who could judge sin and heresy contextualizes why inquisitors persistently constructed accounts of their office and of their own merits; they used them to claim preeminence in the work of judicial discernment in trials of faith. So Páramo, then an inquisitor of Sicily's tribunal lobbying for that court's privileges in Madrid, sought in his 1598 history to tie together all conceivable exercises of Inquisition – past and contemporary – as different faces of a unified system of divine institution; he also sought to build his judicial and institutional authority via arguments (in letters, print, and manuscript) that inquisitorial courts were more just and adhered better to procedure than other ecclesiastical or secular courts. In other contexts, Spanish inquisitors, like Diego de Simancas or the seventeenth-century members of the *Suprema* (who rebuked the Lima tribunal for irregularities), stressed the differences of the Spanish Inquisition from its Roman or Portuguese counterparts. These inquisitors used such comparisons to try to assert the supremacy of their mode of procedure and to bring others into compliance with a particular procedural vision. It remains an open question how much early modern inquisitors perceived themselves as part of a shared inquisitorial culture; the manuals of inquisitorial law indicated the borrowing of practices and precedents between tribunals and sometimes glossed the differing "styles" of Inquisition courts.

Inquisitors were mobile in two senses: social and geographical. To become an inquisitor was a mark of social advancement, part of a successful career trajectory. Closely tied to the ecclesiastical hierarchy and to royal officeholding, inquisitors were part of a process of cross-polination of procedures and experiences between institutions, as individuals were promoted from office to office. One of the primary career aims was appointment as a bishop, an office that Italian, Spanish, and Portuguese inquisitors attained at varying rates across time and place. Inquisitors were also promoted to royal councils, or in the case of the cardinals of the Inquisition, made members of other papal congregations. Inquisitorial experience touched the careers of many attendees at the Council of Trent.

There is dramatic evidence of the possibilities for professional advancement the Inquisitions afforded churchmen in the later sixteenth century. Two inquisitors active in northern Italy, each expelled from Venetian territories during their inquisitorial careers, became prominent popes – the Dominican Pius V and the Franciscan Sixtus V. Paul IV had also been an inquisitor (all three, along with the short-lived Marcellus II, had also been inquisitors in Malta), and the early seventeenth-century Paul V had been the secretary of the Congregation. Still, there is substantial evidence of the limits of this mobility. For the majority of district inquisitors, the acquisition of that office marked the culmination of their careers. And there were hierarchies among the districts. Inquisitors in the Spanish tribunals in the Americas stayed almost exclusively in American posts over their careers, including when they were made bishops; Portuguese inquisitors in Goa, similarly, were almost never promoted to offices in Portugal.

There was a tension between geographical mobility and fixity in the lives of inquisitors. Many served long terms in a single place. With regard to Dominican inquisitors in northern Italy, Michael Tavuzzi suggests that this practice made for an older and perhaps less active cohort of inquisitors; Sara Nalle's work indicates, via Cuenca's inquisitors, that these long terms meant that judges built up substantial local knowledge, including information about those they tried (even as inquisitors were often deliberately posted to places where they lacked pre-existing ties). Inquisitors were also mobile through the practice of conducting visitations – inspections of suspected problem areas and regular tours of their districts, even if the latter practice was already decreasing by the later sixteenth century. This practice not only sought to project authority further afield and drum up judicial business, it was also a way in which inquisitors were asked to behave as pastors, circulating among the flock and acting often as itinerant confessors in the process. Iberian inquisitors, in particular, might travel particularly far afield. In the 1590s, inquisitors were sent from the Lisbon tribunal on inspection tours to Brazil, as well as to the Azores, Madeira, and Angola; this practice persisted into the eighteenth century. To take an especially mobile example from the early seventeenth century, Juan Gutiérrez Flores moved from being the prosecutor of the Spanish Inquisition tribunal in Sicily to an inquisitor in first Mallorca, then Mexico City, and finally Lima, where he died and was buried in the tribunal chapel. Following individual career trajectories might also eventually offer a different vision of the relationships between the three early modern Inquisitions and their subsidiary tribunals. In the later sixteenth century, the Portuguese Antonio Matos Noronha moved from being a district inquisitor in the Spanish Inquisition to the *Suprema*, to being a bishop in Portugal, a councilor of Inquisition there, and finally to serving as the Portuguese Inquisitor General. Significantly, he also spearheaded the compilation of the Portuguese Inquisition's procedural instructions. The future Gregory XIII, trained in canon law, had been sent as a papal legate to Castile during the Spanish Inquisition's trial of Carranza; in the same era, the future Spanish Inquisitor General Gaspar de Quiroga acquired experience in the Roman judicial environment, serving on the Rota. Future cardinals of the Inquisition served as nuncios to Spain (including the future Paul V) and elsewhere; in one case in the 1590s, a nuncio seems to have initiated a Roman Inquisition trial while in Madrid that continued in Rome. Antonio Zapata Cisneros y Mendoza was a district inquisitor in Spain, then a cardinal on the Congregation in Rome, and then became Spain's Inquisitor General (1627–32).

There is also now ample evidence to begin to locate inquisitors as active participants in the intellectual culture of their day – corresponding and conversing with other elites, patronizing artists and younger clerics. They left a variety of writings, both manuscript and print. Tavuzzi's so-called "Renaissance inquisitors" actively produced books, among them important theological commentaries; other sixteenth-century inquisitors in northern Italy, such as Umberto Locati and Leandro Alberti, produced historical and geographical writings in addition to commentaries on inquisitorial law. Early seventeenth-century cardinals and other officials of the Roman Inquisition, especially the theological consultants, wrote in a wide variety of genres, from theological works to poetry. Some councilors of the Spanish Inquisition left works of theology, law, politics, history, or hagiography.

Practicing inquisitors also compiled Inquisition law handbooks – in the mid-sixteenth century the Spanish councilor Simancas and the papal inquisitors Locati and Camillo Campeggi were all printing commentaries on inquisitorial law; it was seemingly not uncommon for officials to generate ad hoc manuals in manuscript. Confronted with cases in district tribunals, other sixteenth- and seventeenth-century Spanish inquisitors also turned to theorizing – among them Arnau Albert, Juan de Rojas, Páramo, and Diego García de Trasmiera, in Mallorca, Sicily, and Valencia. Inquisitors' duties included a substantial written component, of compiling arguments and framing cases that were increasingly related in correspondence between central councils and provincial tribunals. The records reveal not only how inquisitors pursued a variety of strategies to build the authority necessary to exercise their office but also the myriad gaps between the images inquisitors sought to promote of themselves and the course of affairs on the ground. Inquisitors' letters often contain a rhetoric of affliction – officials like Páramo described not only physical injuries sustained in serving their office but also practical hindrances to their judicial work.

Inquisitors also built – and relied in their judicial practice – on libraries. In 1598, the inquisitorial library in Friuli reportedly held around 100 books, among them a variety of inquisitorial manuals. The personal library of Lima's first inquisitor was inventoried at 105 books at his death in 1583, and two members of the Spanish *Suprema* who died in 1572 and 1650, respectively, had around 300 books each. These were in large part ecclesiastical and legal reference libraries, but with a variety of geographical, theological, historical, and other kinds of works among them.

In sum, early modern inquisitors occupied multiple social roles. Historians have cast them as anthropologists and as moderators who complemented and competed with bishops, confessors, and missionaries; they can be envisioned not just as judges but also as archivists, historians, administrators, and pastors in the course of their official lives. Inquiries into their intellectual lives suggest what they had in common with other contemporary elites – including those with whom they disagreed – and perhaps how the persuasive capacities of some inquisitors contributed to the social and political successes of their institutions. As a group, inquisitors were notably well educated and nested in patronage and clientage networks of varying influence. Examining inquisitors themselves suggests how their particular experiences, career aspirations, and ideological affinities could shape the course of trials. To do so complicates more mechanistic visions of Inquisitions that consider mainly the official institutional structures, revealing instead institutions shaped by personal interactions and multiple networks of affiliation. Analyses of inquisitors also hint at how experience was transmitted across continents and hemispheres. Some inquisitors – even though they operated within many constraints – persistently pursued specific judicial priorities for decades. The records also present evidence about inquisitors' transgressions, as the recently discovered deposition of the poet Luis de Góngora in the midst of an inspection of Córdoba's tribunal in 1597 reveals.[5] Góngora sought to spur correction of an inquisitor accused of inappropriate relationships with women and partial judicial treatment of his associates. The archives also yield ample evidence of how the careers of inquisitorial staff crisscrossed over the decades, suggesting the only occasionally glimpsed human relations of those judicial institutions. Attending to the inquisitors thus reveals a range of vocation and preparation for office, of characteristics and personalities. It reveals the persisting contestation of the legitimacy and effectiveness of Inquisitions as a whole and of individual inquisitors in particular – in short, the all too human politics of Inquisitions. And it suggests how inquisitors both generally sought to work within their legal frameworks and how Inquisitions were flexible and adaptable; inquisitors both referred to precedent and improvised as they judged heresy in a wide variety of legal, religious, social, and political environments across the early modern world.

Notes

1 Voltaire, *Philosophical Dictionary*, trans. Peter Gay (New York, 1962), 330. Ibid., 267–68.

2 Julio Caro Baroja, *El señor Inquisidor y otras vidas por oficio* (Madrid, 1968), 15.

3 Inquisitor General (400,000 *maravedís*, to 600,000 in 1568), councilors (150,000 or occasionally 100,000, doubled to 300,000 in 1561), the lowest paid, porters (25,000 each). The district inquisitors of Córdoba drew between 100,000 and 150,000 in the same period. Archivo Histórico Nacional, Inq., lib. 248, fols. 71-181v; José Martínez Millán, "Estructura de la hacienda de la Inquisición," in *Historia de la Inquisición en España y América*, ed. Joaquín Pérez Villanueva and Bartolomé Escandell Bonet (Madrid, 1984–2000), 2:885–1075.

4 Manuel Rivero Rodríguez, "La Inquisición Española en Sicilia," in *Historia de la Inquisición* 3:1212–20; Martin Nesvig, *Ideology and Inquisition: The World of the Censors in Early Mexico* (New Haven, 2009), 274–5; Francisco Bethencourt, *The Inquisition: A Global History, 1478–1834* (Cambridge, 2009), 155–6.

5 *Góngora y el Señor Inquisidor. Un autógrafo inédito de Don Luis en edición facsímil*, presented and transcribed by Amelia de Paz (Madrid, 2012). Cf. John Edwards, "Trial of an Inquisitor: the dismissal of Diego Rodríguez Lucero inquisitor of Córdoba, in 1508," *Journal of Ecclesiastical History* 37 no. 2 (1986): 240–57.

Section D

Inquisition and Consistory Records

10

Consistories

Christian Grosse
Translated by Charles H. Parker

Influenced originally by the combined work of Norbert Elias, Michel Foucault, and Gerhard Oestreich, and then later by the confessionalization thesis of Wolfgang Reinhard and Heinz Schilling, historians since the 1980s have relied heavily on the records left by consistories. The initial studies belonged to a period in which the ideological program of a quantitative history of mentalities, aspiring to identify the "popular" layers of culture, converged with the beginnings of the extensive use of information technology. Historians then devised categories for crimes and sins prosecuted by judicial or ecclesiastical institutions, inserted the cases into patterns of offenses, quantified them, and analyzed them over long periods of time. Thus research combining serial analyses with individual case studies has proliferated since the early 1990s in various collections of consistory records in France, Switzerland, Germany, Scotland, and Holland.

Enthusiasm for quantitative studies and confidence in the objectivity of the conclusions that could be drawn from quantitative data, however, was quickly tempered, thanks to historians of criminal justice who drew attention to the difference between an apparent offense, prosecuted by the courts and therefore recorded in the archives, and an actual event. Consequently, the reliability of observations based on the quantification of cases across time was seriously challenged as strong skepticism about these methods emerged in the 1990s. In all fields where historians utilized quantitative methodology, debates about reliability of the sources and the distortions they presented loomed large. Among historians of criminal justice, discussions about the "dark figure" generated a new field of research devoted to what was called "infra-justice," which considered all informal mechanisms of social regulation outside the exercise of official judicial power and thus absent from archival sources.

Somewhat belatedly, the historiography of Reformed church discipline adopted a critical stance toward the statistical method by identifying the biases in the records of its judicial institutions. In 2002, Judith Pollmann accurately measured the discrepancies between actual consistory activity in Utrecht and the traces it left in official registers. By comparing consistorial accounts with a private journal kept by one of the elders, Pollmann crystallized the doubts on these issues among historians of Reformed Protestantism and revived this discussion. This essay will take up these debates and suggest some alternatives for developing a new perspective on consistory records.

AN UNCERTAIN RECORD

If it is now taken for granted that the information in consistory sources must be handled with care (especially since social factors affected documenting practices, making their reliability uneven), other factors also warrant caution. There was no standard administrative procedure for either compiling or preserving consistory records during the early modern era. The rising "bureaucratic culture," born in urban administrations of the late Middle Ages, had not yet developed standardized procedures of recording and storing information. Such operations remained erratic and uncertain; they depended primarily on the personal oversight of the officials responsible for them. In most cases, this state of affairs explains the fragmentary nature of consistory records that have been preserved. Even those renowned for their completeness contain long breaks. Despite the great continuity of Geneva's consistorial records, we nevertheless lack almost twenty years of its minutes between 1542 and the end of the Republic in 1798; if the collection of records from the Nîmes consistory is almost complete for over a century (1561–1685), the volume spanning the years 1563–77 is missing. Compounding such accidental loss and neglect are cases where these archives were deliberately destroyed, as in France after the revocation of the Edict of Nantes.

Moreover, a significant part of the activity of these ecclesiastical tribunals took place outside of its meetings and therefore left no record. A significant gap existed between recorded and actual disciplinary activity. Just as historians of criminal justice talk of "infra-justice" as Sara

Beam's chapter reveals, we must similarly pay attention to a type of "sub-consistory" covering informal interventions that fell within the sphere of ecclesiastical discipline but do not appear – or appear only indirectly – in the archival sources. This discrepancy emerged from the very way that Reformed churches understood the exercise of discipline; its institutional dimension was seen as a sort of extension of a corrective action begun in everyday social relations, the duty of charity requiring each Christian to lead those who fell into sin back to divine grace.

Between this horizontal supervision, exercised within the fabric of society, and the vertical oversight carried out by the consistory lay a vast gray zone of activities that constituted an important part of church discipline but did not necessarily or systematically leave written traces. Many cases were not resolved at consistory meetings, but through a delegation of ministers, elders, and neighborhood officials (*dizeniers*), often after sermons or during the regular household visits conducted by members of the consistory. In some instances, treating a case through an informal delegation rather than at regular meetings of an ecclesiastical tribunal resulted from a deliberate choice, attempting, for example, to spare members of the social elite from the shame attached to appearing before the consistory. In some areas, such as the county of Neuchâtel, the consistories of individual churches pointedly did not keep any records of their activities. Records kept by "warners" at Nîmes enabled Philippe Chareyre to establish that, in 1670, only 55% of those contacted by the consistory actually appeared at its meetings. Others were convoked in the homes of pastors (21%) or at the end of church services or catechism lessons (24%).

REGISTRATION PROCEDURES AND DISTORTIONS OF INFORMATION

If a sometimes significant part of the disciplinary action taken by a consistory thus remains in the shadows, historians must also take into consideration the fact that the information found in the registers resulted from complex drafting procedures. These could involve several types of mediation and translation from the initial dialogues between different actors from which these records were constructed. Each of these mediations and translations requires filtering because of distortions between the initial oral exchange and the transcription we read today.

The official minutes from consistory meetings frequently resulted from a process of clarifying notes taken during the sessions – in a notebook or on loose sheets – which have not survived. Most of the time, the original rough draft, (*brouillard*), has not actually been preserved, except in Scotland and the Pays de Vaud.[1] This two-stage process of recording minutes – the original rough draft and the final record – might entail not only risking the loss of sources (which may explain some of the gaps identified earlier) and incomplete transcripts of the original notes but also the intentional selection and reorientation of information in them. The "cleaning-up" of draft notes done when the final version was produced usually involved a process of consolidation. What the historian discovers in the consistory records were often a summarized, reduced account, since substantial information was tightened around the critical points of the case – thereby eliminating in the process of redacting a fair share of the circumstances that led to a certain decision. The consistory also some-times stipulated that the parties formally approve the summary of the case. Typically, in Courthézon (principality of Orange), "the elders referred to the register [of the consistory] as the 'book of conclusions.'"[2] In the same manner, the secretary of the Genevan consistory regularly acknowledged that he had abbreviated discussions during meetings by simply noting "and other lengthy remarks" in the record.[3] An edition of two parallel registers of the same meeting by the Genevan consistory (October 13, 1547) verifies that records could vary significantly in relat-ing the specific circumstances of a case by providing more or less descrip-tive detail. The consistory's decisions, however, were rendered accurately in substance, even if they varied in form.[4]

This record, reduced to essentials, derived from a set of norms that determined its form and shaped its content. In the absence of detailed regulations issued by churches on methods for keeping records, we can see that the training of the secretaries who maintained consistory registers played a significant role. This task could certainly be performed by a minister, a schoolmaster or even a local magistrate, but it usually fell to notaries. They followed a particular form of recording minutes and handled them according to customary practices. On the one hand, notar-ies took advantage of such writing techniques as making marginal notes, which allowed them to track decisions and individuals quickly, as well as constructing directories and indices, which contributed greatly to the rationalization, and hence effectiveness, of consistory action. On the other hand, by complying with the formal rules of notarial drafting practice, which required a clear identification of people involved in cases and the rendering of decisions in a synthetic style, secretaries gave greater authen-ticity and authority to the minutes they edited.

This practice explains the attention paid to the verification and preservation of these records since the sixteenth century, even though implementation encountered many difficulties. We know that Calvin himself reread and personally corrected records in order to ensure that they repeated exactly what had been said during a meeting.[5] The decisions made about preserving records also reflected this concern; for example, consistorial regulations for the Pays de Vaud in 1598 specified that the "manual" containing the minutes be kept "secretly" by the minister so that [Bernese] authorities could monitor their "diligence done in chastising vices."[6] Similar regulations in 1758 ordered "cities and communities" to "provide a chest or cabinet in the pastor's home to keep the books pertaining to the consistory or the church."[7] In France, some churches were equipped with cabinets to hold their archives.

If the production of authentic consistory records by secretaries implies that minutes be written in a standard form, the legitimacy of the body's decisions also required that certain information be highlighted and specific formulas adopted in order to clarify the deeds on which the consistory rendered its judgment. This formatting occurred during the transition from the original rough draft (*brouillard*) to the final version and inserted some distance – which could be significant – between the lively discussions at the original meeting and the cold formality of the text that confronts historians. Like the letters of remission studied by Natalie Davis, the minutes of a consistory were a "collective enterprise" that resulted from a process of interaction and negotiation between an oral history, governed by a certain "narrative experience," and a rhetorical framework burdened by technical and literary requirements. A complex translation process intervened during this phase.

We must also remember that the dialogue between ministers, elders, and persons summoned before the ecclesiastical tribunal was held, in many cases, in the local dialect. With a few exceptions, it was later written in the language of the institution and the authorities. The consistories' categorization of sins, so central to the institutions' actions, increased any possible divergences of meaning between consistorial authorities, on the one hand, and the rank and file, on the other. In Geneva, the margins of records listing the names of those suspended from the Lord's Supper employed such terms as "scandal," "rebellion," "calumny," "ignorance," "superstition," "idolatry," "blasphemy," "papist," "abjuration," "enmity," "battery," "theft," "false witness," "lie," etc.

Still other demands intruded to shape the content and form of the records about each case. When an ecclesiastical tribunal had the power to impose fines or compel payment of administrative fees, it became a priority to justify the financial penalties it recorded. Finally, reflecting the activity of an institution working toward "the union of the faithful," consistory records often strove to provide a consensual image of itself. This introduced significant bias in the way the minutes were composed, as they tended to highlight "the sense of perfect accord prevailing in decisions, and the absence of individual views and dissenting voices."[8] This observation indicates that some of the mounting tensions or conflicts that erupted during sessions of the consistory were passed over in silence and consequently lie beyond our knowledge.

THE NARRATIVE DIMENSION OF THE RECORDS

The documentation left by consistories must therefore be evaluated rigorously in order to highlight two things: on the one hand, the limits of their ability to express their institution's intentions and activities accurately; and on the other, to emphasize the many filters and distortions that the process of recording introduced between its real activities and the records it left behind. These critical points of view, however, also require several nuanced approaches. By overstating the randomness of their documentation or preservation and overemphasizing the problems of serial and statistical use of consistorial sources, we risk underestimating the confidence that elders and pastors placed on writing as a tool to reinforce and systematize the discipline they exercised. We have seen that Calvin took great care to proofread and correct these records, and how important they were for Reformed churches and magistrates. Pollmann's careful comparison between Utrecht's consistory registers and the journal of one of its members must be balanced against other research showing how precisely and rigorously cases could be recorded, at least in some Reformed communities at certain periods. In several cases, comparisons between different sources that were recorded simultaneously demonstrate the precise and methodical nature of the available documentation; some consistory members had the ability to produce a trustworthy institutional memory capable of yielding certainty.

Historical criticism of consistory records must get beyond the customary discussion of their limits by attempting to grasp their nature more fully. The usual critiques assess the value of a source from the viewpoint of issues and approaches that historians use to analyze documents. The observations that have been advanced thus focus either on quantitative uses of consistory records as a serial source, or on "qualitative" treatments attempting to uncover examples of beliefs, religious practices, and aspects of "popular culture" in social and material life. None of these critical approaches has yet attempted to grasp the nature of the documents from the viewpoint of those who produced them. However, it is important to consider the meaning that contemporaries themselves attributed to records that perpetuated the memory of consistorial activities.

To understand this dimension, we must take into account the narrative value of consistory records, understood broadly. These books should be seen as providing a collective narrative of "edification" and "sanctification" through the prism of correcting sins – a process that engaged the entire church community and was regarded as always ongoing because of the sinful nature of humanity. Seen this way, the records report on a collective journey, formed by the accumulation of all its individual lapses into sin, repentances, and penances. Calvin captured the spirit of this endeavor well when, responding to Anabaptists who claimed that "there is no church, if it is not perfect," he first acknowledged that perfection is the ideal to be sought, but immediately added, "we walk and run, but we have not yet reached the end."[9] The records thus relate the story of this long journey, whose ultimate outcome will not be reached on earth. The memory preserved in consistory registers was not only repressive. It functioned equally – and just as essentially – to provide witness before God of the Church's diligence in condemning and correcting sin.

The invocations with which consistorial secretaries often began their records in the sixteenth and seventeenth centuries reflect well the idea that all disciplinary activity was undertaken before eyes of God. Their most frequent formula is: "In the name of God, Amen."[10] It referred directly to the opening sentence of Reformed worship ("Our help is in the name of God, who hath made Heaven and earth, amen.") and served to bring together the two major ritual actors: on the one side, the divine author of Creation; on the other, a church community whose liturgical confession, spoken immediately afterwards, characterized itself as inherently sinful. This prayer, which introduced many consistory records, similarly signified that all the activity that the register preserved was conducted in the presence of the divine. Other practices conveyed the same meaning. Several consistories – sometimes in accordance with formal rules – opened their sessions by "invoking the name of God."

Though no particular formula was given, it was very likely taken directly from or inspired by the liturgical formula. The invocation of the divine presence was not, however, a monopoly of ecclesiastical courts. It was also used by some Reformed magistrates, by national and provincial synods, and even by merchants or notaries. Placing institutional or individual activities under divine protection, these prayers aimed primarily at dedicating the endeavor to God so that it would "be to His honor and glory." Moreover, some consistory records even expressed this idea explicitly by starting the volume with the formula "Soli Deo Gloria."[11] Though this initial prayer was widespread, it acquired a particular meaning in consistory records through its metaphorical proximity among contemporaries to the "book of life," the heavenly register that recorded the fate of all souls. This analogy appeared, for example, in both the polemical pen of a sixteenth-century Catholic, Bordeaux magistrate Florimond de Raemond, and in a prayer at the head of a volume from a Vaudois consistory in the late eighteenth century.[12]

Thus, in constructing a memory of a collective disciplinary process that contributed to the history of salvation, consistory volumes belong with other written acts produced by Reformed churches that, like these, recounted a collective narrative. Reformed churches indeed paid attention very early to recording the traces of individual lives, not only between sin and reconciliation in consistory minutes but also between birth and death in civil registers. In these latter sources, the important concern, at least initially, was the integration of the newborn into the spiritual community formed by the Church: it was indeed not the date of birth that was registered, but the date of baptism. Public records also frequently offer more information than a mere list of names and dates corresponding to the major rites of passage (birth, marriage, death).

Organized by nominal entries in the sixteenth century, these records also have a narrative structure that referred frequently to specific life circumstances. In addition, civil registers often functioned as chronicles, recounting notable events in the life of a parish community. Often, moreover, consistory minutes and civil records were merged into a single volume. These different accounts were therefore seen as recording different aspects of the same collective narrative.

This desire to assemble the story of a church community working out its salvation, while taking special care to record the itineraries of its members between sin and repentance, birth and death, connected the concerns of local Reformed communities to recalling the tribulations of the universal Church through printed books. This enterprise was undertaken very early, especially by Jean Crespin's *Livre des martyrs*, then continued in more systematic and comprehensive fashion through the *Histoire ecclésiastique des Eglises réformées au royaume de France* (1580), edited by Theodore Beza and designed to provide the churches of France with a "body of ecclesiastical history."[13] Furthermore, this enterprise took on a truly collective character: beginning in 1563, all French churches were requested to contribute by sending to Geneva "a faithful compendium of everything noteworthy that happened by Divine Providence in places within their jurisdiction."[14] This effort continued after 1580, since in 1612 French churches became responsible for "carefully gathering the stories of pastors and other faithful people who in these latter times have suffered for the truth of God's Son."[15] Consistory records, then, must be considered within a network of texts that complement each other to delineate a history of Reformed churches, which served partly to witness their ongoing submission to divine providence and partly to collect and weave these local histories into a narrative that transcended them and understood them as part of the history of salvation.

Beyond the collective narrative of "sanctification" that they constructed over time, consistory registers also teemed with countless individual stories resulting from the consistory's task of conflict resolution, which formed roughly one-third of its workload. The stories generated by this activity came from two converging processes. Alerted by complaints or rumor, a consistory summoned both parties, requesting them to "state and recount their differences" or to "declare how the thing happened." The parties were thus forced to produce a narrative, that is to say, not only to give a chronology of events but also to arrange the story to make their version appear more convincing. Narrators thus devised an "emplotment" giving meaning to events and providing support for an argument. Consequently, antagonists took care to identify various circumstances – places, times, witnesses, words exchanged, instruments of violence – designed to produce an "effect of reality."[16] Passing off this reconstitution of facts as their faithful reproduction, these concrete pieces of information authenticated their version of events and provided evidence for their adversary's guilt, mentioning, for example, that the incident occurred at night, or on a Sunday, or even "during the sermon," that the other party had been drinking or had grabbed a weapon. Such references particularly stress violations of religious or civil norms in everyday life and were thus intended to guide the consistory's evaluation of the incident.

In this regard, it is striking that the goal of pacifying social tensions which consistories pursued seems to have been achieved, at least in part, precisely through the process of the narration of events and the conflict between divergent stories. In many cases, the record does not even mention a conclusive judgment. It is as if the "emplotment," which required the parties to impose order on the confusion of events, to verbalize emotions that the conflict provoked, and to place some distance between the affair and its retelling, allowed tempers to cool and therefore eased the conflict. Alfred Soman, one of the first historians to pay careful consideration to consistory records, correctly observed that the specificity of intervention in conflicts by Reformed ecclesiastical courts lay precisely in their capacity to mitigate anger. It is likely that the actual effectiveness of consistories in this area resulted partly from their ability to compel both parties to channel their perception of conflicts into a narrative form.

But it should also be pointed out that adversarial parties themselves were keenly interested in producing and recording their own version of events. As David Sabean has noted, anecdotes that historians read today in official records belonged to an era when an intense circulation of stories through gossip and rumor enlivened social life. Given the collection of narratives that challenged and constantly reshaped an individual's honor and reputation, it was essential for anyone accused to register and authenticate his or her own version of events with the institution. This need was particularly strong if it directly threatened one's honor. Both sides would then take pains to ensure that their "denial," in which they challenged the insult, or their "reparation of honor" appeared in the minutes. The consistory register thus attested to their ability to defend their status and rank. If many stories in consistory records resulted from the institution's peacekeeping activities, they also arose from the demands of social actors.

The historical critique of documents – in this instance, records produced by consistories – implies not only discussing their limitations by identifying the processes of reduction and distortion involved in their production but also restoring the meanings they had for their authors and their subsequent users. In the case of consistory records, this critique should also lead us to take into account the full measure of the narrative dimension of these documents. This feature, however, must be further historicized. It is indeed uncertain that they remained stable throughout the *ancien régime*. There are several indications that the status of consistory registers underwent gradual changes. In the eighteenth century, the initial invocations disappeared in most cases. Over time, we can see, at least in French-speaking Switzerland, greater specialization in consistorial activity – namely, the emphasis on suppressing illicit sex. These records reflect less the task of "sanctification" by a church community than families worried about diminutions to their patrimonies through bastards born out of wedlock. Around the same time, the introduction of the right of Genevans summoned before the consistory to be defended by a lawyer – absolutely prohibited before the eighteenth century – is a sign of "judicializing" procedures that profoundly altered the institution's nature. Finally, difficulties in recruiting elders, visible in several places in French-speaking Switzerland, and struggles by eighteenth-century pastors to defend their social rank provide further evidence of the institution's declining prestige. The secretaries of the Geneva Consistory responded paradoxically by creating registers with monumental covers, as if compensating for the weakening of the institution in the minds of their contemporaries through the dramatic presentation of its records. More specialized and more secularized, more judicial and more uncertain about its social function, the eighteenth-century consistory found it difficult to guide an entire ecclesiastical community along the path of its spiritual history.

Notes

1 Archives du Canton de Vaud (désormais: ACV), Bda 126/3; Bda 132/10; Bda 103/10; Bda 103/11; Bda 103/18; Bda 103/19; Dg 260/31; Bda 86/4; Archives d'Etat de Genève (désormais: AEG), R. Consist. R. 77, p. 85, 138–39; and R. 92, p. 41, 45.

2 Françoise Moreil, "Le consistoire de Courthézon au XVIIᵉ siècle," *Mémoires de l'Académie de Vaucluse*, 8 (1998): 516–17.

3 *Registres du Consistoire de Genève au temps de Calvin*, ed. Thomas Lambert, Isabella M. Watt and Jeffrey R. Watt (Geneva, 1996–2012), 3:214 and 217; AEG, R. Consist. R. 7, f. 33, 41, 47; R. 9, f. 86; R. 10, f. 18v, 21v, 23v, etc.

4 *Registres du Consistoire de Genève*, 3: 214–20.

5 *Registres du Consistoire de Genève*, 3: , n. 1273, 1275, 1276.

6 Regula Matzinger-Pfister, *Les sources du droit du canton de Vaud, C. Epoque bernoise 1* (Basel, 2003), 216.

7 ACV Bda 36/1, title page.

8 Danièle Tosato-Rigo, "Registres consistoriaux et images de l'exil," *Bulletin de la Société de l'Histoire du Protestantisme Français* 153 (2007), 657.

9 *Registres de la Compagnie des Pasteurs de Genève*, vol. 1, *1546–1553*, ed. Robert M. Kingdon and Jean-François Bergier (Geneva, 1964), 75.

10 AEG, R. Consist. Ann. 3; R. Consist. R. 57, 62, 64, 69; ACV Bda 8/2; and *Livre des délibérations de l'Eglise réformée de l'Albenc (1606–1682)*, ed. François Francillon (Paris, 1998), 239, 275.

11 ACV Bda 38/2; Bda 34/1.

12 Florimond de Raemond, *L'histoire de la naissance, progrez et decadence de l'heresie de ce siecle* (Rouen, 1618), 997; ACV, Bda 34/1.

13 Jean Crespin, *Histoire des martyrs*, ed. Daniel Benoit, 3 vol. (Toulouse, 1885–1889); Théodore de Bèze, *Histoire ecclésiastique des Eglises reformées au royaume de France*, ed. G. Baum and Ed. Cunitz, 3 vol. (Paris, 1883–89).

14 Marianne Carbonnier-Burkard "'L'Histoire ecclésiastique des Eglises réformées...': la construction bézienne d'un 'corps d'histoire,'" in *Théodore de Bèze (1519–1605)* (Geneva, 2007), 145–61.

15 Isaac d'Huisseau, *La Discipline des Eglises réformées de France ou l'ordre par lequel elles sont conduites et gouvernées* (Geneva, 1666), 183.

16 Roland Barthes, "L'effet de réel," *Communications* 11 (1968): 84–89.

Inquisitions

Kim Siebenhüner
Translated by Heidi Bek

He had come of his own volition – "sponte personaliter comparuit in Palatio S[ancti] O[fficii] Urbis" – noted the law clerk when Francesco Cesasie appeared before the Holy Office in Rome on September 20, 1673 to report his attempt at bigamy. But Cesasie's appearance was not as voluntary as his statement suggested. In truth, his confessor had explained that he had to go to the Inquisition before he could be absolved.[1] Hence the language of the court is quite misleading. The Inquisition called all those who reported themselves *sponte comparentes*. Whether this was a "voluntary" act, however, is an entirely different matter. Through its annually repeated edicts of clemency and faith and its close collaboration with bishops and confessors, the Roman Inquisition exerted such great pressure that numerous offenders "spontaneously" denounced themselves.

The fact that the Inquisition's terminology and the statements of witnesses and accused are not always what they appear to be at first glance are hardly problems confined to Inquisitions. Instead, such problems are inherent in all court records. They all offer methodological challenges, but at the same time hold great potential.

There are many reasons why historians have long been concentrating on court records. First of all, the exploration of these sources has opened up new perspectives for studying history. Historical research on criminal behavior has transformed traditional social history into a social and cultural history of conflict by integrating aspects of everyday life, gender, and religion. Second, court records allow us to access bygone realities from multiple perspectives by combining the history of social norms and legal institutions with the history of the lives of early modern men and women. Third, court records often contain the only traces that ordinary people – cobblers, tailors, shopkeepers, messengers, maids, lackeys, and many others – have left behind. Thus court records open a "window" into the history of these persons – but at the same time, they create the greatest of methodological problems. Contrary to their seeming authenticity, court records represent past actualities only in part, hindered by the constraints of a trial, colored by the interests and fancies of witnesses and defendants, and distorted by the physical and psychological pressure of torture and interrogation techniques. While the petitions for mercy to the French crown studied by Natalie Zemon Davis demonstrate how much depended on telling a persuasive story that would keep one's head out of the noose, ritual murder trials such as the one from Trent in 1475 analyzed by R. Po-Chia Hsia illustrate that almost any confession could be extorted from interrogated persons through the use of extreme physical violence. Moreover, much information was lost during trials, through the translation of spoken into written words or through such procedures as copying or summarizing.

The question of how reliable court records are as historical sources and how plausible the discourses of the accused are is therefore central for all court records, including those of the consistories and the Inquisition. At the same time, the Inquisition was a special institution among early modern court systems. Its records not only reflect the tribunal's idiosyncratic character but have also provoked specific controversies among experts. The object of this essay is to discuss the possibilities and limits of qualitative interpretations based on Inquisition records. For this purpose, the various types of sources left by early modern Inquisitions must be recapitulated before addressing questions about the reliability of these sources, problems of interpretation, and the potential insights they permit. As I demonstrate, a fundamental differentiation must be made between the logic of the court and the situations of the individuals it interrogated.

THE SOURCES OF EARLY MODERN INQUISITIONS

Early modern inquisitorial tribunals have left a variety of different sources, from interrogation minutes, judgments, and resolutions to mandates, instructions, and letters. Since their production was directly connected to the tribunal's working methods and functioning, it is important to recall these institutional structures. They differed significantly from the nature of the consistories and their sources. Early modern Inquisitions were hierarchical bodies, in which center and periphery were closely linked. Letters went back and forth on an almost daily basis between the Spanish *Suprema*, the Portuguese *Conselho Geral*, or the Holy Office in Rome and their local inquisitors. This correspondence forms a significant part of their records because it sheds light not only on the hierarchical relationship between local and central Inquisition tribunals but also on the course of the proceedings and the histories of defendants. In Italy, for example, many local inquisitors reported more or less regularly about current cases, sent summaries of proceedings to Rome, and received instructions from the Holy Office about further courses of action.[2] Similar records have survived for the Spanish and the Portuguese Inquisitions. Apart from comprehensive series with letters, the Archivo Histórico Nacional in Madrid preserves a collection of *relaciones de causas* with more than 40,000 cases.

Since the interrogation minutes have not come down to us in many cases – because they have been lost or destroyed over the course of the archive's complex history – trial summaries often contain the only information about the accused and their trials. The purpose of these two categories was, however, completely different. Whereas summaries informed the governing tribunal about the most essential evidence, arguments, and outcomes of local trials from a purely institutional perspective, interrogation minutes had to record the testimony of the accused and the witnesses as precisely as possible. These sources thus bring the historian in the closest proximity to inquisitorial defendants and the details of their stories, thereby often making them particularly fascinating.

Not without good reason did Gustav Henningsen and Andrea Del Col complain that historians have focused on the Inquisition's interrogation minutes too long and too often. According to Del Col, inquisitorial sources should be investigated as comprehensively as possible in order to understand a trial's legal contexts, its procedures, and its judgments and sentences. Such materials include – in addition to interrogation minutes, letters, and trial summaries – the available series of sentences and judgments, reports about *autos da fe*, decrees of the Holy Office, its edicts and instructions, and more generally, the huge body of canon law (*Corpus Iuris Canonici*), supplemented by papal bulls, letters, and council resolutions. Together with a continuing series of Inquisition manuals dating from the Middle Ages, they formed the basis for the administration of inquisitorial justice. Inquisition manuals and handwritten instructions, in particular, served as a reference for the daily practices at court and the

Inquisition's procedural style. Without some knowledge of these normative sources, the Inquisiton's terminology and judicial procedures become
almost impossible to understand.

Moreover, inquisitors were integrated into a network of players in
both the Catholic Church and secular courts. Various sources document
their contacts with vicars, bishops, or nuncios and with secular authorities and judges. Thus, with many cases of suspected heresy involving
magic, blasphemy, or bigamy, Italian inquisitors had to cooperate with
episcopal or secular judges to decide which of them would try a particular
case. The Inquisition thus produced a variety of different sources, which
shed light on the tribunal's working methods and functioning, as well as
on the lives of those it accused.

THE LOGIC OF THE INQUISITION

One of the most controversial theses about Inquisition records, especially
in Italian research, is Carlo Ginzburg's analogy between inquisitors and
anthropologists.[3] Ginzburg developed this thesis in the background to his
investigation of Friulian *Benandanti,* whom the Inquisition of Aquileia
and Concordia encountered in the sixteenth and seventeenth centuries
because of their agricultural rituals and magical practices. Their beliefs
and practices seemed so bizarre that they provoked in-depth investigations. Ginzburg even believed he detected a dialogue structure in some
interrogation minutes, where it was no longer judge and suspect facing
each other, but representatives of equal rank from mutually foreign
cultures. These moments of dialogue and the abundance of ethnograph-
ical information gathered by the inquisitors led Ginzburg to compare
them to anthropologists exploring an alien culture.

In Italian historiography, Ginzburg's comparison was questioned especially by Del Col, who repeatedly pointed to the self-image of the inquisitors as judges of the faith. Their primary concern was not to explore alien
cultures, but to determine an offense, verify suspected heresy, or sanction
doctrinal error. Overwhelmingly, inquisitors acted as judges and not as
anthropologists.

One need not accept Ginzburg's pointed analogy in order to acknowledge the ethnographic value of these interrogations. Even though not all
minutes are so saturated with information as the Benandanti trials, their
value for understanding the living circumstances of the *inquisiti* remains
substantial. Inquisition historians, therefore, agree that their sources can
shed light on both the history of the institution and the history of the

accused. With respect to the reliability of these sources, however, it is critical to differentiate between their various qualities and perspectives. Interrogation minutes, resolutions, judgments, legal opinions, and instructions all served to orient the court's procedures and decisions, and may, therefore, be understood as "intentional" records of the institution. The majority of these sources primarily clarify the operations of the court and the inquisitor's mental world. Reports about *autos da fe*, sentences, and decrees, instructions, and letters followed the institutional logic of Inquisition law. The fact that the same files may also be read "against the grain" to provide information about the activities of the accused emphasizes their "non-intentional" qualities. How reliable are Inquisition records in their capacity as "intentional" sources? How accurately do they reflect what actually happened at these tribunals?

There are a number of factors which might falsify the image presented of these trials. Besides the loss of entire series, there are even gaps within the records of a particular trial. Records were misplaced, disappeared, or simply lost. For example, in 1577 the evidence collected in Belluno many years previously against a certain Giuseppe could not be used, since the notary in office at that time had taken it with him and later misplaced it after moving to a new position in Milan.[4]

Further losses of information occurred when the statements of the witnesses and accused persons were written down in the course of copying and summarizing. The clerks of the Inquisition were expected to record questions and statements word for word. Nevertheless, they made numerous omissions, inaccuracies, and corrections. In several cases, only the answers were recorded, but not the questions. In part, the notaries took down statements only fragmentarily; they recorded the personal data of witnesses, but wrote down only parts of their testimony, prefaced by the phrase "inter alia dixit." In other cases, corrections were made either in retrospect or already while taking notes; words or partial sentences were struck out, changed, or supplemented. We must also assume on-the-spot translations are occurring whenever Latin phrases appear, or transitions from dialect to high-level language occur suddenly. The same types of issues apply to the relationship between originals, copies, and syntheses. The multiple duplications made of interrogation minutes always contain deviations, even if, as we know today, the original and clean copy were largely congruent. However, substantial differences have been found between the interrogation minutes and the trial summaries; depending on their length and quality, the summaries only compiled the relevant statements and arguments of the person interrogated, conflating circumstantial evidence and proof, and collapsing significant stages of the trial.

Despite all these deficiencies, current research assumes that the various documents from a trial reflect its judicial events fairly precisely – a conclusion that comes close to the findings concerning the consistory records. Even though we cannot expect that the statements of the witnesses and the accused were put into the minutes word for word, the interrogation minutes of the Inquisition contain detailed accounts of the people it affected that are so rich in details, longwinded, and sometimes surprising that they exclude any notion of substantive interventions by the notaries. Not only the presence of the notary, who guaranteed its authenticity with his signature, but also duplications of trial records reduced the danger of encountering false records. Thus, for example, the judgment of a *causa* surfaced in the records of the Roman Inquisition in the series of *Decreta*, in the dossier of the *Causa*, and in the sentence of the case. In the end, the Inquisition simply had no reason to falsify or to invent statements. It neither needed to justify its trials nor possessed any appellate tribunals.

THE STORIES OF THE ACCUSED

While the records of the Inquisition provide a fairly reliable idea of events at its tribunals, the truthfulness of the discourses from witnesses and accused persons is much harder to assess. In this context, research especially on the Spanish and Portuguese Inquisitions has focused on a second controversy. At its heart lie questions about the religious identity of those Jews and their descendants who were forced to convert during the fourteenth and fifteenth centuries through pogroms, persecution by the Inquisition, and finally by the deportation decrees of 1492 and 1497 in the Iberian Peninsula. While Haim Beinart and others interpreted the trials against "Judaizers" in the tradition of Fritz Baer and Cecil Roth as evidence for crypto-Judaism, Benzion Netanyahu, António José Saraiva, Norman Roth, and others radically questioned this view. Subsequently, this controversy has generally subsided. Current historiography has dismissed the idea of a monolithic faith and emphasizes instead how differentiated the religious identity of the *conversos* actually was. Whether a *converso* became a committed Christian, secretly adhered to Judaism, or reconverted openly in exile was first and foremost a matter of individual choice.

Controversies about the identity of the *conversos* were accompanied by debates over the reliability of Inquisition records. Netanyahu, Saraiva, and Roth dismissed these sources as fantasies and lies, which could not be trusted, least of all because they depended upon testimony from anonymous witnesses and confessions coerced under torture – obviously without ever having immersed themselves deeply in the material from the Spanish Inquisition. Although the accuracy of the statements recorded does in fact raise methodological issues, this position is also considered obsolete because it cavalierly denies any value to Inquisition records as a whole. Historians such as Haim Beinart, Jean-Pierre Dedieu, Bartolomé and Lucile Bennassar, Gustav Henningsen, Brian Pullan, and many others have long since shown not only how extraordinarily complex and rich these sources are, but also demonstrated their usefulness for the history of everyday life and its conflicts of faith and identity. Because witnesses and the accused organized, embellished, or even falsified their stories, one must not conclude that they are fundamentally unreliable and useless for historical research.

It is correct that the testimony of witnesses and the accused must be read precisely and critically. Accounts at these tribunals were always influenced by strategic interests, by the concerns and hardships of those under interrogation, and by the physical and psychological pressures of a trial. As we have seen, the clemency edicts exerted subtle pressure on individuals to submit to the Inquisition by reporting oneself. Many confessions of *sponte comparentes* were not voluntary as implied by the title, but rather motivated by anguish about personal salvation or fear of the consequences from being denounced to the Inquisition. During the course of the trial, the accused came under further pressure by being left in the dark about the evidence and testimony against them that was available to the inquisitor. Besides, inquisitorial procedures routinely prescribed torture for those accused of suspected heresy such as reading prohibited books, blasphemy, or bigamy. However, the effects of torture should not be overestimated. Both the *Suprema* and the Congregation of the Holy Office followed a moderate course when using torture and made efforts to prevent any arbitrariness and abuse by local tribunals. On the other hand, it did not rely primarily on torture to terrify its prisoners. Their conditions of imprisonment and the threat of the loss of honor through the trial were already enough to demoralize the accused.

All these factors affected the testimony that inquisitorial tribunals recorded. Instead of a presentation of "truth," we must rather expect a version of reality, accounts which omit certain things and add others, which become contradictory as more people described them, and which are "fictitious" insofar as they furnished events with a plot and legally valid arguments. In the end, it involved fighting one's own court battle or, at worst, saving one's head. Competing variations of a story, as for example those given about Diego Pereira in 1661 to the inquisitors of Toledo, were, therefore, common practice. Two monks had denounced Pereira and stated that they had traveled to Cordoba with him and three others. In the course of their trip, Pereira had increasingly aroused their suspicion by avoiding pork and giving evasive answers to questions. Pereira, however, claimed to come from a family that had been Christian for centuries. But he did lack a thorough knowledge of Catholic beliefs. He counterattacked by claiming that his fellow travelers had insulted him and discriminated against him in public and assumed that he had been denounced by Jews or *conversos*. Thus he revealed his resentment against this group. In fact, the inquisitors did not pursue the case further, either because they believed that Pereira had been slandered by his fellow travelers or because the charge of Judaizing could not be corroborated.[5] In either case, Pereira had successfully used his right to name the persons hostile toward him and thus invalidate their statements. He had thereby introduced a legally valid argument into his defense and woven it into his account. Every story the inquisitors heard was formed in such ways. Pereira was not only a victim of the Inquisition; he also was the protagonist of his own story.

In scholarship, this room to maneuver by the accused has been discussed under the rubric "utilization of justice" (*Justiznutzung*). Although the relationship between judges and the interrogated has always been marked by inequality, the dichotomy of perpetrator and victim, judge and persecuted, narrows our view about the possibilities available to the weaker players for using the tribunal in their own interest. The interpretation of the sources comes with the challenge of uncovering the "literacy" of these accounts – in terms of their chronology, drama, and rhetoric – while simultaneously reviewing them for plausibility. For these purposes, not only does the densest possible contextualization of the respective circumstances help but also the multi-perspectivity of the sources themselves: the more voices we hear in a trial, the smaller seems the danger of being deceived. A final example demonstrates that one and the same protagonist could tell two completely different stories about their religious identity in two different trials.[6]

On February 7, 1623, the milliner Giovanni Domenico Morcante denounced his wife Mariana to the Roman Holy Office for "Judaizing." Mariana had grown up in a Jewish family in Gdansk, who migrated to Tripoli in present-day Lebanon around 1600. Some years later, Mariana

married her Jewish husband and migrated yet again. The couple's
destination was Venice where, however, the ship never arrived. It was
captured by pirates, and Mariana was sold on the slave market on Malta.
She fell into the hands of a Maltese nobleman, who very shortly afterwards had her baptized. Her baptismal certificate from the church of
Santa Maria in Valletta is dated April 3, 1607. Mariana's depiction of
this event is ambivalent. On the one hand, it bears every sign of a forced
conversion. On the other hand, Mariana told the Roman inquisitor that
she had agreed to have the ritual performed.

When Mariana was released some two years later, she had a young
son and decided to start a new life in Naples. Meanwhile, she had no
news at all about her Jewish husband. In Naples, Mariana met Giovanni
Domenico Morcante and married him in 1615. Giovanni had no doubts
that Mariana was Christian. Thus, he was completely surprised when
Mariana admitted to him in 1622 that she had Jewish roots and desired
to return to her previous faith. At this time, the couple was in Vienna.
After years in Naples and Rome, Giovanni agreed to go to Poland with
Mariana, hoping for a better life. But when he came to know her real
reason for the move, he abruptly turned against Mariana. The couple
separated and Giovanni returned to Rome. But neither did Mariana
continue on to Poland. Instead, she and her son sought refuge in the
Venetian ghetto. Witnesses testified that Giovanni and Mariana stayed in
contact through letters. Mariana, however, did not know that Giovanni
had denounced her to the Roman Holy Office in February 1623. Initially
she was not bothered. But in April 1624, she was brought before the
Venetian Inquisition. Thanks to some accident of record keeping, in this
causa both the Venetian and the Roman trial records have been preserved. It is one of the rare cases permitting unusually close observation
of life stories and their adjustments under the constraints of an
Inquisition trial.

In the Venetian portion of the trial, Mariana presented herself as a
crypto-Jewess and claimed that she had never turned her back on
Jewish beliefs. She had only feigned a Christian life from fear of
persecution and because of her affection for her husband Giovanni.
She had adopted certain practices, others she had evaded. Thus, she
had gone to Mass and had adjusted to Christian eating habits, but
avoided going to confession, fasting, and making the sign of the cross.
Consequently Mariana tried to negate the circumstantial evidence for
her Christian identity, and, significantly, kept her baptism on Malta
secret in this account.

Five weeks after her first interrogation, the trial took a surprising turn when Mariana asked to be allowed to travel to Rome and speak with her husband Giovanni. In return, she promised the Venetian inquisitors to get baptized in Rome – an act that had been performed long ago.

As we might expect, Mariana told a different story to the Roman tribunal. Her desire to return to her husband was inseparably associated with a Christian life. Mariana must have been aware of this when she asked for a transfer. To travel to Rome meant that she had to present herself as truly Christian and lead a genuinely Christian life in the future. Now, before the Roman inquisitor, Mariana no longer concealed her baptism; on the contrary, she called it a divine providence and claimed to have always followed the Christian commandments afterwards. Contradicting Giovanni's version, she dismissed her outburst in Vienna as an ill-considered remark in the heat of a marital conflict. When the inquisitor asked why she had then gone to the Venetian ghetto, she explained it through her fear of the Inquisition and her solitary status; only in the ghetto could she live as an honorable woman. Thus, in Rome Mariana replaced the defense strategy she had pursued in Venice with its exact opposite. Instead of portraying everything Christian in her life as dissimulation, she now tried to dismiss all the circumstantial evidence for her Judaizing.

One life – two stories. How should historians handle this? A skeptical position might argue that the accuracy of these contradictory statements cannot be verified. There is nothing, beyond the Inquisition records, which sheds any light on Mariana's religious identity. She might have seen herself as Jewish, but she might just as well have not. Her statements may have been purely strategic, separate from her convictions and based only on her desire to continue to live in the ghetto, or to save her marriage in Rome. Consequently, such a position must lead one to conclude that in this case Inquisition records permit no judgments about the protagonist's faith.

A second position is more complicated. Although asking which of the presented versions was "true" does not offer much insight, the accounts themselves can be understood as signs of ambivalence. Mariana was familiar with two irreconcilable worlds of faith, Judaism and Christianity. Her conversion was primarily a matter of her survival and freedom. But after fifteen years of leading an at least partly Christian life, she was familiar with Christianity's daily rituals and prayers. Her Catholic life was also tied up with a marriage that guaranteed a certain degree of social and material security. The desire to reconvert after so many years, however, argues for the continuity of her Jewish faith.

Instead of assuming that the protagonist lied in her presentation of her story on one occasion, and not on the other, this reading offers the possibility of a contradictory and overlapping identity. In other words, the problems with this source can be understood as symptoms of a complex biography whose accounts were contradictory because the person was herself contradictory. Mariana was torn between the religious worlds, which were also incarnated in the two most important relationships of her life, her son and her husband. This position is less skeptical about the potential of the Inquisition sources and leaves historians with considerable room for interpretation. There certainly is no ideal solution between these two positions. Ultimately, decisions about what significance the records of a specific *causa* have or do not have must be made anew in each case.

CONCLUSION

Overall, current research demonstrates that the controversies about the reliability of Inquisition records have largely subsided. The diverse documents presently available offer a reliable and indispensable basis for studying early modern Inquisitions as institutions and exploring their structures and working methods. In inquisitorial correspondence, in the decrees of the Roman Congregation, in the trial summaries and *relaciones de causas*, in the instructions of the Inquisition, and in the manuals we can hear inquisitors, bishops, theologians, notaries, and *familiares* speak. They acted and expressed themselves according to the logic of the Inquisition. Their perspective was primarily institutional, juridical, and political, dominated by their self-imposed mission of standardizing community life in ecclesiastical matters, and establishing a far-reaching religious and cultural homogeneity. Many of these sources provide information about the *inquisiti* and their stories: in the letters where local inquisitors reported about their cases, in trial summaries, or in the *livros dos autos*. Yet here the judges speak about the accused and filter their original testimony. The voices of the accused themselves can be heard primarily in the minutes of their interrogations or the *sponte comparitiones*. Other sources look deceptively authentic: thus, even though the accused themselves seem to speak in the abjuration documents of the Roman Inquisition, in reality the inquisitors scripted their utterances word by word.

Yet the risk of accepting a misinterpretation has decreased more and more through decades of research; today, historians know the functioning of the Inquisition much better than two decades ago. In fact, our methodological

instruments have been greatly expanded and sharpened through developments resulting from the "linguistic and cultural turn." We have become
more sensitive to linguistic phenomena, discursive strategies, and narrative
elements in the sources – including judicial sources. Historians of consistories and of Inquisitions share this sensitivity for the narrative qualities of the
trial records, as Christian Grosse's essay shows. Moreover, historical
research about criminality has revealed how decisive pre-judicial events
were, since many reports were recorded only after disputes between neighbors, families, or other types of conflicts had escalated. Awareness of this
may also prevent a naive trust, especially concerning testimony from witnesses. Readings of interrogation minutes have become more subtle, more
critical, and more context-oriented. In current research, therefore, the relevance of the Inquisition sources is not an issue in questions beyond the
history of the institution. So many studies about Protestants, *conversos*,
Moriscos, blasphemers, apostate priests, bigamists, necromancers, and
many others have shown how rich the sources of the Inquisition are for
historians of everyday life, culture, society, migration, and gender. The gaps
in their records, the inaccuracies in their minutes, the strategic moves of the
accused, and the *fashioning* of their stories set limits to the interpretation of
these sources. However, through the methods of contextualization and
verification of plausibility, comparison with other cases, analysis of the
discursive and narrative elements of accounts told to these courts – and
some necessary prudence – it is quite possible to gain proximity to living
environments which would otherwise remain inaccessible to historians.

Notes

1 ACDF, stanza storica, M 5-i, fasc. 1673 Roma.
2 BAV, Barb. Lat. 6334–6336 Registro lettere della Congregatione 1626–1628;
Grazia Biondi, "Le lettere della Sacra Congregazione romana del Santo Ufficio
all'Inquisizione di Modena: note in margine a un regesto," *Schifanoia* 4 (1987):
93–108; Guido Dall'Olio, "I rapporti tra la Congregazione del Sant'Officio e gli
inquisitori locali nei carteggi Bolognesi (1573–1594)," *Rivista storica italiana*
105 (1993): 246–86; Pierroberto Scaramella, *Le lettere della Congregazione del
Sant'Ufficio ai tribunali di fede di Napoli 1563–1625* (Trieste, 2002).
3 Carlo Ginzburg, "The Inquisitor as anthropologist," in *Clues, Myths, and
Historical Method* (Baltimore, 1989), 156–64.
4 Nicholas Davidson, "The Inquisition in Venice and its Documents: Some
Problems of Method and Analysis," in Andrea Del Col and Giovanna Paolin
eds., *L'Inquisizione romana in Italia nell' etá moderna: Archivi, problemi di
metodo e nuove ricerche; Atti del seminario internazionale Trieste, 18–20
Maggio, 1988* (Rome, 1991), 117–31.

5 David L. Graizbord, *Souls in Dispute: Conversos Identity in Iberia and the Jewish Diaspora, 1580–1700* (Phildelphia, 2003), 38–53.

6 Kim Siebenhüner, "Conversion, Mobility and the Roman Inquisition in Italy around 1600," *Past & Present* 200 (2008): 5–35. ACDF, stanza storica, M 5-m, fasc. Roma 1624; the documents of the Venetian part are in *Processi del S. Uffizio di Venezia contro ebrei e giudaizzanti*, ed. Pier Cesare Ioly Zorattini, 14 vols. (Florence, 1980–99), here 9:1608–32, 85–94, and vol. 8: *Appendici* (Florence 1997), 137–38.

PART II

CONSISTORIES AND INQUISITIONS IN ACTION

Section E

Programs of Moral and Religious Reform

12

Consistories

Philippe Chareyre
Translated by Charles H. Parker

The consistory in francophone lands, presbytery in Germany, kirk session in Scotland, and *kerkeraad* in the Netherlands had responsibility for the reform of behavior among the faithful, and, in France, the distribution of assistance to the poor. Consistories regularly recorded in their registers the violations of church discipline that came to their attention through extensive networks of surveillance. Pastors and lay elders sought to bring guilty parties to repentance through admonitions and a range of punishments that played to members' sense of belonging to a group, their personal honor, and of course, their individual conscience. The ultimate goal of disciplinary activity was a program of moral and religious reform to produce genuine Christian societies that dealt appropriately with human sinfulness. If disciplinary activities declined in the seventeenth century, the pattern could be interpreted in part as evidence of the success of the reforming enterprise. This chapter thus aims to assess the immediate as well as the long-term effectiveness of the methods used by consistories, taking into account regional differences, within the broad disciplinary program of moral reform.

THE GRID OF ECCLESIASTICAL SPACE

From the 1540s in Geneva and the 1560s in France, the moral program promoted by consistories involved establishing a process for forming new Christian men and women. The earliest deliberations make clear the goal of persuading the entire community to abandon Rome and adhere to the new religion. Then in a second phase, which began with the establishment of Tridentine reform in the late sixteenth and early seventeenth centuries, consistories had to come to grips with the persistent pull of Catholicism. In this period, they established a process of religious exclusion and sharp confessional identification to the point of "biological" separation through prohibitions of inter-confessional marriages.

This process of segregating church members necessitated the creation of a spatial and physical layout to monitor the faithful under the watchful eye of the consistory. The Reformed Church in Geneva created the first supervisory districts in 1537, predating by several years the establishment of a consistory. The *Ecclesiastical Ordinances* (1541) formalized the number of districts at twelve. The practice of carving up urban space, which spread across the Reformed world, was not carried out uniformly. Rather, consistories adapted the management of spatial organization to local circumstances, which encompassed more than simply facilitating ecclesiastical discipline.

The partitioning undertaken by consistories reflected the new church's demand to establish authority over urban space and to impose its own moral standards. This project entailed the elimination of Catholic religious culture located in specific sacred sites (churches and chapels) in order to sanctify the entire community and individual believers. This "disciplinary grid" divided a city into districts under the control of elders and deacons who became the everyday monitors of morals in the program of forming new Christian individuals. The assignment of an elder to oversee a specific location allowed for effective supervision that also fit into the identity of neighborhoods; the consistories of Nîmes and Loudun emphasized the territorial jurisdiction of each elder by prohibiting appeals from those within a district to an elder from another area. An elder was supposed to reside in his district, where he knew the inhabitants and their shortcomings and where he could also depend upon relatives or networks of friends and workers to report events that he did not witness firsthand. The division of ecclesiastical districts along streets and squares also increased the effectiveness of supervision, because their borders fell along the principal municipal axes, so that any disorders occurring in these areas would not escape the eyes and ears of the two elders from adjoining jurisdictions.

This space was the locus of daily Christian activity, rounding out participation with other believers in services at church; the neighborhood was the terrain where the Reformed faith took root. It was in the street or town square that the faithful observed one another's daily behavior, and it was in light of these public observations that elders inquired about "disorders" that occurred in private spaces. Watching the comings and goings from houses and hearing the clamor and noise that projected out into public allowed church authorities to intrude into the domain of family life. This mode of controlling public space attempted to sacralize daily life, which created a structure for sanctifying the street.

MORAL REFORMATION THROUGH CHARITY

Within these reconfigured urban spaces, consistories, especially in France, paid special attention to the poorest within their jurisdiction. Reformed Protestants across Europe envisioned poor relief as integral to a moral society and utilized charity to impose greater discipline on those in poverty. Since the needy were very vulnerable, they came under the dual supervision of the consistory as well as the diaconate. The number and responsibilities of deacons assigned to provide charitable support varied according to churches. Some congregations had no deacons, while other churches accorded them, as in Nîmes and Metz, a prominent place in the consistory meetings. In these latter churches, the deacons' role was very different from their original charitable function. Yet from the outset all Reformed churches gave priority to assisting their neighbors, an undertaking that grew over time.

Consistories in the Swiss orbit, as well as many in the Netherlands, such as those in Delft, Gouda, and Leiden, were not responsible for the direct distribution of charity, although a number of Dutch churches did attempt to take over this function from civil authorities. The French case was different in that consistories engaged directly in providing assistance for members of their churches, a responsibility that ranked second only to disciplinary activity. Through an officer known as the "treasurer of the poor fund," consistories raised money through levy of a "poor tax," recorded donations and collections, pursued the payment of legacies, and managed distribution of aid to the poor.

Alleviating poverty was not considered social work. Rather, it was an expression of Christian faith in keeping with Calvinist theology, and as such it acted as an additional measure of moral education in France as in Holland. It was critical that monetary resources devoted to the poor were not wasted or misused to the disadvantage of those who truly deserved support. Consequently, church officials sought to ensure that relief for the poor did not promote idleness. Discipline guided the allocation of alms so that support could be suspended in the case of moral transgressions. Assistance could be immediate, especially for recent converts, but most often it took the form of weekly payments for the neediest, sick, or disabled who could not provide for their families, widows and widowers responsible for children, and elderly who could no longer support themselves. Boys were placed as apprentices with designated masters, and girls received dowries to help them secure a suitable marriage.

Toward the end of the seventeenth century, particularly at Nîmes and Saint-Jean-du Gard in Languedoc, charitable assistance took precedence over other spheres of consistorial activity. Competition from the Catholic Church seeking to regain lost ground could explain the increased attention to charity. Furthermore, this pattern also prevailed in major cities, especially in industrial areas, where the number of poor increased during this period. The burden of poor relief, which came to occupy the largest portion of the records in a city like Nîmes, left the consistory there with little opportunity to pursue censure of individual members, so that church leaders had to undertake new disciplinary strategies. Still, the exercise of charity served as an occasion to monitor the most vulnerable populations by linking aid to the standards of morality set by ecclesiastical discipline. Thus poor relief functioned as an indirect way of exerting moral authority that does not appear explicitly in consistory registers. In short, poor relief was a key instrument of morals control and communal solidarity.

MORAL REFORMATION OF THE CHURCH

In Reformed churches across Europe, disciplinary procedure unfolded in four stages. The first was the consistory's discovery of alleged misdeeds, followed by an admission of fault by the transgressor, then the administration of punishment, and finally penitence. The process could be rather swift in the event of a simple reprimand and censure, though it could be quite protracted for the most serious cases whose punishment entailed suspension from the Lord's Supper. The process thus was initiated by information that came directly to the consistory through an elder or indirectly by rumor; interrogating witnesses who could possibly contradict the denial of guilt often extended this stage. The second phase commenced with the appearance of the alleged offenders before the consistory where they received an admonition to keep themselves free from immoral behavior; if they denied the charges, they were summoned anew in order to be confronted by witnesses. By calling witnesses and confronting the accused with them, the consistorial disciplining process can be likened to that of inquisitorial procedures, though without the incarceration used by Catholic tribunals. In most consistory cases, the accused admitted their wrongdoing and submitted to the church's judgment, which usually involved a simple censure or a temporary suspension from the Lord's Supper, which would be announced from the pulpit if the transgression was of a public nature. Suspension from communion could also be a precautionary measure if information about the case was incomplete, or if the charge was not yet substantiated, or if the suspect refused to appear, which was equated with rebellion. Finally, as a concluding measure in the most serious cases, sinners had to perform penitence appropriate to their transgressions.

As the most severe ecclesiastical penalty imposed by consistories, suspension from the Lord's Supper evoked the moral program of reform embedded within Reformed discipline. In some territories where the Reformed faith became the official religion, as in Scotland, Geneva, and Béarn, civil sanctions and corporal penalties reinforced ecclesiastical punishments. Some French churches justified denying communion "in order [that sinners] would be humbled and moved to repentance and also to instill fear among others."[1] Between 1561 and 1564 in Geneva, the mere threat of suspension was sufficient to bring 37 percent of accused sinners to repentance and only in 16 percent did the penalty extend beyond two communion services. Depending on the severity and notoriety of the offense, the suspension could be private, simply pronounced in the consistory chambers, or announced publicly from the pulpit on Sunday. As the final step in the process, the censured member underwent a penitential ritual either before the consistory or in public, again depending on the nature of the offense. Full excommunication remained a rarity. In France it was reserved for those who were "obstinate and impenitent over an extended period" and was pronounced after declarations from the pulpit on four consecutive Sundays.[2] This was similar to the "crime of insubordination" pronounced by Inquisitions for the punishment of heresy. Unlike temporary suspension, this level of excommunication was seldom wielded and represented only 3 percent of the cases in the Languedoc sample reconstructed by Raymond Mentzer. For Holland, Charles Parker reported a figure of 2 percent for Amsterdam and only three or four cases in Delft. The formula of final excommunication in France carried the malediction: "Cursed is he who undertakes the Lord's work negligently. Amen. If anyone does not love the Lord Jesus Christ, let him be Anathema Maranatha. Amen." Contained in the national *Discipline of the Reformed Churches of France*, the formula appeared only after the national synod of 1620 and was drawn from a famous ruling given in 1613 at Nîmes.[3] Unlike Inquisitions, consistories, except for Scottish kirk sessions, did not impose sentences that required atonement in the public domain. There were no ceremonies such as the *auto de fe* with its baroque decorum, since censorship, exclusion, and reconciliation were carried out in ecclesiastical space, either in the consistory chamber or the church service.

Suspension from the Lord's Supper as a punishment was neither uniform in practice nor universal in scope. It generated a great deal of controversy in the early years of the Calvinist Reformation. Though the Genevan Church employed suspension, Lausanne rejected it, a decision that provoked the departure of its Reformed pastor, Pierre Viret. Similarly, in the Pays de Vaud, the Bernese state adopted a Zwinglian view and maintained that it should have responsibility for morals control. The debate resurfaced two centuries later when the pastors from Lausanne and the canton of Vaud claimed the right to work toward the purification of society.

In France, suspension from the Lord' Supper occurred very frequently in the consistories of Languedoc, whereas in Loudun this penalty was very rarely applied. It is necessary, therefore, to contextualize the frequency of suspension in different circumstances. When churches were strong, as in Nîmes for example, suspension was common, while in isolated situations or in periods of weakness, consistories were hesitant to stigmatize the faithful out of fear that censured members would turn to Catholicism, thus weakening the Reformed community. This explains why the consistory in Courthézon – the only church of the principality of Orange to have preserved some of its records – avoided the practice in the troubled years before the revocation of the edict of Nantes.

The Reformed practice of suspension from the Lord's Supper denied those censured the possibility of marrying or participating in a baptism for the duration of their proscription, though it did not exempt them from attendance at sermons or catechism lessons. Such exclusion from the sacraments was widely used to great effect by the consistories of southern France. Whether private or public, it was particularly dreaded and served as a deterrent because it required reparation through a demonstration of humility, which, when public, played on the highly sensitive nature of personal honor. In addition, for a society rooted in religious belief and practice, deprivation from the most important sacrament corresponded to an exclusion from the entire community of the faithful.

At the conclusion of the suspension period, which could be imposed for one or more communion services, the sinner had to repent on his or her knees privately before the consistory or publicly before the congregation at the end of the Sunday sermon, depending upon the nature of the offense.

As Margo Todd's chapter points out, staging repentance in Scottish congregations took on special importance, as the guilty might be named
several times from the pulpit and had to sit on a designated bench or "stool
of repentance," several of which have been preserved. "Repentance" was
engraved in large capital letters on the backrest of a seventeenth-century
bench from Holy Trinity Church of Saint Andrews. In the Pays de Vaud,
where exclusion from the Supper was not practiced, penitents in the most
serious cases underwent a type of *amende honorable*, kneeling in the
church barefooted and bareheaded to beg forgiveness. Indeed, repentance
was the central symbolic act because it served as both a deterrent for those
susceptible to temptation and as a means of edification for the entire
congregation, a function that has received too little attention from historians. Performed in the church at the close of the sermon service, public
repentance was in certain respects part of the Reformed liturgy; it was
intended as much to reconcile sinners with the church as to make an
impression on the faithful, reinforcing the moral application of Reformed
discipline and justifying the legitimacy of the Reformation.

The consistory session held on the Friday before the communion
service was known as the "day of the censures," because it represented
the last opportunity for repentance on the part of transgressors as well as
those who had been suspended from the sacrament. Without any amendment, they could not participate in the Lord's Supper. Consistories
followed this practice faithfully so that the sacrament would not be
defiled. Essentially three instruments were at the disposal of consistories
to ensure that the sanctions were applied and the procedures were
observed. The first was the register that recorded pending cases and
sanctions imposed. The second consisted of lists or "rolls," which
included the names of people suspected of participating in sinful group
activities such as dances, charivaris, and carnivals, and above all the roll
of those who were suspended from communion. The third was a token,
made of either lead or tin and known as a *méreau*, which elders distributed in their districts on the eve of the communion service to members
worthy of partaking in the sacrament. Participation was not possible
unless members had a *méreau* to place on the communion table.

All of these procedures, along with the records and lists, aimed not
only at reforming the faithful but also at presenting a unified and pure
community to its Creator. It was, therefore, necessary for the consistory
to demonstrate that it was completely confident in its responsibility as
guardian of the flock and to make sure that the sins of a few did not draw
divine wrath on the entire community. In some cases, when a consistory

was unable to come to a decision, it released the accused to his or her conscience about whether or not to participate in communion, freeing the consistory and the congregation from this moral responsibility. Consistorial pedagogy thus centered on providing good examples and not on punishment as was the case for Inquisitions.

MORAL REFORMATION OF SOCIETY

Consistories immediately applied themselves to the dual task of reforming belief and behavior in congregations founded on the principle of the priesthood of all believers. Deprived of any priestly intermediary, individuals, families, and social groups had to fit into a new mold that permitted them to draw singularly upon divine benevolence. Records from Nîmes, however, reveal clear distinctions in the consistory's disciplinary efforts (see Table 12.1). Concerns with attendance at sermons and the Lord's Supper, as well as appropriate behavior during worship, occupied only a small space in records, as did anxieties about the adherence to Reformed orthodoxy and the persistence of superstitious or Catholic beliefs. Consistories were more concerned with inappropriate devotional activity than heterodox thought; they certainly applied themselves to the complete extirpation of "idolatry," primarily by prohibiting attendance at any "Roman" ceremonies and other forms of devotion. Unlike Inquisitions, consistories played a relatively small role in controlling print media, which fell under the domain of synods and political rulers. The principal disciplinary activity of consistories focused on moral reform and the establishment of a peaceful society through combating violence.

The task of the first consistories was to oversee the transition from the old to the new church, and when they could not abolish Catholicism, they discouraged contact with former beliefs and practices considered as impure and idolatrous. As a result, elders gave special attention to those who continued to attend Mass, frequent other Catholic ceremonies out of curiosity or interest in the renewed splendor of the post-Tridentine Roman Church. Consistories also strongly opposed cross-confessional social interactions, condemning attendance at Catholic baptisms (especially acting as sponsors), yet also at engagements, weddings, and funerals, and sending children to Jesuit schools. These offenses were considered among the most egregious, requiring suspension from the Lord's Supper.

Certainly the primary fear among the Reformed was the prospect that members might renounce their faith in order to marry a spouse of the "opposite religion." Although consistories were quite amenable to the

TABLE 12.1 *Distribution of Discipline Cases before the Nîmes Consistory*[1]

	1578–1604	1605–1634	1635–1674
Attitudes toward worship and communion	15%	14%	10%
Purity of the Church	12%	22%	28%
Social and Moral Order	71%	60%	59%
Indeterminate	2%	4%	3%

Notes: [1] Philippe Chareyre, "Le consistoire de Nîmes et l'Édit de Nantes," in *L'édit de Nantes, sa genèse, son application en Languedoc,* special issue of *Bulletin Historique de la Ville de Montpellier* 23 (1999): 117–28.

conversion of a Catholic party, as attested by numerous conversions recorded just before these ceremonies, they were under no illusions regarding the religious sincerity of the new convert. They recognized that in these cases conversion was an accommodation that reflected a social need rather than a genuine religious impulse. Consistories were equally indignant during repentance rituals that reintegrated those who had temporarily converted to Catholicism at the time of the wedding. These "mixed marriages" frequently appear in the records, so it seems likely that they were a common practice. The danger of mixed marriages for the Reformed community of France, as a minority faith, was demographic decline. The customary practice of raising boys in the confession of the father and girls in that of the mother made a subsequent generation of mixed marriages a likely possibility.

Control over orthodoxy occupied much less attention from consistories most everywhere, though when concerns did arise it was primarily in large towns where there was a Reformed academy. In these locations, consistories monitored not only the moral conduct of students and teachers but also any possible heterodoxy. Pastors and elders reviewed treatises in draft copy, especially those related to theological controversies, to determine whether they were suitable for publication. These rare situations mostly concerned a single quotation from a text, since in France the responsibility for theological review fell more to synods, which dealt with matters related to the general welfare of Reformed Churches.

The family attracted the concentrated attention of consistories, since it was considered the primary and everyday locus for the sanctification of the faithful. The purpose of the family, according to *The Discipline of the Reformed Churches of France*, was to produce children and to prevent fornication. Thus, *The Discipline* stipulated a maximum period of six weeks between betrothal and marriage. In the event of a dispute between the marrying parties, consistories urged them to seek arbitration or otherwise referred the case to civil magistrates. The significant percentage of cases appearing before the consistory involving marriage reveals the vigilance that it brought in seeking to suppress misconduct and promote peace within the process of family formation. It worked to prevent breach of promise in betrothal and marriage vows, and to thwart illicit sexual liaisons before and after marriage, including the extramarital affairs that sow discord within households.

Consistorial efforts at pacifying society were not limited to the family, but extended to society as a whole. Throughout Europe, consistories devoted a significant part of their business from settling disputes and resolving disagreements among church members to condemning duels, intrigues, usury, and whatever else might corrupt and disrupt society. This was the case in Scotland, Holland, and many French communities. This social dimension of discipline was very evident at Nîmes and in the southern French towns studied by Mentzer. In this region, 22 percent of suspensions from the Lord's Supper resulted from social conflict. It was the primary cause of censure at Loudun, thus regulating conflict contributed to social cohesion in this small Protestant community. Likewise, in the rural countryside of southern France, where 41 percent of the censures were meted out for this reason, consistories played a key role in limiting violence.

The accounts of these numerous quarrels, which bear witness to an unchanging level of habitual aggressiveness, are punctuated by an omnipresent and predictable bombast. Faced with impulsive anger that trumped good sense, provoked fights among friends and neighbors, and led to the most regrettable acts, a consistory utilized its chamber as a ceremonial place where quarreling parties were urged to contain themselves in the future, and to reconcile with a handshake in order to live in a peaceful society guided by "civil honesty." Reconciliations such as this were achieved in several ways. The most common means was through a mutual agreement to renounce all animosity, concluded with a handshake or kissing of hands, and a joint declaration to regard one another as a "good man and of good lineage." Suspension from communion remained, of course, a deterrent in dealing with recalcitrant individuals. Consistories distinguished between personal offenses committed in a quarrel from the dispute over material goods, which were referred to arbitrators or the courts. Thus in this difficult work of reconciliation, whether by pastors and elders or by designating arbitrators, consistories played a vital role in restoring violated personal honor. Many consistories experienced great success and had their authority challenged only infrequently, as evidenced by the numerous voluntary requests for reconciliation that came before it. It was this function of "sub-judicial" justice, discussed in the chapters by Todd and Grosse, and the daily pacification of society that church members accepted most readily, which endured for a very long period in consistorial operations across Europe. As a result, in Geneva, domestic disputes still dominated the consistory's business in 1730, a reality that prompted the Lausanne consistory to request the authority to suspend members from communion.

The most spectacular aspect of consistorial activity, though less visible statistically, concerned the discipline of individual and public morality with an eye to preventing greater excesses, especially in matters such as violence and fornication. Consistories sternly condemned sloth, gluttony, and drunkenness, particularly when they occurred in taverns and "cabarets,"considered locales for idleness, debauchery, and gaming. Church leaders regarded the aimless loitering of youths, particularly in the evenings, with suspicion. Any "dissolute" dress attracted the watchful eye of the elders. Women's dress, including low necklines, open blouses, vestments artificially constructed to give attention to the body (e.g. far-thingales), ornate hairstyles, and makeup came under reproach.

The campaign against dancing also mobilized consistories. *The Discipline* stipulated that those who continued to dance or even attend dances after repeated admonitions should be excommunicated. Anne Rulman, a lawyer and elder in the church at Nîmes in 1609 and 1610, described dancing as "the devil's pimp; he had the honor of inventing it," and "[dance] sounds the tocsin of unrestrained liberty to naturally depraved flesh." [4] Consistorial intransigence was even more severe when dances occurred on a Sunday. Taking an equally stern attitude toward traditional folk festivals, such as the Epiphany ritual of the "king drinks," masquer-ades, and carnival, consistories compiled lists of revelers who were often identified despite their masks. Consistories similarly did not take jokes and jesting aimed at sacred texts lightly, for *The Discipline* stated that Scripture is to be used only for preaching.

The *Discipline* also prohibited games proscribed by royal edicts – cards, dice, and other games of chance – and specified the reasons why consistories had to take action. Games promoted avarice, indecency, idleness, quarreling, profanity, and ill-gotten profits, and worse, they often took place during church services. Sports contests, including deck tennis or other ball games, were tolerated, provided that players did not blaspheme or gamble, and not play during church service. The consistory also put up with some other games of skill, such as parrot shooting, because the expertise participants developed could be useful.

CONCLUSIONS

Consistories across Europe did not approach moral discipline in a uniform manner; comparative studies have brought to light important regional differences. A comparison between consistories in Languedoc and the Palatinate, for example, showed that the infractions that came under censorship in these two areas varied significantly, perhaps because of local circumstances. In Germanic territories, elders primarily targeted drunkenness, which was not a priority in Scotland. In Mediterranean regions, comportment, appearance, and dancing trumped other transgressions. Social differences in urban settings also led to practical differences, according to place and time. Dancing, flirtation, and games were often considered to be elite preoccupations, and were a source of friction with artisans and men from the legal professions who frequently served as elders. Finally, it seems that the crackdown on gaming belonged more to the late sixteenth century, while attitudes toward dancing grew more unyielding in the early seventeenth century, but eased somewhat a few decades later. As for "magical" practices, the campaign against them was part of the great wave of European witch hunts during the late sixteenth and early seventeenth centuries.

Historians have noted a decline in the repressive activities of consistories over the course of the seventeenth century. Those who study the Inquisition have observed a similar trend. From this point forward, consistories occupied themselves more with the organization of sermons and the Lord's Supper, and in France with charitable assistance. The apparent success of Reformed discipline, however, may simply mask strategies of adaptation used by church members, similar to those adopted in inquisitorial interactions.

Notes

1 François Méjan ed., *Discipline de l'Église réformée de France annotée et précédée d'une introduction historique.* (Paris, 1947), 233.
2 F. Méjan, *Discipline,* 233.
3 F. Méjean, *Discipline,* 235.
4 Philippe Chareyre, "The Great Difficulties One Must Bear to Follow Jesus-Christ: Morality at Sixteenth Century, Nîmes," in Raymond Mentzer ed., *Sin and the Calvinists: Morals Control and the Consistory in the Reformed Tradition* (Kirksville, MO, 1994), 88.

13

Inquisitions

Doris Moreno Martínez
Translated by Gretchen Starr-LeBeau

Traditionally, Inquisitions have been studied as exceptional ecclesiastical tribunals destined to persecute and punish heresy, instruments of violence in the service of political and religious orthodoxies. Only in the last decades of the twentieth century have Inquisitions been analyzed from the point of view of their social pedagogy and of the tools that they used toward that end. This approach emerged from early modern Europeanists' development of the interpretive paradigms of confessionalization and social discipline. In brief, the religious fissure between Protestants and Catholics brought a concomitant restructuring of religious space, which was intimately connected to the development of early modern nation-states. Beyond the political management of difference, the existence of all these churches (or confessions) confirmed the necessity of reinterpreting traditional customs and beliefs by other methods. Politico-religious unity was sought through intellectual tools and through political means that permitted the recycling or "correction" of thoughts and behaviors. The "subjects-faithful" existed within a structure framed by parameters defined by established powers. Churches got ready for the task of *educating* the faithful and busied themselves with the most effective *methods* for this. They attempted, in the words of Michel de Certeau, to reform the Christian community, to remake the forms of devotion and its practices.

For Catholics, it was the Council of Trent (1545–1563) that established the bases of a program of dogmatic redefinition and, above all, a wide-ranging plan of Catholic renovation that included the moral and religious reform of the community. Early modern Inquisitions played a notable role in that program. Powerful elites, both secular and religious, supported a bureaucratic inquisitorial structure that was already functioning, adding to it the Holy Office's symbolic patrimony of suspicion and fear; above all, they utilized the crime of heresy as pretext. Early modern Inquisitions, for their part, as powers on the rise, anxiously sought hegemony on this newly opened field of labor, successfully confronting bishops and royal ministers.

The inquisitorial pedagogy of Catholic Reform was double-edged. Along one edge ran a pedagogy of fear, as Bartolomé Bennassar wrote, fear of the lingering memory of a loss of reputation, of economic ruin, of having no way to defend oneself before the secret tribunal. But the other edge offered a politics of presence and a pedagogy of exemplars in consonance with the new style of Catholic piety sketched out at Trent. There were many inquisitorial methods, which collectively projected an image of a softer, pastorally motivated Inquisition. Early modern Inquisitions did not abandon their principal task – the coercive, violent persecution of heretics in their own tradition; however, they joined themselves to a wider horizon, diversifying their objectives, their strategies, and their methods, projecting among faithful Catholics an apparently "gentler" image and practice.

This wider inquisitorial horizon occurred because of a reformulation of the concept of heresy ("understanding or interpretation of the Scriptures that did not conform to the understanding and interpretation traditionally defended by the Catholic Church") and heretic ("those who believe or teach things contrary to the faith of Christ and of His church") based on Tridentine emphases and the practices of the faithful.[1] After Trent, Catholicism rained down on the heads of the faithful a series of teachings and precepts so abundant, so all-encompassing in all aspects of social life, that they became a potential battleground between truth and error. All Catholics became potential heretics. All the justifications set forward for this shared an intellectualization of social practices and an application of a rule of suspicion: it presupposed potential doctrinal deviations or heretical intellectual speculation behind errant behavior. Subjects that previously were only the subject of the pastoral concerns of the bishops were promoted to the category of heresy. The hegemonic will of the Inquisition, with its wish not to be a mere adjunct to a process of Catholic reform but instead to exercise a more or less absolute agency, was notable.

BUILDING BEHAVIOR, INTRODUCING SUSPICION INTO CONSCIENCES

From the end of the sixteenth century, superstition, magic, blasphemy, and other subjects began to occupy a more central place among inquisitional objectives. Other concerns also increased in relevance, including false or feigned sanctity, the incorrect use of sacred images, and abuse of the sacraments (such as marriage, confession, and holy orders). Inquisitional responses to sins of a sexual nature were varied. Furthermore, early modern Inquisitions were increasingly occupied by witchcraft and diabolism, those who impeded inquisitorial activity, and the false denunciation of heresy. There were other minor sins that also became integrated into the Inquisition's purview, such as the consumption of prohibited foods on the many Catholic fast days, which became a sign of disobedience to Tridentine rules. It is essential to remember that while moral and religious reform in the Reformed Protestant world fell upon consistories, with their ecclesiastical structure of pastors and elders, their control of urban territory and their expectation of a fundamental role for heads of household, the Holy Office by contrast prosecuted "popular superstitions" and other crimes of customary practice differently. That is, Inquisitions operated from the suspicion of heresy, from the scent of heresy that could emanate from attitudes, words, or deeds. For example, inquisitors' growing preoccupation with fornication was not due to the illicit relations per se, but rather because boasting that it was not a sin to sleep with a single woman if she consented was a threat to the Tridentine sacrament of marriage.

In contrast to consistories, one field in which the Inquisitions had a notable role was that of censorship. In Iberia, censorship was a responsibility of the Portuguese and Spanish Inquisitions, while in Italy a cardinal took responsibility for censorship through a Congregation effectively created in 1571. Censorship not only established what could or could not be read and by whom; it also codified what was permitted. Censors in the three Inquisitions – Portuguese, Spanish, and Roman – varied in their focus.

From the first Index published in 1559 to the end of the seventeenth century, the Spanish Inquisition focused on books of piety and devotion, given their fear of *alumbradismo*, that distinctly Spanish heresy. From the Index of 1612, inquisitorial censorship also increasingly targeted political thought and scientific works. Probably the most characteristic policy of Spanish censorship was the introduction and practice of expurgation from the Index of 1571, and the Expurgatory Index of 1585–86. The Roman Inquisition applied the *donec corrigatur*, the prohibition of a book until its expurgation, although the correction of books never reached a level of bureaucratic systematization. The publication of expurgatory indices, characteristic of the Spanish Inquisition, carried the Holy Office to a dead end: the enormous expurgatory Index of 1586 highlighted the huge task that the inquisitors had placed on their shoulders. From this date on, the principles articulated by subsequent indices attempted to seek out a solution, which led to the proposal that booksellers and/or readers should be those who, using the official indices, should expurgate their books. A further step in this process was the development of *caute lege*. In 1607 the Index of the Master of the Holy Palace, Juan Maria Brasichel, was published in Rome, and in it he articulated the principle of *caute lege*. The slow and polemical debate by the Spanish Holy Office over accepting this principle culminated in the Index of 1640. Read it carefully: the reader is asked to censor his own books according to the criteria of his own conscience – or his own fear – rigidly channeled by the guidelines of the church.

Another of the fields of inquisitorial labor was that of developing good conduct through the intervention of the Holy Office in the practice of confession. In the Tridentine debates confession revealed its double nature: it was an instrument of power and of consolation, a channel of formation and information. From the point of view of the Inquisitions, as with the reforming bishops, what counted was information. The best way of discovering the roots of heresy, and also of preventing it, came from excavating the conscience of an individual; this required a necessary alliance with confessors who initially were disgusted, but soon adopted this alliance naturally. The address of conscience, together with the insistence on the practice of the sacrament, assured an assiduous control over conscience, a systematic redirecting to the right path.

However, resistance to this confessional model was multipronged and profound. The populace had to be compelled to confess. Demands for periodic confession became insistent. Conciliar decrees said it; diocesan synods repeated it; preachers, parish priests, and teachers inculcated it. The insistence of Pope Pius V on this point is well known, and he even came to prohibit doctors from healing the sick if their patients had not confessed first (1566). The pressure on confessors was systematic. The resistance of the bishops was intense, with the notable exception of Portugal. The edicts of the Italian Inquisition insisted in its warnings to confessors that the first step was to question the penitent on whether he had news of any person who had committed heresy – either himself or others – or if he had prohibited books. If the answer was affirmative, the confessor was to send them to denounce themselves before the Holy Office before hearing their confession, as Kim Siebenhüner discusses in Chapter 11. In all the Italian Inquisition tribunals, the inquisitor and his vicars called meetings of all the confessors to inform them that they could not give absolution for the many areas with which the Inquisition busied itself. In the end, confession was subordinated to Inquisition.

Paul IV definitively sanctioned the role of filter and intermediary granted to confessors in matters of heresy and prohibited books. In Spain, the same Pope, born Gian Pietro Carafa, responded to a petition by Inquisitor General Valdés and urged that penitents tell confessors the names of any accomplices for each sin they confessed. Francisco Suárez, in his great theological synthesis (1602), cautiously legitimized this almost police-like use of the confessional. He stated that the penitent should confess the name of any accomplice in his transgression, and authorize his confessor to reveal his deeds to the Holy Office – or even better, that he should present himself to the inquisitors for a "spontaneous confession" or "to relieve his conscience." This was a betrayal of every rule of the sacrament of penance, given that the workings of conscience had moved from being an interior to an exterior act. The Inquisition thus changed from being a tribunal operating as an external forum into an observatory of the movements of conscience, and accustomed itself to intervening using the same means employed by confessors. The debate of whether the penitent or the confessor could reveal the name of an accomplice was a central problem discussed by theologians and canonists. The Inquisition was a protagonist and ally of the Church in generating scruples of conscience, that interior anguish, that shadow of anxiety, that asphyxiating doubt in regard to what was thought, said, acted, read, seen, or heard by others. In the Calvinist world, scruples of conscience had a substantially different weight since ultimately what was in play was not the salvation of the individual but his participation in the unity of the community of the faithful before his Creator.

THE POLITICS OF PRESENCE AND EXEMPLARITY

The absorption of inquisitorial values of religious and moral reform at the local level also aided the business of its own personnel, intermediate figures in the local tribunals and above all, the commissaries (*comisarios*) and familiars (*familiares*) spread across the land. Studies on the sociology of inquisitorial personnel have highlighted how, by the late sixteenth century, familiarship increasingly attracted the interest of rich peasants, the nobility, and the urban bourgeoisie. The theory that familiars systematically denounced transgressions of heresy committed by their neighbors is no longer accepted by scholars. Inquisitorial commissaries, normally parish priests or vicars and members of religious orders, played a much more central role for the Holy Office in its fight for religious reform, especially in regard to superstitious practices of a local religiosity more dependent on community traditions than distant Tridentine directives. The consolidation of this network of inquisitorial commissaries assured the Holy Office a more militant and visible presence and control of the countryside.

Particularly from the end of the sixteenth century, the Inquisitions developed a "politics of presence" in festive ritual spaces. Baroque religious feasts, equal parts festive and theatrical, sought to give physical and sensorial form to the sacred with all its ideological content, while at the same time stimulating religious devotion toward Counter-Reformation fundamentals. From the feast-day stage they launched messages that were intended to take root and grow in the hearts and minds of the community. This was also an era of generating and confirming collective identities. J. A. Maravall has pointed out that the festive culture of the Baroque attempted "to inject into consciences a doctrinal content which enlisted acquiescence, not by means of rationality, but by collective adhesion, by a passion that trumped the will."[2]

Without a doubt, the *auto de fe* was the public ceremony most identified with the Holy Office, especially the general *auto de fe*, the most common type, which was celebrated in public spaces. Like the angel with the flaming sword that guarded the gates of the Garden of Eden, the Holy Office demonstrated its divine legitimacy and its effective power (aided by other powers) through the *auto de fe* to expel the "heretic-Cains" from the Eden of the church-community. At the same time, the *auto de fe* allowed inquisitors to reintegrate repentant souls who had reconciled with the church community and who could now enjoy its mercy and pardon. The theater of the general *autos de fe* became more exaggerated in the seventeenth century even as they became less frequent. The *autos de fe* in Madrid in 1632 and 1680 were spectacles – the latter of the two firmly fixed in memory thanks to the extraordinary painting of it by Rizzi. Although in the sixteenth century Seville witnessed a general *auto de fe* every two years, including two a year in 1573 and 1578, in the following century only four were celebrated, in 1604, 1624, 1648, and 1660.

Printed accounts insured that in the days and weeks following an *auto de fe*, in homes, churches, shops, and squares, individuals would read it aloud to their neighbors, anxious for news – about the exaltation of the Holy Office and inquisitorial values, the names of the condemned and their penalties, and even perhaps some morbid details. They would comment on the familiar name of someone they knew, remembering the feast day of the *auto de fe*, the frugal snack eaten at the midday break; perhaps remembering, too, moments in the pyre, the kind of death the condemned experienced, if they repented or not; or remembering the screams torn from someone feeling the flames on his legs. They would comment on the sermon of the priest charged with the important task of glossing the virtues of the Holy Office and its indispensible role in the fight against heresy. The priest would continue by denouncing the terrible sins committed by the condemned heretics and the dire consequences for the community.

Let us take one example. On January 1, 1624, a spectacular *auto de fe* was celebrated in the Plaza Mayor of Madrid before a large crowd.[3] The royal preacher Cristóbal de Torres took as his base text the healing of the leper by Jesus (Matt 8:1–4) to establish a parallel between Jesus/the Holy Office and the leper/heretic. It was enough that the heretic repented for, like Jesus, the Holy Office extended its hand, touched the heretic and cured him of the leprosy of heresy with some slight penance. But, "if the heretic is obstinate in this heresy ... the rule that the Supreme Inquisitor gives is to cast him out like an apostate son of the Kingdom, into exterior darkness, consigning him to the flames whose smoke causes a temporary lament in his eyes and gives a foretaste of eternity."[4]

In a pedagogical spirit, the preacher went on to define a heretic: "A heretic is a soul without discipline ... Discipline consists ... in subjecting oneself to God with firmness, not presuming proudly to understand more than what God manifests."[5] Friar Cristóbal de Torres laid out with clarity the distinction between the good Catholic, the *disciplined* person, and the heretic, the *undisciplined* person. The heretic granted the law to himself, usurping the magisterium of God and the Church. The former was characterized by obedience, the latter by destructive rebellion. For those in attendance, the *auto de fe* should be many things – a call to attention; a return to discipline, to the obedience of conscience, understanding, and practice; a complete moral reform – in short, the only possible path to acceptance in the present and glory in the future. Heresy and the crime of a lack of discipline, as in the Protestant world, were synonyms, but the consequences from one world to the other were different. Judgment Day had arrived for the guilty. For the Catholic community in general the *auto de fe* ought to be the moment of solemnizing the triumph of divine Providence. Finally, the preacher maintained that divine Providence permitted the existence of such heretics as a lesson to all Catholics who, following their example, could and should commit to improving their thoughts and actions. Among these acts is found the adhesion to the prosecution and punishment of the heretics. This was the path to glory. The inquisitors thus transformed themselves into executors of the popular will, executors of the "good" children of the church.

One inestimable opportunity to give the Holy Office a presence in the streets was offered to it by the confraternities of St. Peter Martyr. Peter of Verona was an apostolic inquisitor murdered in 1252 in Como by a group of heretics. Perhaps a year later he was canonized, and his cult achieved notable success in Italy. Early on, the papacy favored the creation of companies of familiars or *crocesignati* dedicated to the saint. In December 1604 Clement VIII encouraged the creation of new confraternities, direct descendants of those earlier ones. In 1611 Pope Paul V exhorted the faithful to enter the confraternity of St. Peter Martyr and in this way to seek status as a familiar, as a form of connection to the Holy Office. In Spain and Portugal the constitution of confraternities was an initiative of the central organs of the tribunal, especially after 1604.

Only members and personnel connected to the Holy Office across all its territories could belong to the confraternity, creating a prestige and exclusivity that stimulated the participation of elites. Over time, this participation presupposed on the one side a greater intervention by local elites in the tribunals, and, on the other, the extension of inquisitorial messages across informal social networks, the "diffuse Inquisition" spoken of by Juan Ignacio Pulido and an example of horizontal confessionalization.[6]

In addition to providing for these groups' function as a mutual aid society, the statutes of the confraternities regulated their public presence at their own feasts, like those of St. Peter Martyr and the Exaltation of the Holy Cross, or at general ones like the processions of Holy Week and the reception of kings and princes. In any forum, they sought to exhibit and unfurl the image and symbols of the Holy Office on insignias and pendants, actively participating in its social, festive dramatization. The Inquisition knew the power of its image.

In this climate of the politics of presence, the Spanish Inquisition played a strong role in promoting the beatification and canonization of Peter of Arbués, an Aragonese inquisitor murdered in 1485 by hired assassins sent by a powerful group of *judeoconverso* families. From the moment of the assassination, popular religious devotion to the murdered inquisitor began in Zaragoza. In 1619 the Supreme Council of the Inquisition in Spain (*Consejo Superior*) began proceedings to petition for the beatification that was approved by Alexander VII on April 27, 1664. Canonization occurred in 1867.

Sanctity formed part of the Tridentine Catholic program as a way to channel religious sensibilities toward "fresh" saints like Philip Neri in Rome or Carlo Borromeo in Milan. These were saints capable of attracting to themselves intense popular devotional currents – in other words, they were "appropriate" saints who had passed through the filter of Roman control. In Peter of Arbués they had some of the most pertinent and common characteristics that were sought in a Baroque martyrdom: death as *paideia*, as education and as a channeling of deportment, as well as the mandatory post-mortem miracles. The beatification of Arbués in 1664 came to signify inquisitorial success against heresy, a triumph against "Jewish perfidy." The Spanish Inquisition had attained "its" St. Peter, its own inquisitorial saint, opposed to St. Peter Martyr of Verona. The similarity of the two saintly profiles – inquisitors sharing the same name, both killed fighting heresy, assassinated by heretics with swords or axes – allowed for a not very subtle "Peters game" by which the sanctity of the first transferred to the second; this reinforced his inquisitorial, and by extension Spanish, identity. The third Peter, the apostle, founder of the Church, formed together with the other two a suggestive triad for poets, who could take advantage of some of the feasts organized in his honor.

The Supreme Council of the Inquisition in Spain invited all its tribunals to organize multitudinous feasts celebrating the new devotion. The festivities were rigorously structured to exclude all kinds of profane acts. Many printed accounts have come down to us of those feasts celebrated across the Spanish Empire. In all these activities a paean to faith and the Church were closely united by the tribunal, the undisputed protagonist that never abandoned the center of attention. The messages were very explicit: the Inquisition was sustained by the blood of martyrs; the triumph of the martyr was the triumph of the Inquisition; the Inquisition was a bulwark against Judaism; members of the Inquisition were saints; the duration and stability of the church depended on the Inquisition; and the most important popes, including the apostle Peter, were inquisitors. The beatification was an excellent opportunity to generate festive spaces of public cohesion for an elevated sociopolitical impact.

WAS INQUISITORIAL ACTION EFFICACIOUS?

The debate about the efficacy of inquisitorial activity in effecting moral and religious reform has dragged on for decades. Liberal Spanish and Protestant historiography of the nineteenth century argued that it achieved the reform of public morals by persuasion and violence, but that it never succeeded in convincing people to believe in their hearts; rather, they created a country of hypocrites in manifestations of public piety, or perhaps a country of superstitious people. The Scottish Presbyterian Thomas M'Crie wrote in 1829: "in religion, the inhabitants of Spain are now divided into two classes: fanatics and fakes; there is not an intermediate class." For the Scot, inquisitorial vigilance had necessitated a permanent exercise of hypocrisy among all dissident Spaniards. In his judgment, the community remained under the control of a perverted and perverting religion that led the simplest members of the faith to superstitious practices alienated from all reason.[7] The vision of the liberal Spaniard Blanco White is indicative in this respect of the fears that provoked the Inquisition in its last days and the influence that the Holy Office played in the consciences of the epoch. Debates about the effect of the Holy Office in Spanish, Italian, or Portuguese culture occurred throughout the nineteenth century.

Currently, historiographical comment on this theme varies among specific geographic contexts. For Spain, highly divergent views are provided by Jean-Pierre Dedieu for Toledo, Henry Kamen for Catalunya, or Sara Nalle and Miguel Jiménez Monteserín for Cuenca.

The insertion of the Inquisition in Catalan society was so superficial that it was difficult to change society in any aspect. The little changes that Kamen believes he recognizes in the realm of Catholic Reform in Catalunya came, above all, in the exercise of the sacraments, clarification of the liturgical calendar, homogenization of books of prayers, cleaning and embellishing of churches, and so forth. But according to him, those changes did not alter popular culture and the communal practice of traditional religion. William Christian also has reiterated the image of the continuity of local religion in New Castile from the mid-sixteenth century to the end of the eighteenth century. New saints and devotions were assimilated without explicitly renouncing the old pagan piety. In the case of Kamen, this pessimistic reading with respect to the implantation of the new Counter-Reformation model is linked to his assertion that the Inquisition had no contact with more than 90 percent of the villages of Catalunya during the more than three centuries of the existence of the Holy Office.

Dedieu, by contrast, and working from inquisitorial sources, states that more than 75 percent of individuals knew the principal prayers and the rudiments of the Christian faith. Religious education in villages had taken giant steps forward. Dedieu's conclusion regarding the role that the Holy

Office played in this is emphatic: the prestige of the tribunal was used to develop popular mentalities, to impose a new model, to assimilate knowledge defined by the clergy. On the other hand, discipline was felt in the diocese of Cuenca with relatively effective results. But that came with the recognition that the control of space was very limited, that the effort or productivity of the inquisitors was sparing, and overall, that the fear of social conflict resulted in a treatment of local religion marked by scruples and precautions.

In the cultural realm, the efficacy of censorship by the Holy Office remains a great debate. The question posed in recent years has been that of a comparison between theoretical discourse and repressive norms, and its practical application. Various historians have emphasized the contradiction between the theory of inquisitorial repression and its practice. The Indexes with their lists of prohibited books did not create the sought-after ideological *cordon sanitaire*, given that the practice of reading overflowed the narrow channels fixed by prohibited works. It is possible that the ever more intense inquisitorial belligerence in this field was part of a permanent rearguard action. At the beginnings of the seventeenth century the principle of *caute lege* began to be employed in Spain, which in practice involved shifting to readers the activity of censors (*calificadores*). In Italy, during the same period, ecclesiastical censorship was reorganized. Censorship adapted during the seventeenth century to new contexts, and was occupied with new forms of political thought and scientific speculation, acting as an internal Catholic police force in the confrontations between diverse schools of Tridentine Catholic theology. This strategy of control was effective. The Counter-Reformation triumphed in the forge of conscience and religious scruples.

There was, of course, resistance. In Spain during the sixteenth century, some men dreamed of an "other" Inquisition.[8] There were many strategies for surviving the Inquisition. The prohibition of titles and authors at times spurred the publicity of the book, feeding curiosity and fomenting interest in forbidden knowledge. Authors wrote flattering dedications to the powerful, reclaiming a legitimacy that permitted one to elude the shoals of censorship. The prologues were, on many occasions, the site of caution, prudence, or acts of contrition. Maneuvers to reduce the risk of censorship began even before printing with a series of opinions that permitted one to test the limits of tolerance that pertained at that moment. Verbal pirouettes, doubled language, winks to the complicit reader – these were frequent tactics because, as Blanco White also said, "villages subjected to governments that do not permit them to express themselves freely have the alertness of the deaf to understanding themselves by signs."[9]

Before an avalanche of normative prescriptions, that is, of religious regulations in a new Tridentine setting, Catholics of the early modern era developed varied tactics, moving between norms and transgressions. From the perspective of that permeable boundary, the most recent historiography has focused its analysis on the transgressive use of the practice of registering books on the Index. Scholars have also called attention to the resistance to confession according to the Tridentine model and the survival of superstitious practices related to Masses for souls in purgatory, despite several attempts to suppress these unorthodox devotions. They have highlighted the persistence of blasphemy as an inquisitorial transgression in the tribunal of Seville until the middle of the seventeenth century; and they have completed studies that have demonstrated the persistence of beatas, illuminists, *ilusas*, and the possessed, practitioners of a heterodox spirituality that cohabited with orthodoxy on multiple occasions. In the face of discipline as an imposition from the top down, there was an authentic lack of discipline – chronic, quotidian, and resistant to authority.

Finally, we should not dismiss silent resistance, nicodemism, which is so difficult to detect. José C. Nieto studied these "submissive rebels," individuals who did not reject the authority or structures of power but sought alternative survival strategies, those in which the tension between norms and transgressions was resolved in silence. Excellent testimony of "submissive rebels" who opted for the strategy of silence in its original form were, in Nieto's judgment, Friar Francisco Ortiz and Saint John of the Cross.[10]

Certainly, the cohabitation between norms and transgressions adopted various forms, a festival of conduct in continuous negotiation, a true patchwork of the everyday. The result was a reformed Catholic practice more negotiated than any orthodox figure would have wanted to acknowledge, a rebellion more domesticated than any rebellious militant would admit, and a multitude of silences.

Notes

1 Cited in N. Eimeric y F. Peña, *El Manual de los inquisidores* (Barcelona, 1996), 58, 61. See also J. Le Goff (ed.), *Herejías y sociedades en la Europa preindustrial, ss. XI-XVIII*, (Madrid 1987), 310.

2 J. A. Maravall, "Teatro, fiesta e ideología en el Barroco," in J. Mª Díez ed., *Teatro y fiesta en el Barroco: España e Iberoamérica*, Borque (Sevilla, 1986), 87.

3 *Sermón predicado (por orden del Consejo Supremo de la Santa y General Inquisición) en el auto de fe que celebró el Santo Tribunal de Toledo, en la*

Corte de la Magestad Católica, el rey Don Felipe IIII nuestro señor … , a 21 de enero de 1624. Por el Reverendo padre dominico, fray Cristóbal de Torres, natural de la ciudad de Burgos* (Madrid, 1624).

4 *Sermón,* 2r.

5 Ibid., 14r.

6 J. I. Pulido Serrano, *Injurias a Cristo. Religión, político y antijudaísmo en el siglo XVII* (Alcalá de Henares, 2002), 265–67.

7 Thomas M'Crie, *La Reforma en España en el siglo XVI* (Seville, 2008), 353.

8 S. Pastore, *Il Vangelo e la spada. L'Inquisizione di Castiglia e i suoi critici (1460–1598)* (Rome, 2003).

9 J. Mª Blanco White, *El Español,* No. 10, enero de 1811.

10 J. C. Nieto, "Two Spanish Mystics as Submissive Rebels," *Bibliotheque d'Humanisme et Renaissance* 33 (1971): 63–77.

Section F

Victims as Actors

14

Consistories

Timothy Fehler

Consistories were certainly agents of judicial action and moral reformation just as they shaped the narrative of disciplinary cases via detailed recordkeeping. Despite the cautionary tone of Christian Grosse's essay in Chapter 10, consistory records do provide glimpses of the social and cultural history of ordinary people. As was the case with much of the earlier scholarship on Inquisition suspects, consistories too have also been traditionally considered as instruments of discipline over powerless victims. During the past half-century scholars have gone beyond looking to consistories merely to provide fodder for examples of exceptional scandals or illustrations of repressive discipline. This research has uncovered a rich vein of documentation within consistory records that offers intriguing insights into the actions of the "victims" of discipline, even if the narratives are presented from the perspective of the consistory. These interactions show us how people tried to navigate and even manipulate the consistory for their own purposes, while remaining within the framework of Reformed community building and discipline.

    A long-running disciplinary conflict that featured almost twenty-five appearances before the consistory in Emden (Germany) illustrates most clearly the defiance of some church members. In May 1560 the Flemish refugee identified only by the name Proene was summoned to appear before the Emden consistory to substantiate the unspecified charges that she had leveled against the consistory in a "slanderous letter." Yet, when she appeared, her only response to any of the consistory's questions was to cry, "Examine the scripture!"[1] She and her husband Jacob were both

called to the consistory three months later to account again for unspeci-
fied "grave accusations" that they were continuing to make against both
Emden's Reformed pastors and the deacons. They were content with
neither Reformed teaching nor diaconal poor relief, as they made no
fewer than six appearances before the consistory in 1560 and 1561.[2]
Two years later the couple was called by the consistory and accused of
receiving alms from the Anabaptists.[3] During a long discussion before the
Emden consistory in February 1563, Jacob and Proene were asked if they
would agree to separate themselves from the Anabaptists and no longer
accept their alms. Though neither gave a clear reply for a long time, finally
Proene answered contemptuously that she would continue receiving alms
from the consistory's "adversaries," saying that the two of them had not
left the congregation, but rather the Reformed congregation had left
them.[4] Nevertheless, despite Jacob and Proene's harsh criticisms, the
Emden consistory did not give up on them without a fight, as the couple
appeared – sometimes together, other times individually – before the
consistory at least seventeen more times through 1566.[5]

Here we see that the consistory was committed to pastoral care and not
merely to punitive discipline. As Karen Spierling shows in Chapter 16,
such negotiated discipline could involve mutual interactions between
ecclesiastical leaders and their congregants in which neither side was
victorious. In order to explore lay agency, this chapter will take advantage
of the faint whispers of the voices of the accused that we can hear in
consistory minutes in order to focus on women and men called before the
consistory and the variety of their reactions to consistorial discipline.

Scholarship has swung away from the older emphasis on punishment,
but only recently has attention been given to the agency of the accused.
Representative samples from consistorial records allow us to investigate
the circumstances, accusations, and responses of those called before
Reformed consistories for disciplinary questions, especially for this study,
in Geneva, the northwestern German territories, and the Netherlands. Of
course, the most detailed entries in the records typically involve cases
where discipline did not go smoothly. Such cases allow an appraisal of the
agency wielded among those called before a consistory and charged with
deviation from moral or theological norms. How much control could they
exercise in such a position and what specific options were used by men
and women who found themselves before a consistory? There are many
reminders in the consistory records that those who stood before consistories exercised their own unique agency, often in a range of responses in
the middle ground between coercion and resistance.

In addition to each individual's personal circumstances, a number of factors contributed to an accused's reaction to the consistory. The type of accusation and the possible sanctions must be evaluated alongside the accused's relationship to the community. Many complex tensions and competing concerns encased each individual undergoing discipline. Raymond Mentzer's essay in the opening chapter (Chapter 1) reminds us that consistories themselves exercised different levels of autonomy and authority across the Reformed world. Local and supralocal institutions (including regional courts and synodal bodies) had a bearing on the relationship between consistories and secular governments. Without the more standardized legal structures and procedures developed by Inquisitions, consistories offer a greater range of regional variation.

A number of motivations remained consistent from those appearing before consistories. One of the most universal goals was the accused's attempt to avoid or lessen a sanction, whether it was a spiritual punishment from the consistory or corporal or financial punishments from secular authorities. Besides calculations to try to avoid sanction, there were several additional, if related, concerns. While people often sought to remain true to their conscience, there was also great interest in protecting one's reputation or avoiding notoriety. Preserving one's conscience could come into conflict with interests such as avoiding sanction, maintaining one's sense of personal honor, family reputation, and community respectability. These competing goals became even more complicated for poor members of the congregation, as consistories could also raise the threat of withdrawing diaconal alms.

People brought information, petitions, and accusations to the consistory's attention. The carpenter Jacques Charvier sought to use the consistory to safeguard his rights as he approached the Geneva consistory in 1552 with a petition to force a former nun to fulfill her alleged promise to marry him after he had delivered her from a prison in Vienne.[6] Likewise, a distraught member identified only as Antoine approached the Genevan consistory in 1557, urging it to annul an engagement between Philiberte Le Chapuis and her new fiancé Pierre. Antoine wanted the consistory to compel her to marry him as he had been engaged to Philiberte first.[7] Therefore the consistory was not merely an institution to impose top-down discipline; lay people also attempted to use the consistory for their own ends.

Such horizontal policing involved people reporting others' misbehavior for the consistory to investigate. Indeed, third party reports of Pierre Mestrazat's threatened use of "violence with indecent words" reached the Genevan consistory in August 1547, inspiring an investigation into Pierre's two-year engagement to a 10-year-old girl, as well as various scandalous threats made by Pierre.[8] In 1544 the noble citizen of Geneva, Denys Hugoz, was reported to the consistory "because of [his non-attendance at] the sermons, blasphemies in execration and other things giving a bad example to people."[9] Such lay reporting implies an internalization of expected societal and spiritual norms; in this case someone making a report with the hope that the consistory would intervene so that this citizen would not do dishonor to the Reformed community. Hugoz admitted that "sometimes he swears and blasphemes in anger." Yet following his admission of guilt for swearing and giving a bad example, he disavowed any responsibility for the quarrel he was embroiled in over an accusation of "mistreating his wife and managing his household." Hugoz received a reprimand for striking the one who insulted him, but he still wanted to know the source of the consistory's information, saying, "If someone wants to insult him he cannot suffer it, and he would like to hear those who have made the report."

This response offers further insights into motivations behind such manifestations of lay agency, namely using the consistory to settle scores. Hugoz intimated that he could not respond to the charge without knowing who had made the insult, implying an accusation made out of malice. When Jehan Mouri was summoned before the Genevan consistory in 1542 because of alleged fornication, he responded that "he did not fornicate and that someone puts this crime on him because he is examining the rights of the Council."[10] Whatever the validity of such accusations of ulterior personal motivations, the consistory certainly offered individuals the opportunity to report on one another, and even the accused rejected charges as they attempted to exculpate themselves before the consistory. Whereas the constraints of inquisitorial legal procedure generally kept the identities of prosecution witnesses secret, those accused before a consistory in many cases, though not always, knew the source of the accusation against them.

A number of examples of strategies emerged among those who struggled to resist consistorial discipline, or who yielded to it only slowly or reluctantly. Accused church members resisted discipline by resorting to tears, denying charges, appealing to extenuating circumstances, blaming others or the consistory, threatening to leave the congregation, prevaricating, and promising future improvement. Those censured often protested sanctions, which reflected the high value placed on participating in the communion service. But such punishment could hold sway only as long as taking the Lord's Supper was important to the individual. Thus since both inquisitors and consistory elders treated noncooperation as a sign of guilt, the range of punishments available likely affected the accused's calculation of the costs of refusing to participate.

Though it is unclear whether the primary motivation was to take communion or receive alms, Lieven van Vijven wanted to be readmitted to the church after four years of excommunication. The Amsterdam consistory had excommunicated him in 1594 following an adulterous affair, but when he approached the Delft consistory in 1598 asking for admittance and alms, it refused. Despite his appeals that he had done everything possible to conform to the community's standards and that he had repented and publicly confessed, the consistory would not allow him access to communion. His individual reputation, despite his now "troubled conscience," was spoiled enough that it would threaten the reputation of the community if he were allowed to participate in communion.

A similar situation in Emden yielded a different sequence of events. In 1567, after four years of excommunication for his adulterous affair, Rogier van Aetdael approached the Emden consistory to appeal for readmittance to communion. The ministers and elders agreed, but only if he would undergo a probationary period in which he met certain conditions in order to earn back his good reputation and demonstrate moral improvement. Three months later, however, the consistory ordered the deacons to withhold alms because he has "brought the other woman, the adulteress, here against our advice." After an additional three years of excommunication, Rogier came to Emden's consistory and "confessed with tears that he had fallen into the pit of damnation." This time – because of either the long excommunication or the withdrawal of alms or both – he followed the probationary plan and, unlike van Vijven in Delft, was readmitted to the congregation.

Those accused often made promises of future improvement in their moral behavior or agreed to undergo instruction, be it catechism, regular attendance at sermons, or personal consultation with the consistory or individual church officials. Peter de Messeler had already disassociated from the Emden congregation in a dispute over infant baptism; yet he continued criticize the church openly.[11] With an ongoing local Anabaptist threat, the Emden consistory wanted to quiet such public complaints. Despite his withdrawal from the congregation, Peter did appear before the consistory when called, but stressed "that he in his conscience cannot recognize infant baptism as a good thing, because the apostles did no such thing." The ministers and elders wanted to dispute with him and offer him instruction, but he said he had already heard their arguments and would only distance himself from his opinions if he were convinced by instruction directly out of God's word. The pastors agreed to Peter's terms and began such instruction with him, allowing him to set the parameters for the discussions.

Sometimes a self-deprecating response as an excuse could offer an accused person a middle position between formally acknowledging guilt and claiming innocence. Claims of ignorance, poverty, or some other deficiency might be seen as the best means of mitigating an assumption of intentionality when the accused was clearly confronted with undeniable misbehavior. Françoise Loup, for example, appeared before Geneva's consistory in 1542 to account for her continued use of traditional Catholic prayers and words while not knowing the current confession. She answered that she could not retain the words of the preacher despite her attendance at sermons: "her maid indeed says that she has a poor head, and she knows well that she has a poor head and would not know how to pray to God except in the manner that her father and mother taught her, and would not know how to speak otherwise."[12] She attempted to beg off remedial instruction by telling the consistory that it was therefore "too late to teach her" the Lord's Prayer and that she behaved only as a "respectable woman" and thus did not offend Christ with her behavior. Nevertheless, the consistory ordered that she be forbidden communion at the next service and that she report back to the consistory to demonstrate her progress.[13] Such excuses do not appear to have reduced culpability in the eyes of some consistories, but seem intended by the accused to soften the appearance of deliberate misbehavior.

Consistory leaders expected that members of the congregation be in the proper state of mind when participating in communion. Not only did they order people not to partake until they had reconciled or resolved any disciplinary problem; many church members apparently had internalized the norms and voluntarily abstained from communion because they were in conflict with others. They might explain the particular conflict or fight when they were called by the consistory to account for their recent absence. Of course, it is not possible to know the extent to which such justifications were sincere or how much this excuse was simply recognized as a potentially legitimate explanation and thus accepted. The case of Jacques Pape before Geneva's consistory in 1548 certainly raises questions about such calculations. Accused of multiple misbehaviors including frequenting taverns, wasting his family's goods, and beating his wife, Pape was also asked if he had attended the previous sermon. He acknowledged that rather than going to Church that Sunday, he had gone outside the city gates to play a board game (*charret*) with several others. Confronted about not attending communion, however, Pape said he could not attend communion because he was still embroiled in a conflict with another man. It is unclear whether it was *charret* or his proper frame of mind that kept him from communion; nevertheless, Pape obviously knew which excuse the consistory would find more acceptable.

Even if the elders sometimes questioned the sincerity of the accused, the consistory's ongoing negotiations indicate its willingness to try to bring about improvement. Yet, subsequent reports occasionally indicate that people had been disingenuous in their promises or perhaps guilty of outright dissimulation in their interactions with the consistory. When Marquet Du Jusse appeared with his wife before Geneva's consistory in 1556, she had clearly been beaten about her face. Thus, it becomes apparent that Du Jusse had had difficulty keeping his prior promises to the consistory in 1548 and 1552 to improve his behavior regarding domestic violence. Perhaps the consistory's threat to turn the couple over to the Small Council if he continued in this way had more lasting impact this time.

When William, a blind singer, was called before the Emden consistory for an admonition against his bawdy songs, he made an economic appeal: that if they forbad him from such music, he would become dependent on congregational alms.[14] For a decade, he kept his promises to avoid "great misbehavior" in social gatherings, but in the midst several further complaints about his songs ten years later, William stressed that he did not know any other calling through which he could "nourish himself in a godly manner." After several of these interactions, the consistory finally ordered William to avoid absolutely all playing, and they promised to maintain him and not leave his household in any distress. The following week, William had confessed his sins of frivolous playing at lewd dances, promising never to do such things anymore. According to the surviving records, William's promise this time seems to have held.

Consistory records provide numerous examples of individuals whose testimony changed over the course of discussions or as new witnesses appeared. When caught in lies, the accused could either apologize and beg for mercy or sometimes double down with accusations against others. Du Jusse and Blind William might have intended to keep their promises and simply fell back into old habits, but in other cases, the shifting stories or answers provided by the accused indicate a lack of clarity in their minds regarding certain religious questions. These consistory cases could even imply that the accused were dissembling about their beliefs. For example, subsequent events make it clear that Dutch refugees Andries de Braekcer and Jan Cuels claimed various beliefs over a short period of time when the Wesel consistory inquired into their Anabaptist beliefs. Braecker had been a Mennonite before arriving in Wesel. He initiated contact with the Calvinist consistory in 1573 in order to make a confession of faith. The consistory asked if Anabaptism "still troubled" him, to which he offered a simple, "No," and the consistory accepted him with full membership. A mere three months later, Braecker refused to baptize his infant son, though the consistory did finally convince him. More seemingly dishonest in his conversion to Calvinism, the Mennonite Jan Cuels from Leuven married a Calvinist in Wesel in 1577.[15] He attempted to join the congregation, and, after receiving doctrinal instruction on points of contention, Cuels acknowledged his agreement with the Belgic Confession as read by the consistory with a straightforward, "Yes." He then sought the deacons' assistance in getting employment, but in less than a year, Cuels' finances had crumbled, he had left his new wife, and gone home for Amsterdam, where he promptly joined the Mennonite congregation. Such complicated interactions add to the fluid picture of what it meant for an individual to be a confessional adherent while still having religious questions or making compromises. The consistory accounts themselves leave us with an ambiguous understanding of the accused's motives or beliefs.

Of course, one might attempt to escape outright dishonesty by avoiding a direct answer. For instance, when the Geneva consistory asked Marguerite Benella in 1555 whether she was "still papist," she gave the less-than-direct response that she was a "good woman."[16] Marguerite's reply to the main charge that had brought her before the consistory – that "she had played *chez elle* with her servants on Sundays, even during the sermons" – leads us into the most widespread category of nonconforming responses to consistorial charges: the denial. She admitted that she had "certainly seen them playing but denied that it was her."

Such denials of guilt ranged from outright repudiation of the charge, as with Marguerite, to claims of extenuating circumstances to more subtle arguments that the accusation was not really as bad as it seemed. The aforementioned Du Jusse admitted to abusing his wife, but he attempted to justify his wife's bruised face by arguing that she constantly provoked him when she knew he was without money. Similarly François Bonivard understood the biblical mandate that wives obey their husbands, and when called before the Geneva consistory in 1548, he admitted beating her but justified it by stating she had ignored his order to stop visiting a particular man. Such an excuse by an accused as part of the narrative presented to the consistory could offer some mitigation, as the Geneva accepted the explanation as Bonivard's justification for the beating and ordered the wife to obey her husband.

The accused could also downplay the seriousness of the offense or even claim ignorance. The same Bonivard appears in 1543 providing a whole series of excuses to offset a consistorial accusation of gambling. First, he claimed ignorance that some of his games were inappropriate: "It is true that he played checkers as others do publicly, and he had not heard that dice games had been forbidden."[17] Second, he did not create any public problems: he "never played except with respectable and lettered people."[18] And finally, Bonivard, now fifty years old, admitted playing certain games, but justified them as innocuous and necessary pastimes: "that he plays to pass the time a little because of his old age."[19] Similar justifications arise frequently throughout the Genevan records, as when Pierre Truffet answered the consistory by saying "that he has to have fun, and he gambles only for drinks."[20]

Given the number of cases involving long-running negotiations over discipline, it is clear that consistories paid attention to appeals to extenuating circumstances. Particularly common explanations included pleas to one's poverty or illness or family circumstances. The widow Claudaz Dechallon said that she attends the sermons the best that she can in her poverty since she must work for herself and her children.[21] The Genevan locksmith Claude Vuarin explained his poor church attendance on the fact "he must work for himself and his father who is ill."[22]

Church officials also generally took seriously appeals to one's conscience and sought to offer convincing instruction to the accused. Oliver van der Vinct interacted often with Wesel's consistory throughout 1574 regarding his rejection of infant baptism. While the elders were willing to entertain his theological discussions, Oliver maintained that infant baptism was not biblical. He was also annoyed by their response to his question if "he should baptize his son in the established church, in order to avoid the anger of the brothers, even though it was against his conscience?" The Wesel elders acknowledged that they did not want to force him to violate his conscience, but, they went on, by maintaining his position, Oliver had shown that "he did not know what a conscience was, because if he had once tasted it he would not have spoken so." Oliver, the consistory reported, took that statement "very badly," and he went on to describe Reformed infant baptism as "papist superstition." Even though negotiations were deteriorating, Oliver continued to exercise agency, indeed repeatedly postponing issuing a formal written statement as requested by the consistory. Finally, after months of refusing to give into Wesel's consistory over his refusal to baptize his infant son, Oliver van der Vinct suddenly and curiously reversed himself, offering a Reformed confession of faith and promising to bring his child to be baptized. What seems to have changed was the threat of the case being taken over by the town council for his punishment as an Anabaptist (including expulsion and confiscation of property). For its part, however, the Wesel consistory was not fully convinced of Oliver's conversion and it continued to monitor his behavior: in the coming years, Oliver seems to have avoided open opposition to the church while not fully conforming.[23] Thus, making a sincere appeal to conscience might buy one some time and discussion with the consistory even if it might not allow the accused's position to triumph.

Those accused might also blame someone else. Such was the case with Hermann Tymmermann when he and his wife were banned by the Emden consistory in 1578 over a business deal gone bad, in which he blamed the situation entirely on his son having been defrauded and misled.[24] When the consistory refused to accept his argument, he turned to the civic leadership, which seemed more sympathetic to his claims, as he now accused the consistory of misconduct.

By testifying against others, people could create ill will with their neighbors or family. Of course, such reporting on others to the consistory could also stem from preexisting quarrels, settling scores, and business (or romantic) rivalries. The aforementioned case of Jehan Mouri shows that the accused could try to discredit their accusers by claiming that false allegations had been made to the consistory in an attempt to settle a score. While Aimé Rivilliod quickly confessed to fathering a child with his maid, he vehemently denied the additional rumors that he was related to the woman; these rumors of incest, he insisted, had been orchestrated by one of his rivals, who was paying witnesses to testify against him.[25] The case of François Du Frêney and his wife Claudine had been going on before Geneva's consistory for at least nine months with François seeking a divorce because of Claudine's "vicious behavior" involving affairs and pregnancies despite their being separated.[26] Finally in September 1552, Claudine "begged for mercy" to the consistory, which then admonished François, asking "whether he does not want to be reconciled with his wife"; Claudine, for her part, "promised to reform and be obedient to him." François responded, however, that "he would rather abandon the country and be drawn and quartered," and he again asked the consistory for divorce. Now, Claudine decided to settle a score with a scandalous accusation of her own: after having just demurely promised obedience, she made the new scandalous charge that François had slept with his sister and that she had witnesses. Particularly in more protracted cases, a variety of strategies used by the accused person becomes clear as circumstances shifted between the various parties.

As several examples have illustrated, one did not need to be a prominent figure like Bonivard in Geneva, since many poorer members of society were willing to boldly assert their needs and aggressively interact with the consistory. The Emden consistory's imposition of conditions for Anne Jeronimus's poor relief created enough frustration in 1561–1562 that she was twice summoned and admonished for her "blasphemous speech," yet she continued to approach them with requests for support.[27] In 1578 Lenaert Pieterszoon approached the Delft consistory to complain of his inadequate charity allowance; he returned two years later to make the same complaint. When Margeriete Brans had a similar complaint about her alms provision, she ultimately got the consistory's attention by threatening to leave Delft for Catholic Ghent. A week after the Delft consistory prevented Jan Michielssen from partaking in communion due to his public drunkenness, he returned to the consistory to ask them for a large loan. As discussed at the opening of this chapter, Proene and Jacob were willing to confront and accuse the Emden consistory, holding out threats to leave the congregation, which was of course one alternative for avoiding church discipline. Yet resistance is not the same thing as obstinate rejection of a consistory's discipline. Still, the additional connections between discipline and charitable relief complicated the strategies of those on the margins of poverty.

An indication of the limited power of intimidation by the Genevan consistory can be found in the derision expressed by Estienne Tacet in 1563 when it was indicated that he would have to account for his antisocial behavior of grabbing a woman while arguing with her and holding her head between his legs in order to pass gas on her: "What business are my farts to the consistory?"[28] Similarly, it is significant that people from across the social spectrum were willing to complain to and about the consistory. Even those in subordinate positions were not inherently unwilling to confront or question the consistory. A servant, Michée, who in 1556 was alleged to hold Catholic beliefs particularly regarding the Mass, boldly replied to the Genevan consistory that "she does not think that it matters at all because one can be certain of nothing."[29]

The recent interest in and growing accessibility of Calvinist consistory minutes has provided scholars much greater opportunity to examine the nature of Reformed church discipline with a sharper eye on the recipients or targets of the discipline. The fact that the minutes recorded the surviving accounts from the perspective of the consistorial officers raises interpretive problems. Yet, while it is necessary to weigh the value of the accounts, they nonetheless offer a cursory glimpse into the agency of those accused before the consistory, allowing perceptions that go beyond the simple characterization of top-down Calvinist discipline. Even in cases where consistorial discipline was successfully administered, it is not clear whether the parties involved genuinely reconciled or went through the motions of conformity. Likewise, censured members offered a wide range of excuses, some more successfully than others. Without rather structured legal procedures or the guidance of defense attorneys provided in inquisitorial proceedings, the actions of an accused before a consistory can appear even more individualized. Yet Reformed congregants could certainly be aware of typical rhetorical responses that might allow them to meet consistorial expectations. With individual strategies contingent on particular circumstances, it is impossible to establish broad, simple characteristics to describe a clearly defined set of categories. Nevertheless, whatever one thinks about the nature of social control and consistorial discipline, those subject to such discipline were often not passive victims. Thus, the records document people arguing, repenting, accusing, and explaining to the consistory, in ways far more complicated than the simple categories of submission or resistance.

Notes

1 *Die Kirchenratsprotokolle der reformierten Gemeinde Emden 1557–1620*, 2 vols., ed. Heinz Schilling and Klaus-Dieter Schreiber (Cologne, 1989, 1992), 1:112 (May 27, 1560) (hereafter *KRP*).

2 *KRP*, 1:114, 119, 124, and 130–1.

3 *KRP*, 1:159 (February 22, 1563).

4 Archive of Johannes a Lasco Bibliothek, Emden (hereafter a Lasco Bibliothek), *Fremdlingen Diakone Rechnungsbuch*, I (1558–68), folios 50v, 67v.

5 *KRP*, 1:195, 197, 212–14, 220–2, 227, 233–4, 240, 244, and 250.

6 *Registres du Consistoire de Genève au temps de Calvin*, 7 vols., ed. Thomas A. Lambert, Isabella M. Watt, Robert M. Kingdon, Jeffrey R. Watt (Geneva, 1996–2012), 7: 29, 31, and 35 (March 24, March 31, April 7, 1552).

7 John Witte, Jr. and Robert M. Kingdon, *Sex, Marriage, and Family in John Calvin's Geneva: Courtship, Engagement, and Marriage* (Grand Rapids, 2005), 230, and 251–3.

8 Witte and Kingdon, *Sex, Marriage, and Family*, 207,215–16; and *Registres du Consistoire de Genève au temps du Calvin*, vol. 3, 1547–8, ed. Thomas A. Lambert and Isabella M. Watt (Geneva, 2004), 178, 183.

9 *Registres du Consistoire de Genève au temps du Calvin*, vol. 1, 1542–4, ed. Thomas A. Lambert and Isabella M. Watt (Geneva, 1996), 352 (April 8, 1544); and *Registers of the Consistory of Geneva in the Time of Calvin*, vol. 1, 1542–4, ed. Isabella M. Watt and Thomas A. Lambert (Grand Rapids, 2000), 377.

10 *Registres du Consistoire*, 1:135 (2 November 1542); and *Registers of the Consistory*, 143.

11 *KRP*, 1:466 (January 16 and 26, 1573).

12 *Registres du Consistoire*, 1:138 (November 16, 1542); *Registers of the Consistory*, 145–6.

13 *Registres du Consistoire*, 1:156; *Registers of the Consistory*, 164.

14 Timothy Fehler, *Poor Relief and Protestantism* (Brookfield, VT, 1999), 256–8.

15 Jesse Spohnholz, *The Tactics of Toleration: A Refugee Community in the Age of Religious Wars* (Newark, 2011), 152–3.

16 *Registres du Conistoire* (Archives d'Etat de Genève) 10, f. 43 (July 26, 1555).

17 *Registres du Consistoire*, 1:288; *Registers of the Consistory*, 306.

18 *Registres du Consistoire*, 1:289; *Registers of the Consistory*, 307–8.

19 *Registres du Consistoire*, 1: 288; *Registers of the Consistory*, 307.

20 *Registres du Consistoire*, 1:362; *Registers of the Consistory*, 388.

21 *Registres du Consistoire*, 1:143 (November 23, 1542); *Registers of the Consistory*, 151.

22 *Registres du Consistoire*, 1:133–4 (October 26, 1542); *Registers of the Consistory*, 141.

23 Spohnholz, *Tactics of Toleration*, 153–7.

24 a Lasco Bibliothek (Emden), Nellner #501, 13 (May 13, 1578).

25 *Registres du Consistoire de Genève au temps du Calvin*, vol. 2, 1545–6, ed. Thomas A. Lambert, Isabella M. Watt, and Wallace McDonald (Geneva, 2001), 326, 334, 338. Witte and Kingdon, *Sex, Marriage, and Family*, 324, 342–3 (November 11, November 25, December 2, 1546).

26 Witte and Kingdon, *Sex, Marriage, and Family*, 327–8, 350–2 (December 31, 1551, January 7, June 9, June 30, August 25, September 8, September 29, October 13, 1552). *Registres du Consistoire de Genève au temps du Calvin*, vol. 6, 1551–2, ed. Isabella M. Watt and Jeffrey Watt (Geneva, 2012), 227, and 230; and *Registres du Consistoire*, 7:90, 100, 132, 148, 153, and 160.

27 Fehler, *Poor Relief and Protestantism*, 170–1.

28 Jeffrey R. Watt, "Settling quarrels and nurturing repentance: the Consistory in Calvin's Geneva," in ed. S. K. Barker, *Revisiting Geneva: Robert Kingdon and the Coming of the French Wars of Religion*, St Andrews Studies in French History and Culture (St Andrews, 2012), 75–6.

29 *Registres du Consistoire*, 11 (March 31, 1556).

15

Inquisitions

Lu Ann Homza

From a certain angle, scholars of Inquisitions always have been transfixed by the individuals they have seen as "interesting" defendants. Unlike their counterparts who study Protestant consistories, Inquisition historians have fixed on the single cases of provocative suspects since at least the nineteenth century, when Marcelino Menéndez y Pelayo used infamous trials to help trace the challenges to Spanish Catholicism in the early modern period. In the first decades of the twentieth century, Spanish bibliophiles published documentary extracts about celebrated defendants in the *Revista de Archivos, Bibliotecas, y Museos*; in the 1940s and 1950s, a more international group studied individuals whose cases they found unusual or symbolic, or both. Some years later, talented investigators devoted literally decades to studying monumental figures who were prosecuted – also for decades – by either the Spanish or Roman Inquisitions, such as Archbishop Bartolomé Carranza, or Cardinal Giovanni Moroni.

These scholars knew their subjects' trials inside and out. Still, rather than illuminating defense options according to the charges or examining and contextualizing defense rhetoric, they often preferred to transform their defendants into heroes who exemplified timeless moral courage or to prove that their subjects never were guilty of the heresy with which they were charged. Then, the field changed: after Francisco Franco's death in 1975, Inquisition scholarship in Spain headed in a statistical direction, as investigators began to count victims and plumb the Inquisition's structural, institutional history. Investigators of the Portuguese Inquisition experienced a similar liberation, in the sense of being free to ask new questions and read new sources, after the end of the Salazar dictatorship in 1974. Notably, though, the emphasis on victims did not translate into a focus on legal defenses, because scholars engaged in this new track were more concerned with the quantities and identities of the persecuted and whether those quantities and identities changed over time. Yet in a fascinating sort of dialectical movement, by the early 1990s, interest in social history, anthropological attention to local environments, and the Italians' invention of microhistory meant that investigators once again were zeroing in on single trials, though they now wanted their cases to speak to larger concerns about the early modern world.

Unlike an earlier generation, the scholars who carried out Inquisition microhistories generally were not concerned with righting injustices of the historical record or proving the protomodernity of their subjects, though critics pointed out that the risk of anachronism was inherent in micro-history as a genre. Instead, their best efforts produced a heightened awareness of what was possible in legal situations, as well as a more subtle understanding of the ways in which legal processes, and religious and political priorities, might interact on the ground level. Yet if micro-historians also knew the defenses of their subjects backwards and for-wards, they too tended not to comment on larger trends among defendants or across charges, even though their understanding of Inquisition procedure allowed them to detect when the accused were responding to clues in questioning, and to describe how suspects were engaging in a sort of negotiation with prosecutors and prosecution witnesses.

Over the last 150 years, then, we have seen close readings of Inqui-sition cases ebb and flow: they have gone in and out of fashion, with different priorities and motivations on the part of their authors. In order to be persuasive, such close readings imply – indeed, require – attention to every aspect of a prosecution. But no matter what the epoch, more often than not, suspects' defenses have been treated in isolation from each other. For instance, both Italian Cardinal Giovanni Morone (arrested 1557) and Spanish Archbishop Bartolomé Carranza (arrested 1559) exonerated themselves with historical evidence: Morone produced caches of letters to verify his concern with Lutheran heresy while he was bishop of Modena in the 1540s; Carranza's witnesses adduced one anecdote after another to prove he had never encouraged Protestantism in either England or Spain in the early 1550s. Significantly, neither of the master-scholars who investigated Morone and Carranza ever cross-referenced their subjects' defensive strategies. Of course, historians very often prefer to proceed from induction rather than deduction, but our general hesita-tion to draw bigger conclusions is remarkable when it comes to

Inquisition defendants. After all, if inquisitors shared a common legal and intellectual culture which helped them assess proof, it is not so farfetched to imagine that individuals who found themselves on the wrong side of Catholic doctrine and morality would also have been able to summon talking points they believed would be persuasive against their prosecutors. Understanding what the Inquisition was and what inquisitors did was not out of reach for the average inhabitant of Portugal, Italy, and Spain because the Inquisition's infamous policy of secrecy took years to take hold in Portuguese and Roman practice, Inquisition manuals in Spain were printed in the vernacular, and defendants everywhere transmitted information inside and outside of Inquisition jails.

In fact, our hesitation about extrapolating defense strategies to larger conclusions may be due to long-standing skepticism about whether Inquisition suspects had any chance of a defense at all. Earlier scholars such as Henry Charles Lea were convinced that the Inquisitions' offer of a defense was straightforward fraud because defense lawyers were paid by the court itself and enjoined to secure confessions; even into the 1980s, it is difficult to find a historical study that regarded an Inquisition defense as deliberate or effective. Scholars have viewed defendants as so paralyzed with fear, and at such a legal disadvantage, that they very often have treated questions of strategy as out of bounds. But our outlook is changing. More recent work acknowledges that while inquisitors "theoretically" controlled the circumstances and produced the documents, it also finds spaces in the legal process where defendants' own voices could emerge. Defendants did not always follow the legal script, either in terms of content or procedure: where Lea saw only helpless victims, we now are more convinced that the accused's defense was a concoction of rhetorical commonplaces leavened with individual circumstances and priorities, as well as reactions to prosecutors' mistakes. There is no doubt that defendants could be guided by leading questions, but they did not simply, or exclusively, parrot back what inquisitors wanted to hear.

Because any particular defendant's combination of experience, assertion, cliché, and reaction was so individualized, it is not possible, in my opinion, to quantify Inquisition defenses in a persuasively numerical way. Though some defendants may have unequivocally submitted to or resisted the prosecution, large categories of that kind do not capture the subtleties of the Inquisition sources, any more than they do consistory records. Defenses in Inquisition trials contain too many variables, in too many combinations, to be reflected accurately in percentages. Nor do the surviving records lend themselves to quantification by virtue of their format, since prosecutors could add charges at will as trials progressed, and defendants could make endless appearances and statements before their cases were closed. As researchers, we cannot be sure we have captured every detail when we are working with manuscript sources that often run to hundreds of folios; even if we were sure of the specifics, we still would run into problems of categorization. Hence the remarks that follow depend upon qualitative readings that I nonetheless wish to draw toward larger insights, albeit not statistical ones.

Every accused person before an Inquisition court knew that the core of the defense was to prove one's Catholic Christianity. As was the case with consistories, Inquisition defendants too produced tears and repentance. But the Inquisition in Italy, Portugal, and Spain had legal procedures to guide the defense and hence, to circumscribe its content. For example, inquisitors always were supposed to make room for a defendant's confession, in which the accused could explain the misdeed, offer mitigating circumstances, and promise to reform. For example, when Pedro de Villegas was arrested for Judaizing in Ciudad Real in 1483, he was charged both with eating meat during Lent and consuming unleavened bread during Passover. Villegas responded that he had suffered an accident in his work and was allowed to consume meat when it was customarily forbidden, thereby contextualizing one of his alleged offenses by mentioning a past event about which, luckily, there was public talk.[1] When Catalina Díaz came to the Toledo tribunal to confess her blasphemy in 1543, she explained that her swearing ensued from a personal conflict with a neighbor, which others had witnessed; the inquisitors in her case took seriously the circumstances of the offense as well as her sorrow in having committed it.[2]

Even while it presumed guilt, the Inquisition process also allowed two other attempts at exculpation. If the accused wished to combat the charges, they could construct a list of questions, called an interrogatory, for character witnesses; in answering the queries, ideally the defendants' orthodox Catholicism would be attested. The same witnesses could contradict the prosecutor's assertions about heretical behavior. The accused also were permitted to try to "stain" (*tachar*) the prosecution's witnesses with charges of incapability, prejudice, or capital enmity because trials were not supposed to admit the testimony of individuals who wanted the accused dead or had motives to injure them. In the most perfect form of Inquisition procedure, the identities of prosecution witnesses were supposed to be kept secret from the defendant, but in sodomy cases in Aragon, the early period of Inquisition practice in

Portugal, and the first decade of Inquisition practice in Italy, defendants were allowed to know the identities of their accusers. Obviously, such knowledge made the recusation of witnesses, and an effective defense, that much easier to achieve, at least in principle. Nevertheless, heresy trials conducted by Inquisitions allowed a much wider range and quality of witnesses than prosecutions handled by secular authorities and by bishops, including confessed heretics, persons of bad repute (*mala fama*), and underage minors.

Producing character witnesses who would help the defense's case meant naming, as far as possible, older individuals with substantial public reputations who had known the defendant for some length of time. Though the Inquisition accepted less-than-ideal witnesses, they were not "preferred" by either the prosecution or the defense, which does not mean they were not occasionally employed. One of the ways in which Pedro Villegas foiled the charge of Judaizing was by calling middle-aged men of long acquaintance and recognized status to verify his Christian acts and Saturday work habits: luckily for him, he was well-liked by Franciscan friars, parish priests, and fellow weavers, all of whom had known him for more than a decade.[3] Defendants who were new to the community could find it much more difficult to bring forth witnesses who could relay their Christian behavior in believable detail. Deponents who said they "did not know" whether the accused observed feastdays or prayed were not helpful. Sometimes, too, the very interrogatory to which the witnesses were responding could go awry, especially if it included questions about opportunity or intention. In 1494, multiple defense witnesses for Marina González noted that while they had always seen only Christian behavior on her part, she could have acted otherwise if she had so desired.[4]

Significantly, the other defense route available – the disqualification of prosecution witnesses, whose identity had to be guessed rightly by the accused – was also more likely to be successful if the defendant had lived for enough time in one place, or had enough experience in a career, to experience social and economic conflict and thereby create enemies. For example, Marina González's husband attempted to stain witnesses via hatreds that arose from a refusal to extend charity and a rebuke of a sister-in-law for sexual misconduct.[5] Archbishop Carranza successfully recused the Spanish Inquisitor General by documenting the latter's animosity toward him: before his own arrest, Carranza had chastised the Inquisitor General's absenteeism from his diocese in Seville, trapped him into loaning money to King Philip II, and argued for adding theologians to the *Suprema* when the Inquisitor General wanted lawyers.[6]

Suspects who decided they were going to fight the charges, rather than confess, very often spent a good proportion of their defense attempting to disqualify every person they could imagine as a prosecution witness. For instance, after Antonio de Medrano was arrested by the Spanish Inquisition in 1526, he attempted to stain possible deponents against him on the grounds that some were known publicly to be mentally unstable, while others had conspired to take away his ecclesiastical benefices.[7] Of course, simply listing one's opponents was not enough to get their testimony excluded: rather, a defendant not only had to know people who could attest the hostility, but individuals who verified the conflict had to be of sufficient personal weight or sufficiently numerous to make an impact. When Archbishop Carranza challenged the Inquisitor General's ability to monitor his trial fairly, it was no accident that he named as witnesses famous preachers, well-placed academics, and respected members of religious orders.

Eventually, and broadly speaking, the Inquisition in Spain, Portugal, and Italy shared the same structural ingredients: hence, defendants could be expected to use the same general tactics of confession, character witnesses, and recusal on the grounds of enmity. But there were a few other strategies as well that they could employ, which might be more or less effective, depending upon the circumstances. Defendants sometimes would claim that their actions were sanctioned by other religious authorities: when accused of love magic or superstitious healing, they might reply that they had used only customary prayers authorized by the Church itself. If, as women, they drew public attention for their piety and seemed to be elevating their own sanctity, they could insist they were merely following the example of St. Catherine of Siena. If they had eminent connections, they could position them as a counterweight to alleged misdeeds: thus Maria de Cazalla invoked the counsel of her brother, a Franciscan friar, to try to mitigate the charges against her.[8] Meanwhile, Juan de Vergara, secretary to the archbishops of Toledo, tried to trump the inquisitors' version of proper religious behavior by referring explicitly to the different practices of his episcopal friends.[9] Such tactics were not limited to one sex or the other.

At the same time, and unlike their consistory counterparts, no Inquisition suspect could have expected to benefit by threatening to leave the congregation: on the contrary, a promise to depart Catholic Navarre for, say, Calvinist Geneva, would only have worked to cement proof of heresy in the inquisitors' eyes. In another difference from consistory settings, an Inquisition defendant who was a parish priest might try to claim that the relevant bishop should be hearing the case instead of the local Inquisition tribunal. Then there were defendants who not only refused to confess but declined to cooperate with the system, or at least did their best to inhibit its processes. Some rejected calling a character witness or identifying potentially hostile deponents; others waited as long as possible before submitting written replies to the prosecutor's charges.

Flooding a tribunal with paper was a complementary strategy. Sometimes, the accused would pelt the inquisitors with one petition after another, which objected to botched ratifications of witness testimony, claimed that time limits for proof had been overlooked, and raised every other imaginable misstep in the law. Some defendants attempted suicide.[10] In conformity with Inquisition handbooks, those who went on hunger strikes received medical attention; afterwards, doctors testified before the tribunal as to whether a prisoner's neglect of food was intentional or the result of an illness. Inquisitors treated suicidal intent as a sign of the guilt that already was presumed, and reacted as if it were a defense strategy, as if the accused were trying to escape just punishment, though they also were supposed to prevent suicides to the best of their ability. Another way to halt the process, in another possibly injurious way, was to escape the tribunal's jail, or kill the jailer and burn the documentation. In Venice, Abraham Righetto broke loose twice between 1572 and 1573.[11] In 1532, Francisco Ortiz overheard his peers plot to assassinate the Inquisition prison warden in Toledo; the fact that he did not turn them in added to his guilt in the inquisitors' eyes.[12]

Self-injury, murder, and arson aside, techniques such as petitions, complaints, and general noncooperation delayed the trial process and left inquisitors conducting more question-and-answer sessions in hopes of a confession. Such holdups could be to the defendant's advantage if he had contacts inside or outside the tribunal jail who could discover and then transmit information about prosecution witnesses. The more a defendant knew about the prosecutor's deponents, the more likely he would be able to find a way to challenge them. In keeping with this general rule, jailed suspects very often found ways to communicate with each other via holes in prison walls, or through messages carried by servants from one cell to another. If their communication was detected, they might contend they were engaging in spiritual consolation, but to our eyes, and to the inquisitors', it seemed equally plausible that they were consulting over each other's cases.

Though it would have shocked Henry Charles Lea, it is certain that some defense lawyers in the Inquisition system worked assiduously to protect their clients and were very good at their job, despite being court-appointed. The delaying strategies mentioned earlier – especially claims of malpractice and innumerable petitions – seem to have originated with, or at least been endorsed by, some advocates for the defense. Figures such as Licenciado Quemada defended María Cazalla, Luis de Beteta, Rodrigo de Bivar the Elder, and his son, Rodrigo de Bivar the Younger, throughout the 1530s and again in the early 1550s. Quemada was highly effective: none of these particular clients suffered significant penalties.[13]

Of course, in no way is the relative success of defense lawyers going to make the Inquisition system more benign or fair in modern eyes, and it did not in early modern opinion, either. Nor is it ever going to be possible for us to sort out exactly which defense techniques originated with an advocate as opposed to the accused, unless we are lucky enough to discover unmediated transcriptions of conversations or plans between a lawyer and his client, something the Inquisition system tried to prevent. It is important, however, to be open to the possibility of collaboration between defendant and attorney in the Inquisition because the phenomenon heightens our appreciation of the legal knowledge, and the opposition, that was exerted in Inquisition courtrooms and prisons. Along the same lines, I would never suggest that defendants were simply mimicking their lawyers, any more than their speech acts were cued solely by their interrogators. The most plausible approach here is also the most intricate: despite being counseled by advocates or incited by prosecutors, Inquisition defendants very often had time and opportunity in their written and oral statements to initiate, expand, and redirect their attempts to prove themselves innocent.

It seems obvious that charges must have affected defenses because such heresies as Judaizing, blasphemy, and false sanctity involved different offensive actions. Provocatively, though, divergence across crimes was more subtle than I anticipated; unsurprisingly, age, sex, and class also entered into the mix as the accused tried to turn biographical particulars to their advantage. Intention always mattered: someone could accidentally read Martin Luther, accidentally marry for a second time because a spouse appeared to have died in Peru, and accidentally eat meat on a Catholic feast day. Occupations and pastimes counted: blasphemy was more explicable when it occurred with a losing round of cards or a ripped fishing net. Learned suspects could pitch their knowledge against prosecutors' when it came to theological details: intellectuals commonly quoted scriptural incipits as they explained and excused their alleged deviation from Catholic doctrine. Young defendants could imply that they had been misled by their parents, a possibility explicitly recognized by Inquisition manuals, whereas older ones could maintain they had never been instructed. A young woman accused of Judaizing could claim she had been told to follow Jewish rites by her brothers-in-law or some other older relative, and thereby exhibit feminine obedience as well as highlight her youth. Others could invoke subtle stereotypes about their own sex's perfidy and imply that they were persuaded into Mosaic Law via converted women (*conversas*) who were "wicked Christians." Women accused of false sanctity, of indulging in spiritual visions and advice for the sake of fame, could comment on their friendships with local religious authorities, and consequently demonstrate submission and permission all at once. Priests who blasphemed were better off if they were uneducated; the same held for individuals who spread or endorsed Lutheran errors because the Inquisition treated ignorance seriously as an extenuating factor. Given the tremendous interest in the law exhibited by all Spaniards of all social and economic classes in the early modern period, the fact that Inquisition suspects understood what legal buttons to push in their own defense is almost to be expected.

And yet, the most reliable way to avoid the worst Inquisition punishments – galley service and death at the stake – was immediately and straightforwardly to confess with as many mitigating circumstances and proofs of Christianity as a defendant could summon. Thus the question remains as to *why* any accused individuals pursued any alternative to confession, especially if the offense for which they were arrested was their first. The answer would seem to lie in honor and conscience. Like defendants before a consistory, the accused in an Inquisition courtroom fervently wished to avoid even milder Inquisition punishments, which could consist of imprisonment, public penances (and hence public disgrace), and private enclosure in a monastery or convent for re-education. Honor was just as much in play for Inquisition defendants as consistorial ones: despite the Inquisition's rule of secrecy, which prohibited the revelation of what went on in the Inquisition's jails and courts, the community knew when suspects were taken into custody, and it saw or heard what happened when the convicted were released.

As to whether Inquisition suspects explicitly invoked their consciences in their defense, as was very often the case for their consistory peers, the answer is mixed. We know that some accused figures strongly referred to their consciences when they already had been sentenced to death and had nothing more to lose. We also know that references to conscience in Inquisition cases were made across class and gender lines.

Yet it is doubtful whether many Inquisition suspects referred purely to their conscience when defending themselves: instead, their reliance on and belief in their judgment occurred in combination with other, more deferential statements. For example, in the 1530s, María de Cazalla contended she had the right to read the works of Desiderius Erasmus until the Church pronounced otherwise: she thereby fused current discernment with future obedience. In a similar instance, professors from the University of Salamanca argued in the 1570s that the prosecutor was too ignorant to understand their work and then defended their Catholic intentions when they were on trial for elevating the importance of Hebrew scripture and the Old Testament. Francisco Ortiz simply *knew* that his female spiritual director was sent from God.[14] When a Carthusian friar was arrested in Toledo for preaching Lutheran errors, he maintained there were only two sacraments, baptism and the Lord's Supper; he also contended that purgatory was a fraud. Because he then was reconciled by the Toledo tribunal, he must have expressed some degree of repentance for his heretical utterances; nevertheless, after he found himself in the galleys, he tried once again to convert the people around him, who were his fellow rowers. He was sent to the Granada tribunal for trial and executed as a relapsed heretic.[15]

Whether that Carthusian friar consistently believed in Lutheran theology throughout his ordeal is anyone's guess, but it seems clear he was not overawed by the Inquisition. He was not unique. There is evidence that even poor and uneducated defendants were not inevitably terrorized into submission by Inquisition courtrooms and sentences, not only because they answered the prosecution in argumentative ways, but because they practiced and voiced allegedly heretical acts and words after the Inquisition had condemned the same. For example, in the 1520s, male disciples of Isabel de la Cruz ignored warnings and even edicts against illuminism (*alumbradismo*): they not only continued to revere Isabel and promote her talents as a spiritual seer, but openly defied religious superiors who questioned their judgment. Such rebellion was not limited to the Inquisition's earliest decades, nor was it seen only in men.

The meaning of this kind of defiance is open to interpretation: disdain for authority, a sense of inviolability, trust in one's status and connections, religious conviction, or some sort of combination thereof. An appearance before an Inquisition court was never a casual experience, which is what makes attention to defendants so potentially riveting: their behaviors and statements allow us to see contestation – in a variety of guises, assisted by a variety of legal, social, and religious knowledge – against an institution dedicated to spiritual and moral discipline. Inquisition defenses, like consistory ones, establish that the quest to restrain and redirect in early modern Europe was never entirely successful. European Inquisitions did not control religious and intellectual culture in a hegemonic way, for all their modern reputation.

Notes

1 Lu Ann Homza, *The Spanish Inquisition, 1478–1614: An Anthology of Sources* (Indianapolis, 2006), 19, 22, and 23.
2 Homza, *The Spanish Inquisition*, 164–5.
3 Homza, *The Spanish Inquisition*, 17–26.
4 Homza, *The Spanish Inquisition*, 34–6.
5 Homza, *The Spanish Inquisition*, 40–1.
6 Homza, *The Spanish Inquisition*, 204.
7 Javier Perez Escohotado, *Proceso inquisitorial contra el Bachiller Antonio de Medrano* (Logroño, 1526–Calahorra, 1527) (Logroño, 1988), 84–5.
8 See defense statements in Milagros Ortega-Costa, *Proceso de la inquisición contra María de Cazalla* (Madrid, 1978).
9 Lu Ann Homza, *Religious Authority in the Spanish Renaissance* (Baltimore, 2000), ch. 1.
10 Guglielmo Marcocci, *I custodi dell'ortodossia. Inquisizione e Chiesa nel Portogallo del Cinquecento* (Rome: Edizioni di Storia e Letteratura, 2004), 121. Haim Beinart, *Records of the Trials of the Spanish Inquisition in Ciudad Real, 1483–1527* (Jerusalem, 1974–1985), 2:35–7.
11 Brian Pullan, "A Ship with Two Rudders: `Righetto Marrano' and the Inquisition in Venice," *The Historical Journal* 20 (1977): 25–58. For another two-time escapee, see Angela A. Selke, "Vida y muerte de Juan López Celain, alumbrado vizcaíno," *Bulletin Hispanique* 62 (1960): 36–162.
12 Lu Ann Homza, "How to Harass an Inquisitor-General: The Polyphonic Law of Friar Francisco Ortiz" in *A Renaissance of Conflicts: Visions and Revisions of Law and Society in Italy and Spain*, eds. John A. Marino and Thomas Kuehn (Toronto, 2004), 299–336.
13 For Cazalla, Ortega-Costa, *Proceso*; for Luis de Beteta, Archivo Histórico Nacional [AHN] Sección de la Inquisición, Legajo 102, n. 3; for the Bivars, AHN, Sección de la Inquisición, Legajo 213, n. 7; and Jesús Fernández Majolero, *Proceso inquisitorial a Rodrigo de Bivar, 'el mozo', clérigo de Santa María, 1553–1554* (Alcalá de Henares, 1989).
14 Homza, "How to Harass an Inquisitor-General," 299–336.
15 Homza, *The Spanish Inquisition*, 246.

Section G

Negotiating Penance

16

Consistories

Karen E. Spierling

In late 1558 and early 1559, the Genevan consistory repeatedly summoned Claude Dufour for having allowed his daughter to marry a Catholic man outside of Geneva. In his exchanges with the consistory, Dufour defended his decision as financially sound (it had "cost him nothing"), was suspended from the Lord's Supper, and later won readmittance to communion by repenting for having allowed the marriage.[1] But never during the four-month-long case did Dufour bring his daughter back to Geneva or force her to end her Catholic marriage. Dufour presumably would have preferred to avoid engagement with the consistory and suspension from communion, and consistory members clearly preferred that Dufour "do his duty" of "bringing his daughter back from the papistry."[2] Despite the imbalance of power inherent in the situation, the outcome was a negotiated compromise of sorts: Dufour was excommunicated, repented, and was declared a member in good standing, and his daughter continued to live elsewhere as a Catholic. Both sides got part of what they wanted; one might even argue that Dufour got more of what he wanted than the consistory did.

This case exemplifies one type of negotiation in which Reformed consistories engaged: not the wrangling of relatively equal powers across a negotiation table, but ongoing exchanges with variously imbalanced power dynamics, centered on differing priorities and resulting in some form of compromise. Across Europe, consistories' efforts to oversee the processes of repentance and reconciliation within their communities were shaped by several forms of negotiation. First, as Raymond Mentzer discusses in Chapter 1 of this volume, before they could enact or enforce Reformed discipline, consistories had to negotiate with secular authorities regarding their own existence, membership, authority, and limitations. A second negotiating process – the one most impenetrable to historians – is the deliberations among consistory members regarding case outcomes. Occasionally consistory records, especially if one is lucky enough to find a rough draft of minutes, contain voting tallies. But most registers provide only the consistory's final decision, omitting any evidence of the negotiation among consistory members that produced that conclusion.

In developing the theme of negotiating penance, this chapter will focus instead on two other crucial ways that consistories had to negotiate their goals in their communities. First, as in the case of Claude Dufour, consistories sometimes negotiated with the church members who appeared before them as transgressors or as witnesses to another's transgression. And secondly, to fully understand the importance of negotiation in the history of consistories, we must consider the role of consistories as arbitrators of community conflicts and as authorities who "displayed a marked preference for peacemaking rather than punishment."[3] While Reformed leaders viewed consistories as having the common, ultimate goal of preserving the purity of the body of the faithful gathered for communion, the achievement of this end depended upon a variety of different negotiations for each local consistory.

NEGOTIATING CONSISTORIES

From the start of modern work on Reformed disciplinary practices, scholars have recognized that consistories spent significant time negotiating resolutions to quarrels and "scandalous" disputes within their communities. In 1970, Solange Bertheau was already observing that in western France, consistories' concern to maintain "good relations among the faithful, marked by a truly Christian spirit" led them to intervene in familial and neighborly quarrels and to oversee public reconciliations to settle disputes.[4] In 1976, William Monter noted the significant presence of personal conflicts in the Genevan consistory's records but dismissed the gravity of this work, referring to such cases as "low-voltage affairs."[5] As Raymond Mentzer pointed out in Chapter 1, Robert Kingdon during the course of his long career moved toward a viewpoint that emphasized consistories' efforts at conciliation. Similarly, Andrew Pettegree, studying Protestant refugee churches in London insisted that historians needed to consider consistories' willingness to "advise, conciliate, or provide help for members in need."[6] It would take at least another decade, however, before scholars shifted significantly from describing interpersonal conflicts as "low-voltage affairs" or "minor cases" to asserting that such cases were at the core of the consistorial mission and represented consistories' "liveliest success." [7]

A critical juncture in this historiographical development came with Heinz Schilling's 1991 discussion of the "'criminalization of sin,'" which he defined as "the application of church discipline to other than the religious purposes which had formed its core."[8] Schilling viewed certain types of consistorial negotiation – in particular any sort of cooperation with civil authorities – as a degeneration of the consistories' *true* goals. The most pointed challenge to Schilling's distinction between crime and sin came in 1999 from Martin Ingram, who asserted: "In my view it makes better sense to try to understand the experiences of the majority in their own terms, rather than viewing them as a regrettable deviation from an ideal." He went on to say that the "ordinary people" who helped run ecclesiastical courts "were not passive receivers of church teachings, nor did they operate institutions in quite the same spirit as they were expected."[9] This point about "ordinary people" resonates deeply with findings regarding Reformed consistories across Europe, as does Ingram's insistence on not viewing consistorial practices merely as a disappointing "deviation from an ideal."[10]

Since the late 1990s, a variety of scholars have delved further into related questions regarding consistories' interactions and negotiations with state and local authorities, as well as with the members of their local communities. Some of this work has revealed the ways that consistories encountered resistance and set priorities in deciding how to deal with lay transgressors. Equally importantly, this developing conversation often emphasizes consistories' involvement in mediating local conflicts. A number of scholars have begun to analyze the ways that these peacemaking efforts built upon, rather than overturned, traditional avenues of mediation, asserting that an effective mediation role was critical to the overall success and acceptance of Reformed church discipline. Thus, the efforts of Reformed consistories to enforce Christian discipline in their communities always involved some degree of flexibility and willingness to negotiate in the pursuit of a godly, peaceful society.

NEGOTIATING *PENANCE*?

Before examining the variety of ways that consistories engaged in negotiations, it is crucial to address the question: Were Reformed consistories, in fact, negotiating *penance?* The aim of Reformed consistories and kirk sessions certainly was not the Roman Catholic concept of penance: Reformed theologians rejected the idea that penance was a sacrament; consistories did not see themselves as having the power to absolve sins; and Reformed doctrine did not teach that a sinner's acts of penance were required by God for entrance into heaven. Instead, Reformed theologians such as John Calvin emphasized the persistent need for non-sacramental *penitence* as a consequence of original sin and the utter depravity of even the most faithful Christians.

In his 1545 *Catechism*, Calvin included a discussion of good works, in which the child in the dialogue asserts: "The Scripture (*évangile*) is comprised of these two points: that is to say, faith and penitence." When the minister asks, "What is penitence?" the child responds, "It is a dislike of evil and love of good, proceeding from the fear of God and inducing us to mortify our flesh, to be governed and led by the Holy Spirit in the service of God."[11] The same year, in his tract *On the Libertines*, Calvin stated that "penitence, properly spoken of, is nothing other than renouncing ourselves to be new creatures living according to God."[12] In other words, for Calvin – as well as for other Reformed leaders – if the *sacrament of penance* was invalid, the *feeling of penitence* was crucial to faithful Christian life. Such repentance was inextricably tied to the discipline of one's body and person with the aim of living one's daily life in service to God. Ideally, in Reformed communities, before communion, "all hatred and all animosity had to be exchanged for love," a process that required repentance on all sides of community conflicts.[13]

Reformed leaders such as Calvin and Martin Bucer saw the disciplinary work of consistories as a key factor in repairing and reunifying the community of the faithful – a task that required constant repentance on the part of individual Christians and was aided by public acts of penitence. For Bucer, "Public penance ... was meant to satisfy the church of the sinner's repentance, not to satisfy God for sins committed."[14] And according to Calvin's *Institutes*, the reason to call someone before the full consistory was that a transgression was "openly manifest."[15] Thus it was the public effect on the Christian community that led to the need for public reparations. While reconciliation with God was a fundamental element of reconciliation with the earthly community of faithful Christians, God's acceptance of one's repentance was known to God alone. The measurable goal of the consistories in the Netherlands, Scotland, France, and Geneva was, rather, reconciliation between individuals and between an individual and the entire community of the faithful.

All consistorial records demonstrate Reformed efforts to address "public sins" that resulted in "public scandal" in order to bring church members to public repentance and heal any rifts in the community. What is more difficult to determine is how much time consistory members spent facilitating private repentance and reconciliation. Following Calvin's assertions in his *Institutes*, consistory members might first address "private sins" with private admonitions.[16] As Christian Grosse points out in Chapter 10, such exchanges are elusive in the historical record given their private nature. There is substantially more evidence that consistories often chose to require acts of repentance and reconciliation to be performed before the consistory, a semiprivate situation, and that fully public acts of penitence were reserved for the most public and scandalous transgressions. Ultimately, rather than negotiating penance in the sense of debating the best way for a sinner to satisfy God, consistories were negotiating penitence, or in other words, navigating the various routes that would lead individuals to feelings of repentance and would result in acts of reconciliation to restore the peace and unity of the earthly Reformed community.

NEGOTIATING WITH CHURCH MEMBERS

Across the regions where consistories operated, many people recognized consistorial authority, but as Timothy Fehler points out in Chapter 14, within that acquiescence there remained space for negotiating – for defending one's actions, persuading consistories to mete out lighter punishments, or seeking a middle ground between fulfilling the consistory's demands and being excommunicated from the church. In general, consistories were far less willing to negotiate when it came to tenets of the Reformed faith – in no case, for example, would it ever have been acceptable for a Reformed church member to recognize the pope's authority or to defend a believer's baptism. But consistories often demonstrated more flexibility regarding social behavior, as in the Genevan case of Claude Dufour whom the consistory readmitted to communion despite the fact that he never retrieved his daughter from her Catholic life. It was also common for consistories to exercise some flexibility in assigning punishments, depending on the situation and individuals involved, as when the Perth kirk session gave a group of schoolboys who had missed the afternoon sermon only an admonition, given that they had attended an earlier sermon and were generally seen as making an effort to be good.

Honor was a crucial factor in situations where consistories negotiated with individuals. In line with their primary mission of repentance and reconciliation, consistories were trying to counteract the contemporary emphasis on individual honor and reputation. At the same time, in order to be effective, consistories sometimes had to acknowledge the societal emphasis on honor. Traditional notions of family honor and individual reputation could lead people to react against consistorial discipline, as when a Hungarian woman chastised a minister who tried to admonish her daughter for blaspheming, or when Genevan men sent pregnant female servants away from Geneva to Catholic relatives to have their illegitimate children. In the Genevan cases, the men saw their own actions as preserving their individual and family honor by concealing an illegitimate birth from the Genevan community and (in some cases) providing for the mother and child, despite the fact that they were directly contradicting Reformed teachings and expectations.

In other cases, a similar concern for personal honor gave people a reason to engage with the consistory, as when Claude Castain, a Genevan gardener, found himself accused of having impregnated one of his servants. His case initially appeared before the consistory in March 1558, when several people reported that Castain's servant, Ayme, had left his service because she was sick and that they "had heard that she was pregnant." While the married Castain admitted to what the consistory might have considered overfamiliarity with his servant, including sharing meals with her, he denied having committed adultery.[17] Over the course of the next three weeks, he presented a series of witnesses to the consistory to defend his honor. As a result of his efforts, the consistory completely disregarded the issue of inappropriate socializing between Castain and Ayme, despite Castain's admission. Instead, they focused on the false charge of adultery, concluding that Jacques Morellet, Castain's main accuser, was a "calumniator and that he should recognize that Castain is innocent of the thing he has accused him of and that he should satisfy the said Claude in regard to his expenses and the tainting of his honor."[18] Here the consistory's willingness to fully investigate and to consider all sides of the story provided an important instrument for the restoration of the honor of both Castain and his servant, Ayme.

Expectations regarding personal honor affected the ways that consistories negotiated with individuals in a variety of ways. For Reformed church members in Delft, being approved to take communion publicly confirmed one's morality and, thus, honor. While this could give the consistory social power, "the defence of one's honour often embroiled the church council and the disciplined in protracted disputes over both the validity of the charges and public penance."[19] Similarly, Herman Roodenburg argues for Amsterdam that the "constant anxiety about one's 'honour' and 'respectability'" served as a useful tool in enforcing Reformed discipline.[20] In Scotland, kirk sessions recognized concerns about honor by exercising flexibility in "reducing fines or omitting the most public performance of apology, for instance, if the offended party were satisfied without it."[21] In other cases one can observe negotiation at a broader level, as when the consistory of Nîmes, seeking to regulate all gaming, ultimately compromised and allowed "friendly games" in the homes of local elites, even if these involved interactions with Catholics.[22]

Some form of negotiation was frequently at work in cases involving household servants, whether the servants were accused of immoral behavior or were called as witnesses. In a 1546 case the Genevan consistory had to persuade a servant named Jeanne to provide information regarding her mistress's adultery despite the fact that her mistress, Etienna Chappeaurouge, had expressly forbidden her to tell the consistory the truth.[23] While Jeanne ultimately acquitted herself, in the consistory's eyes, with her honest testimony, in other cases servants were more obviously complicit in their employers' moral infractions, as when Jacques Adventura de Morsier lied to a minister who was looking for his master, Jehan Navetta. During the consistory's investigation, Navetta admitted that he had instructed his servant to say that he was not home and that "his servant had done well because when he eats his meal, he likes to be at ease." In this case, the consistory overlooked the servant's lies, reprimanding only Navetta for his habit of blaspheming.[24] Such cases appear regularly in the Genevan consistory records, and while the registers offer no explicit reason for why the consistory chose to overlook servants' sins in certain cases, the consistory's actions suggest a recognition that servants might find themselves caught in a difficult position between the church's moral standards and their employers' expectations that they should help uphold their masters' personal or family honor at all costs.

Finally, in multiconfessional situations consistories were often particularly willing to negotiate in order to stop people from leaving the Reformed church for another local church. In the Netherlands and France, consistories encountered people who apparently were not frightened by the threat of excommunication because they had recourse to other religious communities. As a result, those consistories were more willing to engage in "long, painstaking negotiation" in order to prevent losing a member to a non-Reformed church.[25] Philippe Chareyre has found that French cases involving the disciplining of pastors, in particular, could result in extensive negotiating "among pastors, consistories, and synods" in order to prevent the pastor in question from being wooed by the Catholic clergy.[26] In Delft, the Reformed consistory felt additional pressure from secular authorities to limit excommunication and public penitence. Generally speaking, Reformed churches in multiconfessional regions had to be especially (although not uniquely) willing to negotiate with transgressors and to exercise flexibility and persistence to preserve their Reformed communities.

NEGOTIATING COMMUNAL HARMONY

As noted earlier, scholars have long recognized that conflict mediation was a regular task of consistories across Europe and an important means to pursuing the Reformed ideal of a godly, "pacified and amicable world."[27] Such conflict mediation was also valued by local inhabitants, whether or not they all fully accepted or comprehended the theological underpinnings of the consistory's work. Recently a number of scholars have connected consistorial peacemaking efforts to already-established institutional practices, arguing that conflict mediation helped make consistories not just acceptable but invaluable to their local communities. Suzannah Lipscomb argues, for Languedoc, that the work of the consistories was both dependent upon and limited by the participation of women, who used the consistory "to navigate their way through unpleasant circumstances." In certain circumstances, however, as in France leading up to the Wars of Religion, secular authorities might view this mediating role of consistories as threatening.[28]

In these peacemaking efforts, consistories acted as arbiters of a process of negotiation between injured parties. Christian Grosse has argued that the Genevan consistory offered another important "friendly path" that was potentially a faster and cheaper way to resolve conflicts and was a useful instrument for pacifying society that allowed an important role for local laity.[29] While Grosse sees the arbitration work of the consistory as modeled on the preexisting work of the Genevan City Council, he emphasizes the consistory's particular concern with "mutual forgiveness" and the importance of its religious motivation, as consistory members believed that conflict rendered "the faithful incapable of perceiving the spiritual gift of salvation the promise of which communion attested to."[30] In practice, the reformers' religious concerns were often deeply intertwined with other social and familial issues, as when the Genevan consistory summoned Guillaume Adam, his wife, and her brother, Jean Merlin, and charged them with "not living in good peace." The issues among them included the wife's refusal to go and live with Adam in a Catholic place and a financial quarrel involving Adam's guardianship over Merlin. What is striking in a case like this is the intensity of the consistory's focus on negotiating a reconciliation: the consistory did not even address the question of Guillaume Adam moving to a Catholic place and then returning to Geneva. They raised none of the usual questions about whether he had received mass or engaged in other Catholic practices. Instead, the case concluded when Adam and Merlin agreed to be reconciled and "as a sign of this they gave their hands to one another, and also the wife of Adam to Merlin, her brother."[31]

This role of peacemaker was critical to the achievements of consistories across Europe. In western Hungary, while presbyteries were established relatively slowly, their authority to reconcile personal disputes was accepted early on.[32] In places like Nîmes, where the Reformed community existed within a Catholic state, the consistory became recognized as "the sole authority capable of resolving common disputes and restoring to each his rights while safeguarding the honor of the parties."[33] In the Dutch and French refugee churches in London, the consistories mediated business disputes, including conflicts between masters and servants. In regions as politically different as the canton of Bern, Huguenot communities in France, the Republic of Geneva, the Netherlands, and the kingdom of Scotland, consistories "played the role of a mediator in neighbourhood disputes, and sought to re-establish harmony and reconcile neighbours in dispute with each other."[34]

Consistories did not pursue all of their goals through peacemaking and negotiation alone. Their interest in reconciliation could be limited by the concern to remove ongoing threats to the broader society. And as the other chapters in this volume demonstrate, consistories across Europe spent significant time and energy ensuring that people had learned the tenets of the Reformed faith, trying to prevent the religious corruption of their communities, and disciplining church members for violations of Reformed morality. Nevertheless, recognizing the various ways that Reformed consistories engaged in negotiations – with secular authorities, with individuals, and as the arbiters of quarrels – provides an avenue toward a fuller understanding of Reformed consistories' strategies for balancing the pursuit of their ultimate goal of a godly, orderly, and peaceful society with the need to deal pragmatically with the very worldly relationships that existed among the members of their communities.

Notes

1 R. Consist. 14, f. 121v, 22 December 1558; R. Consist. 14, f. 145, 19 January 1559; and R. Consist. 15, f. 45v, 23 March 1559.
2 R. Consist. 15, f. 45v, 23 March 1559.
3 Raymond A. Mentzer, "Sociability and Culpability: Conventions of Mediation and Reconciliation within the Sixteenth-Century Huguenot Community," in ed. Bertrand Van Ruymbeke and Randy J. Sparks, *Memory and Identity: The Huguenots in France and the Atlantic Diaspora* (Columbia, SC, 2003), 46.
4 Solange Bertheau, "Le Consistoire dans les Eglises Réformées du Moyen-Poitou au XVIIe siècle," *BSHPF* 116 (1970): 529–30.
5 William Monter, "The Consistory of Geneva, 1559–1569," *Bibliothèque d'Humanisme et Renaissance* 38 no. 3 (1976): 471.
6 Andrew Pettegree, *Foreign Protestant Communities in Sixteenth-Century London* (Oxford, 1986), 184.
7 Philippe Chareyre, "'The Great Difficulties One Must Bear to Follow Jesus Christ': Morality at Sixteenth-Century Nîmes," in ed. Raymond A. Mentzer, *Sin and the Calvinists: Morals Control and the Consistory in Reformed Tradition* (Kirksville, MO, 2002/1994), 84.
8 Heinz Schilling, "'History of Crime' or 'History of Sin'? Some Reflections on the Social History of Early Modern Church Discipline," in ed. E.I. Kouri and Tom Scott, *Politics and Society in Reformation Europe: Essays for Sir Geoffrey Elton on his Sixty-Fifth Birthday* (New York, 1991), 303.
9 Martin Ingram, "History of Sin or History of Crime? The Regulation of Personal Morality in England 1450–1750," in ed. Heinz Schilling and Mitarbeit von Lars Behrisch, *Institutionene, Instrumente un Akteure sozialer Kontrolle un Disziplinierung im frühneueitlichen Europa* (Frankfurt am Main, 1999), 93.
10 John McCallum, *Reforming the Scottish Parish: The Reformation in Fife, 1560–1640* (Surrey, 2010), 232.
11 *Le Catechisme de Genève* (1545), col. 51–53, CO VI.
12 *Des Libertins* (1545), col. 202, CO VII.
13 Heinrich Richard Schmidt, "Morals Courts in Rural Berne during the Early Modern Period," in ed. Karin Maag, *The Reformation in Eastern and Central Europe*, St Andrews Studies in Reformation History (Aldershot, 1997), 177.
14 Amy Nelson Burnett, "Church Discipline and Moral Reformation in the Thought of Martin Bucer," *The Sixteenth Century Journal* 22 no. 3 (1991): 451.
15 John Calvin, *Institutes of the Christian Religion*, 2 vols., ed. John T. McNeill, trans. Ford Lewis Battles (Philadelphia, 1960), 4.12.3.
16 Calvin, *Institutes*, 4.12.2 and 4.12.3.
17 R. Consist. 13, f. 19v, March 10, 1558.
18 R. Consist. 13, f. 29v, March 31, 1558.
19 Charles H. Parker, "The Moral Agency and Moral Autonomy of Church Folk in the Dutch Reformed Church of Delft, 1580–1620," *Journal of Ecclesiastical History* 48 no. 1 (1997): 58.
20 Herman Roodenburg, *Onder censuur. De kerkelijke tucht in de gereformeerde gemeente van Amsterdam, 1578–1700* (Hilversum, 1990), 422.

page 214, "Negotiating Penance"

21 Margo Todd, *The Culture of Protestantism in Early Modern Scotland* (New Haven, CT, 2002), 254.
22 Philippe Chareyre, "Jeux interdits, jeux toléré. L'application de la discipline réformée dans la France méridionale," in ed. Maurice Daumas, Adrián Blázquez, Olivier Caporossi, and Philippe Chareyre, *Le plaisir et la transgression en France et en Espagne aux XVIe et XVIIe siècles* (Orthez, 2005), 411.
23 *Registres du Consistoire de Genève au temps de Calvin, (1545–1546)*, ed. Thomas A. Lambert, Isabella M. Watt, Wallace McDonald, and Robert M. Kingdon (Geneva, 2001), 2: 233; R. Consist. 2, fol. 61, May 27, 1546.
24 R. Consist. 5, fol. 2, February 20, 1550; and R. Consist. 5, fol. 5, February 27, 1550.
25 Christine Kooi, *Calvinists and Catholics during Holland's Golden Age* (Cambridge, 2012), 151.
26 Philippe Chareyre, "'Maudit est celui qui fait l'oeuvre du Seigneur lâchement.' Les pasteurs face à la censure," in ed. Raymond A. Mentzer, Philippe Chareyre, and Françoise Moreil, *Dire l'interdit: The Vocabulary of Censure and Exclusion in the Early Modern Reformed Tradition* (Leiden, 2010), 65.
27 Mentzer, "Sociability and Culpability," 54.
28 Suzannah Lipscomb, "Refractory Women: The Limits of Power in the French Reformed Church," in Mentzer, *Dire l'interdit*, 24.
29 Christian Grosse, "Les Consistoires réformés et le pluralisme des instances de regulation des conflits (Genève, XVIe siècle)," in ed. Claire Dolan, *Entre justice et justiciables: Les auxiliaries de la justice du Moyen Âge au XXe siècle*, (Québec, 2005), 641.
30 Grosse, "Les Consistoires réformés et le pluralisme," 643.
31 R. Consist. 14, ff. 117–117v, December 20, 1558.
32 Graeme Murdock, "Church Building and Discipline in Early Seventeenth-century Hungary and Transylvania," in Maag, *Reformation in Europe*, 147–8.
33 Chareyre, "'Great Difficulties,'" 95.
34 Schmidt, "Morals Courts in Rural Berne," 175.

17

Inquisitions

John F. Chuchiak IV

On April 20, 1604, Antonio Gómez, a Portuguese native of the town of Villanueva de Portimán, resident in the city of Puebla de los Angeles in the kingdom of New Spain, sat nervously during the ceremony of the *auto de fe* in Mexico City.[1] Dressed in a pointed penitential cap (*coroza*) and wearing a penitential garment of shame (*sanbenito*) emblazoned with demons and flames, Gómez awaited the reading of his sentence. The Mexican Inquisition sentenced him to relaxation to the secular arm, a sentence of death by fire, for having committed the crime of Calvinist heresy and having vehemently denied the facts compiled against him in his case.[2] As the secretary read his fellow penitents' sentences one by one, Gómez grew ever more anxious and eventually had a change of heart. He stood up from his bench and requested an audience with the inquisitors. Immediately, the constable took Gómez before the inquisitor, Alonso de Peralta, and in the presence of the secretary Gómez gave his confession. He nervously and fully admitted every charge laid against him, and pleaded that "he had not said those things with ill will against the things of our Holy Catholic Faith, nor against any of the articles of faith, but rather out of ignorance."[3] For the Mexican Tribunal, ignorance could serve as a mitigating circumstance. His last-minute confession and pleadings of ignorance convinced the tribunal, and the inquisitors ordered him sent back to the secret prisons of the Inquisition. Gómez had escaped the flames by one simple action: he confessed.

Nevertheless, the inquisitors in this case, with their clemency and lenient treatment of a convicted Calvinist, were in violation of the strictest interpretation of the operating procedures of the Spanish Inquisition. Even the instructions of the Holy Office warned the inquisitors against

"pertinacious renegades who make their confessions at the last minute."
More remarkably in this case, the Mexican inquisitors on March 25,
1605 decided to commute Antonio Gómez's final sentence to the more
lenient punishment of reconciliation. The inquisitors' negotiations toward
a lighter sentence were warranted in this case, as they wrote to the
Suprema in Spain, on the basis of "his sincere confession against himself
and his implication of others"; they justified such mercy "in application
of the general principal of pardon for those who are truly contrite."[4]
The inquisitors argued "extenuating circumstances" existed due to "his
advanced age, his being ill and seeing that he had endured such a long
imprisonment." Nevertheless, it was the statement, "the implication of
others" that might perhaps better explain the inquisitors' willingness
to negotiate Antonio Gómez' final penance. This chapter will examine
the process of the inquisitors' manipulation of and open negotiations
with the accused concerning the outcome of inquisitorial proceedings
and sentences.

INQUISITORS' ATTEMPTS AT INSTILLING FEAR AND REPENTANCE, AND COMMUNITY RESISTANCE TO THEM

Perhaps based on a generalized sense of fear, the Inquisitions in Spain,
Portugal, and Italy often used their awesome power to help negotiate an
end to disputes or otherwise mediate certain contentious social or religious issues. Similar to the negotiated arbitrations of consistories
described in Spierling's chapter, in some cases inquisitors intervened in
disputes between two parties or to quell certain public scandals.

One of the most famous examples of the inquisitors intervening on
behalf of community struggles and issues occurred in the Basque witchcraft cases in the town of Zugarramurdi. The Basque witchcraft hysteria
of the early seventeenth century was probably one of the largest witch
crazes on record with over one thousand people arrested and investigated.
In the end, the Spanish Inquisition ended the hysteria by issuing the Edict
of Silence, an order that forbade anyone to denounce or even speak of
witchcraft without incurring the penalty of an inquisitorial trial for disobedience. The Edict quickly dissipated the hysteria, halting further
accusations. The visiting inquisitor Alonso de Salazar Frías wrote in his
final enlightened report in 1613 that "there were neither witches nor
bewitched until they were talked and written about."[5] In Italy too,
inquisitors attempted to stop any attempts by civil and ecclesiastical
authorities to harshly punish witchcraft. As scholars have shown, the

secular courts in Italy considered the Inquisition too lenient in its prosecution of witchcraft.

The Spanish Inquisition also mediated in the frequent conflicts between members of regular orders such as the Franciscan and Dominican orders. As the monastic orders attacked each other, the Catholic faithful grew uneasy, and the Inquisition served as an authority with power enough to stop these conflicts. In March 1634, the *Suprema* in Spain issued a decree decrying the disorder that arose from these disputes between religious orders. The Inquisitor General proposed to assemble a council of all of the orders and threatened to proceed against any friar or monk who provoked or supported these disputes. Just like the Edict of Silence in the witchcraft craze, in this instance the Inquisition's threat of proceeding against any friar who wrote words or gave sermons and lectures insulting another order brought peace to the dispute. The Italian or Roman Inquisition also served on occasion as impartial arbiters in affairs between two parties, usually in secular and ecclesiastical disputes, or in similar disputes between two religious orders, which frequently occurred.

The generalized fear of the Inquisition in Spain, Portugal, and Italy did not mean that the tribunals lacked resistance and did not suffer from violence at times. In Italy, as Christopher Black noted in his work on the Italian Inquisition, "inquisitors and their officials could face considerable abuse and physical threats," including even murder.[6] For example, two Dominicans linked with the Mantuan Inquisition tribunal were assassinated on Christmas Day 1567 in revenge for the burning of several Protestants. Violence could also break out between inquisitors and members of other Church institutions such as the various bishops and their supporters. In Spain, Mexico, and Portugal, similar instances of physical threats against inquisitors occurred. Not only did some resist the Inquisition by attacking its ministers, but others aided and harbored lay transgressors and suspected heretics, while still others intervened to thwart the Inquisition's proceedings against certain suspects.

UNORTHODOX AND NEGOTIATED DEALINGS WITH THE ACCUSED TO INDUCE OR EXTORT A CONFESSION

From the initial audience with the suspected heretic, inquisitors engaged in a process of open negotiation with the accused, offering them leniency and mercy in exchange for his or her confession. At every stage in a defendant's trial, the inquisitors attempted to hamper the legal defense and set up traps and other tricks in order to elicit or even trick a confession out of the suspect. Antonio del Corro, a Spanish monk and close relative of an inquisitor, wrote an exposé of the Inquisition's operations under the pseudonym "Reginaldus Gonzalvius Montanus" emphasizing the "deviousness and trickery of the interrogation techniques" of the Spanish Inquisition.[7] Although exaggerated to a great extent, the account still fairly accurately follows the actual procedures of Inquisition cases. Moreover, the inquisitorial manuals explicitly instructed the inquisitors to use trickery and deceit as tools toward gaining an ultimate confession. Inquisitors were also not above utilizing jailhouse informants, false setups, and the use of lies in order to gain the all-important confession of the suspect.

If there were too few witnesses and testimonies against a suspected heretic, the manuals urged the inquisitors to carve up the few denunciations into their component parts in order to deceive the defendant into thinking that the witnesses against her or him were more numerous than they actually were. Even if the testimonies against a defendant made no mention of accomplices, the inquisitors tried to make the suspect believe that there were accomplices, so as to pressure him or her to produce names. Furthermore, if during the defense stage of a trial a defendant asked for specifics about the case against him or her, such as the place, date, and time of the suspected crime, here too the inquisitors used deception and incomplete or vague information to hamper the defendant's ability to refute the charges against her or him.

The interplay between requests by the defense for information, and the inquisitor's vague responses, resembled a cat-and-mouse game played out in the audience chamber; it resembled the veiled type of negotiation between unequal power players that Spierling described in consistories. In all of these audiences with the inquisitors, an attempted negotiation occurred with the accused lay transgressor. The earlier a defendant confessed in the trial proceedings, the more mercy the inquisitors offered the accused and the lesser the punishment in the ultimate sentence. The entire process of these multiple interrogations was designed to disorient the accused heretic and make him or her suspect that the inquisitors had much more information and evidence than they actually had.

In a treatise on the Portuguese Inquisition, inquisitor Fray Antonio de Sousa likened anyone who visits, brings food or money, or gives any other succor to the persons on trial for heresy to promoters of heresy.[8] Still, in some cases the inquisitors attempted to summon the relatives and friends of the accused and allow them to visit the prisoner in order to seek their aid in convincing the prisoner to confess. As the sanctions and punishments of a convicted heretic were inherited by his descendants for two generations, the inability of the children and grandchildren of convicted heretics to hold certain positions, pensions, and so forth, served as one sure way to threaten relatives not to commit a crime against the faith. Why did the Inquisition ensure that its penalties and punishments affected two generations of the progeny of a convicted heretic? The answer remained simple as stated by the canon lawyer and jurist Francisco Peña in 1578: "the love of a parent is so beautiful and notable that the parents will many times fear more for the sake of their children than for themselves."[9]

Although our modern sensibilities view the use of torture as abhorrent, in the minds of the inquisitors (and most other contemporary criminal courts of the period), the use of torture remained justified in order to achieve full proof of the crime. The Italian inquisitor Masini, in his manual *Sacro Arsenale* (1621), argued that the use of torture was a fitting instrument in the hands of the inquisitors, stating that the chief beneficiaries of its use were the victims of torture themselves who "by confessing their crimes become converted to God, and through reconciliation save their souls."[10] Still, the Inquisition's use of judicial torture remained moderate in comparison with the civil courts of the time.

Abuses of the use of torture in Inquisition trials and deviations from proper procedures could be punished when discovered. For instance, in 1589, the Roman Inquisition's Cardinal Santa Severina rebuked the vicar of the inquisitor of Florence for his abuses in the use of torture against three female prisoners suspected in a case of sorcery. The cardinal ordered the confessions obtained under torture thrown out, since the evidence compiled against the suspected witches was insufficient to justify the use of torture. The Roman Inquisition was not alone in abuses of the use of torture. In 1645, the visiting judge Dr. Pedro de Medina Rico found the Mexican Inquisition guilty of issues involving improper torture procedures in the questioning of suspected Judaizers. According to the records of the visitation, the Mexican inquisitors had blatantly disregarded the rights of defendants when it came to judicial torture, and these violations "were recorded in gruesome detail both in the glosses of individual cases and in Medina Rico's examination of procedural violations."[11]

As a means of obtaining a confession or naming accomplices in a case with a group of accused suspects, manuals and instructions advised the inquisitors to start out by applying torture to those "whom they judged the weakest," which often meant that they applied torture to women first. In many cases, like a 1594 case in Florence against several monks for sacrilege, the authorities advised the inquisitors to begin the tortures with the suspect from whom "you will judge it easiest to discover the truth."

NEGOTIATING PENANCE IN THE AUDIENCE CHAMBER

Even though disadvantaged from the point of view of power relations, an Inquisition prisoner did have some means of negotiating with the inquisitors and the tribunal in order to change the final outcome of her case. From the moment of a suspected heretic's arrest, she was bombarded by demands to confess. The constable of the Holy Office who arrested her applied the first pressure on the way to the secret prisons as he instructed her "confess your offenses against the faith so that the reverend inquisitors may be merciful towards you."[12]

Even the defense lawyer who advised the defendant reminded the suspect that a full confession was the best way out. As one defense attorney of the Portuguese Inquisition warned his client, "there is no other way out ... he who does not confess remains in prison for many years and at the end will either be executed and burnt or come round to confessing anyway, like all the rest of them."[13]

When it came time for the defendant and his attorney to answer the charges, the defendant often found a coherent defense difficult as he was not given the names of the prosecution's witnesses. As one defense attorney apparently counseled his client when it came time to attempt to disqualify the prosecution witnesses for animosity toward the accused, "put everyone into your list, prisoners of the Inquisition and free people, because we do not know who has been or is going to be arrested during your imprisonment."[14]

Although many Inquisition defendants attempted to acquiesce to the inquisitors' demands for a full confession by implicating others, the ultimate negotiation of the outcome of a trial or confession was up to the inquisitors. Besides, not all collaboration and information served to mitigate a suspect's sentence. In 1657, for instance, in Portugal, Maria Mendes, a resident of Elvas, had confessed immediately after her arrest and denounced all of her children, relatives, and as many people as she knew by name. Apparently, she denounced more than six hundred people and in spite of this rapid confession and the implication of others, she was sentenced to death as an "incomplete confessant."[15] As often occurred when a defendant's information and denunciations did not serve to help negotiate a lighter sentence, Maria quickly revoked her testimony saying that her denunciations were false and she had only named names in the hopes of saving her life. Maria's attempt to negotiate her sentence with the inquisitors by means of denunciations failed.

Still, a convicted heretic's desperation at the thought of execution often led him to continue his denunciations even at the *auto de fe* and up to the foot of the stake where he was to be burned. During the *auto de fe* of 1657, Maria Mendes's own daughter reportedly shouted out the names of other distant relatives for her mother to denounce to save her life, and Maria called back in response as the authorities led her to the place of execution, "My daughter, there are no names left to denounce in Castile or Portugal ... I went through them all and it availed me nothing."[16]

Another case in Portugal, on the other hand, illustrates how even convicted prisoners who had committed perjury, been tried twice and convicted, might still ultimately negotiate their final punishments if they showed enough contrition. The notary Bautista Franguerio Cabras, sentenced initially to death by fire in 1667, successfully had his death sentence commuted by denouncing others. A year later in 1668, he managed to also gain temporary relief from his commuted sentence of hard labor, arguing that his asthma, eight poor children, and his repentance merited this mercy. By decision of the Inquisitor General, in April 1673, the rest of his galley service was commuted to three years of banishment.[17]

In Inquisition trials, denunciations and testimonies taken after the prisoner's arrest, either by fellow prisoners, spies, or prison guards, also counted as "proofs of guilt." Prison guards and fellow cellmates of the accused were not disinterested observers, but their testimony often contributed to the prosecution's case. Offering up testimony against a fellow prisoner could provide corroborating evidence of a suspect's contrition. Many Inquisition prisoners attempted to offer their services as spies and jailhouse informants in the hopes of negotiating a better outcome in their own case. As an anonymous treatise by a secretary of the Portuguese Inquisition noted, "solely because he feels himself slighted and shamed, a defendant in his confession will denounce the one who stubbornly maintains his innocence, or if he is more cautious, tries to induce other prisoners to make the denunciation."[18] Still, serving as a spy or informer could be a dangerous business. In 1583, for instance, an important witness and Inquisition informant of the Barcelona tribunal, Guillem Marti, was found murdered in his prison cell.[19]

Furthermore, even active and complicit informers often found out at the end of their own trials that informing on their fellow prisoners did not help them to negotiate a lighter sentence. The case of Gaspar de Alfar before the Mexican Inquisition is a good case in point. As one inquisitor deprecatingly commented, Alfar was a disagreeable suspect of crypto-Judaism who "never stopped talking."[20] Gaspar served as the inquisitors' spy on his fellow cellmates for several years, handing over routine testimonies and information against a large number of suspected Judaizers. Apparently, even his loyal service as an Inquisition informer did not allow him to ameliorate his own final sentence because the same inquisitors sentenced Gaspar de Alfar to appear in the 1648 *auto de fe* "as a penitent, with a green tapered candle in his hand, a noose around his neck, and a white *coroza* on his head." The inquisitors also meted out a rather harsh punishment for their loyal informer, sentencing him to make an abjuration *de vehementi* and receive 300 lashes and then serve as a galley slave perpetually in Spain at the oars without a salary or the possibility of his sentence being commuted."[21]

Other prisoners resisted the urge to serve as a spy on their fellow prisoners, though some testified out of fear of reprisals. In Valencia, a Morisco prisoner eventually testified under torture against his co-conspirators in a 1589 riot against inquisitorial officials in the town of Gea. Although he resisted at first, he claimed before the inquisitors that he did not inform on his fellow citizens at first out of fear "because the other Gea Moriscos made signs that they would tear him to pieces if he confessed."[22] Nevertheless, fear for his own sentence outweighed his fear, and he implicated fifty of his fellow villagers who had participated in the riot.

Still, if a defendant was able to resist the torture session without confessing, he would not only escape the death penalty normally reserved for people who denied their guilt, but he would also be let off, at the *auto de fe*, with a fine, costs of the trial, penances, and a short period of confinement and Catholic re-education. The fine and length of imprisonment depended on how convinced the inquisitors were of the defendant's guilt. Withstanding torture, especially more than once, could persuade the inquisitors that the suspect was not guilty of heresy and this often led to the prisoner's release or to a less serious ruling of unintentional heretical actions or statements made out of ignorance.

Some inquisitorial officials were also not beyond seeking bribes or other influence from wealthy prisoners in order to aid them in their cases. For instance, Simón López Rivas, the jailer of the secret inquisitorial prison in Santiago de Compostela, Spain, often invited wealthy prisoners to dinner and informed them of the progress of their cases, no doubt in expectation of some emolument.

CONSULTANTS, *VOTOS*, AND NEGOTIATING
THE FINAL SENTENCE

Regardless of their self-perceived powers, the reality was that the inquisitors could not impose sentences themselves in isolation, or even administer torture in a case without the agreement and a formal vote by an entire body of secular and ecclesiastical advisors who together formed a collective body that held formal consultations of the faith (*consultas de fe*).

At the end of a trial, inquisitors in Spain, Portugal, and Italy all had to submit the trial transcripts for judicial review by the tribunal's consultants and their legal and theological advisers. At the meeting of these advisers, the chosen consultants reviewed the entire case and the evidence collected against the accused to determine if the inquisitors and the other officials had proceeded correctly in the processing of the case. The jury or body of consultants and advisers consisted of both religious and secular officials, specialists in theology and both canon and civil law. The number of consultants varied from tribunal to tribunal, but each tribunal counted on anywhere from six to ten consultants for the judicial review and sentencing in their cases.

Once the consultants completed the judicial review and approved the inquisitors' proceedings in the case, the inquisitors turned to a jury of advisers to help them determine the verdict in the case. The official deliberations of this type of jury, called a *consulta de fe*, included the opinions of the inquisitors, a representative of the local bishop, and several legal or theological advisers (*consultores*), who together decided upon the guilt of the accused heretic and jointly decided on the sentence to impose. These advisers then made a formal decision of innocence or guilt in the case of the accused heretic. Without this vote and decision, the inquisitors could not issue a sentence.

Limitations in sentencing did exist, especially in cases of formal heresy that merited a death sentence. In cases where the prisoner might be condemned to death, the final decision and definitive sentence had to be unanimous on the part of the inquisitors and their advisers and consultants. If only one of the Inquisition's advisers voted against it, the accused could not receive a sentence of death. This helps explain the gradual reduction in the numbers of those condemned to death after the application of these regulations. However, for sentences that did not include a death sentence, a simple majority among the inquisitors and the advisers and consultants decided the final verdict. A few inquisitors, such as Alonso Ximenéz de Reynoso, inquisitor of Cordoba in 1597, were the object of sanction for their abuses and negligence. Still, abuses like these were the exception, not the rule in inquisitorial proceedings.

Although required by law to have a representative of the local bishop in consultation during the conclusion and sentencing of an Inquisition case, many times local inquisitors slighted the bishop's vicar or representative, known as the ordinary. The bishop's representative had a decisive and important vote in cases of crimes against the faith. For example, during the voting that approved final sentences in these cases, the ordinary voted after the legal consultants and before the inquisitors. The ordinary also had to vote on all requests for the administration of questioning under torture. As the theoretical and actual ecclesiastical official who had control over all members of their bishopric, the ordinary had a deep interest in observing the proceedings in cases when votes of torture existed. The ordinary also had to be present while the suspect underwent torture to safeguard against abuses. The participation of the ordinary signified the consolidation and cooperation of the secular diocesan church in the inquisitorial activities of the tribunals of the Holy Office.

The instructions also stated that the inquisitors should share all of their trial proceedings in the case with the ordinary, and with the consultants, without leaving out any substantial detail. Still, in some of the Inquisitions this cooperation was not always forthcoming. In the Italian Tribunal of Pisa, for instance, the inquisitors had requested the presence of the archbishops' representative at a public abjuration ceremony for a convicted witch, but the vicar refused to attend, claiming that the inquisitors had not shown him the documents in the case, which was a requirement by law.

Many inquisitors throughout the Spanish, Portuguese, and Italian world chose a policy of minimal consultation with the local bishops and their representatives in order to avoid the necessity of having to negotiate the final sentences of their cases, or accept the interference of the ordinary. Nevertheless, inquisitorial law required the presence of the representative of the local bishops and even the aid of local theological and legal consultants to participate in the final votes on requests for the use of torture and the final definitive sentencing of the cases.

Unlike consistorial archival records which as Spierling notes seldom preserved records of the votes of their members, inquisitorial documents recorded in minute detail all of the discussion and votes on each of the sentences executed. Special books of votes (*libros de votos*) exist in many inquisitorial archives. In the first *Libro de Votos* of the Mexican Inquisition, for instance, all of the votes on the use of torture and on the definitive sentences of the heresy trials undertaken by that tribunal still exist. Minute details and the actual record of each vote, as opposed to the records of the consistories, had to be recorded in detail as a requirement of the regulations of the Inquisition. For instance, in the February 7, 1601 vote and sentence in the case against Rodrigo Franco Tavares as a Judaizer, the Mexican inquisitors and their consultants' votes are meticulously recorded. The record even notes that one of the inquisitors, Don Alonso de Peralta, "was ill this day and in bed with poor health, but was also of the same vote and opinion."[23]

Unlike the Spanish Inquisition, the Roman inquisitors conducted their sentencing in private. In the Italian Inquisition, local bishops intervened more often, and conflicting jurisdictions were more likely to occur in Italy than in Spain or Portugal. Nevertheless, as some scholars have shown, the Roman Congregation of the Inquisition and its cardinal inquisitors often "mixed harshness with comparative mildness" apparently at their own whim.

In the Italian and Spanish Inquisitions, unlike the Portuguese one, appealing one's sentence did not automatically lead to a suspension of the sentence. The inquisitors justified the lack of suspension of sentences based on the fact that the convicted heretic would not know about his or her final sentence until it was imposed at the public *auto de fe*, making any appeal irrelevant. If the sentence was to submit the defendant to torture, however, the Spanish Inquisition and especially its distant tribunals in the Americas were instructed by the Inquisitor General on February 5, 1569, to allow the prisoners to "appeal the sentences of extraordinary punishments and the sentences of torture."[24]

Just as the Reformed consistories engaged in facilitating private repentance and reconciliation for some of their repentant members, as Spierling notes, the Inquisition also had the ability to facilitate private acts of abjuration or individual particular *autos de fe* in which a convicted heretic was permitted to make her or his abjuration in the secrecy of the tribunal's audience chamber before only a few witnesses. Although few records exist for these types of private ceremonies of repentance in the consistory archives, ample evidence for this type of private acts of faith exist in the archival records of the Spanish, Portuguese, and Italian Inquisitions. The final sentences might occasionally be issued privately to an individual in cases of guilt for minor offenses, but for most of the convicted, the sentences were issued publically at the *auto de fe*.

Similar to the actions of the consistories, as Spierling notes, the Inquisitions also reserved the fully public acts of faith for the prominent sentencing and punishment of the most publicly scandalous transgressions. Nevertheless, the goal of the consistories in these cases was to "lead individuals to feelings of repentance" that resulted in "acts of reconciliation to restore the peace and unity of the reformed community." The goal of the Inquisitions, on the other hand, focused on publicly punishing the guilty parties, regardless of their repentance, so that the general public would abhor the sins and crimes of the convicted heretics. As the Spanish jurist and inquisitorial commentator Francisco Peña noted, "we must remember that the main purpose of the trial and execution is not to save the soul of the accused, but to achieve the public good and put fear into others."[25] It was this "pedagogy of fear" that the scholar Bartolomé Bennassar described in his own work, and that the Inquisitions cultivated, to facilitate social control. Thus, the Inquisition through its *autos de fe*, did not attempt to "restore" the peace and unity of the religious community as the consistories apparently attempted to do, but by means of its public punishments of lay transgressors, the Inquisition "maintained" the continued public unity of the Catholic faithful by means of exemplary public punishments and the *auto de fe's* concomitant didactic theater of final judgment.

In the end, as we have seen, inquisitors were not passive receivers of Catholic dogma, but they interpreted the rules and regulations and operated sometimes against modern-day expectations (such as in the cases of the suppression of the witchcraft craze). By cajoling, tricking, or manipulating the accused into implicating others, or aiding them in creating mitigating circumstances for themselves, the inquisitors often rewarded those who cooperated during their proceedings and this often led to eventual negotiated sentences in Inquisition trials.

Like their consistory colleagues, inquisitors throughout Spain, Italy, and Portugal often were willing to negotiate the final outcome of an Inquisition trial with the accused lay transgressor. Although it is unarguable that power imbalances existed in the inquisitorial courtrooms, spaces did exist, inside and outside of the courtroom, within which both the inquisitors and the accused could actively negotiate the final outcomes of inquisitorial trials. For the convicted heretics, a belated confession and implicating an accomplice for other acts of heresy combined with an apparent act of contrition could serve to save their lives; while the same act also served the inquisitors' ultimate purpose of gaining complete "full proof" of the heretical crime committed and valuable testimonial evidence of the crimes of others. It was in the negotiated benefit of both parties to enable the convicted heretic to avoid a final sentence of death and bring him or her back into the bosom of the church. For the condemned it meant continued life, while for the apparent "merciful" inquisitors the ultimate confession meant a final victory in the realm of inquisitorial "truth" and justice. In the end, both sides won something in these negotiated exchanges inside and outside of the tribunals' audience chambers.

Notes

 1 Archivo Histórico Nacional [AHN], Sección de la Inquisición, libro 1064, f. 401.
 2 AHN, Inquisición, lib. 1064, ff. 379r–402v.
 3 See AHN, Inquisición, libro 1064, f. 402.
 4 Antonio García Molina Riquelme, *El Régimen de penas y penitencias en el tribunal de la inquisición de México* (Mexico City, 1999), 204.
 5 Gustav Henningsen, *The Witches' Advocate: Basque Witchcraft and the Spanish Inquisition (1609–1614)* (Reno, NV, 1980).
 6 Christopher Black, *The Italian Inquisition* (New Haven, CT, 2010), 109.
 7 Edward Peters, *Inquisition* (Berkely, CA, 1989), 133.
 8 Fray Antonio de Sousa, *Aphorismi inquisitorum in quatuor libros distributi: cum vera historia de origine S. Inquisitionis Lusitanae*, Lisbon, Pedro Craesbeeck, 1630, Libro I, capitulo XXV "De fautoribus hareticorum", párrafo 12, folio 70v.
 9 Carlos Cavallero and Ricardo Juan Cavallero, *Justicia Inquisitorial: El Sistema de Justicià Criminal de La Inquisicion Espanola* (Barcelona, 2003), 74–5.
10 John Tedeschi, "The Roman Inquisition, the Index and the Jews : New Perspectives for Research" in *The Roman Inquisition, the Index and the Jews: Contexts, Sources, and Perspectives*, ed. Stephen Wendehorst ed. (Leiden, 2004), 193.
11 Richard E. Greenleaf, "The Great Visitas of the Mexican Holy Office 1645–1669," *The Americas* 44 no. 4 (1988), 399–420.
12 António José Saraiva, *The Marrano Factory: The Portuguese Inquisition and its New Christians 1536–1765*, trans. rev. and augmented by H. P. Salomon and I. S. D. Sassoon (Leiden, 2001), 68.
13 *Noticias Reconditas y Posthumas del Procedimiento de las Inquisiciones de Espana y Portugal con sus Presos* (London, 1722), 46; Also see Saraiva, *Marrano Factory*, 71.
14 Ibid., 72.
15 *Noticias Reconditas*, 96
16 Ibid., 97.
17 Antonio Borges Coelho, *Inquisiçao de Evora* (Lisbon, 1987), no. 2314.
18 *An Account of the Cruelties Exercised by the Inquisition in Portugal* (London, 1713), 16.
19 E. William Monter, *Frontiers of Heresy: The Spanish Inquisition from the Basque Lands to Sicily* (Cambridge, 1990), 118.
20 Eva Alexandra Uchamany de la Peña, "Simón Vaéz Sevilla," in *Estudios de Historia Novohispana* (Mexico, 1987), vol. 4, 67–93 (84).

21 "Relación del tercer auto particular de fe de 1648," in *Documentos inéditos sobre la inquisición*, 200–9.
22 Monter, *Frontiers of Heresy*, 205.
23 Archivo General de la Nación [Mexico], Ramo de Inquisición, vol. 254, exp. 4.
24 AHN, Inquisición, libro 352, fols. 4v–10v.
25 Francisco Peña's commentary to Eimeric's *Directorium Inquisitorum*, 1578.

Section H

Gender on Trial: Attitudes toward Femininity and Masculinity

18

Consistories

Jeffrey Watt

The study of consistorial records can provide insight into the types of sins for which women and men were summoned and into the attitudes toward masculinity and femininity of both judicial authorities and the laity. To date, however, there has been far more gender analysis of Inquisitions than of consistories. As Allyson Poska shows in Chapter 19, scholars have been able to study in detail the beliefs of women who were questioned by early modern Inquisitions. In effect, inquisitors' aggressive questions actually served as a means of preserving the voices of some early modern women. By contrast, no consistory record reveals any case even remotely resembling that of Teresa of Avila, who effectively used the Spanish Inquisition as a forum to defend her spirituality and female independence and eventually became a very significant actor in the Counter-Reformation. Heresy, which was so central to the concerns of inquisitors, was usually not even under the purview of consistories. For example, neither Jerome Bolsec nor Michael Servetus, the two most prominent "heretics" in Calvin's Geneva, ever appeared before the consistory; their cases went directly to the Small Council. Moreover, while Inquisitions sought religious uniformity in word, deed, and thought, consistories were most concerned with the actions and practices of the laity and generally refrained from trying to probe their inner beliefs. Although consistories might convoke someone who, for example, openly rejected predestination, people who were summoned were often asked to recite the Lord's Prayer and the credo, perhaps even the Ten Commandments, but were virtually never subjected to lengthy interrogations concerning theological or spiritual nonconformity.

Be that as it may, consistorial records do lend themselves to meaningful gender analysis. Certain types of cases that were commonly heard by consistories pertained directly to gender, most notably those related to marriage and sexuality. In many places, among the most common of consistorial actions were those taken against illicit sexuality. In handling cases of fornication and adultery, consistories definitely did not appear to maintain a double standard. Reformed authorities pursued male and female fornicators with the same aggressiveness – males actually comprised almost 60 percent of those convoked for fornication or adultery in Geneva for the years 1568–82 – and sentenced them to the same penalties. In Geneva, first-time unmarried offenders were generally excluded from the Supper and sentenced by the Council to three days in jail on bread and water. Interestingly, consistories in southern France took one form of police action exclusively against women, ostensibly to impede illicit sexuality: in the 1580s and 1590s, they convoked a number of women for dressing or coiffing themselves provocatively. In such cases, consistories urged women, at times with the threat of public censure, always to be attired in a modest manner. Such actions can be interpreted to mean that members of consistories believed that women bore primary responsibility for sexual misconduct.

In many ways, Reformed Protestantism enhanced patriarchy, but the greater responsibilities attributed to men could actually bring certain benefits to women. Calvin and other Reformed leaders strongly affirmed that men were, by divine decree, the heads of households and responsible for the welfare of all members of their families, including children they fathered outside of marriage. Consistories, in conjunction with secular authorities, made much more aggressive efforts than their Catholic counterparts to oblige men to support all children they fathered. At times this meant that they raised their illegitimate offspring in their own households, at others that they provided financial support to the mothers of their children born out of wedlock. Reformed leaders wanted to avoid having illegitimate children become a financial burden on the state, but the consistory of Geneva also took actions against men who, in order to shield themselves and their families from dishonor, had sent their children to be raised outside Geneva. In so doing, Calvin and his colleagues showed not only that they wanted these children to be brought up Protestants rather than Catholics but also that they expected men to recognize their faults and to fulfill their responsibilities as fathers.

Consistory records in most Reformed areas show that disputed marriage contracts were the most common form of matrimonial litigation in the sixteenth and seventeenth centuries. Contrary to what one may expect, women did not always comprise the majority of plaintiffs to enforce alleged marriage contracts. Women did file three-fourths of such suits in Basel, but men comprised the majority of such plaintiffs in Neuchâtel. In certain areas, such as in Neuchâtel and Geneva, authorities insisted that promises that had been properly made had to be respected; a couple could not simply decide that they no longer wanted to marry. To modern sensibilities, it seems cruel and imprudent to force people to marry someone they no longer desired as a spouse, but this amounted to a continuation of the tenet from canon law that marriage contracts were binding from the moment of consent, not from the consecration in church.

Protestants introduced the possibility of divorce and remarriage, but divorce remained quite rare throughout Europe in the sixteenth and seventeenth centuries. Grounds for divorce were essentially limited to adultery and desertion, the latter requiring a very lengthy period (usually at least seven years) during which the abandoned spouse received no news from the one who had left. After that time, a divorce was granted on the assumption that the absent spouse was likely deceased. Significantly, evidence from Reformed areas consistently shows that adultery was cited as a ground for divorce much more often by male than by female plaintiffs, whereas women comprised the majority of those who filed for divorce for desertion.

Why the contrast? The most common proof of adultery was the birth of an illegitimate child; quite often these involved married women whose husbands were away for extended periods and returned to find their wives with babies they could not possibly have fathered. If an unfaithful husband did not actually get caught in the act, he ran the risk of being discovered only if his partner revealed his name. Consistory records also show that the number of men convicted of adultery was much larger than the number of women who divorced their husbands for their infidelity. This could have meant that women were indifferent about their husbands' infidelities, that they were hurt but willing to forgive their husbands' foibles, or that they feared the economic consequences if they suddenly found themselves without a male head of the household. In support of this last hypothesis, it is important to note that rarely do the registers indicate how the divorced woman was to be supported henceforth. The silence of most cases on the question of financial settlements accompanying divorces provides a clue that there may have been strong economic incentives to remain married. Most likely, the majority of women could not afford to separate from their husbands. A case before the consistory of Geneva during the time of Calvin provides palpable evidence of how even battered women feared being abandoned by their husbands. In August 1542, the consistory convoked Claude Soutier and his wife, Martina, because of their domestic turmoil. Four months prior to this appearance, Claude had beaten Martina so severely that he blinded her in one eye. Martina, however, had not wanted to appeal to the authorities out of the fear that Claude would get angry and abandon the household, leaving her and their children destitute.[1]

A theory stressing the importance of economic concerns fits comfortably with the fact that abandonment was the most common ground for divorce cited by women. Most often these women complained that their husbands had left them with no financial support. If their husbands had left behind few assets, clearly there were no economic deterrents to divorce. The sole financial hope for many was to remarry.

Quite significant is the fact that nowhere in Europe was cruelty recognized as a ground for divorce in the sixteenth and seventeenth centuries. True, Reformed authorities did convoke people for domestic violence, one of the few types of consistorial actions that were clearly made primarily for the benefit of women. That said, the protection that consistories offered women from abusive husbands was quite limited. The consistory of Geneva censured two men – Claude Soutier, mentioned earlier, in 1542 and another in 1561 – for having beaten their wives so severely that they put out one of their eyes. In both cases, however, the consistory also ordered these women to obey their husbands and to live peacefully with them; neither man spent a day in jail for this brutality.[2] Members of consistories disapproved of excessive domestic violence and took steps to deter it, but cruelty, unlike adultery, did not undercut the very essence of marriage, as they understood it. I know of no consistory that recognized cruelty alone as a ground for divorce in the sixteenth century. Only once during the ministry of Calvin did Genevan authorities grant a separation, and that case involved a man, Bertin Beney, who had repeatedly been reproached for domestic violence that was so extreme that his wife's life was in danger. In 1553 his long-suffering wife was permitted to go live with her mother indefinitely, and she finally received a divorce in December 1555, but only because Beney was convicted of adultery.[3] In the sixteenth century, women who were the victims of domestic abuse would have been much more likely to receive separations in Catholic rather than in Protestant areas. Catholic judicial authorities had long approved of granting separations on certain grounds, including abuse. Protestant reformers, however, believed that it was immoral to subject innocent parties to indefinite separations that forbade remarriage. But barring the very limited grounds for divorce – essentially adultery and abandonment – they expected married couples to live together until death did them part. All told, although unwed mothers likely received more support in Reformed than in Catholic areas, the protection that consistories provided to married women was quite restricted.

Reformed leaders enhanced patriarchal responsibility in overseeing the mores and the religious education of family members. If, for example, a baby had not been baptized, morals courts almost always held the father of the child as most responsible for this omission. With its emphasis on patriarchal authority, the consistory of Geneva on occasion also ordered men to give their children (almost always their sons) a good whipping for their misbehavior. Calvin's consistory was known to convoke men and ask them how they instructed not only their children but also their wives in religion. For example, in 1542 a merchant was summoned because his wife and his mother were not attending church; in March of the following year, suspecting that a woman was saying "popish" prayers and the rosary, members of the consistory called her husband to ask him how he instructed his wife and children.[4]

Although men were deemed principally responsible for the behavior and religious education of family members, this is not to say that consistories paid little attention to the religious practices of women. Indeed, consistories often showed a special concern for the religious behavior of women, in part out of fear that women were more likely than men to remain tied to various Catholic beliefs and practices. Evidence suggests that there was basis in fact for this concern. In the first two years of extant records (February 1542 – May 1544), the consistory of Geneva convoked twice as many women as men for attending Mass in neighboring states, saying prayers for the dead or to the saints or to the Virgin Mary, fasting for religious purposes, or observing other similar vestiges of "popery." Some of the discrepancies for specific offenses are quite remarkable. During those two years, the consistory convoked twenty-four women but only two men for possessing a rosary or Catholic literature, twenty-three women and three men for celebrating Catholic holidays, and twenty-nine women and thirteen men for saying prayers to the Virgin Mary. To be sure, the consistory took action against those men who attended Mass or said prayers to Mary, but the unavoidable impression from the earliest extant records is that Genevan women remained more closely tied than men to certain Roman Catholic practices. During Calvin's ministry, such cases declined in number as residents learned to distinguish acceptable from unacceptable rituals for Reformed Protestants.

Records indicate that consistories convoked more men for certain sins and more women for others, and these variations more often than not do not appear to be simply a product of the gendered prejudices of these all-male institutions. In Geneva, for example, men comprised the large majority of people who were accused of drunkenness, blasphemy, and violence. Men almost certainly were more prone than women to over-indulge in alcohol, gamble, blaspheme, and commit violent acts, and they were certainly more apt to commit such indiscretions in public. Almost all those accused of wasting time and money in taverns and of gambling were men. Taverns were essentially a male domain, whereas women who imbibed too much were likely to do so at home and might thereby escape the notice of the consistory. Most broadly, consistories tended to exclude from the Supper far more men than women; no surprise since men dominated public life and consistories tended to resort to excommunication when misbehavior resulted in public scandal. The evidence from consistories shows that in Reformed as in Catholic areas, conflicts between men often ended in physical violence, whereas quarrels between women were much more likely limited to verbal disputes or, at worst, less violent forms of physical altercations.

The consistory of Nîmes convoked almost three times as many women as men for insults, and studies of consistories in Languedoc suggest that gossip was primarily a female activity. Women were not taking part in gossip solely out of malevolence or prurience. Rather, through gossip, they were helping establish what was acceptable behavior and were actively engaged in policing morality, especially in regard to the sexual behavior of other women. Consistories strived to eliminate the public unrest and animosity that were engendered by insults and took action against those who slandered others. Be that as it may, consistories accepted rumors as viable evidence concerning sexual misbehavior. In so doing, consistories, while trying to strengthen patriarchy, were unintentionally providing important avenues for female agency. An unintended consequence of attempts to regulate sexuality was that Reformed women in southern France played an important role in policing behavior through their gossip; as accusations spread by word of mouth, people who violated prevailing mores could suffer a loss of reputation, especially their sexual reputation, which was central to a woman's honor.

Interestingly, Judith Pollmann finds that discipline was actually an important means of attracting women to the Dutch Reformed faith. In the religiously pluralistic society of the Netherlands, no one was obliged to be a member of any church. Females comprised the majority of church members, and unmarried women – widows, older single women, and fatherless younger single women – were especially overrepresented. Pollman quite plausibly explains this trend by noting that organized religion provided one of the few means of "institutional sociability" available to females. More important, joining the Reformed church was an important means of protecting the honor of women, especially those who did not have husbands or fathers to defend them. Being permitted to participate in the Supper affirmed their moral good standing in the community, and women were much more willing than men to submit to the discipline of the consistories; doing so amounted to restoration of their honor.

Women and men had vastly different professional opportunities, a reality that was evident in consistorial actions. Consistories generally summoned far more men than women for laziness and dissipation of goods. In November 1558, for example, the consistory of Geneva rebuked Michel Bonivard of the village of Vandoeuvres and ordered him to "work for a living without spending his goods in laziness and in filing suits, as Messieurs [of the Council] have ordered him and [as they] always advise all their citizens, Bourgeois, and [legal] residents."[5] The words that the consistory carefully chose in rebuking Bonivard indicate that the civil and religious authorities regularly exhorted all Genevans to be industrious and to eschew prodigality as well as indolence. In October 1560, the consistory expressed its alarm and sent to the Small Council a list of fourty-four young men who led a life of debauchery and hedonism; they were described as loafers who did not want to do anything other than wander about aimlessly and consume the small amount of goods left to them by their parents. Calvin and his colleagues became increasingly convinced that Geneva was plagued by an ever-growing number of lazy, irresponsible men.[6]

It is not surprising that consistories subpoenaed far more males than females for laziness or profligacy. Men were expected to be the principal breadwinners, and they had far greater opportunities than women did to make a decent living. While women most definitely worked long hours and made indispensable contributions to the early modern economy, they generally did not go through formal apprenticeships. Moreover, in urban areas where Reformed Protestants so often lived, the work of women tended to be performed at home – in their own homes or in the homes of others, most often in domestic service – where indolence was less likely to come to the attention of authorities.

Like the Inquisition in Italy and Spain, consistories tried to suppress practices considered superstitious or magical, and these cases also shed light on attitudes toward femininity and masculinity. Among the most common of such cases were those attacking therapeutic magic. In Geneva, women were in the majority (twelve out of nineteen) among those called before Calvin's consistory for allegedly engaging in cures that were deemed magical. Although this may in part reveal the prejudices of the male authorities who passed judgment, it also reflected the fact that women bore the primary responsibility of tending to the sick. An excellent example of such a case involved the widow Jeanne Fassoret, who had already been cited in the consistory for being a *guérisseuse* in 1547, 1550, and 1551.[7] In 1553, Fassoret was summoned as a witness in the case of Guillauma Gros, who was accused of adultery and of having contracted a venereal disease. When asked if she had provided cures to Guillauma, Fassoret replied that she had not because Ami Gros, Guillauma's husband, was a dishonest man and that the couple habitually did not pay for services they received. She did say, however, that she "taught them how they had to deal with this illness," adding that the malady afflicting Guillauma was definitely syphilis. She also unabashedly confessed that she had treated about twenty other sick people.[8] When she first appeared for this case, Fassoret certainly gave the impression of being an expert witness. She spoke as if she were a physician, and it certainly seemed that the consistory itself took her testimony quite seriously, accepting it as evidence that Guillauma Gros had indeed committed adultery. By contrast, five weeks later, in July 1553, the consistory convoked Fassoret to reproach her for her "hypocrisies and superstitions in examining and trying to heal the ill."[9] To a certain extent, the registers suggest that members of the consistory themselves had difficulty in distinguishing acceptable medical treatments from those considered superstitious.

Closely related to magic is cursing, which has been described as "a verbal form of harmful magic." A study of rural areas in early modern Berne shows that morals courts subpoenaed more men than women for "heavy cursing," but four times as many women received harsh punishments for these curses. These figures show unequivocally that judicial authorities were much more likely to associate cursing with possible harmful magic if the malediction was uttered by a female. They not surprisingly accepted the stereotype that witchcraft was predominantly a crime of women.

When reading the registers, one often has the impression that these disciplinary institutions were trying to impose certain forms of behavior that were widely unpopular among the population at large. One must always remember, however, that these registers, like all court records, are skewed toward the negative, and testimony of witnesses often reveals that many laypeople shared the convictions of the pastors and elders that certain forms of behavior should be suppressed. In one case, seven witnesses, three men and four women, affirmed that they bluntly told a group of women riding in a cart outside Geneva to stop singing unseemly songs.[10] In Calvin's Geneva, many residents also clearly felt that it was their moral responsibility to reprimand, even publicly, blasphemers. In April 1551, a certain Pierre Papa appeared in the consistory for having blasphemed and having refused to kiss the earth when ordered to do so by bystanders, a clear indication that anyone who witnessed a blasphemy was obliged to tell the miscreant to get on his knees and kiss the earth as a sign of contrition.[11] Apart from self-denunciations, which were not uncommon in some areas, authorities depended on the Reformed population in general to inform on those who had strayed from the straight and narrow path. Unfortunately from the historian's perspective, consistory records, like those of the Inquisition, almost never give the names of the accusers.

One should not overemphasize the penal nature of consistories. Since, as noted earlier, consistories were in many ways more akin to compulsory counseling services than tribunals per se, it is not surprising that consistories were generally less aggressive than Inquisitions were in dealing with religious nonconformity. Reformed morals courts were trying to root out certain religious practices that had long been accepted or even promoted by Roman Catholicism. Moreover, while Inquisitions in Spain and Italy generally functioned farther from the front lines of Protestantism, most consistories operated in cities that were in close proximity to Catholic areas, and excessive zeal in pursuing moral shortcomings could result in provoking some simply to abandon the Reformed faith and move to a neighboring Catholic community. Moreover, a chief aim of the consistories was to reconcile feuding parties, be they neighbors, siblings, or husbands and wives. Consistories sought to maintain peace among the faithful and ultimately to help them interiorize Reformed mores and suppress (or at least channel) feelings of anger and hatred. Though a coercive institution, consistories ordinarily promoted values that were largely shared by the Reformed population in general. Consistories defended a form of patriarchy in which women and children were to be subordinate to their husbands and fathers. They espoused concepts of femininity and masculinity that seemed to dovetail more or less with the values of the laity. One can find a few examples of women who seemed to want to break out of the constraints placed on them – the healer/physician Jeanne Fassoret was an obvious case in point, and some of the women convoked for marital discord were surely rebelling against the overbearing authority of their husbands. As evidence on gossip in Languedoc shows, women demonstrated a form of agency that members of consistories had not foreseen and no doubt did not entirely welcome. By and large, though, the patriarchal hierarchy espoused by consistories seemed to be widely accepted by both women and men. Consistory registers provide far fewer examples than Inquisition records of women who tried to circumvent or rebel against the gendered restrictions placed upon them.

Consistory records will never be the bases for monographs on Reformed equivalents of Teresa of Avila, and the terse nature of consistorial sentences and the absence of dissenting and concurring opinions will preclude studying in detail the mindset of individuals who served on these morals courts. There is nonetheless much to be done in regard to the gender analysis of these fascinating sources. We definitely hope to see more work of a comparative nature, studies that juxtapose the findings from not only different consistories but also from other disciplinary institutions, including of course Inquisitions. Such research will reveal variations among tribunals in the numbers of men and women who were prosecuted, in the sins or crimes that female and male defendants reputedly committed, and in the sentences passed. To date much of the research on consistories has understandably focused on the confessional age. As Joke Spaans and James E. Wadsworth illustrate in Chapters 24 and 25, it would be most fruitful to see more research on the late seventeenth and eighteenth centuries to trace changes over time in the types of cases heard, the norms concerning femininity and masculinity promoted by these all-male institutions, and the attitudes toward gender of the women and men appearing before them.

Notes

1 *Registers du Consistoire de Genève au temps du Calvin, 1542–1544*, ed. Thomas A. Lambert and Isabella M. Watt (Geneva, 1996), 1:104:5.
2 Achives d'Etat de Genève (hereafter AEG), Registres du Consistoire (hereafter R. Consist.) 18: 178v (23 December 1561).

3 *Registres du Consistoire de Genève au temps de Calvin, 1553–1554,* ed. Isabella M. Watt and Jeffrey R. Watt (Geneva, 2014), 8: 111, 115–6. Procès criminels, 2ᵉ série, n. 1019 (6 July 1553); Registres du Conseil Particuliers 7: 100v, 104r-v, 105v–106r, 107r-v (10, 14, 17, 18, 20, 21 July 1553); *Registres du Consistoire de Genève au temps de Calvin, 1555–1556,* ed. Jeffrey R. Watt and Isabella M. Watt (Geneva, 2016), 10: 271.
4 *Registres du Consistoire de Genève,* ed. Lambert and Watt, 1:139, 190–1.
5 AEG, R. Consist. 14: 97r (24 November 1558).
6 AEG, R. Consist. 17: 159r-v, 164r, 167v, 172r (3, 17, 24, 31 October 1560); AEG, R. Consist. 17: 35r (21 March 1560).
7 *Registres du Consistoire de Genève au temps de Calvin, 1547–1548,* ed. Thomas A. Lambert and Isabella M. Watt (Geneva, 2004), 3:34, n. 228; *Registres du Consistoire de Genève au temps de Calvin, 1550–1551,* ed. Isabella M. Watt and Thomas A. Lambert (Geneva, 2010), 5:51; *Registres du Consistoire de Genève au temps de Calvin, 1551–1552,* ed. Isabella M. Watt and Jeffrey R. Watt (Geneva, 2012), 6: 176.
8 *Registres du Consistoire,* ed. Watt and Watt, 8: 90, 100.
9 *Registres du Consistoire,* ed. Watt and Watt, 8: 120.
10 AEG, R. Consist. 14: 38v–39r (30 August 1558).
11 *Registres du Consistoire,* ed. Watt and Watt, 6:76, 313.

19

Inquisitions

Allyson M. Poska

More than thirty years ago, in 1979, Claire Guilhem offered what seems to have been the earliest scholarly discussion of gender and the Inquisition. In a chapter on the devaluation of the feminine word in Inquisition trials, she provided a basic overview of women who challenged religious authority and the response of the Inquisition, which, according to Guilhem, was to label them as crazy. Somewhat of an outlier in a collection of essays that otherwise did not deal with gender, her work presaged what would develop into an exciting new subfield in Inquisition studies. Indeed, during the next decade, the vibrant intersection of social history, women's history, and literary analysis gave rise to what we may look back on as the golden age of studies of the Inquisition and gender. Mary Elizabeth Perry, Alison Weber, Anne Jacobson Schutte, María Helena Sánchez Ortega, and the many others who followed in their intellectual footsteps would provide scholars with an entirely new perspective on a long-studied institution, as well as deeper insight into the complicated nature of gender expectations in early modern Europe.

First and foremost, gendered analysis has demonstrated that the Inquisition was, in every way, a masculine institution. The orthodoxy that it was created to enforce was conceived and articulated by men. Its structures and processes were formulated and implemented by the men who served the institution, from the lowliest of jailers and familiars to the Inquisitor General. As such, the process of taking denunciations by Inquisition officials was not a gender-neutral activity. The decision to denounce one's self or someone else involved willing participation in and submission to a gender hierarchy in which the entirely male group of clerics and other officials who called for and recorded the denunciations were situated as the moral and intellectual superiors of all of the men and women who appeared before them. It could not have been lost on either the men or the women making denunciations that as a result of a combination of class and gender (and, at times, race), they could never be in that superior position.

For most Europeans, visitations were the first moments of encounter with the Inquisition; however, it is unclear the degree to which the masculine nature of the institution influenced the participants' perspective on gender. Did men feel more comfortable participating in the visitation than women or did women see Inquisition officials as their adversaries in competition for authority in their communities? Were women cowed more than men by the spiritual and cultural authority that these literate clerics exercised over them during the visitation?

In the process of calling for denunciations, the Inquisition became the mouthpiece for a certain set of European gender expectations. The Edict of Faith, which varied somewhat in content but was read at the beginning of every Inquisition visit in Spain and sometimes by other tribunals, generally used gender-neutral language to describe heretical acts; however, in some cases, the edicts explicitly linked gender and heresy. For instance, an Edict of Faith issued in Mexico City in 1616 specifically noted that "many people, and *especially women*, are easily given over to superstitions which gravely offend God, our Lord."[1] Even when gender was not mentioned, the lists of heresies nevertheless evoked particularly gendered associations. As I will discuss in more detail later, many of the heretical acts of *conversos* and *moriscos* fell undeniably within the female sphere. Based on the large numbers of men denounced, listeners seem to have associated other heresies, such as bigamy and declarations that nonmarital sex was not a sin (simple fornication), much more often with men than with women.

During a visit from the Inquisition, local men and women could use the heresies listed in the Edict of Faith to voice their disapproval of women who failed to conform to a particular set of feminine ideals, usually some combination of female submission, humility, silence, modesty, and/or chastity. For instance, accusations of blasphemy allowed neighbors to condemn a woman's sexual behavior or other unfeminine acts and to solicit the intervention of authorities to admonish or constrain that inappropriate behavior. Thus, as much or more so than heresy, when a woman like nineteen-year-old María Afonso was denounced for saying that she preferred her earlier years in concubinage to her unhappy current marriage, her denouncers were expressing their anxiety about both her earlier nonmarital sexual activity and her current conflictive relationship.[2]

Once denounced and investigated, the masculine apparatus of the institution certainly had different implications for the women and men who appeared before it. Stacey Schlau has recently noted that while women were held in Inquisition prisons, the constant male surveillance under which they lived deprived them of the usual protections due to them as "respectable" women. Accused of witchcraft, Suor Maria Deodata Fabri was raped and impregnated by her jailer in Faenza.[3] Out of sight and vulnerable, she could not have been the only woman to be victimized by Inquisition staff. Moreover, as Mary Giles pointed out, when the accused was a woman, interrogations could easily become pornographic, as men performed torture on seminude female bodies, while other men watched. The sexualization of the spectacle was further highlighted when convicted women were stripped to the waist and whipped in front of crowds. For men accused of heresy, the sexual humiliation was less pronounced, but the social/cultural humiliation was intensified. When nonelite men appeared before the Holy Office, the encounter was a stern reminder of the highly stratified nature of early modern society in which some men were clearly subordinated to others. The torture of one man by another further reinforced class and moral hierarchies. When elite men were accused of heresy, the prosecution challenged their status and compromised their masculinity vis-à-vis their social equals.

Despite the pressure to submit to masculine authority, during their trials, when women stood face to face with inquisitors, rather than confess to accusations of heresy and recant their beliefs, many women stoically defended their connections to the holy and the correctness of their faith. Their testimonies indicate that they understood the gender expectations of the inquisitors and strategically employed gender stereotypes in their own defense. Alison Weber has demonstrated how Teresa of Avila's rhetoric of feminine subordination eventually convinced church authorities of her orthodoxy, but such rhetorical skills were not unique to this famous nun. According to Richard Kagan, Lucrecia de León's argument that she was a weak woman manipulated by men, "suggests that she was fully prepared to exploit sixteenth-century conceptions of women as a means of strengthening her defense."[4] Similarly, the accused Judaizer Bernarda Manuel relied on stereotypical feminine norms to plead for her life.[5] Even peasant women were resolute in their female knowledge, fearlessly explaining to inquisitors how no matter what the church taught, they knew from experience that the Virgin birth was impossible and that singleness was better than a bad marriage. More often than not, the inquisitors conceded and let them go.

There is no evidence that the presence of the Inquisition deterred or suppressed mystical or other unconventional religious activity often associated with women. Although inquisitors often characterized women's mystical activity as demonic and connected discernment with femininity, both women and men continued to engage in these intense forms of spirituality. Indeed, the Inquisition often had difficulty deciding which visions were orthodox and which were not; as a result, not all accused mystics were found guilty of heresy. Thus, early modern women did not necessarily become victims of a male-dominated religious culture, but rather were primary actors in the Catholic Reformation and the evolution of Catholic Reformation spirituality. In fact, in the long run, the Inquisition served less as a mechanism to stifle women's religious activity, than as a means to preserve their experiences and ideas about reform for successive generations.

Moreover, there is no evidence that the existence of or interaction with the Inquisition altered the behaviors or ideas of ordinary Europeans. For instance, despite an assertive campaign by the Spanish Inquisition against simple fornication, illegitimacy rates did not decrease in the seventeenth century. Even as prosecutions for these "minor heresies" diminished in the mid-seventeenth century, scholars believe that it was due to changes in Inquisition priorities not changes in the behaviors of the Spanish population.

More than any other group of women female converts from Judaism and Islam, *conversas* and *moriscas*, suffered terribly at the hands of their Old Christian neighbors who used the Inquisition to cleanse their communities of people whom they perceived of as threats to Christian society. Indeed, it was their responsibilities as wives and mothers that brought *conversas* and *moriscas* to the attention of suspicious neighbors and servants, often also women, who then denounced them to the Inquisition. For instance, when officials called for parishioners to denounce anyone engaging in supposedly Jewish acts, such as "preparing on Fridays the food for Saturdays in stewing pans on a small fire" and "placing clean linens on beds and clean napkins on the table," it is likely that they visualized the Judaizing heretic as female, not male. The same was true as the Edict of Faith warned of the potential heresy involved in washing the blood off meat and various burial rituals. However, gendered analysis has also complicated the image of converted women as token victims of Catholic fervor. Although women's domestic responsibilities were often the basis of accusations against them, women's responsibility for food preparation, the education of children, and even laundering could also be a means of subverting efforts at assimilation by maintaining traditional religious beliefs and practices within the protected space of the home.

Gendered analyses of Inquisition sources have provided for a substantial reconsideration of the relationship between women and magic. Twenty years ago, María Helena Sánchez Ortega argued that communities saw women healers as a "source of evil." However, more recent scholarship has articulated a more nuanced perspective. The masses of southern Europeans relied heavily on female healers and wise women to diagnose and cure their ills, seeing them as critical intermediaries between the natural and the supernatural. Women's abilities in terms of love magic were believed to be even stronger. As long as the interventions "worked," people believed that female healers were merely conduits for God's will, but early modern people differentiated between healing magic and *maleficia*, and when the spells, balms, and potions failed to achieve the desired results, some women were accused of engaging in malicious and evil activity. However, in Inquisition territories, people were less convinced about the relationship between women and witchcraft than their Protestant counterparts. Indeed, the numbers of men prosecuted as healers and for magic on the Iberian Peninsula were surprisingly high compared to prosecutions in other parts of Europe. In Galicia in northwestern Spain, about one-third of the accused were men. In the Aragonese tribunal, men made up about 30 percent of the accused of witchcraft, and in Toledo, the average was about 38 percent.[6] In Italy, there was significant variation. In Venice, approximately 70 percent of the accused were women, but the Friulian Inquisition reveals no particular association between women and magic.[7] In fact, in her study of those trials, Luisa Accati has argued that men who engaged in magic did so based on a different set of assumptions.

As men's bodies had no particular powers, male magic was dominated by "tools and knowledge." By the eighteenth century, Friulian men were more likely to be accused of magic related to money than love or seduction. Even then, inquisitors demonstrated little interest. In Portugal, men made up a significant proportion of the accused during the most intense prosecution of *curandeiros*, folk healers, during the eighteenth century, ranging from only 30 percent in Coimbra to 48 percent in Évora.[8] However, the ratio of women to men is less important than the overall prosecution rates. It is important to keep in mind that, in general, inquisitorial skepticism about the existence of witches led to few prosecutions

and even fewer convictions in comparison with the witchhunting associated with other judicial systems in early modern Europe.

It is particularly interesting that when it came to lesbians and people
whose genitalia did not match their gendered performances, inquisitors
played the role of sexual investigators and not necessarily enforcers of
particular gendered ideas. Elena/Eleno Cespedes and others did not
receive harsh punishments for their gender bending, rather their trials
indicate that inquisitors worked to find adequate resolution for what to
them was a complicated physical and social, but not necessarily a heretical issue. Sherry Velasco argues in her recent book on lesbians in early
modern Spain that more than anything, the Inquisition was confused by
sex acts between women and, as a result, was inconsistent in the way it
dealt with female sodomists. Certainly in many of the trials of people
whose gender bended, the Inquisition was more concerned about acts that
compromised a sacrament, not their complicated sexuality or sexual
interactions per se.

For all the fascinating research on women and the Inquisition, men
made up the majority of those brought before the tribunals. In Spain, the
fact that Contreras and Henningsen's statistical analysis of Inquisition
cases did not include gender as a category of analysis makes it very
difficult to make general statements about the Spanish Inquisition;
however, studies of individual tribunals indicate that men were far and
away the majority of the accused. For instance, in Toledo, except for the
earliest years of the Inquisition during which large numbers of women
were prosecuted for Judaizing and *alumbradismo*, women never made up
more than one-third of the defendants.

Thus, the Inquisition also served as a mechanism used by powerful
men to enforce a certain set of masculine gender norms on other men. In
Spain and Portugal, Jewish and Muslim converts were the easiest targets.
Accusations of effeminacy were common against myriad enemies, and in
Spain, religious and racial hierarchies designated Christian men as
masculine in contrast to their feminized Jewish and Muslim counterparts.
During the reconquest Christian men reinforced the feminization that
came with defeat. According to Mary Elizabeth Perry, in 1492 "victorious
Christian warriors 'feminized' the defeated Muslims, stripping them of
their masculine markers by prohibiting them from carrying knives and by
denigrating their culture."[9] When those Jewish and Muslim men became
Christians, they rejected the feminine characteristics that, from a
Christian perspective, were part and parcel of their former faiths; however, when they relapsed, they implicitly chose to revert back to their

feminine and feminized past. In that context, it is not surprising that inquisitors dealt harshly with that conscious rejection of both Christianity and early modern masculinity.

Race and class were often implicated in the enforcement of masculine norms as a part of the prosecution of sodomy. From 1509 in Spain, the *Suprema* forbade the prosecution of sodomites without evidence of other heresy, as it was not clear to authorities that the *pecado nefando* constituted heresy in and of itself. Although, as Luiz Mott has noted, "Sodomites always disturb the stability of heterosexual patriarchal society,"[10] only the Aragonese and Portuguese tribunals had jurisdiction over the crime. Even then, the Inquisition generally only intervened when the sex act raised the specter of status and racial difference in ways that challenged the masculine hierarchy. For instance, as soon as it obtained permission to add sodomy to the list of heresies, the Valencian tribunal took action against accused sodomites who most challenged masculine norms. They defrocked and executed two Trinitarian monks for sodomy and a *morisco* who attempted to rape a Catholic boy was whipped and sentenced to the galleys for ten years.[11] Similarly, the Aragonese tribunals disproportionately prosecuted *moriscos* and slaves, who, like women, were viewed as social subordinates and characterized by a lack of physical control. When there were class differences among the participants, noblemen fared substantially better than their nonnoble sexual partners. Inquisitional interventions reestablished the equilibrium in the social hierarchy that many homosexual relationships disrupted.

Beyond sodomy, the Inquisition clearly articulated a masculinity based in self-control, as is evident in both local denunciations of sexual impropriety and the Inquisition's prosecution of simple fornication and bigamy in which men far outnumbered women. In the Galician tribunal, 86.2 percent of the accused were men. In Toledo, more than 90 percent were men. As Ann Twinam has noted, "A traditional masculine priority was the protection of their partner's honor, rather than any advertisement of their own sexual exploits."[12] Men who had multiple wives and/or bragged about their sexual exploits failed to conform to expectations of masculine discretion and marital chastity that the Inquisition was trying to instill.

An argument about the Inquisition's emphasis on male self-control can also be made about blasphemy accusations. Here too, men were by far the majority of the accused. In Seville, only twelve women appeared on blasphemy charges between 1560 and 1638.[13] Men who called the Virgin a whore or Christ a "cuckolded faggot"[14] often faced time in the galleys, even if their outbursts were not meant as challenges to orthodoxy, but were rather the uncontrolled expletives of men who were drunk, angry, or frustrated. Even without evidence of a serious religious misunderstanding or heretical belief, inquisitorial intervention reasserted the expectation of masculine moderation and control.

The prosecution of charges of clerical solicitation and the Aragonese tribunal's trials against clergy for sodomy provide further evidence of the attempt to punish male promiscuity by inquisitors who valued sexual self-control as an indicator of both sacramental piety and masculinity; however, these prosecutions also indicate some ambivalence, as both denunciations and conviction rates remained low. Only 188 clerics appeared before the Sicilian tribunal between 1500 and 1782.[15] Stephen Haliczer found only 223 complete solicitation cases from seven tribunals between 1530 and 1819. The tribunal in Cuenca, Spain heard more solicitation cases in 1576–85 than it had a decade before, but few of the accused were convicted. When push came to shove, inquisitors proved more willing to impose their masculine expectations on men with whom they shared less in common.

Finally, the expectation of male self-control may be behind the more frequent convictions and more serious punishments for men than for women. According to Anne Schutte in her study of the Venetian Inquisition's prosecution of pretense of holiness cases, "even when a female defendant had inspired a male who was prosecuted with her, men were judged to be more culpable than women and sentenced more harshly."[16] If it is in fact true that men were punished more harshly for the same crime across the tribunals (and we do not know that for certain), then that differential may be attributed not only to the inability of inquisitors to assign women full responsibility for their actions, but also to the challenge to or failure to comply with masculine expectations that the trials exposed.

Thus, the Inquisition has proven ripe for gendered analysis; however, there is much more work to be done. First, we need a well-theorized study of the gendered nature of the institution and its processes. As I have indicated, some scholars have raised these issues, but thus far no one has taken up the challenge to examine the gender ideologies of the institution as a whole or even of individual inquisitors. Second, scholarship would benefit from more meta-analysis of the Inquisition, including an examination of the issue of gender across tribunals and indeed across the entire system of tribunals. As was true of most other categories of accused, were there some tribunals more likely to deal with accusations against women than others? Under what conditions and for what heresies? That type of analysis presents us with the opportunity to argue something specific about the institution as a gendered entity. What about change over time? What was the ebb and flow of accusations against women? We tend to hold gender constant, but did the institution's ideas about women evolve in any way? We also need deeper, more explicit discussions of masculinity. As I have asserted, the Inquisition was deeply involved in the enforcement of masculine norms. Beyond sodomy trials, other accusations and the interactions between male accused and inquisitors during trials might provide some indication about the expectations of men in the same way that they have provided insight into expectations about women. Moreover, understanding the expectations of men helps us better understand the expectations of women. Finally, it is almost shocking how many recent works on the Inquisition fail to even mention gender as a category of analysis. Even if gender is not central to the argument, it is critical that we push scholars to acknowledge both the bread and depth of scholarship on the issue and the complications that gendered analysis can bring to any argument.

Although the Inquisition was established to eliminate heresy, a crime ostensibly unconnected to gender, it initiated interactions that were profoundly gendered – between accusers and accused, between male inquisitors and female accused, and between male inquisitors and the men brought before them. Gendered analysis allows us to complicate early modern understandings of orthodoxy and heterodoxy, and the power relations that accompanied their enforcement, while at the same time offering a new perspective on the role of gender in early modern society.

Notes

1 Emphasis mine. "Edict of Faith that Requires all to Denounce the Practitioners of Astrology, Necromancy, Geomancy, Hydromancy, Pyromancy, and Chiromancy, as well as anyone who Possesses Books on these Themes," in *The Inquisition in New Spain, 1536–1820: a Documentary History*, ed. and trans. John F. Chuchiak IV (Baltimore, 2012), 112.

2 Archivo Histórico Nacional (Madrid), Sección Inquisición, legajo 2042, no. 54 fol.1 (1613).

3 Anne Jacobson Schutte, *Aspiring Saints: Pretense of Holiness, Inquisition, and Gender in the Republic of Venice, 1618–1750* (Baltimore, 2001), 109.

4 Richard L. Kagan, *Lucrecia's Dreams: Politics and Prophesy in Sixteenth-Century Spain* (Berkeley: University of California Press, 1989), 160.

5 Lisa Vollendorf, *The Lives of Women: A New History of Inquisitional Spain* (Nashville, 2005), chap. 2.

6 Jean-Pierre Dedieu, *L'administration de la foi: L'inquisition de Tolède* (XVI-XVIIIè siècle) (Madrid, 1989), 256, tableau 41.

7 Ruth Martin, *Witchcraft and the Inquisition in Venice, 1550–1650* (Oxford, 1989), 226; E. William Monter and John Tedeschi, "Toward a Statistical Profile of the Italian Inquisition," in *The Inquisition in Early Modern Europe: Studies on Sources and Methods*, ed. Gustav Henningsen and John Tedeschi, with the assistance of Charles Amiel (DeKalb, 1986), 135.

8 Timothy D. Walker, *Doctors, Folk Medicine and the Inquisition: The Repression of Magical Healing in Portugal during the Enlightenment* (Leiden, 2005), 349.

9 Mary Elizabeth Perry, *The Handless Maiden: Moriscos and the Politics of Religion in Early Modern Spain* (Princeton, 2005), 47.

10 Luiz Mott, "The Misadventures of a Portuguese Man in Seventeenth-century Brazil," in *Pelo vaso traseiro: Sodomy and Sodomites in Luso-Brazilian History*, ed. Harold Johnson and Francis A. Dutra (Tucson, 2007), 328.

11 E. William Monter, *Frontiers of Heresy: The Spanish Inquisition from the Basque Lands to Sicily* (Cambridge, 1990), 137.

12 Ann Twinam, "The Negotiation of Honor: Elites, Sexuality, and Illegitimacy in Eighteenth-Century Spanish America," in *The Faces of Honor: Sex, Shame and Violence in Colonial Latin America*, ed. Sonya Lipsett-Rivera and Lyman Johnson (Albuquerque, New Mexico, 1998), 87.

13 Michel Boeglin, *Inquisición y Contrarreforma: El Tribunal del Santo Oficio de Sevilla (1560–1700)* (Seville, 2007), 197.

14 Monter, *Frontiers of Heresy*, 166.

15 Andrea del Col, *L'inquisizione in Italia dal XII al XXI secolo* (Milano, 2006), 241.

16 Schutte, *Aspiring Saints*, 201.

PART III

ECCLESIASTICAL DISCIPLINE'S EXPANDING
REACH AND DECLINE

Section I

Disciplinary Institutions in the Atlantic World

20

Consistories

Mark Meuwese

Although they were confronted with similar challenges, the Reformed Church greatly differed from the Catholic Church in how they responded to them. Whereas the Catholic Church was able to build on and utilize the medieval institution of the Inquisition for the purpose of implementing orthodoxy in the Iberian colonies, the Reformed Church lacked a comparable institutional framework. In the Dutch Republic and its overseas possessions, the institution primarily responsible for ensuring religious orthodoxy was the consistory. Furthermore, contrary to the state churches in the Spanish, French, and Portuguese Atlantic where the Catholic faith was the only permitted religion, the Reformed Church in the Dutch colonies, as in the Dutch Republic, was a public church. While the Reformed Church was the only religion allowed to hold public services, each individual in the Republic and in Dutch overseas possessions was given a degree of freedom of conscience. This practice was also different from Puritan New England where there was a strong overlap between church and state, especially in the seventeenth century. In the Puritan colonies of New England, secular and religious authorities closely collaborated to punish individuals for straying from orthodox Protestant beliefs. In Puritan New England, the congregational church at the local level as well as local and provincial officials imposed church discipline on church members, rather than a consistory.

Similar to the Reformed Church in the Republic, the Calvinist churches in the Dutch Atlantic were expected to hold public services for all Christians and to baptize and marry any Christian who so desired. The only religious ritual from which non-Calvinists were excluded was the communion service, which was reserved for full church members. Because of the noncoercive character of the Reformed Church, membership in the Calvinist churches in the Dutch Atlantic remained fairly small. For example, in New Netherland in North America perhaps 20 percent of the colonial population was a member of the Reformed Church. In Dutch Brazil, about a quarter of the total colonial population were full church members. These numbers were a bit lower compared to church membership levels in the Dutch Republic, which were 37 percent around 1650.

In return for serving as the public church for all Christians, the Reformed Church was financially and politically sponsored by the West India Company (WIC), the private trade company that received a monopoly in 1621 to establish and govern colonies in the Atlantic world from the States General, the assembly of the seven provinces comprising the Dutch Republic. All religious personnel were appointed and paid by the Company. Reflecting the prominent role of Amsterdam in the WIC, most church personnel in the Dutch Atlantic were recruited in coordination with the Amsterdam consistory. For example, ministers and lay preachers selected for New Netherland were first nominated by the Amsterdam church council and then appointed by the Amsterdam chamber of the WIC. As the WIC empire greatly expanded in the first half of the seventeenth century, the Classis of Amsterdam, the Classis of Walcheren in Zeeland, and provincial synods also became involved in the recruitment of church personnel. Because the WIC had the final say in the appointments and in the payment of the salaries, it was essential for the Reformed Church to maintain a good relationship with company directors in the United Provinces and with WIC officials in the overseas territories.

While it is true that the WIC did not establish extensive and ambitious missionary programs among the indigenous peoples such as were attempted in New France, New England, Brazil, and New Spain, the Dutch trade company was actively involved in the promotion of the Reformed Church in all of its colonies in the Americas and West Africa. The substantial support of the WIC for the Reformed Church in the Atlantic can be illustrated by two examples. No fewer than fifty ministers served in Dutch Brazil from 1624 to 1654, forming twenty-two congregations and several classis organizations. Likewise, by the time of the English conquest of New Netherland in 1664 there were eleven Reformed congregations in the North American colony.

Rather than trying to provide a comprehensive overview of church disciplinary practices in all Dutch Atlantic possessions, this chapter analyzes Calvinist regulatory practices in the WIC colonies of Brazil, New Netherland, and Surinam – all prominent sites in the development of the Dutch Atlantic. While Brazil was the cornerstone of the WIC's empire in the early seventeenth century, Surinam was a valuable plantation colony during the eighteenth century. Seventeenth-century New Netherland, meanwhile, was the only colony in the Dutch Atlantic with a large European settler population. Furthermore, the religious life of New Netherland and Dutch Brazil have recently been the subject of sophisticated scholarship. This comparative study of three colonies shows that time, place, and the support of secular officials decisively shaped the extent to which consistories and the Reformed Church were able to promote religious uniformity and impose church discipline on Christians, Jews, indigenous Americans, and Africans.

DUTCH BRAZIL

Although the WIC colony in Brazil was short-lived, Dutch Calvinists viewed it as a prestigious enterprise. The Reformed Church in Brazil was sufficiently strong to organize two classes (presbyteries), one for Pernambuco in 1636 and one for the neighboring province of Paraiba in 1637. In the 1640s the Reformed Church in Brazil even held four synod meetings. As a result, in Dutch Brazil the classes rather than the consistories worked to maintain religious discipline in the colony. The main explanation for the meteoric rise of the Reformed Church in Brazil is that at the time of colonization, the church was dominated by a strict orthodox (Counter Remonstrant) faction that was eager to strengthen its brand of Calvinism in the Republic and in the Dutch Atlantic. For the Counter Remonstrant faction, Brazil was a unique opportunity to show that the Calvinist faith was superior to that of the Catholic religion, which had a long-established network of priests, churches, monasteries, and missions there.

In this militant spiritual context it is not surprising that the Reformed Church in Brazil was greatly concerned about instilling discipline among its followers. People who attended Reformed Church services in Dutch Brazil mostly consisted of army personnel, WIC officials, and low-level employees. In 1639, the WIC employed 10,000 men in Brazil, the majority of whom were soldiers and sailors. To lower the costs associated with paying the large army, the company reduced the number to 4,000 in 1642 after the conclusion of a truce with Portugal.

There were relatively few Protestant settlers and families in Dutch Brazil because the continuing Iberian resistance made the colony unattractive for settlement. Moreover, the Dutch were dependent on Luso-Brazilian settlers for the exploitation of the sugar mills. Most of the Protestant settlers resided in coastal towns, especially in the capital Recife in Pernambuco. While the senior WIC positions were usually occupied by Dutchmen, the lower ranks were filled with Germans, Frenchmen, and men from the British Isles. Most of the soldiers were Protestants from various denominations; English and French Protestants held their own services.

Because of the dominant presence of many rowdy and poorly educated soldiers, sailors, and other male personnel in the colony, the Reformed Church was greatly concerned about the moral and spiritual well-being of Protestants. The Reformed Church in Recife urged the secular government to issue public ordinances calling on church goers to keep quiet during church services. Similarly, on several occasions the colonial government renewed the prohibition on serving alcohol on Sundays. A related disciplinary issue for the Reformed Church was the widespread presence of prostitutes in Recife. In August 1637 the consistory of Recife even wrote a letter to the central board of WIC directors in the Republic to do something about this pressing problem. Not surprisingly, classis and synod meetings in Dutch Brazil frequently deliberated on the many immoralities committed by Protestant soldiers and sailors. Apart from discussing the expected problems of swearing, prostitution, and drunkenness, the classes and synod also reprimanded WIC personnel for living together with unmarried women. The Reformed Church insisted that these couples formally marry in church. The zealous French Calvinist pastor Vincent Soler, who hoped to install a theocracy in Brazil, even complained in private correspondence about the licentiousness of fellow ministers and secular officials in the colony. The Brazil Classis was generally also disappointed about the quality of elders in the consistories of the colony. Because most Protestants were soldiers or other Company personnel who returned to the Republic after their three-year service, it was difficult to find adequate elders to serve in the consistories.

In addition to instilling moral discipline among Protestants, the Reformed Church in Brazil was also preoccupied with the large numbers of Catholics in the colony. Throughout the entire period of Dutch rule, the Luso-Brazilian population outnumbered the Protestant population at least two to one. Since the Luso-Brazilians had indispensable know-how about the workings of the sugar mill industry, the WIC could not afford to alienate them. Even dedicated Calvinists in the colonial government accommodated Catholics by granting them the right to hold public services, though most Catholic clergy were expelled. Following the truce of 1642 the central board of Company directors allowed Catholic priests, except Jesuits, to return to Dutch Brazil as long as they swore an oath of loyalty to the colonial government. While Catholic services could be held in existing churches, public processions were prohibited. The Classis of Brazil was predictably alarmed at the continuing presence of Catholic priests whom they blamed for the failure of Catholics to convert to the Calvinist faith. Even if Catholic priests had been absent, it is doubtful whether many Catholics would have embraced the Reformed Church. For the Luso-Brazilians the Calvinist religion was always associated with the hated Dutch invaders. The Luso-Brazilian settlers' uprising in 1645 was so successful in part because it appealed to widespread anti-Protestant sentiments among them.

Another pressing issue for the Reformed Church in Brazil was the large Jewish community. A considerable number of New Christians lived in Portuguese Brazil before the Dutch invasion. After 1635, when the WIC consolidated control over Pernambuco and neighboring provinces, many New Christians in Dutch-held territory began to openly practice their traditional faith that had been prohibited by the Catholic Church. In doing so they were inspired by the growing Jewish community of Amsterdam, which gradually gained the right to worship in public during the 1630s, and even sent some members to Brazil to encourage their former co-religionists. As the WIC expanded its hold in northeastern Brazil, more Jews migrated to the colony where they mostly worked as traders. Because of their vital role as commercial middlemen in the colonial economy, the Jewish community received permission from the WIC government to build its own synagogue in Recife in 1636, the oldest one in the Americas. By the mid-1640s the Jewish community in Recife counted approximately 1,450 persons, which was as large as the Jewish population in Amsterdam.

The Reformed Church was frustrated with the growth of the Jewish community in Brazil. Although the Jewish community in Amsterdam was allowed to practice its religion in public by that city's government, elsewhere in the Republic municipal councils dominated by Counter Remonstrant Calvinists prohibited Jews from worshiping in public. Reformed ministers in Brazil tried to do everything possible to prevent the Jews of Brazil from obtaining the same privileges that their counterparts had received in Amsterdam. The consistory in Recife protested the construction of the synagogue in 1636, but to no avail. When another synagogue was being built in the province of Paraiba two years later, the provincial government of Paraiba, undoubtedly with approval of the Classis of Brazil, forced the synagogue to be constructed on the outskirts of town rather than in the more visible center. In 1646, the Classis of Amsterdam petitioned the central board of Company directors to repeal the freedom of public worship granted to the Jews in Brazil. Despite all these petitions and complaints, the WIC, concerned about the vital economic role of the Jews, continued to uphold the right of Jews to publicly practice their faith in Brazil.

The final groups in Brazil whose spiritual and moral well-being drew the attention of the Reformed Church were indigenous Brazilians and imported African slaves. When the WIC invaded Brazil, the Dutch came into contact with Tupi-speaking indigenous peoples who lived in Jesuit mission villages. Converting the Catholic Tupis to the "true religion" was seen as a prestigious task for the Reformed Church. Ironically, the fiercely anti-Catholic Calvinist preachers found it convenient to use the mission system established by the Jesuits in order to convert the Tupis more quickly. Dutch ministers eagerly adopted the mission villages that Jesuits had established to better supervise the semi-nomadic Tupi Indians. Not all tactics used by the Jesuits were favored by the Reformed ministers, however. The Reformed Church personnel involved with the mission program among the Tupis refused to practice mass-baptism as the Catholic missionaries had done. Instead the Calvinist missionaries emphasized education and catechization. For this purpose a catechism was translated into Tupi in 1641 but the Classis of Amsterdam prevented it from being used because of theological inaccuracies in it. Although a sizeable number of Tupi groups lived in the mission villages during peace time and a handful of Tupis even became salaried schoolteachers, the Reformed Church was disappointed in the slow progress of converting the Tupis. In 1644, the Recife church council was shocked to find that many Tupis continued to paint their bodies. The church councillors also found it necessary to prohibit the Tupis from "going to the papists or any other heathenish servants, whoever they may be, in order to obtain letters, beads, or crucifixes of St. John from them for superstitious practices."[1] The WIC supported the mission program among the Tupis because the company viewed them as useful auxiliaries. The Calvinist missions collapsed after the outbreak of the Portuguese rebellion in 1645 although some Tupis continued to associate with the Reformed Church after the surrender of Dutch Brazil in 1654.

The Reformed Church had a more ambivalent attitude toward African slaves in Brazil. In the late 1630s, as the importation of African slaves into Dutch Brazil began to increase rapidly, the classis of Brazil argued that the slave trade was morally justified because it enabled the Africans to become Christians. Indeed, the baptism register of the Reformed Church in Recife includes the names of several Africans. However, the French minister Vincent Soler was one of the very few Reformed preachers who actively worked to catechize and educate African slaves. Moreover, because of their high status in colonial society, Reformed ministers received household slaves from the WIC. Additionally, the Classis of Brazil complained that many imported slaves led immoral lives and continued their African dances. To remedy this situation the classis called on the colonial government to order owners to bring their slaves to Sunday mass and to outlaw the African dances performed by the slaves. It is unknown but unlikely that the colonial government supported this request because the sugar planters, most of them Catholics, were indispensable to the economy of Dutch Brazil.

NEW NETHERLAND

Like the WIC, the Reformed Church devoted fewer resources and personnel to New Netherland than it did to Brazil. Until 1674, only twelve ministers served in New Netherland, the majority of them arriving after 1650. In contrast to Brazil, a classis never formed in New Netherland until well after the English conquest of the colony in 1664. One important reason for the unpopularity of New Netherland among Dutch ministers was that the WIC was notoriously slow in paying church salaries. The growth of the Reformed Church in the colony was a reflection of the development of the colonial population. Before 1630, New Netherland remained largely a fur-trading colony. When permanent settlement increased in the late 1630s, a period of warfare with the indigenous peoples broke out which only ended in 1645. After this time, New Netherland quickly developed into a settler colony with a European population of around 10,000 by the time of the English conquest in 1664. Unlike Brazil, New Netherland did not have a Catholic population. A very small number of Jews arrived, but only after the fall of Dutch Brazil in 1654. The overwhelming majority of settlers were Protestants, many of them from Scandinavia, Germany, and the Low Countries. Beginning in the 1630s New Netherland also became attractive to disaffected English Protestants from neighboring New England.

Because of the colony's homogenous religious character, the Reformed Church in New Netherland was primarily concerned with maintaining church discipline in Protestant ranks. Before the rise of non-Calvinist

Protestant groups in the colony in the late 1640s, most issues of church discipline centered on the relationship between church and state. The first ministers in New Netherland during the 1620s and 1630s often had a difficult relationship with secular officials because the colony was governed by inexperienced WIC employees. Additionally, some of the ministers in this early period were uncompromising Calvinists influenced by the Counter-Remonstrant movement. In 1634, Lubbert Dincklagen, one of the senior officials in the colony, was excommunicated by minister Everardus Bogardus. At issue was a dispute over whether the church or the secular government had the supreme authority in the colony. By mid-century, as the Counter-Remonstrant movement had weakened and as WIC officials became more experienced, relations between church and state in New Netherland markedly improved. This was exemplified during the tenure of director-general Petrus Stuyvesant from 1647 to 1664. As the most senior WIC official in the colony, Stuyvesant consistently supported the Reformed Church in matters relating to church discipline.

Unfortunately, little documentation has survived relating to the implementation of church discipline by the consistories in New Netherland. The few available sources indicate that the Reformed Church in the colony was concerned with the legality of marriages and with couples who had children without being married. There are also several references in the surviving consistory records related to drunkenness and nonattendance at church services. In 1662, the consistory in the town of Breukelen (Brooklyn) temporarily excluded a church member from communion after having found that he had cut down fruit trees during a day of prayer. Although it is not realistic to draw firm conclusions from this limited evidence, the smattering of evidence does indicate that the consistories in New Netherland after 1650, when the colony grew in population, functioned in the same manner as their counterparts in the Republic.

Much better documented and more revealing about the preoccupation of the Reformed Church in New Netherland were the fervent campaigns against Lutherans, Quakers, and Jews in the colony. As New Netherland transformed into a settler colony, the WIC directors feared that the colony could be destabilized by religious factionalism. For this purpose the WIC instructed local officials in the colony to strictly uphold the Reformed Church as the only public church. In remarkable close cooperation between church and state, the Reformed Church was repeatedly successful in preventing the sizeable community of Lutherans and the smaller groups of Quakers and Jews from holding public services. Religious toleration only came to New Netherland after the English conquest.

In contrast to Brazil, the Reformed Church in New Netherland attempted only on several occasions to convert the indigenous peoples to the Calvinist faith. During the period when the colony was a fur-trading outpost, the few Counter-Remonstrant ministers who were present, such as Bogardus, were ambitious but lacked the linguistic and intercultural skills to attract the indigenous population. Although some indigenous people occasionally attended the sermons of minister Johannes Megapolensis out of curiosity, almost none of them were seriously interested. Things did not improve during the brutal war between the Algonquian groups and the Dutch from 1638 to 1645. Ten years after the war ended, the Reformed ministers in New Netherland reported to the classis of Amsterdam that the program to convert the native peoples of the colony had to wait until the Dutch had asserted more control over them. As long as the Indian communities remained independent, the Protestant ministers did not think they stood much chance.

Partially because the comparatively small population of slaves in New Netherland was firmly under colonial control, the Reformed Church was initially more successful in converting Africans there. By the mid-1650s, almost sixty African slaves had been baptized. Some Africans also married in the Reformed Church on Manhattan. Africans exposed to Catholicism in Angola and Congo, the main places of origins of the New Netherland slaves in the 1620s and 1630s, were more likely to convert to Calvinism. When the WIC began to transport to New Netherland African slaves from the Lower Guinea Coast where Catholicism had not penetrated, the Reformed ministers found it much more difficult to convert the slaves. By the mid-1650s the Reformed preachers refused to baptize Africans any longer because the slaves were now perceived as only being interested in becoming Christians in the hope of gaining their freedom. According to minister Henricus Selijns in 1664, the Africans were no longer interested in "pursuing piety and Christian virtues" but only in advancing the freedom of their children through baptism.[2]

SURINAM

The English colony of Surinam was captured by an expedition launched by the province of Zeeland during the Second Anglo-Dutch War (1665–67). At the time of the conquest, Surinam was an emerging sugar plantation colony of 4,000 people, most of them African slaves. When Surinam was granted to the Republic and New Netherland to England at the Treaty of Breda in 1667, most English planters left Surinam, taking their slaves with them and leaving behind a ruined colony. From 1667 to 1682, Surinam was governed by Zeeland. Faced with abandoned plantations and a destructive war with Carib Indians, Zeeland eagerly sold the colony to the WIC in 1682. As the WIC was itself confronted with financial problems, the company sold a portion of the colony to the city of Amsterdam and to the aristocratic Van Aerssen van Sommelsdyck family. These three groups united as the Society of Surinam which governed Surinam from 1683 until 1791. After 1700, Surinam developed as a major plantation colony. The number of private plantations grew from 171 in 1713 to more than 400 in 1800. The population reflected this growth, going from 1,000 Europeans in 1700 to almost 2,000 in 1755. The African slave population grew from 10,000 to 35,000 during the same period. In addition, the colony was inhabited by several maroon communities (runaway slaves) and a number of indigenous groups.

The position of the Reformed Church in Surinam is often characterized as that of a *handelskerk* or trade-church in which the priorities of the Reformed Church were subordinated to commercial concerns of the planter class. This is correct for the eighteenth century when the Surinam plantation economy greatly expanded. For example, in 1733 the influential planters who sat in the consistory of Paramaribo, the colonial capital, forced minister Jan Willem Kals to leave the colony because he had shown too much interest in converting the slaves.

However, from 1667 to 1683, when the religiously conservative province of Zeeland ruled Surinam, the Calvinist church tried to play a prominent role in the public life of the colony. In this era the Classis of Walcheren, the church body responsible for coordinating Calvinism in Zeeland, also controlled religious affairs in Surinam. Similar to the situation in New Netherland, the Classis of Walcheren and the colonial government closely cooperated in implementing moral discipline. The Classis of Walcheren appointed the zealous minister Johannes Basseliers as the first minister to the colony in 1668. Basseliers quickly established the basic infrastructure for the Reformed Church in Surinam by organizing the first consistory in 1669. By 1680 there were three churches in the colony. The close cooperation between church and state was expressed by prohibitions against the sale of goods and alcohol on Sundays and by issuing ordinances against licentiousness.

Calvinists also tried to limit the rights of the colony's Jewish community. Jewish planters, many from Dutch Brazil, had been in Surinam since the English period and had received the right to publicly worship under English rule in 1665. When the Zeeland expedition conquered Surinam in 1667, the Dutch commander confirmed the existing privileges for the Jews. Two years later, when Surinam was still in ruins and desperately needed settlers, Governor Julius Philips Lichtenberg even permitted Jews to work on Sundays. However, the States of Zeeland rejected Lichtenberg's tolerant measure. In January 1675, the Jews again petitioned the colonial government to be exempt from the prohibition to work on Sundays. Despite Jewish petitions, this measure remained into effect until the Society of Surinam took over the control of the colony from Zeeland in 1683. Unlike conservative Zeeland, the Society of Surinam was dominated by more liberal Amsterdam. Since many of the Jews in Surinam in the early 1680s were planters who owned slaves, and thus were vital for the struggling colony, the Society of Surinam allowed Jews and their slaves to work on Sundays. In 1685 the Jewish planters were even permitted to construct a synagogue.

The Calvinist church also encountered problems in converting the Indians and African slaves. The Classis of Walcheren had instructed Basseliers to devote attention to this task, but he soon concluded that there were serious obstacles, such as the ongoing war with the Caribs, the unwillingness of indigenous parents to part with their children, and the inability to find adequate schoolteachers.

After the Society of Surinam took control, the public church was quickly subordinated to the colonial state. The colonial government ensured that the Reformed Church did not undermine slavery and interfere with economic developments. Except for individuals such as the minister Kals, the Reformed Church did not challenge but supported the racial hierarchy in the colony. When one minister converted several slaves in 1767, the colonial council reprimanded him for not having asked permission from the governor to do so. The colonial government occasionally supported the Reformed Church in enforcing anti-Jewish measures. After complaints from the Surinam consistories in 1718, the government prohibited Jewish shopkeepers in Paramaribo from displaying their wares on Sundays. At the same time, the colonial government continued to uphold the religious and social privileges for the sizeable Jewish community. Additionally, officials allowed the Lutherans in 1744 to build their own church, which was completed in 1747.

The Reformed Church was also powerless to prevent the Society of Surinam from contracting Moravians in 1734 to stimulate the colonial economy. In addition to the rise of religious pluralism, the Reformed Church was disheartened by the constant immoralities committed by

Protestant planters. Instead of attending church on Sunday many planters took leisurely boat trips with their mulatto mistresses. Clearly, when the States-General assumed direct control of Surinam in 1791, the influence of the consistories on colonial society had become minimal.

In short, the Calvinist church was not negligent in trying to instill orthodoxy in the colonies of Brazil, New Netherland, and Surinam. The Reformed Church and its consistories and classes consistently tried to regulate the behavior and morals of Christians and non-Christians in the Dutch Atlantic. In this respect the Reformed Church was not that different from the Catholic Church in the Iberian colonies of the New World. Like their Catholic counterparts in the Atlantic, the extent to which the Reformed Church was able to impose religious discipline in Dutch Brazil, New Netherland, and Surinam depended on time, space, and the relationship between church and state in each colony.

Although the Reformed Church invested considerable energy and manpower in Brazil, the various Classes of Brazil had a hard time regulating morals and beliefs in the multicultural and multiconfessional colony. Above all, the WIC was never able to fully stabilize the colony except for a brief period in the early 1640s. Moreover, most of the Protestant population consisted of soldiers and sailors who were neither the easiest groups to discipline nor were seen as well-qualified to serve as consistory members. Near-constant warfare and the presence of a large Catholic and Jewish population who were indispensable for sugar production made it practically impossible for the Reformed Church to implement Calvinist orthodoxy in the colony.

In New Netherland the Reformed Church was remarkably effective in maintaining hegemony. In the absence of a Catholic community and faced with a very small Jewish community that only arrived in the mid-1650s, Calvinist leaders and their supporters in the consistories had a relatively easy task in suppressing religious pluralism. Moreover, as New Netherland became a settler society that closely resembled the motherland the exercise of church discipline through consistories also became similar to that of the Republic. In Surinam, on the other hand, support from the secular authorities for the Reformed Church was sorely lacking, except for the brief period when the plantation colony was governed by Zeeland. After 1683, when the Society of Surinam assumed control and economic development was prioritized, the influence of the Reformed Church in the colony quickly declined. Whereas consistories in New Netherland were increasingly occupied by urban and rural immigrants from the Republic whose moral concerns sometimes overlapped with that of the Reformed

Church, in Surinam the consistories were dominated by the planter class which was little concerned about instilling moral discipline in the colony. Overall, the three case studies demonstrate that support from secular officials proved crucial in enforcing Calvinist discipline in the Dutch Atlantic. Although directors and officials of the WIC sometimes supported measures to implement Reformed discipline in the colonies, in most cases practical and commercial considerations trumped religious concerns for the Dutch trade company.

Notes

1 Dutch National Archives, 1.05.01.01, Archive of the Old WIC, inv. nr. 70: Daily Minutes of the High Council in Recife, September 20, 1644, section 1.
2 Evan Haefeli, *New Netherland and the Dutch Origins of American Religious Liberty* (Philadelphia, 2012), 129.

21

Inquisitions

Allyson M. Poska

In many ways, the American tribunals replicated the priorities and activities of their peninsular counterparts. They struggled to ensure Catholic hegemony through the prosecution of Lutherans and New Christians and worked to enforce orthodoxy through the pursuit of minor heresies among the Old Christian populace. As was true on the peninsula, the tribunals were subject to the vagaries of local politics and had very little influence in rural areas. However, the Inquisition tribunals in the Americas evolved in ways that reflected the many threats to early modern imperial authority, as well as the demands of regulating the diverse racial and ethnic populations of the Americas.

The earliest Inquisitions in the Americas took place during the Franciscan evangelization of the Aztec empire. In 1524, when the first Franciscan missionaries arrived on the mainland, they came with papal authority to conduct Inquisitions based on the bull *Exponi Nobis* (known in Spanish as the *Omnímoda*), which allowed regular clergy to perform all episcopal functions except for ordination. Of course, the ability to conduct Inquisitions was of little use in those first years of the evangelization, as the majority of the population had not yet been baptized. Nevertheless, there is evidence that the Franciscan Martín de Valencia prosecuted and executed a few newly converted indigenous Mexicans for having relapsed into idolatry and human sacrifice.

In 1525, the *audiencia* (the provincial judicial tribunal) of Santo Domingo and the Inquisitor General in Spain transferred inquisitorial authority to the Dominican Order. First, Tomás Ortiz and then Domingo de Betanzos established an episcopal-type Inquisition, which prosecuted a number of conquistadors for blasphemy and ordered Hernando Alonso and Gonzalo de Morales burned at the sake for Judaizing in an *auto de fé* in October 1528. By focusing on the Spanish rather than the Indigenous population, these prosecutions were part of a multifaceted attempt to assert control over Hernán Cortés and his supporters.

These monastic Inquisitions would be short lived, as the monarchy quickly moved to establish formal ecclesiastical structures in Mexico. In the Americas, the Spanish Crown, not the Catholic Church, was the primary actor in this regard. In 1486, the Papacy had granted Ferdinand and Isabel the *Patronato*, the right to present (that is, select) appointees for clerical office in the not-quite-conquered kingdom of Granada. Then, in the wake of *Inter Caetera* (1493), which gave the Spanish monarchy exclusive rights to evangelization in the Americas, the Papacy extended the *Patronato* to the Americas in 1508. Not only would the monarchy receive all tithes in perpetuity (ostensibly to fund the evangelization efforts) but it had the right to present all cathedrals and benefices in the newly conquered lands.

Based on the *Patronato*, Charles V established the first diocese in Mexico in 1527, appointing Juan de Zumárraga as bishop. Zumárraga had some prior experience conducting inquisitional investigations in northern Spain, and beginning in 1536, he zealously undertook his role as inquisitor in Mexico, prosecuting at least 120 cases between 1536 and 1541, the majority of which involved blasphemy, bigamy, and Judaizing.

During the ensuing decades, the conquest extended Spanish territorial control across Mexico, Central America, and Peru. That expansion in combination with the dramatic decline of the indigenous population from disease and challenges to royal authority from conquistador elites led the Crown to reorganize inquisitional authority in the Indies. In 1570–71, Philip II established formal Inquisitions in the viceregal capitals of Mexico City, whose first Inquisitor General was Pedro Moya de Contreras, and Lima where Antonio Gutiérrez de Ulloa took the reins of the institution until the end of the century. These tribunals faced serious obstacles. First, they held jurisdiction over vast territories and enormous populations. The Mexican tribunal was charged with ensuring orthodoxy from Zacatecas in the north to Honduras in the south, and eventually its territory included the Philippines. The tribunal in Lima prosecuted heresy in all of the Spanish territories in South America until 1610 when a third tribunal was established in Cartagena de Indias. That tribunal had jurisdiction over New Granada, the Caribbean islands, and Spanish Florida. Second, from their moment that they were established, the American tribunals faced challenges to their authority from other secular and ecclesiastical authorities. Mexican and Peruvian Inquisitors struggled against the constraints imposed by the *Suprema* in Madrid, while viceroys and the *audiencias* regularly clashed with Inquisition officials. The Holy Office also faced opposition from local elites and regular clergy. Finally, all of the tribunals were compromised by poor staffing, inefficient communication, and fiscal problems.

The situation in Brazil was substantially different. Although the Portuguese monarchy also had complete authority over the church in its empire based on its version of the *Patronato*, the *Padroado*, no permanent tribunal was ever established in Brazil. Rather, Brazil fell under the jurisdiction of the Lisbon tribunal, and inquisitors from the peninsula visited only three times during the colonial period. In the first visit, the Visitor General D. Heitor Furtado de Mendonça heard denunciations and confessions in Bahia and Pernambuco from 1591 to 1595. His investigations resulted in the prosecution of nearly 200 men and women, mostly for making heretical propositions. Without a permanent inquisitor, the accused were not tried in Brazil, but were sent back to Lisbon for prosecution. During the entire seventeenth century, an inquisitor from Portugal visited only once, venturing to Bahia in 1618 to 1620. In lieu of regular visitations, the Inquisition developed a network of *comissários* and *familiares* to act in its stead. As that network solidified, inquisitional activity increased. In fact, most of the activity of the Inquisition in Brazil took place in the first decades of the eighteenth century.

Considering the expanses of territory and large populations, few people were prosecuted in the Americas. In all of Spanish America, probably no more than 5,000 people faced inquisitorial scrutiny over the course of nearly 250 years, and only 1,076 trials of Brazilians were held between 1519 and the dissolution of the tribunal in the nineteenth century. Moreover, as was true across the Iberian empires, executions were rare. No more than fifty executions took place in Mexico and in Lima only forty-eight people burned at the stake over two and a half centuries. Despite all these issues, the four tribunals played a critical role in the extension of imperial authority and the imposition of imperial control in the Americas.

CONTROLLING THE EMPIRE: INDIANS, LUTHERANS, AND
NEW CHRISTIANS

Although it was clear to everyone that the new territories in the Indies would require an Inquisition just like the rest of the Spanish kingdoms due to the ongoing threats from Protestantism and New Christians, from the beginning the Spanish Crown was ambivalent about using the Inquisition to ensure orthodoxy among the newly converted indigenous peoples of the Americas. That ambivalence stemmed from its experience on the peninsula. In 1526, Charles V, worried that forced conversions of his Muslim subjects in the kingdom of Granada would prompt violence against the Crown, came to an accord with the Muslim community under which the Holy Office would be lenient with the Muslim converts for a period of forty years. Of course, at the same time, the early evangelization in Mexico by the Franciscans, which was also based on mass baptisms with little or no prior religious instruction, bore striking similarities to that of Granada. Based on the Granadan case, many expressed concern that the use of the Inquisition to pressure Indians into religious conformity would lead many to reject the faith and/or revolt against royal authority. Thus, in 1538, Charles also exempted Indians from inquisitional jurisdiction.

The king and other officials may have hoped that the exemption would allow for more extensive instruction of indigenous converts, but in Mexico, suspicion and distrust among indigenous elites and Spanish clerics quickly led to inquisitorial intervention. Only a year later, Zumárraga began to pursue Nahua leaders, *caciques,* for worshipping indigenous gods, rejecting Christianity, and encouraging others to return to their native beliefs. Among those prosecuted was Don Carlos Ometochtli of Texcoco who was denounced by political opponents and whom Zumárraga convicted of heresy and burned alive. His execution precipitated an outcry from Spanish religious and secular authorities, as well as indigenous elites. In response, the Council of the Indies stripped Zumárraga of his inquisitorial authority, admonished the American clergy to treat the indigenous people with kindness, and reiterated their exemption from inquisitorial jurisdiction. Nevertheless, the policy that forbade using inquisitorial procedures against new converts was contravened again two decades later. The Franciscan Diego de Landa was an enthusiastic and driven missionary, who played a central role in the establishment of the church in Yucatán. However, by 1562, he became frustrated by evidence that the local population in Maní was continuing to worship its indigenous deities. In response, de Landa initiated a violent campaign against idolatry, torturing thousands of Maya men and women and killing some in the process. He also burned dozens of Mayan codices and destroyed thousands of Mayan religious "idols" in an *auto de fé* on July 12, 1562. Fortunately, the newly arrived bishop of Yucatán, Fray

Francisco de Toral, immediately realized the dangers of de Landa's zeal. He ended the campaign against idolatry and reprimanded Landa for his use of violence.

After the establishment of the Holy Office in 1571, these extirpation of idolatry campaigns were waged mostly under the auspices of archiepiscopal authorities. In Peru, the Extirpation, as it became known, employed an Inquisition-like apparatus, headed up by a *visitador general de las idolatrías* who had extensive powers to visit, investigate, and sentence offenders. Its activity was completely dependent on the interest of the archbishop of Lima. Some of Lima's seventeenth-century archbishops like Bartolomé Lobo Guerrero (1608–22) and Pedro de Villagómez (1641–71) were zealous campaigners, while others like Hernando Arias de Ugarte (1630–38) were not. In addition to episcopal zeal, a key factor in these idolatry trials was the complicity of indigenous people in both the perpetuation of native devotions and the denunciation of friends and neighbors to authorities. Scholars used to argue that extirpation campaigns declined after the mid-seventeenth century, as religious authorities became more tolerant of native devotions and the indigenous population became fully acculturated to Christianity. However more recently scholars have demonstrated that in both Peru and Mexico the 1660s was not a transitional moment in relations between the church and its native flock; rather both native devotions and extirpation trials continued well into the eighteenth century.

With at least 75 percent of the population exempt from prosecution, the Inquisition turned its time and energies to broader imperial priorities. In the broader sixteenth-century context, the crown was more concerned that the tribunals in the Americas ensure that neither Lutherans nor relapsed converted Jews escape to the newly conquered lands to proselytize and practice their heretical beliefs.

In the mid-sixteenth century, Protestants represented the most serious threat to the Catholic Church and the Spanish monarchy. Thus, in the early years, Mexican bishops acting as inquisitors tried a number of mostly foreign men for heresies related to Protestantism all of whom they referred to as *luteranos* (Lutherans), with little regard for the theological differences among Protestants. With the establishment of the Holy Office, French corsairs and English and northern European sailors and traders faced the most scrutiny. In the first year alone, the Mexican tribunal led by Moya de Contreras conducted more than sixty-eight trials of Protestant heretics. At the end of the sixteenth century, there was another wave of prosecutions, this time against presumed Calvinists. At an *auto de fé* in

1601, thirty-two *luteranos* appeared and four were burned at the stake. By the seventeenth century, prosecutions for Lutheranism were uncommon in Mexico and Peru, but the Cartagena tribunal periodically battled the plague of Protestantism, as Caribbean commerce, both licit and illicit, brought foreigners into their jurisdiction. However, when international commerce pressured the Spanish king to grant a modicum of toleration to English and Dutch merchants, the Inquisition complied. Censorship was also a key factor in the Inquisition's attempt to control the spread of heresy in the Americas. Although some clergy attempted to constrain access to prohibited books by urban elites, in general the tribunals were never particularly effective at controlling the consumption of heretical texts by colonial readers.

As the expulsion of the Jews occurred the same year as Castile's acquisition of much of the Americas, the Crown feared that relapsed New Christians would flee to the Indies to evade their newly installed Inquisition. Thus, all emigrants were required to provide a certificate of purity of blood, *limpieza de sangre*, a bureaucratic measure that ostensibly would prevent New Christians to the third generation from embarking for the Indies. However, as we have already seen, some of the first prosecutions in Mexico were against accused Judaizers. In the last years of the sixteenth century, the tribunal made the prosecution of Judaizers a priority, arresting members of a powerful political family, the Carvajal, for Judaizing in 1596. During his incarceration, Luis de Carvajal (the younger) wrote an autobiography and letters to his mother and sisters that articulated dedication to his Jewish faith. Nine members of the family were eventually executed at an *auto de fé*.

In the seventeenth century, the prosecution of Judaizers in the Americas was intricately linked to both imperial and peninsular politics. After the edict of expulsion in 1492, many Spanish Jews, known as Sephardim, fled to Portugal until the establishment of the Portuguese Inquisition in 1536 forced them to flee once again. Some went to the Netherlands, but others sought refuge in other parts of the Portuguese empire, all of which came under Spanish rule in 1580. In the following decades, the Spanish grew increasingly suspicious of not only Portuguese loyalty to the Spanish monarchy but also the Portuguese tolerance of New Christians and the success of Portuguese New Christians in the Atlantic trade. In fact, for many, being New Christian and being Portuguese became synonymous. Increasingly economic success became evidence of Judaizing, and many feared that the diaspora of Jews and crypto-Jews would aid each to the detriment of Old Christian merchants. At the same time, the Spanish monarchy recognized the economic potential that came with New Christian communities. Under Philip III, New Christians were allowed to settle and trade in the Americas (after paying an enormous fee) and they negotiated a papal decree in 1605 that pardoned relapsed Jews across the Iberian empires. The policy of tolerance for New Christians continued during the tenure of King Philip IV's favorite, the Count-Duke of Olivares.

When the Dutch took Bahia in northeastern Brazil in 1624, many Spaniards believed that Portuguese New Christians would naturally ally with the invaders because of their economic connections in the Netherlands and Dutch tolerance for Judaism. Peruvian inquisitors were attuned to the fact that that would place a community of relapsed Jews on their border and potentially within their jurisdiction. In this atmosphere of fear and distrust, rumors of Portuguese/Jewish heresy abounded and led to the "discovery" of *la complicidad grande,* the Great Conspiracy. Between 1635 and 1639, the Lima tribunal arrested more than 100 men and women for Judaizing, and in a spectacular *auto de fé* in 1639, 72 were punished, 11 of whom were relaxed to the secular arm for execution.

The anti-*converso* sentiment quickly spread to Mexico. The Portuguese revolt against Spain in 1640 again called into question the loyalties of the *converso* population and Olivares's fall from favor left New Christian communities without royal protection. Among others, Blanca Méndez de Rivera and her family were arrested by the Inquisition in 1641 as a part of both a broader crackdown on suspected Judaizers and Archbishop Palafox's personal concerns about his own "great conspiracy." The Mexican Inquisition conducted four *autos de fé* between 1646 and 1649, executing thirteen for Judaizing in 1649. In Cartagena de Indias, where a significant community of New Christians had emerged in conjunction with the slave trade, the "great conspiracy" led to the prosecution of at least thirty-nine Judaizers. Of course, no great conspiracy ever existed, but the fantasy of intrigue on an imperial scale (similar rumors spread on the peninsula) and the violent repercussions that it provoked were powerful reminders of both the power of the Inquisition and the tenuous position of New Christians across the Iberian world.

Initially, authorities in Lisbon demonstrated little interest in the New Christians whose economic success was driving Portuguese growth. However, the same imperial rivalries that provoked anti-*converso* activity from the Spanish-American tribunals eventually affected the New Christian community in Brazil. After northeastern Brazil was returned to Portuguese control in 1645, the Jesuit Manoel Fernandes led an extensive visitation that produced 118 denunciations mostly for minor heresies; however, 73 percent of the accused were New Christians.

As the Inquisition in the Spanish territories fell into decline during the eighteenth century, the Portuguese Inquisition demonstrated renewed vigor, particularly in its prosecution of Judaizers in Brazil. The 470 defendants made up more than 40 percent of the total cases tied to the Inquisition in Brazil, half of the Brazilians burned at the stake, and two-thirds of the women tried by the tribunal. This burst of inquisitorial activity can be closely correlated with the discovery of gold in Minas Gerais. As New Christian merchants provided an array of goods to participants in the gold rush, economic success was again equated with Judaizing.

From the beginning, the activity of the Inquisition tribunals in the Americas reflected the imperial concerns of the Spanish monarchy. Faced with a Muslim threat on the peninsula and concerned that the prosecution of new converts might lead to the violent rejection of Christianity and Spanish governance, Indians were quickly exempted from inquisitional authority. At the same time, royal anxieties about the spread of Protestant heresy and the authenticity of New Christians led to sporadic prosecutions of Lutherans and Judaizers across the Americas. Although the Dutch conquest of northeastern Brazil briefly heightened those concerns as Inquisitors faced the specter of a significant New Christian/Jewish community adjacent to its territory, the most intense prosecutions of accused Judaizers came not in Spanish America during the Dutch crisis, but in eighteenth-century Brazil, long after that the withdrawal of Portugal's Protestant rival from the region.

RACE, GENDER, AND THE AMERICAN TRIBUNALS

Even as it acted as an arm of imperial politics, the majority of the Inquisition's efforts in the Americas went to enforcing orthodoxy among the general population through the prosecution of minor heresies. During the sixteenth and seventeenth centuries, nearly 70 percent of the cases brought before the tribunal in Mexico involved minor heresies and in Lima and Cartagena, the figure was closer to 75 percent. Most of the denunciations and prosecutions were for blasphemy. In the early days of the conquest, blasphemy was a particular concern for the clergy in the Americas, as they feared that heretical utterances by Spaniards could hinder the evangelization of the natives. Moreover, prosecuting blasphemy was a critical way for the Spanish Crown to police the hypermasculine and antiauthoritarian behavior of conquistadors and early colonists. However, by the end of the century, although prosecutions for blasphemy increased, with the consolidation of both secular and religious institutions, inquisitors were generally lenient with offenders. While some colonists made dangerous denials of the efficacy of Christian rituals and beliefs, Stuart Schwartz has argued that many others were denounced for making more benign and commonly accepted expressions of religious tolerance and challenges to the church's ideas about sexuality.

Bigamy was the next most frequently prosecuted of the minor heresies by all of the tribunals. Of course, the church was profoundly interested in protecting the sacrament of marriage and ensuring that sexual activity was confined to the marriage bed. However, in the early modern world, bigamy was the paradoxical expression of the intersection between piety and love. As the church forbade divorce, when a marriage failed or a spouse found a new love, there was no legitimate way to extract oneself from the marriage. Annulments were difficult to obtain and even on the relatively rare occasions when episcopal authorities granted separation of bed and board, that form of Catholic divorce did not allow either spouse to remarry. Generally couples merely separated informally and took up with new partners, a decision made easier by the long distances and lack of either ecclesiastical or secular supervision in much of the Americas. At the same time, it is striking evidence of the cultural power of the sacrament of marriage that, despite clerical injunctions and the threat of inquisitorial denunciation, many people chose to marry a second or even third time. However, multiple marriages were not only a sin against the sacrament, but they also threated civil society, whose laws presupposed the primacy of patriarchal family. By far, the majority of those accused of the heresy were men, at least half were white, indicating that inquisitors viewed its prosecution as key to controlling the sexual activity of the Spanish population and preserving the integrity of the Spanish nuclear family.

Although the intensity of tribunals' prosecution of blasphemy and bigamy was similar in the peninsula, their interventions into the daily lives of colonial subjects affected the racially diverse population of the Americas in radically different ways. For instance, in the process of investigating and adjudicating the denunciations, inquisitors became involved in the complex process of defining racial identities, particularly since Indians were exempt from its jurisdiction. When Francisco Rojas was accused of bigamy by the Mexican tribunal, he claimed that he was Indian, and therefore exempt from inquisitorial jurisdiction. Others, however, described him as mestizo.

Of course, the work of the inquisitors was made more complicated by the fact that the process was dependent on ordinary people's often flexible definitions of race and cultural normativity, as well as their conceptions of heterodoxy and orthodoxy. Such obstacles often frustrated the bureaucratically minded Inquisition staff. In Francisco's case, inquisitors eventually issued a sentence that reflected their inability to resolve the issue. They both freed Rojas (indicating that they believed that he might be Indian, and thus exempt) *and* admonished him not to return to his second wife under threat of punishment (indicating that they believed that he might be mestizo, and thus subject to their jurisdiction).

It was also important for inquisitors to identify the racial/ethnic origins of the accused in order to better understand the degree to which African or indigenous devotions may have "tainted" his or her Christianity. Inquisitors drew a sharp dichotomy between a "pure" Christianity and anything "tainted" by African or indigenous beliefs; however, trial records reveal that across the racial spectrum, colonial subjects had a much more complex understanding of the relationship between Christianity and non-Christian devotional practices and beliefs. Witness testimonies reveal that Christianized peoples of all races and ethnicities believed that a wide variety of ritual and beliefs could be easily coopted into one's religious activity without compromising one's Christian faith, and those same acts or ideas might be denounced to the Inquisition as heretical when they failed to produce the desired result.

Without jurisdiction over indigenous peoples, the Inquisition took particular interest in the religious activities of enslaved Africans and their descendants (both free and enslaved). Approximately half of those whose ethnicity is evident in the documentation of the Mexican tribunal and about 27 percent of those charged by the tribunal in Cartagena fell into that racial category. Slaves were frequently charged with blasphemy, as the debilitating subjection and violence of slavery elicited an array of heretical outbursts. At times, blasphemes were used strategically. María Blanca, a Congolese slave in Mexico, renounced God and the saints as she was flogged by her mistress in an attempt to end the punishment. Slaves also blasphemed in order to use their audience with the Inquisition as a forum to publically criticize violent masters. At the same time, the tribunal reinforced the slave system, acting as a mechanism for controlling slaves when coercion by their masters failed.

As they exposed the complicated intersections of race, status, and heresy, Inquisition trials have proven to be a remarkable resource for broadening our understanding of the people and ideas that moved around the Iberian

Atlantic. Domingos Álvares, an African spiritual leader and healer, was taken as a slave from Africa and worked in Brazil, where he continued his healing practice. He eventually achieved his freedom, but his fame (or infamy) as a *feitiçero*, "sorcerer," led to his denunciation for witchcraft. Álvares was then sent to Lisbon for trial, where at his first *auto de fé* he was sentenced along with an Angolan woman and a Tupinambá Indian man. Although men and women of all races flocked to these healers, inquisitors believed that the spells, cures, and divinations that emerged from the Portuguese empire's multiracial, multicultural synthesis had diabolical origins.

Inquisitors also became arbiters of appropriate female behavior. Although it seems from a general overview of cases that the Inquisition was generally lenient with women of all races, it is also clear that some women faced increased scrutiny. Women accused of *alumbradismo* like Marina de San Miguel and the "false" mystics studied by Nora Jaffary were usually admonished for transgressing gender norms as much or more than committing heresy. Sexualized expressions of religious ecstasy and inappropriate intimacy with followers were, for inquisitors, indicators of women whose piety had moved beyond the limits of acceptability.

Witchcraft was more extensively prosecuted by the American tribunals than on the peninsula. In Cartagena, these trials made up approximately one-third of the cases in the seventeenth century, and in Mexico and Peru, closer to 15 percent. The prosecutions often had both a racial and a gendered component, as the majority of the accused were people of color and many were women. In fact, in Cartagena, all of those charged with witchcraft were of African descent. These defendants' trials were doubly racially charged as not only was their orthodoxy suspect because of their skin color, but many inquisitors came to associate blackness with the devil and African defendants with devil worship.

Scholars have debated the degree to which the Inquisition empowered or disempowered those accused of witchcraft. On the one hand, Inquisition investigations and punishments advertised and at times even legitimated the accused's ability to access supernatural power. On the other hand, inquisitors defined colonial witchcraft in ways that connected poor women's commercial activity to heresy and often redefined them as threats to both church and state. Even then, many women skillfully maneuvered through the inquisitorial system. Three different trials before the Cartagena tribunal did not stop Paula de Eguiluz, a freed slave, from providing love magic those who sought her services.

Finally, although all of the tribunals in the Americas attempted to constrain the illicit sexual activity that pervaded colonial society, the

Spanish American tribunals did not have jurisdiction over sodomy, despite their organization under the Inquisition of the Kingdom of Aragón. As a result, although from time to time sodomists were erroneously denounced to the Inquisition, inquisitors only prosecuted them in conjunction with other heresies. However, the Portuguese Inquisition did have jurisdiction over both sodomy and bestiality, and tried at least fifty Brazilian men and women for the crime. Although the number of cases was not very large, scholars have used the trials to produce an extensive literature on homosexual activity in colonial society. Moreover, Brazilian scholars have participated in a vigorous debate over whether the inquisitors viewed the sodomitical act itself as heretical or was merely associated with other more serious forms of heresy.

Although scholars have devoted more than fifty years to the study of the Inquisitions in the Americas, there is still much to be done. In particular, comparative analyses could provide greater insight into the function of the Inquisition in colonial society writ large. As it stands, the divisions among scholars as Mexicanists, Andeanists, and Brazilianists tend to exaggerate the differences among the tribunals by favoring the local over the broader institutional context. For instance, comparative analysis could help us better understand if the interactions of AfroMexicans were similar or different from their African counterparts who stood before inquisitors in Peru. In addition, the tribunal in Cartagena offers a slightly different trajectory of prosecutions which also need to be considered in the broader American context.

It is also important to juxtapose the experiences of the people of color who interacted with the Inquisition with the experiences of whites. We know surprisingly little about the religious lives of the white population in either Spanish America or Brazil, although whites were always the majority of those prosecuted. Scholars might look to their European colleagues for examples of how to use Inquisition texts as windows into daily religious practice among the white population and then analyze the degree to which those practices differed from those of the population of color.

In recent years, there has been a movement within the Latin American scholarship toward transatlantic and broader imperial analyses. Such a perspective is particularly important when studying the Inquisition, as from an institutional perspective, the Inquisition was *not* divided into colonial and peninsular tribunals. Scholars have tended to differentiate the activities of these tribunals based on modern dichotomies of colony and metropole, but officials of the Holy Office in Seville would not have understood their charge to be any different from officials in Peru or

Mexico. In fact, it is striking how closely the American tribunals followed the same trajectory as peninsular tribunals. Along those same lines, and this has been clearly demonstrated in recent work on the Portuguese Inquisitions, in order to understand the Inquisition as a global institution, we need to conceptualize it as one piece of a world-wide empire through which people, both in Iberia and around the world, struggled for spiritual and political authority.

Section J

Disciplinary Institutions in an Asian Environment

22

Consistories

Hendrik E. Niemeijer

Across Asian outposts, the employees of the Dutch East India Company (VOC) were preoccupied on a daily basis with purchasing and packing textiles, fine spices, opium, coffee, and tea. Nevertheless, there was a religious dimension to the Dutch maritime empire, albeit less strongly evident than in Portuguese and Spanish overseas expansion. Many of the company servants who professed the Calvinist faith in their home village or town carried their Reformed religion with them to Asia. Since many of these Dutchmen were posted overseas for at least several years, the company felt the need to have the Dutch Reformed Church transplanted to their temporary homes. Consequently, colonial territories were not only subject to Dutch law and VOC decrees; they were also transformed into "Christian republics" in which the Reformed Church exercised an important influence in morals control.

It did so through institutions such as a consistory, a diaconate, an orphanage, an almshouse, and a school system. Local VOC governments for the most part were limited to trading ports, such as Cochin in India, Melaka on the Malay peninsula, or Semarang on Java's northeast coast. Sometimes the VOC also gained jurisdiction over much larger territories, including the Moluccas or the coastal regions of Ceylon. In all cases, the governments took charge for upholding Reformed Protestantism as the only authorized religion in their domain. To ensure all went according to the VOC's wishes, a special political commissioner attended consistory meetings, and all charitable institutions had to submit their annual financial reports to the colonial government in Batavia for approval. In a nutshell, Reformed consistories and institutions formed part of the local backbone structure of the Dutch overseas empire under the VOC.

The most heavily stressed component in studies on Calvinism in VOC territories thus far has focused on the influence of churches in the Dutch Republic. In colonial areas, the Reformed Church was accorded the same protected status as the state-protected church in the Dutch Republic. Yet recent scholarship on empires has called attention to the importance of overseas networks in the functioning of colonial projects. Kerry Ward, for example, has proposed that early modern empires consisted of durable networks of trade, administration, settlement, and legal and forced migration. Certainly, interconnections between Reformed churches and consistories in VOC establishments comprised a religious network within the larger matrix of empire. The VOC depended on this religious network in the recruitment and financing of ministers, chaplains (*krankenbezoekers*), catechists, and schoolmasters. Following this approach, I will argue in this chapter that a Reformed religious network formed a practical factor in the rise of the early modern Dutch empire. Within the context of slavery, forced migration, and deportation, all of which threatened to undermine social stability, religious discipline provided a modicum of moral and social order.

From the early seventeenth century until around 1740, the VOC's religious policies led to the establishment and maintenance of approximately 240 churches in its Asian territories. By no means did all local churches, however, have consistories. The first overseas consistory appeared in December 1620 after the VOC conquered the port city of Jakarta (renamed Batavia) in West Java in 1619. This consistory in the VOC's headquarter in Asia functioned as the central coordinating body for all other churches in VOC settlements across Asia. Over the course of the seventeenth and eighteenth centuries, consistories emerged in a number of locales across the East Indies, Formosa, Ceylon, and other areas.

Across the Moluccas, three consistories were established in the early seventeenth century at Banda, Ambon, and Ternate. Ceylon followed the same pattern after the conquest of Portuguese Colombo in 1656. Three consistories were established in the government towns of Colombo, Jaffna, and Galle. Cochin on the Malabar coast of India (conquered in 1663) was considered to be the fourth government town in Ceylon. The Reformed Church also established itself at the Cape of Good Hope in the mid-seventeenth century, forming consistories in Cape Town, Stellenbosch, and Drakenstein.

Compared to Roman Catholic missions in Asia, Calvinist missionary efforts were modest in scale and scope. The VOC was a trading organization that calculated the expenses and profits in each of its territories and towns, including the costs incurred by ministers and schoolmasters. In the VOC's pragmatic vision, maintaining religious services in its territories did not necessarily mean it felt a strong compulsion to expand religious activities beyond its territorial borders. Therefore the number of Dutch ministers working overseas was always held in check and depended on the need of pastoral care in the territories directly under VOC control, usually urban-maritime towns and cities. During the seventeenth and eighteenth centuries, a total of no more than 605 Reformed ministers were sent to Asia on board a total of 4,720 ships that sailed under the auspices of the VOC. This ratio breaks down to an average of one minister every three years, which was nothing like the thousands of Franciscans, Dominicans, and Jesuits who were sent to Asia as missionaries.

The consequence of VOC parsimony was that the establishment of consistories in maritime southeast Asia was restricted to the communities of believers in a number of port towns such as Ambon, Ternate and Banda-Neira in the Moluccas; Makassar and Timor-Kupang in eastern Indonesia; Padang in west Sumatra; Batavia, Semarang, and Surabaya in Java; and Melaka on the Malay peninsula. In mainland southeast Asia and the Far East, the Dutch made no attempt to promote Reformed missions in such places as Ayutthaya (Siam), Tonkin (Vietnam) or Deshima (Japan), where it was even forbidden by the Japanese emperor. The only exceptions to the VOC policy of restraint were Dutch missions in Formosa (Taiwan) and in the Moluccas, prompted by a strict policy to prohibit Roman Catholicism that was introduced by the Portuguese and Spanish. In Ceylon, the consistory of Colombo supervised around 1,000 members in the town itself, and dozens of small churches populated the island during the course of the eighteenth century.

The religious network linking all of these consistories in Dutch Asia was quite active. The ministers often rotated service in different locations, thus contributing to the unique identity of the Asian-Reformed church. VOC personnel or free burghers (European, mestizo, and Asian) moving from one place to another often requested an *attestatie* or testimony of good standing from the local consistory before boarding a VOC ship. Only after handing over this proof of membership and certification of a moral life could one be recognized as a church member and participate in the celebration of the Lord's Supper. Moreover, it was much easier for a VOC official to gain promotion when he could demonstrate church membership in writing. For high VOC officials, membership in the Reformed Church was even a prerequisite for their appointment. Church membership lists in various locations indicate that many Dutch men and their families traveled from one post to another with an *attestatie*. Consistories in VOC ports administered their congregations carefully, recording the movement of their members. All this recordkeeping created a well-documented religious network within the larger framework of empire.

Of all the VOC towns and territories, Batavia's history is best documented since it served as the central headquarters of the company's operations in Asia. Maintaining a congregation of believers in a bustling, overseas garrison town such as Batavia – a port with constant traffic, in a multiethnic slave society composed largely of soldiers, sailors, and uprooted slaves – was a completely new experience for the Reformed Church, a far cry from the disciplinary work it carried out in the orderly towns of the Dutch Republic. Within the Reformed religious networks across the Dutch Asian empire, Calvinist morals promoted by consistorial discipline, catechism instruction, and poor relief emerged as important elements in the formation of this colonial society. In this urban environment, the Dutch Reformed Church gained prominence in a new type of society.

CONSISTORIAL DISCIPLINE IN BATAVIA

After conquering Jakarta, the VOC constructed a well-defended castle complex and walled town. Although the first Calvinist minister, the Rev. A. Hulsebos, had already been a resident of the VOC lodge since 1616, it was only two years after the conquest, on January 3, 1621, that forty VOC staff and free burghers living in and around the new castle celebrated the Lord's Supper for the first time in Asia. A provisional consistory had been elected only a few weeks earlier. The list of this first group of church members who partook in the celebration of the Lord's Supper reveals that Jan Pieterszoon Coen, the Governor General, was the first communicant. In 1658, more than thirty years after this first celebration, the church claimed 500 members at its communion service. A decision by the consistory in 1648 to allow all baptized adults (mostly privately owned or company slaves) to participate in communion created more growth. Prior to 1648, Asians who had been baptized as adults were not admitted to the Lord's Supper until they had undergone more extensive religious education and passed an additional examination.

The practice of religious discipline in Batavia was based on the Church Ordinance of 1624 and reaffirmed in a revised church order in 1643. The articles related to discipline were taken from the Synod of Dordt (1619). These regulations were also intended for the other churches in the Dutch East Indies, though in practice every church followed its own locally written ordinances. Supervision by a classis or even a synod was simply not realistic given the distances between the churches.

Studies on Reformed discipline in the Netherlands have shown that it exerted primarily an "exemplary function" in Calvinist congregations. Thus, one would not expect that in a rough-and-tumble colonial town like Batavia, the Reformed church to exercise a great influence on the lives of soldiers and sailors or on the everyday comings-and-goings of free burghers, let alone mestizo and slave populations. A close analysis of the church records, however, shows the opposite: the Batavian consistory held considerable sway over a large portion of the European, mestizo, and Asian populations. Naturally, it was in the interest of the VOC to develop an international, principally Asian merchant city that would accommodate those from different religious persuasions. At the same time, a Christian population contributed considerably to social and societal stability and political loyalty to the company. Therefore, the implementation of Calvinist discipline in the VOC's colonial cities had at least the same appeal to a local colonial government as it had to local European magistracies. The key questions include: How did the church wield its instruments to exercise moral control? How did the consistory deal with the great variety of social classes, ethnicities, slaves, and all the other concomitant characteristics of this multiethnic colonial society?

OBSERVING AND SUPERVISING THE CHURCH DISTRICTS OF BATAVIA

The *Nederduytsche stadskerk* or Dutch Reformed city church was situated in the center of Batavia. Located on the west Ciliwung river quay, east of the town square, this monumental cruciform church attracted a couple of thousand believers every Sunday. The Malay-speaking congregation held church services in a special hall in the city hospital. The Portuguese-speaking *Mardijkers* (free Asians mostly of Indian descent) were provided with a church both inside the city walls (the *Portuguese Binnenkerk*) and outside the walls on the eastern side of the city (the *Portuguese Buitenkerk*), founded in 1695. All these churches and their own congregations fell under the authority and member administration of one central Dutch consistory, of which only Dutch men could be its ministers and elders.

The growth of the church in the second half of the seventeenth century placed increasing demands on Reformed pastors. In the last quarter of the seventeenth century each minister had his own district to supervise. From 1674 to around 1700, church membership increased from 2,300 to about 5,000. Eight or so Dutch ministers, assisted by a lay elder from their church district (*kerkewijk*) were responsible for the pastoral care and moral supervision of the members in their district. Their own monitoring was complemented by several people who assisted them in the church organization. Foremost among these helpers were pastoral caretakers or chaplains and indigenous catechists (*inlandse leermeesters*) whose work was spread over several different districts. Only with their regular assistance was a minister able to keep a close eye on the moral lives of the 250 to 600 church members in a given church district.

Other help was also at hand. Various examples in the consistory records indicate that slave-owners proved vigilant in reporting any misbehavior among slaves who had converted to the Reformed faith. Given the power wielded by slave-owners, it is not surprising that the minister's auxiliaries hardly ever reported a slave-owner's transgressions in cases of maltreatment of slaves. Only in a very few cases of extreme corporal punishment did reports about the abuse of slaves ever reach the meetings of the consistory, an indication that church discipline was not intended to be used as a tool to criticize even the excesses of slavery. Since ministers had their own slaves and the church did not speak out against slavery, it was thought normal to discipline one's slaves. In short, Batavian church discipline supported the practice of slavery and ignored even its abuses.

It is difficult to determine how intensively ministers monitored the lives of members in their districts. The consistory records only register those cases that a minister brought before the consistory. As the essay by Christian Grosse in Chapter 10 demonstrates, disciplining often involved informal actions that did not appear in the records; these also formed an important part of morals control in Batavia. Visitation in various districts and reports on members' transgressions were made only four times a year as a part of the preparation of the celebrations of the Lord's Supper. The service was held on every first Sunday in January, April, July, and October. Two weeks before the service, a minister would announce the upcoming event in the church and on the Monday following the announcement, the consistory would meet to make its first review of the church membership lists. In these meetings, each minister would read the membership list of his district aloud, and after each reading, the lives of suspect members would be discussed. After these deliberations, the minister would set aside a few days to walk through the streets of his district, visit each member personally, and extend a personal invitation to attend the next celebration. When he had completed his rounds, the minister reported his findings to the consistory. During a second consistory session, the various people who had transgressed the moral boundaries were reprimanded in the consistory chamber. After an admonishment, those members who repented from their sins and/or reconciled with their neighbors were admitted to the sacrament. Those who remained "stubborn" were suspended from communion until they had undergone a change of heart. No single case of excommunication can be found in the Batavian consistory records.

The deacons, using the same consistory chamber in the *stadskerk*, provided charity to poor members on a monthly basis and also concerned themselves with the moral behavior of "outdoor" recipients (*buytenarmen*) who received a maintenance outside the alms house. These mostly Asian or mestizo Christians had to give proof and gain the support of their district minister, family, and neighbors that they were truly living in poverty. Next to the consistory, the Batavian diaconate also served as an institution for the moral control of church members. Annual inspections of hundreds of poor gathered in the church, and monthly house visitations by two deacons put pressure on the moral comportment of the poor.

Social historians have attempted to determine the intensity of church discipline and its effects on individual and collective behavior in early modern European societies. As Chapter 1 by Mentzer and Chapter 10 by Grosse have pointed out, one methodology usually adopted is statistical analyses of the consistory records (*notulen*). Despite the appropriate reservations about assuming that the records accurately reflect all disciplinary action, attention to disciplinary trends within the records can at least call attention to the concerns of consistories over time. Because of ink corrosion, some pages in the consistory register are largely illegible; nevertheless, it appears that for the period 1677–91, a total of 1,509 persons were summoned to appear before the consistory. This annual average of approximately 100 accused remained fairly constant over these fifteen years, despite the fact the number of church members rose considerably. Of the 1,509 summoned members, around 819 were admonished and, in around 554 of these cases, people were suspended from partaking in one or more celebrations of the Lord's Supper.

SINS AND SINNERS

Of the 819 cases, 294 concerned expressions of illicit sexuality such as concubinage, adultery, and prostitution. An examination of the toponyms of the accused makes it clear that most cases of sexual transgressions concerned slaves and freed slaves in the poorer districts. An explanation for this is that these people were a lot easier to summon to the consistory than European, high-class members who often refused to appear in front of the church council. Furthermore, poverty and marriage were not easy bedfellows, and among these poorer Asian members one can detect a "civilizing process" promoted by church and colonial authorities, which Norbert Elias, Heinz Schilling, and others have identified in Europe.

The second most prominent category, "social conflict," involved a variety of threats to public order including fighting, swearing, drunkenness, petty arguing, and thievery. Of these 273 cases, most transgressors whose ethnicity can be identified were Europeans and mestizos of a relatively high social standing (161), while Mardijkers and lower-class mestizos (illegitimately born) comprised a significant minority (79). Cases of marital conflict (106) indicate the same pattern: about sixty-two Europeans and forty-two mestizos and Mardijkers. The seventy-four transgressions in the field of religion (nonattendance at church services and defying the consistory) were committed by fifty-six Europeans, ten Mardijkers and eight slaves. Table 22.1 shows the percentages (the category "other" is omitted as many cases proved impossible to identify).[1]

This brief analysis raises the question of how significant was the influence of an active consistory in its campaign against sin in this colonial society? After all, 100 cases per year or an average of 25 cases before every celebration of the Lord's Supper out of a total of 2,300 (1674) to 5,000 (1700) church members seems fairly insignificant. On the other hand, the number of Christian groups (Europeans, Mestizos, and Mardijkers) hovered around 8,112 in 1673. As the total population amounted

TABLE 22.1 *Ethnic Identity of the Censured in Batavia*

	Europeans/ mestizos	Mardijkers/ mestizos	Mardijkers/ slaves
Sexuality	10%	42%	48%
Social	59%	29%	12%
Marriage	58.5%	39.5%	2%
Religion	76%	13%	11%

to around 27,000 residents in the town and its immediate vicinity, it would probably be fair to say that around 25 percent of the Christian population were members of the church. Looking at society at large, about 12 percent of the total population was subject to direct morals control by the consistory. One might conclude that the influence of the Batavia consistory was fairly significant, although it is difficult to measure this on the basis of an analyses of church records only. Moreover, the fact that the number of cases remained fairly constant over the years 1677–91 despite the growing number of members might be an indication that the ministers had reached their physical limitations. The constant numbers certainly do not mean that the consistory finally gained more control over Asian and mestizo females. It is much more likely that church discipline, as had occurred in many Dutch and European cities, had become more "exemplary" and less "systematic" in the sense that it was more difficult to monitor the lives of all church members in a district comprehensively.

SINS IN A COLONIAL SOCIAL CONTEXT

The differences between European cities like Amsterdam and a colonial city in Asia should not be underestimated. From their own moral perspective, westerners condemned every form of sexual contact outside government- or church-sanctioned marriage. Southeast Asian societies at that time, however, recognized many different forms of formal and informal liaisons between men and women, and these expressions can be found in a multiethnic port city full of Asian immigrants including Indians, Chinese, and different peoples from the Malay-Indonesian archipelago. Thousands of notarial contracts in Batavia contain all sorts of transactions involving debt relations (*bondage*). Apart from common Asian forms of social relations, the importation of thousands of female slaves from the Indian subcontinent (in particular from Bengal) and placed in European households created many illegal forms of sexual engagement between European men and female slaves.

In particular, lower-caste "black" female slaves from the Indian subcontinent were subjected to racism, misogyny, and discrimination by the European and mestizo communities. They were called *negros* or *swarten* (blacks) and appeared in contemporary Dutch descriptions as despicable women, abhorred by white (*totok*) or newcomers. Many of these women, however, reached a higher social status through marriage when still young with a Mardijker, a mestizo, or even a European, and entered the free Christian Mardijker community. The most direct way to this advantageous marriage was often through concubinage, though it could also result in a life of continuous maltreatment.

For concubines, marriage and church supervision offered a way out of poverty, maltreatment, and exploitation. Religion in a multiethnic slave society could function as a safe haven. A legal marriage supervised by the spiritual leaders of the city's church districts could improve a troubled life without any rights that all too often characterized the plight of immigrant women. It was certainly no coincidence that the Batavian church consisted of approximately 75 percent women, as the 1673 membership list reveals.

In this multifaceted Asian and colonial culture, it comes as no surprise that the Batavia consistory over the years dealt with hundreds of cases of prostitution, bigamy, abandonment, and other sexual sins. Indeed, the decision to permit the first minister in Batavia (December 1620) was taken shortly after a protracted deliberation about the increasing evil of concubinage.[2] A public decree forbade sexual intercourse with female slaves and public prosecutors were given the power to monitor this policy.[3] The Marriage Law of 1622 included the death penalty for bigamy. Although this was also the customary punishment in the Dutch Republic, colonial authorities in Batavia justified its strict enforcement on the supposition that tropical climate stimulated sexual desire. An additional concern was for Batavia's moral reputation in the eyes of other nations, since colonial authorities considered it a "totally derisory and ridiculous matter" should they punish such sins more lightly, "even were we Christians to hold the honor of our women less than the Turks, Moors and Heathens." A third rationale was that European immigrants were regarded as lowliest of the low. One edict referred to them as the "dirtiest and most despicable people, in few of whom – God help us – can one find any [traces of] reasonableness, suitability, and purpose."[4]

The effort to control sexuality was an interminable process, though the consistory never gained complete control over Asian and Mestizo members and the problematic social circumstances that affected these people. This is not to say that all females suffered from a male-dominated racial society. On the contrary, southeast-Asian women showed a remarkable energy and independence, running small businesses by themselves and employing their own female slaves. In particular, Muslim communities protected the property rights of women.

CATECHISM AND SOCIAL CONTROL

Thus far this study of church discipline has focused on the analysis of consistory records, but it is also useful to incorporate documents that provide a different glimpse at the wider practice of neighborhood control, and catechism instruction in the respective districts. In 1648, after experimenting with instructing company slaves in the catechism with Asian lay catechists, the consistory decided to admit all practicing, converted, and baptized Asians to the sacrament of the Lord's Supper. Admission to both sacraments was normal practice in Calvinist churches in Europe but not implemented by the Batavian church until 1648. One of the principal reasons for this decision was the growing number of requests from slave-owners to supply them a sufficient number of catechists to give oral instruction in devotional texts to their domestic slaves. On Sundays these domestic slaves accompanied their owners to church, and people were coming around to the idea that it was no longer useful to exclude them from the Lord's Supper if they were well enough versed in the catechism and had passed a final examination.

In 1652 the whole city was divided into catechism districts, each supplied with its own Asian catechist who maintained a register of the number of houses he attended. Catechists were trained in the repetition of questions and answers from a shorter version of the Heidelberg Catechism in Portuguese or Malay. By 1665 the consistory was supervising eighteen indigenous catechists, the majority of whom were Mardijkers. The catechists reported monthly to the minister in their districts and showed him the lists of candidates for baptism. Most of their pupils were either slaves, recently manumitted slaves, or Mardijkers. When they were considered advanced enough, they were designated as "competents." Three weeks before the celebration of the Lord's Supper, a cohort of "competents" could register for a final catechism examination in the church.

The Asian catechists were known as *mèstèr keliling*, which means the "masters making their rounds" (in the neighborhoods). One of the tasks of these *mèstèr keliling* was to update the lists of church members in their minister's district. In 1682, for instance, the consistory ordered the catechist of the Rev. Gueynier to deliver an updated list of members every month and he was also directed to become familiar with them to ease the work load of the pastor.

This system of house-to-house catechism instruction and simultaneous moral supervision of members reached enormous proportions by the end of the seventeenth century. In 1706 a contingent of thirty-four Asian catechists were making their daily rounds, drumming the fundamentals of the Christian faith (the Lord's Prayer, the Twelve Articles of Faith, the Ten Commandments, and assorted prayers) and a shortened version of the Heidelberg Catechism into the heads of an almost incredible number of 4,873 slaves and Mardijkers. Some 4,440 persons learned the catechism in Portuguese, 323 in Malay and only 110 in Dutch.

Although consistories experienced difficulty in controlling the catechists and dealing with the high demand for catechism instruction from private persons, undoubtedly the catechism system in Batavia did increase control of morals in certain neighborhoods. The biweekly visits yielded information about the moral lives of candidates. The frequent visits by the catechists were a direct help to the supervision of members in ministers' districts. This might have compensated for the lack of social cohesion in Batavian neighborhoods, which were far more fragmented than those in European cities. Half the population was composed of slaves of diverse ethnic backgrounds, restrained by harsh forms of corporal punishment. The fact that 4,440 candidates were instructed in Portuguese, the lingua franca of Batavia, indicates that these candidates did not yet belong wholly to a congregation of confirmed believers. Rather, they remained part of a mixed community of slaves, recently manumitted slaves, or Mardijkers who were only partially integrated into the Christian community of Batavia.

CONCLUSIONS

The establishment of consistories in Asia in VOC-controlled colonial port cities and territories formed part of a religious overseas network in which thousands of overseas Dutch participated. The frequent trafficking of church members, ministers, pastoral carers, and other Christians between the trading settlements kept this network dynamic and led to archival documentation. Batavia as a *Christelijcke Republiek* was promoted by both the colonial authorities and the consistory of the Reformed Church. The actual implementation of Calvinist church discipline acquired greater significance after 1648, following the abolition of the separation of the sacraments. When the number of church members increased drastically during the last quarter of the seventeenth century, church discipline in Batavia became an important instrument to attempt to control the lives of Asian and mestizo citizens, in particular women who had committed sexual offenses. Church discipline was also an important instrument to further regulate the personal lives of domestic slaves. This transformation of Dutch consistorial practice under the influence of the particular social circumstances found in colonial slave society meant that religious discipline became just part of the larger institutional mechanisms in place to uphold moral norms in a multiethnic population of Europeans, mestizos, free Asians, and slaves. The hierarchy it underpinned was quite clear-cut. Calvinist slave-owners were never admonished for the maltreatment of their slaves, a common practice. Members of the European elite were seldom humiliated by being summoned to the consistory chamber but always questioned discreetly in their own homes.

The control of morals by the consistory was supported by two other areas of church work: catechism instruction in private homes and poor relief to the paupers qualified to receive monthly alms at home. Candidate members were watched closely by the Asian catechists, neighbours, district heads, and ministers had the right to assess the quality of life of the applicant for poor relief before alms were distributed. Surveying all the activities of the church, it could be said that in the dynamic interactions between the elite of the VOC and their subjugated Asian and mestizo peoples, the power to exercise social and moral control in colonial settlements was central to the age of Dutch expansion.

Notes

1 Hendrik E. Niemeijer,*Calvinisme en koloniale stadscultuur: Batavia 1619–1725* (Amsterdam, 1996), 224.
2 National Archives (hereafter NA) The Hague, 1.04.02, VOC inv. nr. 1072, fols. 187–200, resolutions of the Supreme Government December 11, 1620.
3 Ibid.
4 NA, nr. 1076, fols. 246–287, resolutions July 4, 1622.

23

Inquisitions

Bruno Feitler

The Portuguese Holy Office of the Inquisition was created in 1536 on the same basis as its older Spanish sister, founded approximately fifty years earlier. Aiming at the eradication of heresy in general but mainly of crypto-Judaism, it expanded its direct action to the Asian Portuguese Empire in 1561 with the arrival of the first two inquisitors of the local tribunal to the city of Goa, the head of the Portuguese dominions in Asia (the so called *Estado da Índia*). The only extra-European Portuguese inquisitorial court had jurisdiction over all the very discontinuous and scattered Portuguese territories in East Africa and in Asia.[1]

The history of this tribunal, in its general aspects, is well known: abolished for the first time in 1774 by the Marquis of Pombal, it was recreated four years later, to be definitely closed down due to British pressure in 1814. If it was created mainly to persecute crypto-Jews, it very quickly became overwhelmed by cases of crypto-Hinduism that practically monopolized its activities from the beginning of the seventeenth century on, with a total of more than 16,000 processes. Most of the Goan tribunal records were destroyed in the context of its final abolition; however, this chapter uses the existing historiography, as well as published sources and extant documents kept in Portugal and Brazil, not only to study the Indian Inquisition's rhythm of persecution and its original role in conversion but also to understand how it operated in such a vast space, and its place as a source of power among other local Portuguese political and religious institutions.

The Portuguese presence in Asia, inaugurated in 1498 with Vasco da Gama's arrival at Calicut on the Kerala coast, took on an imperial cast about fifteen years later, with the conquest of its main outposts: Goa in

1510, Melaka in 1511, and Hormuz in 1515. Being a mixed commercial and colonial empire, the Portuguese establishments in Asia expanded and retreated continuously, and at their maximum, spanned from Mozambique and Mombasa in eastern Africa, to Macao and Nagasaki in the far East, with important establishments in the Coromandel coast, Gujarat, and Ceylon. Besides the official trading posts staffed through traditional Portuguese institutions such as a captain named by the king, a municipal chamber, and religious brotherhoods, it is also important to remember that many Portuguese established settlements out of the reach of the empire, sometimes in spontaneous and informal colonies, as happened on the Bengal coast, where they lived as merchants or soldiers. It is estimated that in the first half of the sixteenth century, an average of about 3,500 Portuguese arrived in Asia per year, an average that increased during the Hapsburg dominion of Portugal (1580–1640) to 5,500, and diminished in the following period (1640–1700) to 2,500. These numbers, of course, cannot be taken at face value, since many returned to Europe or died. The real annual average of Portuguese in Asia can be estimated at its height (1571–1610) as between 667 and 1,239, depending on whether one counts immigrants from Asia or from Portugal. But the inhabitants of the Portuguese outposts and territories were far from being solely of European origin. A contemporary source estimated in 1635 the total population of the main Portuguese settlement of Goa and its territories (Bardes, Salcete, Chorão, Divar and Jua) at 100,000 people.[2] Of that total approximately 60 percent were Christian, and only about 800 purely European households. All of them were, nevertheless, under the jurisdiction of the local inquisitorial tribunal.

The creation of the Asiatic tribunal in 1560, together with that of Coimbra five years later, stabilized the network of Portuguese inquisitorial courts. It happened in the wide context of the intensification of repression and of the religious grounding of the Iberian monarchies in the aftermath of the Protestant Reformation. The necessity for a better definition of theological principles by the Roman Catholic Church resulted in a narrower space for negotiation by the Portuguese monarchy when dealing with different populations, and consequently also by its agents, either lay or ecclesiastic.

In the specific context of Goa and the other territories of the *Estado da Índia*, this political stiffening resulted in strong limits on non-Catholic religious ceremonies and observances, which as we shall see later led to the destruction of mosques and Hindu temples and mass conversion among the local population. It also resulted in increased limits on the roles occupied by non-Catholic subjects of the Portuguese monarch.

The creation of the Indian tribunal served clearly to reinforce this intolerant policy toward "New Christians" (the converted descendants of the Jews), and also toward the "Christians of the land" (*cristãos da terra*), that is, the local Asian populations that converted to Catholicism.

This chapter aims to examine how the Inquisition (amid other Catholic institutions) adapted, or rather reacted, to specific cases concerning the local native population of the *Estado da Índia*, a space subject to different political and social situations than in the European motherland. The first part is an examination of the strategies created by the Holy Office to deal with the local Asian situation. It focuses on the problem of the *cristãos da terra* that apostatized from Catholicism and the solutions found to take them back to the fold. The second part examines the specific situation of the important number of non-Christians arrested and judged by this tribunal, which usually had jurisdiction only over baptized people. Those responses were thus a peculiar way of demonstrating the Inquisition's concern not only with the maintenance of Christendom's purity but also with the expansion of the Catholic faith in the context of Portuguese Asia.

Before the creation of the local inquisitorial court in 1560, the prosecution of heretics and apostates was led by episcopal tribunals that traditionally had jurisdiction over heresy. Nevertheless, some religious orders, such as the Jesuits, could also deal with heresy cases in very specific conditions, described in different papal bulls. In fact, there were only a few reports of strict surveillance over local religious practices before the 1560s. Indeed, in descriptions of native people worldwide written by different authors of the sixteenth and the seventeenth centuries, Indians were positioned in the middle of a scale that went from the very refined Japanese to the more barbaric native people of South America. Accordingly, Catholic authors counseled that Indians should be treated with thoughtfulness, taking into account what they saw as a natural difficulty to understand the mysteries of the Christian faith. The establishment of the Inquisition was preceded, therefore, by the demand for moderate treatment of the recently converted, fearing that "no one will convert if the Inquisition has jurisdiction over them."[3] In fact, the main concern of the religious authorities at that time was rather to prosecute Judaizers. The first trials focusing on religious charges concerned New Christians living in Goa and Cochin.

Sources mention indigenous apostates abandoning Goa when they went to live outside Christian territories as early as 1553, but coming back repentant and publicly performing their reintegration to the church, possibly under the care of Jesuits. After the controversial events in Mexico described by Allyson Poska in Chapter 21, converted native peoples of the Americas were finally exempt from inquisitorial jurisdiction by royal and inquisitorial decisions from 1568 (Castile) and 1579 (Portugal). Apparently this possibility was never suggested for people of Asian origin, and as soon as the Inquisition was created in Goa, and in increasing numbers thereafter, *cristãos da terra* were tried by the Holy Office for various offenses. Inquisitors nevertheless took into account the "freshness" of their conversion, and little by little, with the support of the central institutions of the Holy Office they established an *ensemble* of procedures specifically designed to judge local converts in a way that took into account their recent integration in Christendom, but always with respect for canon law requirements to prosecute heresy.

This legal concern is illustrated, for instance, in the issue of recidivism for heretical offenses. Following canon law, inquisitors judged that someone who had relapsed into heresy or apostasy, no matter how repentant he or she was, should be burned at the stake. Inquisitorial authorities knew that if they followed that regulation, not only would they convict an outrageous number of people but also that such severity could prevent other people from converting to Catholicism. Many of the letters exchanged between the inquisitors of India and various inquisitors general – and even the first regulations of the Asian tribunal, dated from 1559 – raised the issue.[4] Nevertheless, rules regarding recidivism were unchanged ten years later. For example, the inquisitor Aleixo Dias Falcão wrote in January 1569 to inquisitor general cardinal Henrique reminding him to provide a papal brief authorizing an exemption for capital punishment for relapsed indigenes. For Dias Falcão it was not only a matter of mercy but also a wider missionary concern, since "this [exemption] seems convenient with respect to the conversion and the new Christianity of these parts."[5] In 1585 the bull had still not been issued, and inquisitor Rui Sodrinho de Mesquita tried to include in it "Moors and Jews baptized as adults," which ultimately did not happen.[6]

While local inquisitors awaited the bull, the improvised solution was to diminish the rigor of a first *processo* opened against those recently converted, or simply to maintain the procedure as inconclusive, as inquisitor general cardinal Henrique ordered again in 1576 specifically in cases of Muslim recidivism. This same letter mentions another important instrument for taking back to the fold those who "within their heart or only by exterior ceremonies" converted to Islam. Inquisitors should publish an edict of grace specifically regarding those cases, granting not only mercy but also release from corporal punishments or the confiscation of property to those who in thirty days presented themselves to the inquisitors.[7] This procedure was inspired by the previous example of the Portuguese North African territories, and might have been used for the first time in India following an order sent by cardinal Henrique in 1572.[8] There, as in Asia, inquisitors had to use alternative methods, adapted to the specific political situation.

North African Portuguese possessions were surrounded by Muslim territories where the Inquisition and its delegates had little space for action. The Holy Office, well known for its persecutory and punitive methods, had for once to make use of persuasion.

In March 1585, the inquisitor general Jorge de Almeida, at the request of the Goan inquisitor, once more sent him an edict of grace, accompanied by the necessary royal decrees that exempted those who presented themselves to the inquisitors from the confiscation of their goods. Given the vast geographic breadth of the *Estado da Índia*, this edict of grace was valid for six months instead of the usual thirty days.[9] In March 1596, on the demand of the archbishop and other clergy, inquisitors published in Goa and in some of the northern fortresses an edict of grace of three months for those who had left Goa for the mainland, but with little effect; very few people came forward and confessed.[10] The publication of edicts of grace and the remission of the penalty of confiscation was used many times, apparently with the same poor results, as admitted by the local inquisitors in 1669.[11]

In 1597, Goan inquisitors wrote to Lisbon about many men who shortly after converting left for the mainland, forgetting the Catholic faith. They eventually returned to Goa, where they showed little or no knowledge of Christianity. Inquisitors suggested that in those cases they should use "the old regimen," meaning that these people would not be immediately formally charged, but instead would be placed "somewhere" where they could think about their offenses and be instructed in Catholicism. The inquisitors added furthermore that if they were going to prosecute all those people, "the cases would be infinite." They also declared that the return of these men to Christian lands was not always completely spontaneous. It was necessary to promise them safe conduct to make them return, and probably when the case regarded a minor heresy, inquisitors would simply send them to their parish priests.[12]

And in fact, a letter dated November 22, 1574 mentions the possibility of a more expeditious procedure for native Christians. They should simply confess to a parish priest, who would instruct them and then send them to the inquisitorial court to have their case solemnized and dispatched.[13] This method was indeed in use a few years later. Inquisitor Bartolomeu da Fonseca related in 1576 that "the Christians of the land who come to confess are heard and immediately sent to the Jesuit 'father of the Christians,' who has them instructed. The penitent then comes back to us with a written declaration [that he had been educated], is acquitted and his case registered."[14]

Different inquisitors general reminded Goan inquisitors of the mildness with which they should treat the "newly converted." Cardinal Alberto did it in a letter dated March 20, 1591, arguing that harsh treatment would scandalize the gentile population (that is, people such as Hindus, who were not members of an Abrahamic faith) and create a barrier to their conversion. Nevertheless, he implied that this treatment could cease once the awaited papal bull concerning the second lapse was published.[15]

The papal brief, issued in January 1599, finally arrived in India that same year. It allowed Goan inquisitors to reconcile local apostates to the church not once, as fixed by canon law, but twice and even thrice before releasing them to the secular court to be executed. It also established that the defendant's possessions should not be confiscated in those first offenses, as was normally the case. Local inquisitors did not appreciate this last novelty, and might also have by that time tempered their earlier desire to be merciful. Marcos Gil Frazão and Antonio de Barros, while discussing the reception of "one of the briefs concerning the neophytes," considered that the policy was "indeed very benign and well-inclined toward these local people. Now, however, they will more easily go to the mainland, knowing that they will not lose their possessions, which before was the only obstacle to their apostasy."[16] The brief was in any case respected but, as happened with many different papal decrees, this one was only valid for five years and had to be renewed by request of the inquisitor general. In 1606, with the brief largely expired, inquisitors were still waiting for its reissue, and they wrote to Lisbon asking what should they do in the case of recidivism.[17] The new brief finally arrived by 1608, but another question surfaced, this time related to the interpretation of the papal document. At the same time that the Goan inquisitors were stating their will to apply the papal bull, inquisitor general Pedro de Castilho received information that the "blacks of the land" baptized as infants, even educated in religious institutions, were not being relaxed to secular justice or having their goods confiscated. In a letter from 1610 he reminded them that the special conditions set by the bull should only be applied to those who were baptized as adults and badly instructed in Catholicism.[18]

The shift in perception of how to deal with the local population is apparent in the letter signed by Jorge Ferreira and Gonçalo da Silva in December 1611, in which they commented on the specific case of Muslims and Hindus who, after their arrest by the Inquisition, converted to Catholicism in exchange for a dismissal of the process. The numerous cases of apostasy in the lands out of reach of the inquisitors (in fact just across the river from Goa) made them wish to use more rigor "following the Doctor's common opinion," since their prior benevolence was practically fruitless.[19] But the fear of repulsing possible conversions by a rigorous procedure, together with the poverty of the locals and the Portuguese belief that locals could not convert to Catholicism and practice it without error, meant that for most of the time the inquisitors' policy toward those arrested for gentile practices was one of general condescension. It is noteworthy that in 1732 the brief was still being applied in some cases,[20] though inquisitors condemned people to death for gentilism or Islam. The first case of capital punishment for gentilism dates from the *auto da fé* of 13 September 1587, when the effigy of Luis Pereira (who was lucky enough to escape Portuguese lands) was burned at the stake.[21] Until then, almost one hundred persons had been condemned to the bonfire in Goa for crypto-Judaism, but the number of people relaxed to secular justice for gentilism only increased over time, and the Goan court would use the maximum penalty frequently until its first abolition in 1774. In the last *auto da fé*, out of more than one hundred convicted, three persons and the effigies of five other were burned at the stake for gentilism.[22]

Other dilemmas surfaced for the Goan inquisitors besides the problem of relapsed heretics. In 1584 they informed Lisbon that "many mestizo Portuguese, slaves, and Christians of the land" went to non-Christian lands to escape territorial law, or in the case of slaves, to escape their Malabar masters. There they would accept Islam to curry favor with local kings or simply out of "weakness or necessity." Once back in Christian lands, they would frequently say that their acceptance of Islam only happened in acts and not "in their heart," perhaps because that was really the case, but probably also because they thought that this kind of behavior was less serious than a full acceptance of Islam. But that was not how inquisitors, with their legal minds, saw the issue. They, to the contrary, saw these kinds of confessions as extremely suspicious and insincere, and sought advice from Lisbon on how to deal with those who denied their "intention," meaning that they did not intend to convert fully to Islam or Hinduism, but only to participate superficially in their ceremonies. Inquisitor general Jorge de Almeida answered that those who confessed "having believed in those sects" should be received with much mercy and reconciled, while those who denied their "intention," (as proven by witnesses), should be relaxed to the secular authorities and burned at the stake as false penitents. But he also mentioned a series of conditional situations that would in practice leave to local inquisitors the responsibility for deciding if defendants were being sincere or not.[23]

Cases concerning neophytes or apostates to Hinduism grew over time. In 1603 inquisitor Jorge Ferreira complained that "this island of Goa is all infected and full of idolatry, and if the inquisitorial court was to treat the people of the land in the ordinary way, they would have a lot to do in the next couple of years."[24] The increase in workload made the inquisitors ask for a third notary in 1640, and ten years later for a third inquisitor, who was granted by the king, who paid the inquisitorial stipends.[25]

Gradually, as had happened previously with Jewish New Christians, the converted population (and their descendants) of the main Portuguese territories in India came roughly to understand inquisitorial procedure and make *en masse* confessions as a way of obtaining special reconciliation conditions. In January 1649 inquisitors wrote that "all the inhabitants of [the island of] Juá either spontaneously presented themselves or are indicted." They then asked the inquisitor general for an edict of grace as a way to avoid "ravaging the place," and also to prevent the confiscation of their modest properties, the fear of which caused their flight "to the other side."[26] A list of the 111 people (mostly first-generation converts) who abjured their errors in an *auto da fé* celebrated in Salsete in 1686 indicates that in most light cases of heresy – showing respect for local traditions considered pagan – inquisitors chose to use a more expeditious procedure that included entrusting their power to commissaries.[27] As with other issues, inquisitorial policy of deputizing commissaries varied over time. After initially granting wide powers in 1621 that enabled commissaries in distant places to investigate as well as to reconcile some specific cases, these powers were rapidly withdrawn in 1632.[28] The use of commissaries seems to be definitely established by the beginning of the eighteenth century, when inquisitor Manuel João Viana, while leading a visit to the northern territories in 1701 and 1702, issued a regimen that local inquisitorial commissaries should follow.[29]

It is difficult to know the specific offense with which these "people of the land" were being charged. The list of all the processes for "Gentile practices" and related offenses, such as adoring or consulting Hindu images or temples (*pagodes*), searching for treasures, divination ceremonies, judged by the Goan court until 1623, account for almost half of the 3,438 total cases. Nevertheless, a plurality of those cases were simply designated as "Gentile practices" (circa 660 cases), with no further explanation about what they were.[30] The existing *auto da fé* lists, which run from the 1680s until the final abolition of the Goan tribunal in 1821, seem not only to confirm that data but also to show that this generic designation of "gentile" acts was even more generalized.[31] What might those "gentile" acts have been? An edict of the Goan Inquisition of 1736 provides a good idea not only of what those acts were but also what was the main concern of the tribunal: controlling every detail of the acts of local Christians, but also, as we shall see, of the local non-Christian population.[32] This exceptionally long edict gives a thorough description of different matrimonial, birth, and funerary ceremonies, and food and clothing habits that were seen as pagan. These included, among many others, having food cooked by "the principal woman or women wearing wet cloth," or planting the *tulosi* plant (that Hindus adored) in their "home gardens, house yards, coconut gardens or other properties." The edict opens with the interdiction of cohabitation between Christians and non-Christians, pointing out the fact that the authorities desired the total "Lusitanianizing" of the local Catholic population. If we juxtapose this edict with the commissaries' regimen of 1702 and the numbers of processes for gentilism, we might conclude that by the eighteenth century the Inquisition had become a kind of customs police, with merciful admonishments but also with the full use of the justice's rigor, depending on the case. Because of the virtually total loss of the Goan processes, it is difficult to determine in detail what would account for the difference in treatment, except for the case of those converted to Catholicism in adulthood who thus benefited from the 1599 papal bull's continuous re-editions.

There was also clearly an economic factor in determining punishment, even more when the culprits lived far from the tribunal headquarters. Goan inquisitors tended to resubmit to trial only persons that would have the means at least to pay the costs of imprisonment, depending also on the gravity of the offense.

Inquisitorial tribunals were created with the specific purpose of returning Christians to the fold who had, in one way or another, betrayed what had been promised on the baptismal font, namely that they would follow the teachings and commandments of the Catholic Church. This implies that non-baptized people, such as infidels (i.e., Jews and Muslims) and pagans (Africans, Native Americans, Indians, and so forth), were not under the jurisdiction of the tribunal of the faith. Nevertheless, some rare cases exist in which non-baptized Jews of Portuguese origin living secretly in Catholic lands for many years were judged for "making as if baptized," and the same happened in Modena, where Jews were tried by the local Inquisition "for endangering Christianity with their behavior." What was unusual in the European or American Portuguese context, namely that non-Christians were judged by the Inquisition for heresy, seemed to be a priority in the Indian world.

The specific Asian context, where small and scattered Portuguese territories were surrounded by Hindu and Muslim territories and states, and also inhabited by non-Christian populations, was very different from that of Europe or America. The Inquisition was thus led in time to deal directly with that non-Christian population, mainly Hindus who lived in Catholic lands. In that sense, in India, Inquisition and mission frequently tended to merge. In the first violent years, marked by wars, sieges, and revolts fed by an everyday resistance to Portuguese Catholic power, the Holy Office was immediately seen as a powerful supplement to proselytizing activity. Among its responsibilities was judging offenses committed by converted locals who escaped to the other side of the border to apostatize. What is more interesting is that the tribunal punished without distinction Christians and non-Christians who impeded the conversion of infidels or endangered the frail faith of local Christians. Those powers, confirmed by the *Mesa da Consciência e Ordens* in 1569, were nevertheless frequently used in a distorted and arbitrary way. Among the trials opened against gentiles or infidels between 1561 and 1623 (62 "gentiles" and about 26 "Moors" out of a total of 3,438 cases), some would end with the concession of absolution or forgiveness in exchange for the respondent's conversion. As early as 1568, the *naiak* Vitul, from the parish of São João, and his family converted to Catholicism so he would be forgiven for selling a Christian slave to a Muslim master.[33] Likewise, the Hindu Antecamotim was condemned on August 10, 1575 for taking some Christians to the mainland to reconvert to gentilism, but then was pardoned when he himself converted to Catholicism.[34] The *Reportorio* of *processos* judged before 1623 contains many other similar cases of non-Christian persons judged for "impeding the faith," some of whom finally converted to Catholicism. Also, some rare cases of infidels judged for sodomy show that the Inquisition was ready to use any means to attain the goal of a purely Catholic Portuguese India, as if it were a mirror of the Portuguese European territories. Amet and Encenè, Muslims from Baçaim (one of the Portuguese Northern territories in India), were arrested and tried for sodomy, and the charges dropped on January 27, 1612 once they decided to convert to Catholicism.[35]

These activities of the local Holy Office were noticed by the Jesuits who, perhaps fearing the briskness with which these people were being converted, wrote to the Inquisitor General in Portugal, Cardinal Henrique, asking for his intervention. In a letter dated March 1580, the now king Henrique wrote back to the inquisitors acknowledging their "care and zeal in favoring and helping the conversion of the local gentiles." He also wrote that "what they had done in that sense served not only as good example, but also as an action that was done in service of God." In a delicate way, King Henrique asked for prudence in that matter, and ordered that the inquisitors be sure, before administering the sacrament of baptism, that there was no hint of gentilism in those who converted to Catholicism.[36]

Over time, the authority of local Catholic institutions grew, and the practice of Indian rites and customs was increasingly restricted in Portuguese territory in the wake of the polemics surrounding the Malabar rites controversy from 1610–30. In 1615, inquisitors were already managing (through authorizations given by them) the celebration of Hindu marriages in Portuguese territories, and one year later, they were opening procedures against Hindus who performed "affirmative gentile ceremonies" such as sacrifices.[37]

The Inquisition thus seems to have claimed jurisdiction over these events, and ended up judging increasing numbers of non-Christians who showed little respect for the prohibition against public or even private Hindu or Muslim rituals. The almost total disappearance of documentation regarding persons tried between 1623 and the mid-1680s keeps us from discerning precisely when these cases began to have the numerical relevance that they would have at the turning point of the late seventeenth or eighteenth century. But all the lists of *autos de fé* completed from 1685 on contain an impressive number of Hindus (and some Muslims) sentenced for practicing prohibited rituals on Portuguese territory, some of whom ended up converting, such as the impressive case recorded in Goa that same year.

On July 22, 1685 many non-Christians were arrested for celebrating a Hindu wedding in the island of Goa. While their trial was still in process, they requested baptism, and the criminal procedure ceased. After being instructed in the mysteries of the faith by the Jesuits in the college of Saint Paul they were baptized by the *pai dos cristãos* Luis de Abreu. A list of these various baptisms, ordered by inquisitor Manuel Gonçalves, shows that they were performed in different ceremonies between February and October 1686 in different parishes of Goa, accounting for exactly 102 persons registered by family groups: father, mother and children.[38] The lists of *autos de fe* two years later do not make clear reference to this type of conversion, but the not infrequent cases of "absolute [gentiles] by court," without any other qualifier, could point to this practice.[39]

Those cases of Hindus arrested for practicing marriage ceremonies, having Hindu images at home, or more generally, for being present in "gentile ceremonies in our lands," or for participating in "offers and sacrifices to the Devil done in our lands,"[40] which were practically non-existent in the sixteenth century, became frequent by the end of the seventeenth century. Gentilism was a major cause of *processos* during the first half of the eighteenth century, until they started to diminish before finally disappearing in the 1770s, when Hindu and Islamic practices were again authorized in Portuguese India, to the displeasure of the local inquisitors.[41]

Thus, during a good part of its long existence in the *Estado da Índia*, and unlike what happened in Portuguese territories in the Atlantic, the Inquisition worked directly with local populations, whether converted or unconverted. This unique quality of the Goan Inquisition in the Portuguese Asian territories led the institution to assume a much more all encompassing disciplinary character than its Atlantic counterpart. But beyond its traditional threatening and punitive character, it also assumed – above all in the second half of the seventeenth century, and parallel to the proselytizing activity of the regular and secular clergy – an auxiliary missionary function, supervising the local population, both Christian and non-Christian.

Notes

1 Abbreviations: ANTT: Arquivos Nacionais da Torre do Tombo. CG: Conselho Geral. Baião I: António Baião, *A Inquisição de Goa. Tentativa de Historia da sua origem, estabelecimento, evolução e extinção* (introdução à Correspondência dos Inquisidores da India 1569–1630) (Lisbon, 1945); Baião II: António Baião, *A Inquisição de Goa. Correspondência dos inquisidores de Goa (1569–1630)* (Coimbra, 1930). Reportorio: *Reportorio geral de tres mil oito centos processos, que sam todos os despachados neste sancto Officio de Goa …* [1623]; BNL: Biblioteca Nacional de Portugal – Lisbon, BNRJ: Biblioteca Nacional do Rio de Janeiro.
2 See Sanjay Subrahmanyam, *The Portuguese Empire in Asia 1500–1700. A Politic and Economic History.* Chichester, 2012), 228–36.

3 Melchior Carneiro to Francisco de Borja, Dec. 6, 1555 (Ioseph Wicki (ed.) Documenta Indica. Romae: apud Monumenta Historica Soc. Iesu, 1948–1988 (18 vols), 3, #. 65).

4 Cunha, *A Inquisição no Estado da Índia*, 126–9, 299–300.

5 Aleixo Dias Falcão to Inquisitor General Henrique, Goa, January 3, 1569. Baião II, 4.

6 Rui Sodrinho de Mesquita to the General Council of the Inquisition, Goa December 24, 1585. Baião II, 99.

7 Inquisitor General Henrique to Inquisitor Sebastião Pinheiro, Lisbon February 13, 1576. ANTT, CG, Livro 298, pp. 27–9.

8 ANTT, CG, Livro 207, fl. 281.

9 Inquisitor General Jorge de Almeida to Goa, March 12, 1585. ANTT, CG, Livro 298, pp. 27–9.

10 Barros and Frazão to Inquisitor General António de Matos de Noronha, Goa December 19, 1596. Baião II, 251.

11 ANTT, CG, Livro 101, fol. 179v.

12 Antonio de Barros and Marcos Gil Frazão to Inquisitor General António de Matos de Noronha, Goa December 1, 1597, in Baião II, 259.

13 Bartolomeu Dias to Inquisitor General Henrique, Goa November 22, 1574. Baião II, 11.

14 Bartolomeu Dias to Inquisitor General Henrique, Goa November 8, 1576. Baião II, 25.

15 Inquisitor General Cardinal Alberto to the inquisitors of Goa, March 24, 1589; ANTT, CG, Livro 298, p. 94–5.

16 Antonio de Barros and Marcos Gil Frazão to Inquisitor General António Matos de Noronha, Goa December 16, 1600, in Baião II, 287.

17 Ferreira to Inquisitor General Alexandre de Bragança, Goa December 15, 1603, in Baião II, 319. See also Ferreira and Gonçalo da Silva to Inquisitor General Pedro de Castilho, Goa December 15, 1605, in Baião II, 333. The same happened in 1624 and 1634; Baião II, 610, 625 and ANTT, CG, Livro 101, fol. 60.

18 Inquisitor General Pedro de Castilho to the inquisitors in Goa, Lisbon March 13, 1610. ANTT, CG, Livro 298, p. 298.

19 Ferreira and Silva to Inquisitor General Castilho, Goa December 23, 1610. Baião II, 456–7.

20 BNL, cód. 201, fol. 139.

21 *Reportorio*, fol. 450.

22 BNL, Livro 202, *auto da fé* list of Feb. 7, 1773.

23 Inquisitor General Jorge de Almeida to the inquisitors of Goa, Lisbon March 24, 1584; ANTT, CG, book 298, 78–81.

24 Jorge Ferreira to Inquisitor General Alexandre de Bragança, Goa December 22, 1603: Baião II, 327.

25 ANTT, CG Livro 101, fols. 107, 177.

26 ANTT, CG maço 31 doc. 32, fol. 5.

27 *Ibid.*, doc. 3.

28 BNRJ, 25, 1, 3, n. 204 and 25, 1, 4, n. 9.

29 BNRJ, 25, 1, 5, n. 132.

30 *Reportorio*. A database on this document is available at www.i-m.co/reportorio/
   reportorio/home.html.
31 An important series of those lists in BNL, cód. 201 and 202.
32 BNRJ, 25, 1, 8, n. 226.
33 *Reportorio*, fol. 639v.
34 *Reportorio*, fol. 105.
35 *Reportorio*, fol. 152 and 297v.
36 ANTT, CGSO Livro 331, fol. 46.
37 Baião II, 531 [597–8], 545 and 610.
38 ANTT, CGSO, maço 31, doc. 28.
39 BNL, cód. 201, *passim*.
40 BNL, cód. 201, fol. 17, 9v, 11.
41 BNL, cód. 201, 202, 866 and ANTT, CGSO maço 31, *passim*.

The Endgame: The Decline of Institutional Correction

24

Consistories

Joke Spaans

It is almost a commonplace in Protestant church history that ecclesiastical discipline waned in the course of the seventeenth century. Quantitative studies support this view: in the records of consistories all over the Reformed world, the number of cases declines. The same sources indicate that the attention of consistories shifted: a recent comparative international overview of the practice and effects of ecclesiastical discipline in the Reformed Churches of early modern Europe until the end of the seventeenth century suggests that church discipline was strict only in the first decades after the Reformation, in order to safeguard the purity of the congregations, and especially of the communion table. Gradually, however, the function of ecclesiastical discipline shifted toward inculcating civic virtues. Its focus narrowed toward sins against sexual morality and Christian brotherhood, and its activities increasingly aimed at civilizing the lower orders.

A closer look, however, shows that church discipline was more tenacious than the perceived decline of religious fervor would suggest. Generalizing impressions about "decay in influence and activity" or "waning interest," although not totally unfounded, still do not quite do justice to this subject. Maintenance of public morality remained important, to churches, secular authorities and often the bulk of the common people as well. The fear that toleration of public sins would provoke divine wrath, descending upon entire populations in the form of epidemics, crop failure or other large scale disasters, only gradually and slowly gave way before more "scientific" explanations in the course of the eighteenth century. Moreover, a prudent use of church and social discipline contributed to harmonious relations between neighbors. Church discipline, therefore, did not disappear. Its eighteenth-century manifestations varied, however, from place to place, dependent on local perceptions of the necessity, propriety and usefulness of church involvement within social discipline as a whole. These differences had developed out of the religious regimes built over the preceding centuries.

Unlike Catholic Inquisitions, Protestant institutions for discipline operated on a local or regional level. It would be interesting to compare them to the disciplinary efforts of Counter-Reformation bishops. Within the scope of this essay, however, I will limit myself to comparing Reformed discipline with its equivalent in other Protestant confessions, as far as the availability of case studies allows, and looking at its relation with secular social discipline. Both aimed at shaping and maintaining Christian commonwealths as did Catholic forms of discipline, which pertain to the primary concern of this volume. Although by the eighteenth century the Reformation was a thing of a distant past, everywhere church discipline remained recognizably the heir to medieval canon law. Protestant princes had largely assumed the responsibilities formerly held by bishops, among other things for jurisdiction over *res mixtae*: religiously and socially unacceptable behavior once comprised under canon law and adjudicated by ecclesiastical courts like heterodoxy, blasphemy, profanation of the Sabbath, neglect of worship and sacraments, usury, adultery, fornication and marriage within the forbidden degrees of consanguinity and affinity. In public preaching the churches inculcated Christian values in the hearts and minds of the population. Ministers and representatives from the congregation privately admonished those suspected or found guilty of public or private sins. The obstinate faced measures ranging from "medicinal" temporary exclusion from communion ("the lesser ban") to public penance in order to be rehabilitated within the religious community. The incorrigible were excommunicated. Where secular officers were represented on the benches of local or regional ecclesiastical courts, they imposed secular, retributive and exemplary punishments. Those suspended from communion or excommunicated were often also excluded from election to public and ecclesiastical office and could not act as godparents at baptisms, marry before the church or be buried with full church ritual, a remnant of the lesser and greater bans of canon law. Ideally "medicinal" discipline was in the purview of the church, whereas the sharpest measures were reserved for secular courts. In practice, however, jurisdictions overlapped, and the measure of cooperation between the ecclesiastical and the secular varied from place to place. The kind of punishments considered proper for the various degrees of sinners also changed over time, under the influence of societal or cultural changes.

Whereas the institutional changes and the initial introduction of church discipline are often well-researched, in both qualitative and quantitative studies, especially for the Reformed churches that considered discipline as essential for true religion, this is not the case for the second half of the seventeenth and the eighteenth centuries. The later early modern period in general has attracted far less scholarly interest than the period of Reformation, Counter-Reformation and the Wars of Religion. Consequently case studies on church discipline within the wider context of a more general campaign against immorality and vice are few and far between. In many cases information about the workings and impact of church discipline has to be gleaned from studies into state formation, legal systems, sex and marriage or lay agency. In what follows I will piece together what these studies have to offer, focusing on four different types of disciplinary regimes and sketching the eighteenth century survivals and transformations in church discipline. Finally, I want to suggest some directions for further research, looking at how changing theological justifications, religious functions and popular perceptions of church discipline may have produced variations in practices.

PENANCE, PUNISHMENT, AND HONOR

In Reformed Scotland, local consistories (or kirk sessions) of ministers and elders were an integral part of secular authority, and even meted out corporal punishments. Church discipline was brought to bear not only against strictly religious offenses but also against everything that caused scandal. As Margo Todd argued in Chapter 3, churches would try to bring sinners to repentance and reconciliation with their neighbors in civil conflicts through public rituals of humiliation, but could also impose fines or incarceration, as retribution for scandals committed and as a deterrent. Those who could not be brought to repentance and improvement of behavior were handed over to secular justice. In a sense, church discipline was the lowest level of law enforcement.

Research into illegitimacy in early modern Scotland, based on extensive use of church records, has shown how the kirk, in close conjunction with secular authorities, kept up a very strict policing of morality, especially in sexual matters, but also in mediating conflicts and punishing slander and violence, far into the eighteenth century. The kirk wielded an extensive repertoire of admonitions, forms of public penance and punishments like fines, exposure on the pillory and incarceration. Even those outside the membership of the established church were not immune. The continued vigor of the "performance of repentance" appears to stem from the support of the Scottish population itself. Although the public shaming of sinners was feared, people from the middle groups of society often willingly submitted to it, as an accepted and effective means to repair one's honor and standing in the local community. Only those whose honor was guaranteed by noble birth or those without honor in the first place defied the judgments of the kirk.

Ecclesiastical discipline collapsed only after 1780, as a result of incisive changes in Scottish society. Secession movements and massive immigration from Catholic Ireland undermined the public function of the Church of Scotland. At the same time, the introduction of large-scale production methods both in agriculture and industries destroyed the traditional web of relations based on honor. The hierarchies of the work floor, the school, and the army exercised their own particular forms of discipline, and took over from the kirk.

A similar situation, with church discipline as the first stage of social discipline and secular law enforcement for a wide range of offenses, could be found in the semiautonomous *seigneurie* of Valangin, part of the Swiss principality of Neuchâtel. Here, however, local consistories had to leave the higher degrees of discipline to a regional tribunal, the seigneurial consistory, mainly composed of secular officials, supplemented by a few ministers as representatives of the church. This tribunal heard cases involving moral infractions, most of them for dissolute living, especially when resulting in illegitimate births, insults and disputes, disrespect for the church manifesting itself in working on Sundays, staying away from worship services or ignoring the admonitions of the local consistory, but also in apparent apostasy to Catholicism and suspicions of witchcraft. The consistory could suspend sinners from communion and demand public performances of penitence before the entire community or, in less serious cases, only before the ministers and elders, before readmittance. However, it also imposed secular punishments: fines, exposure to public scorn in the pillory, jail sentences, or even banishment.

In the early eighteenth century, this tribunal split into two separate courts with similar powers, one specifically for matrimonial cases, and the other for the remaining moral offenses. Marriage courts had sprung up all over the Swiss Confederacy in the early sixteenth century, as replacements

for episcopal jurisdiction, and, like their predecessors, they often decided
a broader range of *res mixtae* than marriage alone. Because their field of
expertise was secular as well as religious, they always included ministers
and could impose forms of ecclesiastical as well as secular discipline,
notably exclusion from communion. Here again, the distinction between
secular justice and church discipline was fluid. These courts remained
active until the very end of the *ancien régime*. In the eighteenth century,
however, arguments from natural law came to prevail over the strict
application of theological precepts. Enlightened philosophies and the
introduction of industrial wage labor enabled a shift from communalism
to individualism. Marriage came to be seen as a contract between con-
senting adults, reducing the influence of the family and incidentally
allowing divorce for incompatibility of character.

It should be noted that church discipline as a first stage of civil justice
was not specifically Reformed. In this later period, Lutheran principalities
in the German Empire often show the same disciplinary policies as their
Reformed neighbors. A well-researched example is the large and populous Duchy of Württemberg. Here, from the middle of the seventeenth
century, *Kirchenconvente* were installed with far-reaching jurisdiction
over many aspects of everyday life. They enforced attendance at worship,
corrected moral faults and adjudicated marital conflicts. The courts saw
to it that parents sent their children to school and Sunday catechism
lessons. From 1722 confirmation became obligatory. These *Kirchenconvente* were staffed by church elders and secular officers, and presided over
by the local sheriff. Pietist ideals about practical theology, inspired by
Calvinist Geneva, as well as political pressure toward the maintenance of
peace and order after its breakdown in the Thirty Years War went into
their making. These courts could admonish and withhold access to
communion, but also impose fines and sentence delinquents to the pillory
or a stay in a House of Correction. Church discipline in Lutheran Württemberg was fully integrated in secular jurisdictions.

This form of church discipline changed, in conjunction with economic
and cultural transformations, but did not necessarily decline or wither in the
eighteenth century. It proved a useful component of social discipline.
Although spontaneous submission to church discipline seems unique for
Scotland, the disciplinary efforts of local churches and the supralocal mixed
courts seem to have been broadly accepted by the population. A survey of
cases of resistance to the orders of ecclesiastical courts in Württemberg
produced many cases of passive disobedience, for instance when poor
parents kept a daughter out of school to mind younger siblings while they

themselves went to work. Active defiance was often based on a perception of incompatibility between biblical teaching and the demands of the authorities, whether in regard to Sunday rest, marital duties, the exercise of clerical power, or military conscription. Yet, popular protest against social discipline remained "embryonic" during the eighteenth century.

PUBLIC PENITENCE BETWEEN SPIRITUAL AND SECULAR DISCIPLINE

In a number of Reformed and Lutheran principalities within the German Empire, church discipline could apply spiritual sanctions only. However, ecclesiastical censure did often confer civil disabilities. Here also, sinners suspended from communion could not be appointed for public office, could not be taken as godparents at baptisms, marry before the church, or be buried in the church or churchyard. Unlike in the cases discussed before, the supralocal *(Ober)Konsistorien*, which could impose full excommunication and secular punishments for sinful crimes in *res mixtae*, were staffed and presided over by princely officers only. Although church and state had separate jurisdictions, in practice church discipline was exercised in close conjunction with the secular authorities and their enforcement of social discipline. Here again, differences between Lutheran and Reformed churches were often negligible. In principalities where the confession of rulers changed over time, and immigration brought confessional pluralism as well, the situation could become quite complicated. In the eighteenth century the Dukes of Pfalz-Zweibrücken upheld both Lutheran and Reformed church orders. Institutions for ecclesiastical discipline for both confessions were in place and worked together with the princely judicial system. Occasionally they even invoked the assistance of Catholic priests to keep wayward subjects in line.

Once these higher church courts had pronounced judgment and administered appropriate punishment, the sinner had to be reconciled with his or her local church. This reconciliation involved a public appearance in the church, sitting or kneeling under the pulpit during the sermon, a public confession of sin and humble request to be readmitted to the sacraments, the so-called *Kirchenbuße* – a procedure not unlike the Scottish performance of repentance. After the Peace of Westphalia in several principalities the rules were tightened and strictly enforced to bring back order after the chaos of protracted warfare. However, the *Kirchenbuße* could often be evaded by paying a fine, usually in alms for the poor. As the higher social orders gladly opened their purses to evade the humiliating ritual of reconciliation, and the *Kirchenbuße* weighed increasingly heavily on the lower orders, its original meaning was lost. Soldiers would rather desert than submit to the ritual in the church of their garrison town, and the prospect of being held up for public condemnation drove serving girls impregnated by employers or other men they did not want or dare to denounce to suicide or infanticide. Critics claimed that it was ineffective against the willfully immoral, unacceptable as a corrective measure against the social elite because it undermined social hierarchies, and in its selectivity unduly harsh against the penitent and the well-meaning.

From the 1730s, one after another German principality abolished the formal *Kirchenbuße* and replaced it with a more private ceremony before minister or local presbytery. The same happened in Swiss Valangin after it had come under Prussian rule in the eighteenth century. Some Lutheran principalities, however, held on to the *Kirchenbuße* even after 1800. The abolition of the *Kirchenbuße* did not spell the end of ecclesiastical discipline as such. On the contrary, presbyteries and consistories continued their work into the nineteenth century. However, the nature of discipline changed. The much more private procedure after the abolition of public *Kirchenbuße* effectively uncoupled political and spiritual jurisdictions. This change seems to imply that ecclesiastical jurisdictions and punishments that too closely resembled secular ones lost credibility and were tacitly entrusted to secular law enforcement agencies. Especially in cases of private sins that had not caused public scandal, suspension or admission to communion were increasingly left to the consciences of those involved.

SPIRITUAL JURISDICTION

The Dutch Reformed Church seems to present a rather exceptional case. From the introduction of the Reformation, ecclesiastical discipline had been strictly separate from secular jurisdictions. The Reformed Church never gained the adherence of the entire population. Access to membership and communion was limited to those who declared full assent to its teachings and were willing to submit to ecclesiastical discipline. The Reformed church in the city of Emden found itself in a similar situation until the end of the eighteenth century. The local consistory could admonish sinners, suspend them from communion, and excommunicate them, but these exclusions did not entail social disabilities. It could not impose secular punishments. The same applied to the tolerated religious communities. The regulation of marriages, litigation and everything pertaining to economic life including usury, and even the enforcement of public respect for Christian values including Sunday rest, regulation of luxury, prevention of public indecencies, and suppression of blasphemy and overt atheism were the exclusive preserve of the secular authorities.

Church historians have almost unanimously claimed that the discipline of the Dutch Reformed church went into sharp decline from the middle of the seventeenth century. Most authors simply assume a general decline in religious fervor in conjunction with the emergence of new philosophy and science. Herman Roodenburg's sociological study of Reformed discipline in Amsterdam, however, presents exactly the opposite view. Although quantitative data show a marked decrease in the number of disciplinary cases from 1650, this is interpreted as a sign that the concerted efforts of church and urban magistracies after the introduction of the Reformation had rather effectively suppressed offenses against Christian morality in the public sphere. Ecclesiastical discipline limited itself to the supervision of personal morality, especially targeting premarital sex and adultery, and from 1680 separations and divorces.

Despite its exclusively spiritual jurisdiction, the Reformed Church did claim for itself a role as guardian of public morality. Time and again it reminded the political authorities of their duties in maintaining secular laws and regulations against public sins. Especially in times of national crisis, because of military threats, epidemic disease, or other natural disasters, ministers asked for strict observance of existing laws against profanation of the Sabbath and frivolous entertainments, blasphemy, and the publication and sale of dangerous books, and petitioned for the proclamation of days of public prayer and fasting. Most of the time the political authorities responded favorably. Beginning in 1713, the days of public prayer and fasting would even become an annual ritual, initiated by the Provincial States and celebrated in the churches of all confessions and the Jewish synagogues with suitable prayers and sermons. These events drew massive audiences. But also in periods of calm and prosperity, the Reformed Church could expect secular law-enforcing agencies to undertake, on their own initiative or upon request, specific action against undesirable behavior in *res mixtae*. In the middle of the eighteenth century, classes and synods even successfully lobbied for new legislation against mixed marriages between Protestants and Catholics.

Discipline changed but did not disappear in the eighteenth century. It even gained importance in enforcing not only Christian morality but above all in inculcating diligence and sobriety among the poor who received assistance from the church deacons. Dissolute living could result in the withdrawal of support, temporarily or permanently. Deacons closely monitored the recipients of their welfare, as did the trustees of all other types of poor relief. They expected regular attendance in church and for the children of the poor at catechism classes, as well as honest application at whatever gainful employment was within the powers of all members of poor households. Churches did not apply secular punishments, but the possibility of losing one's allowance must have been a formidable threat. Strict discipline over the recipients of welfare ensured the continued willingness of the citizenry to contribute alms to finance the system. For the nonpoor, church discipline evolved into spiritual counseling and moral guidance, supporting enlightenment values of civility and civic virtue as the Reformed mainstream increasingly equated morality with politeness. This may partly explain the decrease in recorded disciplinary cases, as such more private proceedings needed no recording.

Occasional glimpses into eighteenth-century religious culture show that discipline retained considerable impact. An order from the consistory to abstain from communion was considered a stain on one's respectability. Church members took the trouble to appeal to the regional classis or even criticize the consistory in print when their minister had not made the customary house visits to invite them to the celebration of the Lord's Supper. This was resented as a slight to one's honor. For all practical purposes, however, withholding the formal invitation left it to members' consciences to determine whether they were worthy to join the congregation at communion. Enhancing the role of the individual conscience also gave church members a measure of agency. In some congregations the exhortation to scrutinize one's conscience before partaking of the sacrament was taken so seriously that the majority would voluntarily abstain. Abstention, once imposed as a serious disciplinary measure now became ambiguous: Was it either a sign of a bad conscience or of exemplary piety?

AN ENDGAME? SUGGESTIONS FOR FURTHER RESEARCH

If we see a decrease in the number of recorded cases of ecclesiastical discipline, that is all we see. We have to allow for considerable under-registration, even in the supposed heyday of the practice in the late sixteenth and early seventeenth centuries, when Protestant religious fervor was supposedly at its peak. As time progressed, congregations grew, and habit and bureaucratization took their toll, the dark number of nonregistered cases must have risen. Especially in confessionally homogeneous societies where notions of what constituted decent Christian conduct were widely shared, some form of church discipline remained in effect for the entire early modern period, and often even beyond.

Although the phenomenon did not disappear in the eighteenth century, it did change in character. Generally speaking, eventually the Reformed and the Anglicans followed the Lutheran and Zwinglian pattern that conferred formerly episcopal jurisdictions to the secular authorities. Historians are only beginning to identify the implications of this shift. My impression is that the change is at least partly due to an inner dynamic in the Protestant churches themselves. As churches developed their own bureaucracies with their inevitable legalistic regulations and routines, church discipline was increasingly perceived as mere duplication of secular law enforcement. Moreover, what formerly had been *res mixtae*, public misconduct that transgressed both secular and religious laws, increasingly became secularized. Especially in marital affairs, traditional religious rules and prohibitions without clear biblical underpinning, as in the case of divorce, could be seen as a leaven of popery, to be rejected by true Protestants. The focus of disciplinary activity shifted toward mediation of civil conflicts and punishment of illicit sexuality, the latter especially in the poorer segments of society. Although this was fully compatible both with contemporary notions of social propriety and ideals of Christian brotherhood and ritual purity, the cultivation of civility and legitimating social order seem to have taken precedence over theological arguments. Instead of enforcing a penitential regime still based on medieval ideals of the Christian commonwealth, church discipline now reinforced social control in the service of enlightened religion. A similar development is also discernible in the decline of the Inquisitions.

Several studies address the question whether ecclesiastical discipline contributed to a process of civilization, and most answer it in the negative. Discipline may have reformed individuals, but it did not change human nature. Human culture, however, did change ecclesiastical discipline. In England, toleration resulted in religious plurality in the public sphere and in the impossibility of enforcing discipline formerly wielded by the established church. Lay vigilantes organized themselves in societies that claimed a role in the policing of public morals, with an appeal to Christian values, but in practice bringing infractions of 'Christian' values to the attention of secular jurisdiction. In Scotland new forms of social discipline in the emerging nation state undercut ecclesiastical discipline as it had been practiced until the late eighteenth century. In the Dutch Republic the heavy involvement of church deacons in public welfare resulted in vigorous disciplinary regimes in all churches, specifically over the morality of the poor. My suggestion would be to direct further research toward developments in church-state relations, economic diversification, and intellectual culture that led to changed disciplinary regimes, ecclesiastical and otherwise, to understand how their conjunction contributed to social and religious change.

Another aspect of discipline that has been underresearched is its transformation under the influence of enlightened thought on human agency in personal morality. Most studies focus on the *public* discipline of churches, often as an aspect of early modern state formation or confessionalization. If we look not only at the division of labor between secular and ecclesiastical jurisdictions in the combat against public sins but also at the tools wielded by local churches against "secret" sins, that is, those that had come to the notice of the church without being public knowledge or causing public scandal, the picture becomes much more vague. In several German principalities public shaming of sinners in the ritual of *Kirchenbuße*, once considered such a salutary medicine for the soul, was abolished, first for the social elite, but eventually also for commoners, as external force was no longer considered effective in producing inner conversion. Still, this inner conversion remained the mission of all churches, and we should ask how they redirected their efforts. In general churches seem to have left more to the individual conscience as the eighteenth century progressed – the scrupulous avoidance of communion as practiced in some Dutch Reformed congregations may have been a rather extreme manifestation of this trend. Broadening out comparative research on ecclesiastical discipline toward developing notions about the individual conscience, and the localization of religion in the human heart would be very useful.

Finally, few studies make a connection between early modern practices and the renewed emphasis on ecclesiastical discipline in neo-orthodox Protestant communities in the nineteenth century – and, for that matter, in Pentecostal churches worldwide in the twenty-first century. This in itself belies the assumption that church discipline belongs to a distant past. Several authors on early modern church history deplore the "secular" functions of church discipline as ways of the early modern state to (ab) use the churches for their own purposes. Often, their evaluation is based on modern theologies rather than on an analysis of changing cultural configurations and their consequences for churches and religion. Instead of concluding that church discipline waned in the eighteenth century, we should probably look at how emerging ideas about citizenship and civility, and about religious distinction and ritual purity played out in the self-perception of churches from the eighteenth century into the present.

25

Inquisitions

James E. Wadsworth

If we are to understand the abolition of the Inquisitions, we must approach the subject from the perspective of the long eighteenth century – roughly the 1690s to the 1820s. The Spanish, Portuguese, and Italian Inquisitions faced a long series of threats to their prestige and power from the late seventeenth century on that forced them to reimagine and reinvent themselves in ways that paradoxically permitted their ongoing utility and sowed the seeds of decline. The Italian Inquisitions proved less successful in reinventing themselves. They endured ongoing political challenges that left most of them impotent or suppressed by the end of the eighteenth century. This history has not been well studied, nor can I examine it in the detail it deserves in this short chapter. I have sought, therefore, to lay out the broad comparative outlines while highlighting important moments in this evolution.

ITALIAN INQUISITIONS

The slow suppression of the Italian Inquisitions was due largely to reasons of state as political entities began to reshuffle the balance of power between church and state. Secular officials sought to restrain church power and enhance their own resulting in the gradual marginalization, secularization, and circumvention of the Inquisitions throughout the eighteenth century.

The early suppression of the Italian tribunals provided the model for later attempts to limit or suppress the Inquisitions in Spain and Portugal by slow suffocation – systematic reduction of the tribunal's jurisdiction and activity without actually abolishing it. The slow starvation of resources, personnel, and jurisdiction ensured that the tribunals became hollow shells of their former selves and increasingly irrelevant to the rapidly changing intellectual, political, social, and religious transformations sweeping Europe and its colonies.

Sardinia fell first in 1708 when anti-Spanish forces seized the island during the wars of the Spanish Succession. In 1718 the House of Savoy, which gained control of the island, returned inquisitional jurisdiction back to the bishops. The more rapid spate of abolitions began in 1746 with Naples followed by Parma in 1768, Milan in 1775, Tuscany and Sicily in 1782, and Modena in 1785. The French invasion brought about the suppression of more (1796–1800 Venice, Genoa, Malta, Bologna Genoa and Turin). The rest came in 1805–10.

As early as 1737 in Florence, the Count of Richecourt began to formulate plans to "reduce the power of the Inquisition." In July 1737 the Council of Regency refused the assistance of the secular authorities to ecclesiastics. In January 1738 it restricted the right to bear arms. The 1739–40 controversial trial of Freemasons caused widespread scandal. In 1754, lay assistants were introduced to supervise inquisitorial trials. Finally, in July 1782 Peter Leopold abolished the Inquisition in the Grand Duchy of Tuscany.

In the Duchy of Modena the suppression of the Holy Office began at least as early as 1758 with the appointment of a special magistrate tasked with protecting the laws of the state. This measure was followed in 1772 by the creation of the Tribunal of Jurisdiction that monitored the proceedings of ecclesiastical courts. The tribunal of Reggio nell'Emilia was suppressed in 1780 and placed under the jurisdiction of Modena. Hercules III finally abolished the tribunal of Modena in September 1785.

The move toward abolition in Parma began in 1765 when the government created a new junta to police the activities of all episcopal courts. It gained steam when the junta abolished the titles of *crocesignati* (volunteer lay functionaries; literally, "crusaders") and was finally precipitated by the new inquisitor of Piacenza who refused to comply with the orders of the junta and continued to "imprison suspects without authorization." The Minister du Tillor of the Duchy of Parma finally abolished the tribunals of Parma and Piacenza in February 1768.

In Milan the assault began at least as early as 1768 with the Chancellor Kaunitz who described the Inquisition as arbitrary, barbaric, fanatical, bloodthirsty, and incompatible with the authority of the state and the bishops. In August of 1771 Maria Theresa presaged abolition by suppressing the titles of the *crocesignati*, confiscating the property of the Order of the *Crocesignati*, and refusing to fill any vacancies within the

Inquisition. The complaints of the papal nuncio regarding the refusal to accept a new inquisitor appointed to Pavia precipitated the abolition in March 1775, which declared the Inquisition to be incompatible with public law and redundant since bishops and the civil government held jurisdiction over religion and morality.

CRISIS, REFORM, AND REINVENTION OF THE IBERIAN INQUISITIONS

For both the Spanish and the Portuguese Inquisitions the moment of crisis arrived long before the ideas of the Enlightenment took root in Iberian soil. In both cases the papacy played a fundamental role in the demise of these institutions. The Portuguese Inquisition experienced its moment of crisis two decades earlier than that of Spain. It entered into a long and heated jurisdictional dispute with the papacy between 1674 and 1681 that resulted in the papal suspension of inquisitional activity in Portugal between August of 1679 and August of 1681.[1]

Inspired either by the visible signs of its own weakness or by the wish to turn the struggle to its advantage, the Portuguese Inquisition responded to this crisis by reinventing itself in a two-pronged strategy – first, it reasserted its authority over heresy and second, it broadened its base of popular support. Over the next fifty years (1690–1740), and especially between 1735 and 1745, we see an increase in inquisitional activity against New Christians as if the inquisitors hoped to demonstrate their ongoing relevance.

The caseload never recovered from the papal suspension, but the Inquisition had already undergone a fundamental adjustment to its activity away from repression toward providing social advancement for its functionaries through their qualification for inquisitorial office. The Portuguese Inquisition remained relatively active into the 1760s, but after 1690 much of its manpower and resources were oriented toward qualifying candidates for office rather than in prosecuting heretics. Thereafter, the appointment of officials dominated inquisitional activity in Portugal until the institution itself was abolished.

Thus, the Inquisition pursued a clear strategy of strengthening its popular support among the aristocracy and upwardly mobile classes by throwing the doors of inquisitional office wide open. In doing so, inquisitorial bureaucrats responded to the push from below as merchants, public functionaries, and other upwardly mobile sectors of the population sought appointments to gain access to privilege and prestige. This happy arrangement made the Inquisition more relevant than it had ever been to a much wider sector of the population, increased the visibility of the Inquisition, brought in much needed revenues, and gave the Inquisition a new lease on life.

The next major blow to the Portuguese Inquisition came in the 1740s, though its results would not be felt for some decades. The Jacobin movement fought the Inquisition's attempts to increase its authority, causing the bishops to withdraw their support from the Inquisition and to reclaim their authority to police the orthodoxy of their flocks. For the Spanish Inquisition, the opening of the eighteenth century inaugurated a prolonged period of crisis. The wars of the Spanish Succession and the rise of the Bourbon monarchy fundamentally shifted the balance of power between church and state. The Bourbon absolutist state was jealous of its power and the allegiance of its subjects. The church found itself being forced to take sides in royal disputes with the papacy over "jurisdiction, revenues and appointments."

Philip V (1700–46) asked the intellectual Melchor Rafael de Macanaz to examine the differences between the church and the state. His *Proposiciones* of December 1713 declared royal power to be above the church in jurisdiction and absolute power over temporal affairs in his kingdom. Melchor de Macanaz also proposed that the Inquisition be transformed into a purely ecclesiastical tribunal with its power of censorship restricted. This proposal formed the backbone of royal policy toward the Inquisition for most of the eighteenth century.

Bending under the weight of this assault, the Inquisition tried to rejuvenate itself, or at least to demonstrate that it was not irrelevant, by showing that the crypto-Jewish threat remained. Between 1721 and 1725 it prosecuted 950 Judaizers out of 1,091 trials, applying the death penalty to 165 of them. But this spurt of inquisitional activity did not last long. The reign of Ferdinand VI (1746–59) witnessed a growing apathy in inquisitional procedure. Edicts of Faith were not issued, punishments became more lenient, and few cases of Judaizing were tried. Most dealt with heretical or scandalous propositions.

Still, reining in the Inquisition became one more cog in the broader Bourbon campaign to subordinate the church, often spearheaded by powerful royal ministers. Charles III (1759–88) used his sovereignty over the Inquisition more vigorously than his predecessors. He pursued policies proposed by the Count of Campomanes who argued that happiness should be defined in terms of economic progress, free trade, and market forces. He hated privilege and followed an absolutist agenda only because a strengthened state could give him the power to control the people and resources necessary for his reform agenda. In 1768, Campomanes accused the Inquisition of being "pro-Jesuit, pro-papal, hostile to regalia rights and arbitrary in its procedure."[2]

The crown continued to restrict the jurisdiction of the Inquisition throughout the 1760s, 1770s, and 1780s while the Count of Florida-blanca proposed the abolition of the *limpieza de sangre* (purity of blood) statutes. But Charles III's measures were inconsistent, laced with a desire for reform and a penchant for tradition. Consequently the Inquisition persisted and even experienced temporary moments of resurgence.

Under Charles IV (1788–1808) the powerful minister Manuel Godoy continued the assault on the church including the September 19, 1798 order for "the sale of the property of all charitable institutions at public auction," which included inquisitional property.[3] Gaspar Melchor de Jovellanos distilled much of the sentiment of the intellectual community regarding the Inquisition in 1798 in his famous *Representación a Carlos IV sobre lo que era el Tribunal de la Inquisición*. This work signaled the growing desire among intellectuals and even government officials to curtail the power and influence of the Inquisition. In it, he argued that the power and jurisdiction the Holy Office was "restricted to questions of faith." He criticized the secrecy of inquisitional proceedings and the ignorance of inquisitional officials, and he recommended the restoration of jurisdiction to the bishops in matters concerning faith.

The ongoing regalism of the Bourbon monarchy and the fiscal assault on church property revealed the divisions within the church and within the Inquisition. Some officials held clearly liberal inclinations while others refused compromise at all costs. While liberals relied on regalism and absolutism in their cause for reform, the conservatives demanded respect for traditional institutions and privileges. The conservative segments eventually came to see liberalism as a new heresy and the Inquisition as essential for the survival of Catholicism and the social order. They gained a new lease on power after 1791 as the radical and conservative Secretary General of the Inquisition Juan Antonio Llorente led the charge against liberals, Jansenists, and Francophiles. He rode the waves of the religious backlash fueled by the French Revolution, a punishing war, epidemic disease, and corruption.

Meanwhile, the newly reinvigorated Portuguese Inquisition plodded along for another half-century until the chief minister under Dom José I, the reform-minded, regalist Sebastião José de Carvalho e Melo, later known as the Marqués de Pombal, assumed office in 1750. Pombal reformed the colonial administration and economy and sought to limit the power of the church. His policies toward the church and the Inquisition had less to do with anticlericalism or antagonism toward either institution than with a specific political agenda that was a combination of regalism, secularization, and economic nationalism laced with anti-papist and anti-Jesuit sentiments.

Pombal fell out with the papal nuncio over the wedding of the heir apparent in June of 1760. The ensuing schism lasted until 1770. Pombal used the time to firmly subordinate the church to the crown without papal interference. In 1768, he stripped the power of censure from the Inquisition investing it in a new institution called the *Real Mesa Censória* (although one inquisitor was supposed to sit on the new mesa). In the same year he began his campaign to eliminate the distinction between New and Old Christians by destroying all the lists of *fintados* (or those who had paid the Jewish tax) and by ordering that all references to infamy be erased from the books of genealogy.[4] In January of 1771, Pombal also moved to eliminate the distinction between New and Old Christians, which was at the core of the purity of blood laws. It went into effect in May 1773.

These reductions in inquisitional authority and changes in the legal statutes meant that the 1640 *regimento* (bylaws) that governed the Inquisition was out of date. Still, the 1774 *regimento* retained much of the original wording of the 1640 *regimento*. It placed new limits but did not fundamentally alter either inquisitional procedure or the tribunal's capacity to go after heretics. Indeed, it may be argued that the inquisitors successfully manipulated the political environment through strategic acts of submission to reform while still preserving and even expanding their powers. The new *regimento* probably helped rejuvenate the Inquisition by bringing it up to date with current enlightened philosophical and political ideas, which gave it at least the façade of legitimacy and perhaps a fifty-year lease on life. Francisco Bethencourt has termed this strategy "low profile" survival.[5] In 1774, the Inquisition of Goa also became a casualty of Pombaline politics. The Inquisitor General argued that Portugal had lost most of its Asian empire leaving Goa with only a tiny jurisdiction, which meant it was superfluous.[6]

IBERIAN INSTITUTIONS DIVIDED AGAINST THEMSELVES

The Inquisitions in both Spain and Portugal reinvented themselves as bastions of conservative social and religious thought in the last quarter of the eighteenth century, placing themselves on a collision course with the tide of political change. But the officials of the Inquisitions never fully embraced the anti-liberty, anti-equality strategy. Within their ranks, from top to bottom, disunity reigned. Unfortunately, the conflicts within the Inquisition during that last half-century of its life have not been well studied. Still, some tantalizing evidence suggests that internal struggles were occurring and that they weakened the institutions' ability to respond to rapidly changing times. Both inside and outside the inquisitional edifice a cultural reaction against the Inquisition began to form in the late eighteenth century. It manifested itself in declining interest in inquisitional office, refusal to honor inquisitional privilege or respect inquisitional authority, and in a lack of vitality in inquisitional procedure.

The response to the abolition of the purity of blood requirements in 1774 was almost immediate in Portugal, though delayed by almost twenty years in Brazil. The number of applications for inquisitional office plummeted. The rising middle ranks of society discovered that the cost of an inquisitional appointment could no longer be justified since it could no longer produce the prestige and honor it had once done. The ongoing decline in tax exemptions and special privileges also undercut popular support for the Spanish Inquisition, drying up the applications of those seeking appointment.

Inquisitorial judges and functionaries remained deeply divided over liberal ideas and policies, which meant that they could never formulate a coherent agenda. Stephen Haliczer notes that we can see these divisions and the power of liberal opinion inside the Inquisition in the large number of licenses issued by the Inquisition for reading prohibited books. The same is true for Portugal, though censorship had been largely taken from the Inquisition between 1768 and 1787. The censorship board granted many licenses to read prohibited books. Booksellers also avoided inquisitional censure by importing forbidden books in false covers. Indeed, most liberal publications circulating in Brazil were contraband. The vast number of licenses undermined the Inquisition's efforts at censorship and facilitated the spread of liberal ideas. Hence, the inquisitional failure to prevent the new ideas from taking hold arose, at least in part, from internal divisions and inconsistencies.

In Portugal and Brazil local leaders refused to honor inquisitional privilege.[7] Governors in Brazil forced familiars to serve in the local militias even though they had the right to join the private *Companhia dos Familiares*.[8] Priests refused to allow access to their records for investigations.[9] Familiars refused to fulfill their obligations.[10] Parish priests refused to post the Edicts of Faith arguing that it contradicted the people's right to free will.[11] In the Canaries, parishioners refused to hang sanbenitos on the walls of their churches.

The Inquisitions also became more lax in their investigations. Rather than carrying out inquiries in both the place of birth and the place of residence, Portuguese inquisitors began to order quick investigations done in Lisbon. In 1820, the more liberal Inquisitor General Azeredo Coutinho simply dismissed one applicant from any investigation at all and gave him an appointment.[12] Haliczer has shown that even though the tribunal of Valencia enjoyed considerable royal favor it proved unwilling to pursue denunciations with much vigor or even to punish offenders. The *Suprema* also regularly intervened in provincial tribunal affairs and lost crown support in disputes with royal courts. Evidence of inquisitional decline can be seen in Toledo where the inquisitors only heard three or four cases a year in the late eighteenth century.

There were only 4,000 cases in 100 years, 10 percent of which dealt with Judaism and Protestantism. The death penalty was only carried out four times. Haliczer notes that the Zaragoza tribunal suffered a similar decline with only four cases per year after 1700. He argues that this decline was related to the virtual disappearance of its target population, rapidly rising crime rates, and a shift in the pattern of crime from heresy to things like fraud, counterfeiting, and smuggling.

Another poorly researched area but one certainly relevant to the decline of the Inquisitions in Spain and Portugal is the fiscal vitality of the tribunals. Haliczer argues that the Inquisition might never have been abolished had it not been for the "grave economic and fiscal crisis brought about by the Franco-Spanish conflict of 1793–1795 and the Anglo-Spanish wars of 1796–1802 and 1804–1808." The 1799 order to sell inquisitional property left the Spanish Inquisition without the financial independence it needed to survive.[13]

The Portuguese Inquisition may also have suffered a fiscal crisis in the eighteenth century. Though the financial history the Portuguese Inquisition has yet to be studied, there are hints that the push to appoint large numbers of officials may have been driven partly by fiscal need. Though New Christians remained the primary fodder for the Portuguese Inquisition until the late eighteenth century, it did extend its prosecutions of bigamy, sodomy, and witchcraft.

Fewer confiscations and confiscations of lesser value meant less revenue to the coffers of the Inquisition. Bigamy, sodomy, and witchcraft, though certainly not confined to the lower classes, were largely concentrated there. This meant that the practice of having the accused pay for their imprisonment simply did not function well or yield much revenue.

The large number of applications for inquisitional office helped offset this fiscal crisis. All candidates had to pay for every detail of their investigation. Likewise, once appointed, they had to pay the entrance fee to the Brotherhood of Saint Peter Martyr as well as the yearly dues. Again, the history is not clear, but the Lisbon tribunal may have occasionally borrowed from these funds to cover their operating costs.[14]

THE END GAME

The Inquisition in Spain never recovered from the gargantuan disruptions caused by the French invasion, the occupation of the country, and the fiscal crisis that ensued. But the French Revolution also gave the Inquisition a new, though short-term, lease on life. The Inquisition reinvented itself as the defender of tradition and religion from the "heresies of liberty and equality." It regained its power to censure and went after Spain's enlightened intellectuals, many of whom fled to France in exile.[15]

But even as the Inquisition ratcheted up its attack on liberals, the French invasion and Napoleonic abolition of the Inquisition in 1808 cut the campaign short. The liberal *Cortes* at Cádiz that attempted to govern the country in the absence of its king also declared that the Inquisition was "incompatible with the new constitutional order" in 1813.[16] Some speakers declared that it was not necessary for the survival of the church, that the *Cortes* could abolish it because it had been imposed by the crown and the pope, that it was intolerant and universally hated by all enlightened men, that government was not a theocracy, and that the *Cortes* could not permit the existence of a state within a state.

The suppression of the Inquisition stimulated outrage from bishops and traditionalist clerics for whom restoration became a mantra. Ferdinand VII fulfilled their aspirations in 1814 when he returned from exile and undid the work of the *Cortes* of Cádiz. But Ferdinand did not bring about the theocratic revolution the traditionalist clergy had hoped for. Nor did he liberate the church from the state. He did, however, share the church's desire to discredit and destroy liberalism. The restored Inquisition set about this business as part of a new alliance of power between the "Throne and Altar." But the alliance could not last.

A revolt led by Rafael de Riego in 1820 forced the king to accept the Constitution of 1812 and to abolish the Inquisition once again. This abolition lacked the heated debate of 1812, and most clerical leaders simply let the Inquisition die a quiet death. The Inquisition's persistent affiliation with the extreme right had made it vulnerable to the liberal recovery after 1820.

Ferdinand, however, also came to fear that the extreme right hoped to use a restored Inquisition to attack those who supported the king. His fears seemed confirmed when a new campaign to restore the Inquisition began in 1823 led by conservative clerics and bishops. But Ferdinand had come to mistrust the ultra-conservatives whom he increasingly saw as a "threat to the Crown's independence."[17] With the support of a French army that crossed the Pyrenees in 1823, Ferdinand rescinded his decrees of 1820 and toppled the liberal government, which, by implication, also reinstated the Inquisition. But Ferdinand was unwilling to reinstate it formally.

The clerics responded to his foot-dragging in 1824 with episcopal Inquisitions called "Juntas of Faith." These juntas were not officially recognized, but they picked up the work of the Inquisition against liberals even managing to execute the liberal school teacher, Cayetano Ripoll. But Ferdinand moved against them, and by 1827 they had ceased to function. Still, the final definitive abolition of the Inquisition in Spain came only on July 15, 1834 when Queen Mother Cristina acting as regent for Isabella II suppressed the Inquisition, appropriated its property, reverted inquisitional jurisdiction back to the bishops, and compensated its employees.

In Portugal, the downfall of Pombal in 1777 slowed the assault on inquisitional autonomy. The Goa Inquisition was reestablished in 1778, though finally abolished in 1812. The crown fled to Brazil to avoid the French invasion in 1807. The French did not move against the Portuguese Inquisition, but the period of the French occupation interrupted inquisitional business with the colonies. Then in 1820 a constitutionalist rebellion erupted in Portugal. The king D. João VI was still in Brazil. The leaders of the rebellion formed a council and began drafting a liberal constitution. In October 1820, the liberal junta required the General Council and the inquisitors to swear an oath of loyalty and obedience to the new government and the future constitution. On February 8, 1821, Francisco Simões Margiocchi introduced a motion to abolish the Inquisition. The inquisitor present at the debate declared that the Inquisition arose from a culture of intolerance and persisted because of "the moral causes that retarded the progress of human understanding." The delegates approved the motion on March 24, 1821, and the formal order became public on April 5 of the same year. The order abolished the entire

bureaucracy, laws, regulations, etc. governing the Inquisition. All authority for spiritual crimes reverted back to the bishops and the rest to the civil
authorities. All inquisitional property was delivered to the national treas-
ury. All inquisitional documents were sent to the national library to be
inventoried. Finally the doors of the inquisitional palace were thrown
open and the public gained access for the first time to the sacred precincts,
including the secret prisons.

SURVIVAL OF THE ROMAN INQUISITION

Though the Roman Inquisition had been suppressed temporarily during
the Napoleonic occupation, it survived. The Inquisition had been abolished by the Roman Republic in 1799 and again from 1800. From
1809 to 1814 the Papal States were officially part of French Empire,
and the Inquisition was abolished again. By the eighteenth century, its
influence outside the Papal States had collapsed. It now dealt primarily
with censorship and clerical immorality. Even then censorship remained
limited to Latin, French, and Italian versions of books listed in the 1758
Index, which lasted until it was abolished in 1966. In 1860 the Roman
Inquisition suffered a further setback when the Italian national state
restricted ecclesiastical authority. From then on the Congregation played
mostly an advisory role even during the move against Modernism from
1907–8.

In 1908 the papacy changed the name of the Inquisition to Congregation of the Holy Office and merged it with the Congregation of the
Index. This did not change until 1965 when Paul VI changed it to the
Sacred Congregation for the Doctrine of the Faith. It remains the main
advisor to the papacy on disciplining clerics and theological questions.
From 1848 to 1965 it played a crucial role for clerics who feared the rise
of secular governments and nineteenth-century anticlericalism. But it also
allowed the enemies of the papacy to drag up images of the Inquisition as
the symbol of papal ruthlessness and ambition.

CONCLUSION

The abolition of the Inquisitions in Spain, Portugal, and Italy must be seen
in the context of a series of broad structural changes that began before the
Enlightenment took hold, but that merged with and cross-fed the new
political, economic, and social critiques produced by the Enlightenment.
The Reformation had thrown open the doors to intellectual and religious

questioning. Long-standing popular attitudes of tolerance resurfaced and became more public, finding their voices in the language of the Enlightenment. States no longer needed religion to legitimize power. Holy warriors of all stripes came to be seen as increasingly irrelevant in the national and international affairs of Europe. Bishops in Portugal withdrew their support from the Inquisition. Papal conflicts exacerbated political instability and inspired internal reforms. Chief ministers found in the Enlightenment useful tools to employ in their ongoing battles to subordinate the church. The faithful found the Inquisition increasingly irrelevant as it lost its ability to supply honor and prestige and ideas of tolerance came to dominate public discourse. New forms of social control emerged that were distinct from church discipline.

Most explanations for the decline and abolition of the Portuguese and Spanish Inquisitions focus on the increasing political and cultural irrelevance of the institution, which is certainly true. But the cultural changes brought about by the Enlightenment also created an atmosphere in which the Inquisition came to be seen, paradoxically, as an important regulator of social tensions as well as a threat to individual liberties. For this reason, the Enlightened absolutists of Spain and Portugal initially chose to reform the tribunals and subordinate them to the will of the crown rather than completely disrupt the balance of institutional power.

The argument put forward here is that it is simplistic and anachronistic to lay abolition solely at the feet of Enlightened thought. We must take a long historical view to understand both the persistent efforts of government officials to reduce the autonomy and power of the tribunals of faith and the political, cultural, and internal ruptures that contributed to institutional instability and decline. The secular authorities in Italy developed a method of slowly starving the Inquisitions of manpower, jurisdiction, and revenues, which was mimicked in both Spain and Portugal. Consequently, the inquisitional leaders in Spain and Portugal responded by reinventing themselves, which, for a time, gave them a new lease on life. The political and military instability in the Italian states meant that the Italian Inquisitions had much less room to maneuver and reimagine themselves, which contributed to their much earlier decline.

All of these cases demonstrate how closely the Inquisition was tied to secular authority. Indeed, the Inquisitions remained so dependent on secular support that when it was restricted or withdrawn, the Inquisitions simply could not function. Perhaps this best explains not only the timing of suppression in the Italian states but also the survival of the Roman

Inquisition, which remained under the political jurisdiction of the papacy. These political winds may have arisen earlier in Italy than in Iberia because in much of Italy by the eighteenth century the Inquisition was seen as an imposition of a foreign power (either Rome or Spain) that pursued political objectives behind the façade of religion.

To a certain extent the increasing secularization of the Inquisitions paralleled the increasing secularization of Protestant consistories. For the Inquisitions this was part of an intentional political strategy on the part of the state to weaken the tribunals. For the consistories it was more of a shift in political and social perceptions regarding the right to punish. The consistories lacked formal hierarchical and centralizing institutions, were more local in nature, relied more heavily on the laity, and focused more strongly on public sin. But the Inquisitions were much more deeply entrenched bureaucratic institution with formal structures of power. For these reasons the abolition of the Inquisitions must be approached from an institutional and political perspective, whereas the evolution of the consistories may be more fruitfully examined with a bottom-up approach that emphasizes broader shifts in public perceptions.

Despite the abolition of all but one of the tribunals of the Holy Office by the middle of the nineteenth century, the influence of the Inquisitions lives on. They have left indelible marks on the modern nation-state and have been resurrected in exaggerated mythical tropes trotted out to defend freedom of conscience. Whether consciously or not, the general patterns of intolerance pioneered by the Inquisition have also resurfaced in conservative movements by those who seek political power through the control of narratives of race, religion, and history. The Inquisitions may have fallen prey to historical change, but their history remains as relevant as ever.

Notes

1 J. Lúcio de Azevedo, *História dos Cristãos-Novos Portugueses*, 3rd ed. (Lisbon, 1989), 312–26; and ANTT (Arquivos Nacionais da Torre do Tombo. CG: Conselho Geral), Armário Jesuítico Maço 30, no. 74, 76–80, 85.
2 John Lynch, *Bourbon Spain, 1700–1808* (Cambridge, MA, 1989), 288.
3 Lynch, *Bourbon Spain,* 401.
4 ANTT, IL (Inquisicao de Lisboa), Numero de Transferencia 2158. See ANTT, IL, m. 24 no. 18; Elias Lipiner, *Terror e Linguagem: Um dicionário da Santa Inquisição* (Círculo de Leitores, 1999), 114.
5 Francisco Bethncourt, *The Inquisition: A Global History, 1478–1834,* trans. Jean Birrell (New York, 2009), 353.
6 ANTT, MNEJ (Ministério dos Negócios Eclesiásticos e da Justicia), Livro 4, 88–89v, 116–21.

7 ANTT, CGSO (Conselho Geral do Santo Ofício), m. 4, no. 12; ANTT, CGSO, NT 4156; CGSO, m. 28, nos. 98, 99; ANTT, NT 4156 and CGSO, m. 53. See also ANTT, CGSO, NT 4188; ANTT, CGSO, m. 17, no. 3 and IL, NT 2133; ANTT, MR (Ministério do Reino), m. 362; AHU (Archivo Historico Ultramarino), Bahia, cx. 52, docs. 10021–27.

8 ANTT, CGSO, Livro 381, fol. 168; ANTT, CGSO, NT 4152; AHU, Pernambuco, cx. 62, doc. 5347.

9 ANTT, HSO (Habilitacoes do Santo Ofício), José, m. 57, no. 885; ANTT IL, 319 and 320.

10 ANTT, CGSO, m. 6, no. 27; ANTT, HI, Luís, m. 26, no. 130.

11 ANTT, IL, Processo 14321. See also James E. Wadsworth, *In Defence of the Faith: Joaquim Marques de Araújo, a Comissário in the Age of Inquisitional Decline* (Montreal & Kingston, 2013).

12 ANTT, HSO, Francisco, m. 95, no. 1572; and James E. Wadsworth, *Agents of Orthodoxy* (Lanham, MD, 2006), 221–2.

13 Stephen Haliczer, *Inquisition and Society in the Kingdom of Valencia, 1478–1834* (Berkeley, CA, 1990), 347–8.

14 "As esmolas de São Pedro Mártyr," ANTT, Inquisição de Lisboa, Livro 154, fol. 113.

15 Helen Rawlings, *The Spanish Inquisition*, (Malden, MA, 2005), 138–9.

16 *Spain under the Bourbons, 1700–1833: A Collection of Documents* , ed. W. N. Hargreaves-Mawdsley (Columbia, SC, 1973), 242–3.

17 William J. Callahan, *Church, Politics, and Society in Spain, 1750–1874* (Cambridge, MA, 1984), 138.

Conclusion

Reformations of Penance and Scholarly Renascences of Disciplinary Institutions

E. William Monter

PROTESTANT AND CATHOLIC REFORMATIONS OF PENANCE

When Martin Luther launched his publicity campaign against the sale of indulgences for the dead in 1517 that grew into the Protestant Reformation, he began by attacking the sacrament of penance. The first four of his famous 95 theses bore directly on this sacrament, for which he could find no Scriptural foundation; the implications for indulgences emerged later. But, as with much of the Lutheran Reformation, it proved easier to critique existing practices than to replace them. What might be called "the Reformation of Penance" evolved in divergent ways within major forms of organized Protestantism. Catholics, meanwhile, soon acknowledged part of Luther's critique by prohibiting the sale of indulgences, but the Council of Trent firmly upheld its tradition of formal penances as a sacramental obligation for all Christians. Fulfilling penitential obligations imposed after confession to ordained priests continued to be necessary before receiving communion.

At the same time, post-Tridentine Catholicism also attempted to remove abuses in the administration of penance, especially those arising from physical intimacy between female penitents and male clergy. One might argue that the most important Catholic "Reformation of Penance" after Trent took a specifically architectural form. In order to provide greater privacy to the laity during confession while physically separating them from clergymen, Catholics added a new piece of church furniture, the confessional, placing a grill between priest and penitent. It inhibited, without completely eliminating, the sexual solicitation of penitents by priests during confession. Imitation being the sincerest form of flattery, one also finds rudimentary forms of confessionals in some Lutheran or Anglican churches; however, Protestant versions seem primitive alongside the numerous surviving examples from Baroque-era Catholicism.

Although agreeing with Catholics that only God could forgive sins, mainstream Protestantism rejected the traditional Catholic doctrine that priests absolved sinners only after imposing appropriate penances. Since both Luther and Reformed Protestants emphasized Adam's original sin, they saw all humans as necessarily sinful; although some sinners were saved solely by Divine grace, and penance was not a sacrament, some form of individual repentance continued to be necessary for all Protestants, particularly before receiving communion. Because Protestants generally celebrated the Eucharist far less often than Catholics (rarely more than four times a year), they placed great weight on moral readiness as a prerequisite for participation in this basic and fundamental moment of union for a Christian community. But to whom should ordinary Protestants admit their failings when preparing for this supreme religious experience? To their local clergyman who would perform the ceremony, or directly to God himself, who alone could forgive them?

As so often among Protestants, answers varied. At one extreme stands England's schismatic national church. Its famous founder, Henry VIII, had published a defense of the seven sacraments against Luther, for which the papacy awarded him the title of "Defender of the Faith." Straddling the gap between Luther and Rome, his successors divided Christian sacraments into two fundamental obligations – baptism and communion, both of which appear unambiguously in the New Testament and therefore called "Sacraments of the Gospel" – and five minor ones, including penance. Although a prerequisite for the "great" sacrament of communion, penance can be performed in several ways, including corporately during worship.

At the opposite extreme stood the continental Reformed tradition, where members normally confessed their sins directly to God rather than clergymen, but where the very seriousness of congregational communion required some degree of communal supervision to prevent unworthy members from receiving it. Unlike Luther, Calvin considered properly enforced "discipline" to be a necessary mark of the true church, and in 1541 he made the establishment of an ecclesiastical disciplinary institution a prerequisite for his return to Geneva. From then on, the Reformed tradition distinguished itself from other forms of Protestantism by the intensity of its officials in enforcing discipline. Its version of the "Reformation of Penance" required the most notorious sinners to make elaborate and extremely public forms of repentance. The polar opposite of the ultra-private Baroque confessional is another piece of early modern church furniture, a "stool of repentance" in Scotland.

Reformed consistories arguably offered a form of disciplinary institution superior to other possibilities available to Protestants. Our best evidence comes from the homeland of the Protestant Reformation, the Holy Roman Empire of the German nation, where the Reformed tradition arrived late and made mostly minor inroads. Germany is unrepresented in this collection and generally remains marginal in consistorial scholarship; on the Catholic side, its papally appointed inquisitors had already been reduced to laughingstocks before Luther acquired notoriety. Nevertheless, since German scholarship originated two concepts that seem relevant to this enterprise, "social disciplining" and tightly interlocking church-state "confessionalization," it seems worth glancing briefly at the "Reformations of Penance" in the intensely confessionalized heart of central Europe. An excellent cross-confessional guide, Ronnie Hsia, notes at the outset of a chapter on the "Moral Police" that "all Christians believed in maintaining a certain degree of church discipline," adding immediately that "separatist communities persecuted by the state, in fact, upheld the strictest discipline, as did communal congregations such as Wurttemberg Pietists and Emden Calvinists." Among the major confessions, Hsia asserted that "moral discipline was most effectively enforced among urban Calvinist communities, due to a high degree of ... communal participation in the supervision."[1] Unexpected corroboration comes from pre-Pietist Wurttemberg near the end of the Thirty Years War, when a Lutheran theologian, Johann Valentin Andreae, tried to improve discipline by establishing individual parish consistories on the Genevan model. His innovation was soon abandoned; however, imitation remains the most sincere form of flattery, especially when one recalls the bitter attacks on "crypto-Calvinism" by German Lutherans.

Although confessional differences matter, all types of Christian disciplinary institutions shared an important attitude: public acknowledgment of the sinner's guilt was always and everywhere a prerequisite for his subsequent reintegration into the Christian eucharistic community. As we are repeatedly reminded throughout this collection, reintegration, not punishment, remained the primary goal. Permanent expulsions from a Christian community required exceptional circumstances. John O'Malley has recently reminded us that at the conclusion of the Council of Trent, the Fathers warned the papacy to wield the sword of excommunication only "with great reserve and caution."[2] While we cannot be sure how well this sage advice was followed, it seems pertinent that the records of the major Catholic Inquisitions reveal that permanent expulsions of imprisoned heretics through "relaxation to the secular arm" ended only a tiny minority (about 1.5%) of cases between the Council of Trent and the eighteenth-century Enlightenment. Similarly, consistorial scholarship has also noted the extreme rarity of permanent excommunications among almost all Reformed communities.

For Protestants and Catholics alike, some sins were far more serious than others. Usually these involved harmful actions toward fellow Christians, both within and beyond his family. The most severe among them required public acknowledgement before the sinner could be reintegrated into a Christian community. For post-Tridentine Mediterranean Catholics, so-called "reserved sins" could not be absolved by ordinary priests or even by their diocesan superiors, but instead required intervention by the Holy Office of the Inquisition. In such cases, the cozy newfangled confessionals in which such sins were originally revealed could lead to shaming rituals that were every bit as public and humiliating as those inflicted on Scottish Presbyterians. The workings of this system in Italy have been explored magisterially by Adriano Prosperi, and it reappears in numerous cases of misleadingly labeled "spontaneous" penitents preserved in records of the royally operated Iberian Inquisitions.

The vast majority of penitents appearing before early modern public disciplinary institutions, whether Catholic or Reformed, were considered capable of reintegration. A different fate awaited the very few who had committed the ultimate unforgivable sin: obstinate heresy. The Iberian Inquisitions had been created in order to root out the most toxic forms of heresy among baptized Christians of Jewish ancestry by punishing the most serious offenders through a "pedagogy of fear" carried out with maximum publicity and extreme severity, including death. Executions of such apostates were terrifyingly numerous in the first few decades of the Spanish Inquisition, and they persisted until the very end of the Portuguese Inquisition.

Nothing similar ever developed among Protestant churches, for several reasons. One is simply that "mainstream" Protestant authorities, unlike their Catholic counterparts in Mediterranean Europe, never confronted numerous converts from either Jewish or Muslim backgrounds. Another is that Luther's famous slogan about the "priesthood of all believers" not only limited definitions of what constituted heresy or apostasy but also crippled ecclesiastical hierarchies. Profound institutional differences separated penitential Catholic inquisitions from penitential Reformed consistories. Modern inquisitions were "top-down" structures, dependent ultimately on papal authorization, with effective central controls over the operations of their local components; Reformed consistories, however, were autonomous "bottom-up" organizations with no meaningful hierarchy. Modern Inquisitions possess central archives (which may be severely truncated, as at Rome), but archives of Reformed consistories have civic origins.

Protestants occasionally agreed with "papists" about what constituted major heresy – for example, adult baptism. Thus we find early Anabaptists put to death by both Zwinglian and Lutheran authorities, while Catholic authorities crushed the Anabaptist "New Jerusalem" at Münster with Lutheran approval. Similarly, Calvin's condemnation of Servetus's extreme antitrinitarian doctrines as heretical evoked a Protestant consensus that was fully shared by Catholics (who had arrested Servetus first). But with rare exceptions, Protestant theologians generally avoided elaborate definitions of heresy and apostasy.

Because the principal Holy Offices confronted large numbers of hypocritical Catholics (including Protestants, who provided the original reason for creating the Roman Inquisition), they developed elaborate information-gathering techniques that combined private sacramental confessions to clergymen with public requests for denunciations of heretics, delivered annually from local pulpits. At the opposite extreme stands Calvin's Geneva, where neighborhood gossip served as a functional replacement for collecting information about suspicious or religiously unacceptable behavior. This homely and informal method, however, produced results that seem at least equally effective in terms of the detection, public shaming, and ceremonial repentance of especially sinful penitents. Somewhere in the middle, once again, are the Protestant schismatics of England, who maintained a network of episcopal courts that seem surprisingly effective over a long time, as Martin Ingram reminds us.

Among Protestants and Catholics alike, the punishment of such exceptional sinners required some degree of collaboration between ecclesiastical and secular authorities. Indeed, the need for such collaboration increased in direct proportion to the seriousness of the moral infraction. Historians of the early modern era have long noted the overlap between two categories that we habitually distinguish, "sin" and "crime." These terms were virtually interchangeable in the sixteenth century, but today's readers of early modern documents must remember that "sin" was the more important term for the writers, whereas "crime" is now the more important term. Christian clergymen admonished and pardoned sinners, but by virtue of their profession they could not shed blood. Always and everywhere in Christendom (except in tiny and remote Anabaptist communities) their physical punishment remained the exclusive responsibility of Christian magistrates. Language, of course, varied: inquisitors "relaxed" prisoners to the "secular arm," while Geneva's Consistory "remanded" many penitents to the Republic's magistrates – whose membership, Naphy reminds us, overlapped with theirs.

"RENAISSANCES" OF INQUISITORIAL AND CONSISTORIAL STUDIES

This collection of studies of Catholic Inquisitions and Reformed consistories presents them as parallel institutions, both with sinister reputations, that were responsible for the public humiliation and eventual reintegration of sinners whose actions menaced the solidarity of their religious communities. It is very much a child of our ecumenical time. As someone with experience in both academic specialties, I believe that Inquisitions and consistories have experienced parallel recent scholarly revivals, each collaborative and multinational in scope. However, the differences between their respective historiographies reflect other differences that are both geographical and chronological.

First, geography. Both Inquisitions and consistories were international enterprises, but the European nations involved are completely different. 'Inquisitorial' scholars concentrate on three permanent, centrally directed Holy Offices created in Mediterranean Europe (Spain 1478, Portugal 1536, and Italy 1542). The first two soon became global, with branches operating in American and Asian colonies by 1570. At the opposite extreme, consistories remained extremely nonhierarchical local institutions created by Reformed churches located primarily in four places: French Switzerland, France, Scotland, and the Netherlands, with minor outposts in Germany and Hungary.

Their respective locations have helped orient historical investigations of each institutional group in different directions. Compared to the study of the modern Mediterranean Inquisitions, the study of Reformed consistories benefits from two advantages: superior resources and friendly mentors. With the possible exception of Scotland, the best-documented consistories cluster in prosperous parts of Europe with top-notch research centers, making it predictable that French, Dutch, and Swiss experts will play vital roles in studying them. Moreover, some key consistorial experts come from friendly confessional backgrounds; the American godfather of the "consistorial renaissance," the late Robert M. Kingdon, offers a perfect example.

However, the situation is reversed with the major Mediterranean Inquisitions. Here a venerable tradition, dating from the great seventeenth-century Dutch scholar Philipp van Limborch and continuing through Henry Charles Lea in nineteenth-century Philadelphia, decrees that their major scholarly investigations have been conducted by physically distant foreigners who are overwhelmingly hostile to Tridentine Catholic orthodoxy. With few exceptions, this tradition continues in this volume, which includes some locally based experts but no apologists for the Holy Office.

Second, chronology. These recent scholarly revivals have not been synchronic. The ongoing "renaissance" of inquisitorial studies preceded the "renaissance" of consistorial studies by about fifteen years, a circumstance that helps explain some aspects of this collection. One side features several younger, "second-generation" inquisitorial experts, while the other includes some senior scholars who have been contributing to the consistorial conversation for almost two decades. Although purely fortuitous, this difference mirrors their respective institutional chronologies. The Spanish Inquisition held its first *auto da fe* before Luther was born, while the Vatican organized the last major Mediterranean Inquisition shortly after the oldest Reformed consistory held its first session at Geneva in December 1541.

Their recent historiography also reveals some similarities. For example, each scholarly "renaissance" had an isolated prelude. In 1965, in the Franco era, Henry Kamen made a pioneering attempt to write a history of the Spanish Inquisition that tried to explain it rather than vilify it; eleven years later came my preliminary exploration of Geneva's early consistory. Neither was followed up for many years, although Kamen subsequently published two major revisions of his original work in 1985 and 1997. In retrospect, it seems fair to say that the ongoing renaissance in inquisition studies began in 1972, when a Danish ethnographer, Gustav Henningsen, first realized the peculiar riches of the 44,000 case summaries preserved by the central headquarters of the oldest Holy Office. One can similarly argue that the ongoing renaissance in consistorial studies dates from 1987, when Robert Kingdon began assembling the human and financial resources to prepare a critical edition of the oldest surviving records of the Genevan Consistory.

Each scholarly "renaissance" has celebrated its progress through various international congresses, held irregularly but assembling many leading scholars. Obviously, inquisitorial congresses began first, holding two parallel meetings in 1978: a large one in Spain commemorating the 500th anniversary of the Spanish Holy Office, and a smaller but more multinational meeting (also in Spanish) organized by Henningsen in Denmark to publicize the first results from his documentary break-through. The publications resulting from each enterprise continue to form part of the intellectual infrastructure of this volume. The Spanish venture published its key contributions at Madrid in 1980, but the principal goal of its organizers was to plan a comprehensive modern history of the Inquisition in Spain and America that would require three volumes and twenty years to complete. Meanwhile, the principal papers from the Copenhagen congress finally appeared eight years later – in English, and in America.

The "inquisitorial renaissance" accelerated during the 1980s and 1990s, holding numerous congresses, mostly in Spain or Italy but occasionally in America. In 1987, a splashy LusoBrazilian congress on the Portuguese Inquisition in Lisbon and São Paulo eventually attracted 700 people from fifteen countries. In contrast, international congresses spawned by the "consistorial renaissance" have been relatively modest and late-blooming affairs, beginning well after the first collaborative volume on the subject had appeared in 1994. So far, four of them have been held, all in France or Switzerland. Their subsequent publications, especially from the most recent one in 2009, suggest that comparative studies of consistories have now reached maturity under a relatively stable body of scholarly elders, several of whom reappear in this collection.

Having begun much earlier, inquisitorial studies also reached maturity sooner, about two decades after their beginnings. One important measure is the appearance in 1995 of a thoroughgoing comparative institutional history of all three modern Inquisitions composed by a single author, Francisco Bethencourt. No single expert has yet attempted an institutional synthesis of Reformed consistories, perhaps because the situations of the two most important non-Francophone Reformed churches in Scotland and the Netherlands seem so utterly different, and neither closely resembles the original Genevan model.

An appropriate conclusion to the "inquisitorial renaissance" took the form of an unprecedented international summit congress in 1998. It was hosted by the ongoing institution that had formally created all of them, the Papacy, which had moreover just opened the records of its own Holy Office to outside scholars. (Reformed Protestantism being strongly averse to hierarchy and having avoided international theological gatherings since the Synod of Dort in 1619, no analogous summit conference for "consistories" is even imaginable.) The Vatican requested historical experts to help its theologians prepare a formal apologia for the sins of 'its' Inquisitions in time for its forthcoming millennial Jubilee. Those who attended the Vatican conference remember it well – when else do historians address an audience composed entirely of professional theologians? – and its help was duly noted in the formal papal *mea culpa*. However, unlike the aftereffects of the 1978 conferences, its published proceedings have been ignored by the current generation of inquisitorial scholars. Two reasons help explain this neglect. Its presentations, only 10 percent of them in English, were not embalmed in print until 2005. Moreover, some of its best-known participants, who played major roles in its debates and ordinarily write in English (e.g., Henry Kamen, John Tedeschi, or Carlo Ginzburg), made no formal presentations.

Despite the asymmetrical stages of current historiography on Inquisitions and consistories, both groups of experts seem acutely aware of the difficulties in interpreting the surviving records of these institutions. Reading the methodological caveats raised in Chapters 10 and 11 by two Swiss academics (Siebenhüner and Grosse) enumerating the many significant obstacles confronting contemporary interpreters of early modern disciplinary institutions evokes the diatribe of a distinguished American essayist and unabashed champion of Calvin, Marilynne Robinson:

> Records, of course, are biased toward the literate and the official and must always be assumed to be flawed by the methods and circumstances of record keeping and the accidents of preservation and accessibility. The interpreted past incorporates all these difficulties and adds new distortions having to do with the motives, enthusiasms, sensibilities, talents, and scruples of interpreters.[3]

One is tempted to extend the Augustinian doctrine of original sin, which was probably shared by many inquisitors as well as by all Reformed elders, to include modern scholars of consistories and Inquisitions.

But awareness of total human corruption never prevented either inquisitors or elders from going about their duties – and keeping records of their activities. Later in the same essay, Robinson observes that "I have no conclusion to offer in place of the old one, except that history is very strange and beautiful *and instructive* [my italics] in the absence of all conclusion."[4] Aware of our limitations, we must keep trying our best to make sense of our expanding range of information about these institutions, because doing otherwise only prolongs obsolete and pernicious stereotypes.

As our ecumenical age confronts the long record of a divided Christendom, this attempt to compare and contrast Inquisitions and consistories suggests some additional lines of inquiry. To my mind, our single greatest need is a better understanding of both the explicit and implicit reasons why both Catholic and Reformed churches eventually consigned their respective disciplinary institutions – which were, by and large, still performing their assigned tasks with some success – to the scrapheap of history. The central reason for establishing such institutions had not changed; Christian churches required some form of effective penance before admitting the most notorious sinners to communion. But coercive institutions to discipline them disappeared. The last remaining vestige of the early modern "Reformations of Penance" is the Catholic confessional, whose history remains unwritten because these are still in use.

Notes

1 R. Po-chia Hsia, *Social Discipline in the Reformation: Central Europe, 1550–1750* (London, 1989), 123, 124.
2 John W. O'Malley, *Trent and All That: Renaming Catholicism in the Early Modern Era* (Cambridge, MA, 2000), 237.
3 Marilynne Robinson, *The Death of Adam* (New York, 2005; first ed., 1998), 126.
4 Ibid., 146.

Bibliography

GENERAL WORKS (CONSULTED IN MULTIPLE CHAPTERS)

Abbott, William M., "Ruling Eldership in Civil War England, the Scottish Kirk, and Early New England: A Comparative Study of Secular and Spiritual Aspects," *Church History* 75 1 (2006): 38–68.

Alberro, Solange, *Inquisición y sociedad en México, 1571–1700* (México, 1988).

Alcalá, Angel ed., *The Spanish Inquisition and the Inquisitorial Mind* (Highland Lakes, NJ, 1987).

Ames, Christine Caldwell, *Righteous Persecution: Inquisition, Dominicans, and Christianity in the Middle Ages* (Philadelphia, PA, 2009).

Baião, António, *A Inquisição de Goa: Tentativa de história de sua origem, estabelecimento, evolução, e extinção*, 2 vols. (Lisbon, 1949).

Barker, S. K. ed., *Revisiting Geneva: Robert Kingdon and the Coming of the French Wars of Religion*, (St Andrews, 2012).

Benedict, Philip, *Christ's Churches Purely Reformed: A Social History of Calvinism* (New Haven, CT, 2002).

Bennassar, Bartolomé, "La Inquisición o la pedagogía del miedo," in *Inquisición española, poder político y control social*, Bartolomé Bennassar et al. eds. (Barcelona, 1984), 94–125.

Bethencourt, Francisco, *The Inquisition. A Global History, 1478–1834*, Jean Birrell trans. (Cambridge, 2009).

Black, Christopher F., *The Italian Inquisition* (New Haven, CT, 2009).

Brambilla, Elena, *La Giustizia Intollerante. Inquisizione e tribunali confessionali in Europa (secolo iv-xviii)* (Rome, 2006).

Calvin, John, *Institutes of the Christian Religion*, 2 vols., John T. McNeill ed., Ford Lewis Battles trans. (Philadelphia, PA, 1960).

Calvini, Ioannis, *Opera quae supersunt omnia*, 59 vols., G. Baum, E. Cunitz and E. Reuss eds. (Brunswick, 1863–1900).

Cavarzere, Marco, *La Prassi della Censura nell'Italia del Seicento. Tra Repressione e Mediazione* (Rome, 2011).

Chuchiak, John F., *The Inquisition in New Spain, 1536–1820. A Documentary History* (Baltimore, MD, 2012).

Contreras, Jaime, *Sotos contra Riquelmes: regidores, inquisidores, y criptojudíos* (Madrid, 1992).

Croq, Laurence and Garrioch, David eds., *La religion vécue. Les laïcs dans l'Europe moderne* (Rennes, 2013).

Davidson, Nicholas D., "The Inquisition," in *The Ashgate Companion to the Counter-Reformation*, Alexandra Bamji, Geert H. Janssen, and Mary Laven eds. (Farnham and Burlington, VT, 2013), 91–108.

Dedieu, Jean-Pierre, *L'administration de la foi: l'inquisition de Tolède, XVIe – XVIIIe siècle* (Madrid, 1989).

Del Col, Andrea, *L'Inquisizione in Italia. Dal XII al XXI secolo* (Milan, 2006).

van Deursen, A. Th., *Bavianen en Slijkgeuzen: Kerk en kerkvolk ten tijde and Maurits en Oldenbarnvelt* (Franeker, 1997).

Errera, Andrea, *Processus in causa fide: l'evoluzione dei manuali inquisitoriali nei secoli XVI-XVIII e il manuale inedito di un inquisitore perugino* (Bologna, 2000).

Estèbe, Janine and Vogler, Bernard, "La genèse d'une société protestante: étude comparée de quelques registres consistoriaux languedociens et palatins vers 1600," *Annales: économies, sociétés, civilisations* 32 (1976): 362–88.

Fehler, Timothy, *Poor Relief and Protestantism* (Brookfield, VT, 1999).

Feitler, Bruno, *Inquisition, juifs et nouveaux-chrétiens au Brésil. Le Nordeste, XVIIe-XVIIIe* (Louvain, 2003).

Flynn, Maureen, "Mimesis of the Last Judgement: The Spanish Auto de Fe," *Sixteenth Century Journal* 22/2 (1991): 281–97.

Giles, Mary E. ed., *Women in the Inquisition. Spain and the New World* (Baltimore, MD, 1999).

Ginzburg, Carlo, "The Inquisitor as Anthropologist," in Clues, Myths, and the Historical Method, John and Anne Tedeschi trans. (Baltimore, MD, 1989), 156–64.

   The Night Battles. Witchcraft and Agrarian Cults in the Sixteenth and Seventeenth Century, John and Anne Tedeschi trans. (Baltimore, MD, 1983).

Givens, Bryan, *Judging Maria de Macedo: A Female Visionary and the Inquisition in Early Modern Portugal* (Baton Rouge, LA, 2010).

Gowing, Laura, *Domestic Dangers: Women, Words, and Sex in Early Modern London* (Oxford, 1996).

Graham, Michael F., *The Uses of Reform: "Godly Discipline" and Popular Behavior in Scotland and Beyond, 1560–1610* (Leiden, 1996).

Grosse, Christian, *Les rituels de la Cène: le culte eucharistique réformé à Genève (XVIe-XVIIe siècles)* (Geneva, 2008).

Grosse, Christian, Tosato-Rigo, Danièle, and Staremberg Goy, Nicole eds., *Sous l'oeil du Consistoire: sources consistoriales et histoire du contrôle social sous l'ancien régime* (Lausanne, 2004).

Henningsen, Gustav, *The Witches' Advocate: Basque Witchcraft and the Spanish Inquisition, 1609–1614* (Reno, NV, 1980).

Henningsen, Gustav and Tedeschi, John eds., *The Inquisition in Early Modern Europe: Studies on Sources and Methods*, ed. (Dekalb, IL, 1986).

Holt, Mack P. ed., *Adaptations of Calvinism in Reformation Europe: Essays in Honor of Brian G. Armstrong* (Aldershot, 2007).

Homza, Lu Ann, *Religious Authority in the Spanish Renaissance* (Baltimore, MD, 2000).

The Spanish Inquisition, 1478–1614: An Anthology of Sources (Indianapolis, IN, 2006).

Hsia, Ronnie Po-Chia, *Social Discipline in the Reformation: Central Europe 1550–1750* (New York, 1989).

Hughes, Philip Edgcumbe ed. and trans., *The Register of the Company of Pastors of Geneva in the Time of Calvin* (Grand Rapids, MI, 1966).

Huisseau, Isaac d', *La Discipline des Eglises réformées de France ou l'ordre par lequel elles sont conduites et gouvernées* (Geneva, 1666).

Ingram, Martin, *Church Courts, Sex and Marriage in England, 1570–1640* (Cambridge, 1987).

"History of Sin or History of Crime? The Regulation of Personal Morality in England, 1450–1750," in *Institutionen, Instrumente und Akteure Sozialer Kontrolle und Disziplinierung im frühneuzeitlichen Europa*, Heinz Schilling and Lars Behrisch eds. (Frankfurt, 1999), 87–103.

Janin-Thivos Tailland, Michèle, *Inquisition et Société au Portugal. Le cas du tribunal d'Évora 1660–1821* (Paris, 2001).

Kagan, Richard, *Lucrecia's Dreams: Politics and Prophecy in Sixteenth-Century Spain* (Berkeley, CA, 1990).

Kagan, Richard, and Dyer, Abigail eds. and trans., *Inquisitorial Inquiries. Brief Lives of Secret Jews and Other Heretics* (Baltimore, MD, 2004).

Kamen, Henry, *The Phoenix and the Flame: Catalonia and the Counter Reformation* (New Haven, CT, 1993).

The Spanish Inquisition. An Historical Revision (London, 1997).

Kaplan, Benjamin J., *Calvinists and Libertines: Confession and Community in Utrecht, 1578–1620* (Oxford, 1995).

Kingdon, Robert M., *Adultery and Divorce in Calvin's Geneva* (Cambridge, MA, 1995).

"The Control of Morals in Calvin's Geneva," in *The Social History of the Reformation*, Lawrence. P. Buck, Jonathan. W. Zophy eds. (Columbus, 1972), 3–16.

"Social Welfare in Calvin's Geneva," *American Historical Review* 76 (1971): 50–69.

Kingdon, Robert M. and Bergier, Jean-François eds., *Registres de la Compagnie des Pasteurs de Genève, vol. 1, 1546–1553* (Geneva, 1964).

Kooi, Christine, *Liberty and Religion: Church and State in Leiden's Reformation, 1572–1620* (Leiden, 2000).

Lambert, Thomas A. and Watt, Isabella, M., eds., *Registers of the Consistory of Geneva in the Time of Calvin*, vol. 1, (Grand Rapids, MI, 2000).

Lambert, Thomas A., Watt, Isabella M., Kingdon, Robert M. and Watt, Jeffrey R. eds., *Registres du Consistoire de Genève au temps de Calvin*, 6 vols. (Geneva, 1996–2012).

Lea, Henry Charles, *A History of the Inquisition of Spain*, 4 vols. (New York, 1906).

Lenman, Bruce, "The Limits of Godly Discipline in the Early Modern Period," in *Religion and Society in Early Modern Europe*, Kaspar von Greyerz ed. (London, 1984), 124–45.

Lipscomb, Suzannah, "Crossing Boundaries: Women's Gossip, Insults and Violence in Sixteenth-Century France," *French History* 25 (2011): 408–26.

Llorente, Juan Antonio, *Histoire critique de l'Inquisitio d'Espagne* (Paris, 1817–18).

Lualdi, Katherine Jackson and Thayer, Anne T. eds., *Penitence in the Age of Reformations* (Aldershot, 2000).

Lynn, Kimberly, *Between Court and Confessional: The Politics of Spanish Inquisitors* (Cambridge, 2013).

Manetsch, Scott M., *Calvin's Company of Pastors: Pastoral Care and the Emerging Reformed Church, 1536–1609* (Oxford, 2013).

"Pastoral Care East of Eden: The Consistory of Geneva, 1568–82," *Church History* 75 (2006): 274–313.

Marcocci, Giuseppe, *I Custodi dell'Ortodossia. Inquisizion e Chiesa nel Portugallo del Cinquecento* (Rome, 2004).

"Toward a History of the Portuguese Inquisition: Trends in Modern Historiography (1974–2009)," *Revue de l'histoire des religions* 227 3(2010): 355–93.

Mayer, Thomas F., *The Roman Inquisition, A Papal Bureaucracy and its Laws in the Age of Galileo* (Philadelphia, PA, 2013).

McCallum, John, *Reforming the Scottish Parish: The Reformation in Fife, 1560–1640* (Farnham, 2010).

Méjan, François ed., *Discipline de l'Église réformée de France annotée et précédée d'une introduction historique* (Paris, 1947).

Mentzer, Raymond A., "Le consistoire et la pacification du monde rural," *Bulletin de la Société de l'Histoire du Protestantisme Français* 135 (1989): 373–89.

"*Disciplina nervus ecclesiae*: The Calvinist Reform of Morals at Nîmes," *Sixteenth Century Journal* 18 (1987): 89–115.

"Morals and Moral Regulation in Protestant France," *Journal of Interdisciplinary History* 31 (2000): 1–20.

"The Reformed Churches of France and Medieval Canon Law," in *Canon Law in Protestant Lands*, R.H. Helmholz ed. (Berlin, 1992), 165–85.

"Sociability and Culpability: Conventions of Mediation and Reconciliation within the Sixteenth-Century Huguenot Community," in *Memory and Identity: The Huguenots in France and the Altalntic Diaspora*, B. Van Ruymbeke and Randy J. Sparks eds. (Columbia, SC, 2003), 45–57.

ed., *Sin and the Calvinists: Morals Control and the Consistory in the Reformed Tradition* (Kirksville, MO, 1994).

Mentzer, Raymond A., Chareyre, Philippe, and Moreil, Françoise eds., *Dire l'interdit: The Vocabulary of Censure and Exclusion in the Early Modern Reformed Tradition* (Leiden, 2010).

Mills, Kenneth R., *Idolatry and its Enemies: Colonial Andean Religion and Extirpation, 1640–1750* (Princeton, NJ, 1997).

Monter, William E., "The Consistory of Geneva, 1559–1569," *Bibliothèque d'Humanisme et Renaissance* 38 3 (1976): 467–84.

Frontiers of Heresy: The Spanish Inquisition from the Basque Lands to Sicily (Cambridge, 1990).

Moreno Martínez, Doris, *La Invención de la Inquisición* (Madrid, 2004).

Münch, Paul, *Zucht und Ordnung. Reformierte Kirchenverfassungen im 16. und 17. Jahrhundert (Nassau-Dillenburg, Kurpfalz, Hessen-Kassel)* (Stuttgart, 1978).

Murdock, Graeme, *Calvinism on the Frontier, 1600–1660: International Calvinism and the Reformed Church in Hungary and Transylvania* (Oxford, 2000).

Nalle, Sara, *God in La Mancha: Religious Reform and the People of Cuenca, 1500–1650* (Baltimore, MD, 1992).

Mad for God: Bartolomé Sánchez, the Secret Messiah of Cardenete (Charlottesville, VA, 2001).

Naphy, William G., *Calvin and the Consolidation of the Genevan Reformation* (Manchester, 1994).

Nesvig, Martin Austin, *Ideology and Inquisition: The World of the Censors in Early Mexico* (New Haven, CT, 2009).

Paiva, José Pedro, *Baluartes da fé e da disciplina. O enlace entre a Inquisiçâo e os bispos em Portugal (1536–1750)* (Coimbra, 2011).

Parker, Charles H., "Enregistrer les péchés pour favoriser la réconciliation. Les archives des consistoires des Eglises réformées de Hollande," *Philippe Chareyre trans. Bulletin de la Société de l'Histoire du Protestantisme Français* 153 (2007): 613–34.

"The Moral Agency and Moral Autonomy of Church Folk in the Dutch Reformed Church of Delft, 1580–1620," *Journal of Ecclesiastical History* 48 (1997): 44–70.

The Reformation of Community: Social Welfare and Calvinist Charity in Holland, 1572–1620 (Cambridge, 1998).

Parker, Geoffrey, "The 'Kirk by Law Established' and the Origins of the 'Taming of Scotland': St. Andrews 1559–1600," in *Perspectives in Scottish Social History: Essays in Honour of Rosalind Mitchison*, Leah Leneman ed. (Aberdeen, 1988), 1–32.

Pastore, Stefania, *Il vangelo e la spada. L'inquisizione di Castiglia e i suoi critici (1460–1598)* (Rome, 2003).

Pérez Villanueva, Joaquín, and Bonet, Bartolomé Escandell eds., *Historia de la Inquisición en España y América* 3 vols. (Madrid, 1984–2000).

Perry, Mary Elizabeth, and Cruz, Anne J. eds., *Cultural Encounters: the Impact of the Inquisition in Spain and the New World* (Berkeley, CA, 1991).

Peters, Edward, *Inquisition* (Berkeley, CA, 1989).

Pettegree, Andrew, *Foreign Protestant Communities in Sixteenth-Century London* (Oxford, 1986).

Pollmann, Judith, "Off the Record: Problems in the Quantification of Calvinist Church Discipline," *Sixteenth Century Journal* 33 (2002): 423–38.

Religious Choice in the Dutch Republic (Manchester, 1999).

Prestwich, Menna ed., *International Calvinism, 1541–1715* (Oxford, 1985).

Prosperi, Adriano, *Tribunali della coscienza. Inquisitori, confessori, missionari* (Turin, 2009).

Prosperi, Adriano ed., with Vincenzo Lavenia and John Tedeschi, *Dizionario storico dell'Inquisizione*, 4 vols. (Pisa, 2010).

Pullan, Brian, *The Jews of Europe and the Inquisition of Venice, 1550–1670* (London, 1997).

Romeo, Giovanni, *Inquisitori, esorcisti e streghe nell'Italia della Controriforma* (Florence, 1990).

Roodenburg, Herman, *Onder Censuur. De kerkelijke tucht in de gereformeerde gemeente van Amsterdam, 1578–1700* (Hilversum, 1990).

Roth, Cecil, *The Spanish Inquisition*, 2nd ed. (New York, 1996).

Saraiva, António José, *The Marrano Factory: The Portuguese and its New Christians, 1536–1765*, H. P. Salomon and I.S.D. Sassoon trans. (Leiden, 2001).

Scaramella, Pierroberto ed., *Le lettere della Congregazione del Sant'Ufficio ai tribunali di fede di Napoli 1563–1625*, introduction by John Tedeschi (Trieste, 2002).

Schilling, Heinz, *Civic Calvinism in Northwestern Germany and the Netherlands: Sixteenth to Nineteenth Centuries* (Kirksville, MO, 1991).

"'History of Crime' or 'History of Sin?'" in *Politics and Society in Reformation Europe*, E. I. Kouri and Tom Scott eds. (Basingstoke, 1987), 289–310.

Schilling, Heinz, and Schreiber, Klaus-Dieter eds. *Die Kirchenratsprotokolle der reformierten Gemeinde Emden 1557–1620*, 2 vols. (Cologne, 1989–1992).

Schutte, Anne Jacobson, *Aspiring Saints: Pretence of Holiness, Inquisition and Gender in the Republic of Venice, 1618–1750* (Baltimore, MD, 2001).

Schwartz, Stuart B., *All Can Be Saved: Religious Tolerance and Salvation in the Iberian Atlantic World* (New Haven, CT, 2008).

Seitz, Jonathan, *Witchcraft and Inquisition in Early Modern Venice* (Cambridge, 2011).

Silverblatt, Irene, *Modern Inquisitions: Peru and the Colonial Origins of the Civilized World* (Durham, NC, 2004).

Soyer, François, "Nowhere to Run: The Extradition of Conversos between the Spanish and Portuguese Inquisition during the Sixteenth and Seventeenth Centuries," in *The Conversos and Moriscos in Late Medieval Spain and Beyond*, Kevin Ingram ed. (Leiden, 2012), 247–74.

Spierling, Karen E., *Infant Baptism in Reformation Geneva* (Aldershot, 2005).

Starr-LeBeau, Gretchen, *In the Shadow of the Virgin: Inquisitors, Friars, and Conversos in Guadalupe, Spain* (Princeton, NJ, 2003).

Tausiet, Maria, *Abracadabra omnipotens: magia urbana en Zaragoza en la Edad Moderna* (Madrid, 2007).

Ponzoña en los ojos: brujería y superstición en Aragón en el siglo XVI (Madrid, 2004).

Tedeschi, John, *The Prosecution of Heresy. Collected Studies on the Inquisition in Early Modern Italy* (Binghamton, NY, 1991).

Todd, Margo, "Consistoire, guilde et conseil: les archives des consistoires écossais et l'urbanisation de la culture paroissiale," *Bulletin de la Société de l'Histoire du Protestantisme Français* 153 (2007): 635–48.

The Culture of Protestantism in Early Modern Scotland (New Haven, CT, 2002).

Villa-Flores, Javier, *Dangerous Speech: A Social History of Blasphemy in Colonial Mexico* (Tucson, AZ, 2006).
Wachtel, Nathan, *The Faith of Remembrance: Marrano Labyrinths*, Nikki Halpern trans. (Philadelphia, PA, 2013).
Wadsworth, James E., *Agents of Orthodoxy: Honor, Status and the Inquisition in Colonial Pernambuco Brazil* (New York, 2008).
Watt, Jeffrey R., *The Making of Modern Marriage: Matrimonial Control and the Rise of Sentiment in Neuchâtel, 1550–1800* (Ithaca, NY, 1992).
The Scourge of Demons: Possession, Lust, and Witchcraft in a Seventeenth-Century Italian Convent (Rochester, NY, 2009).
"Women and the Consistory in Calvin's Geneva," *Sixteenth Century Journal* 24 (1993): 429–39.
Witte, John Jr. and Kingdon, Robert M., *Sex, Marriage and Family in John Calvin's Geneva, vol. 1, Courtship, Engagement and Marriage* (Grand Rapids, MI, 2005).
Wouters, A. Ph. F. and Abels, P.H.A.M., *Nieuw en ongezien: kerk en samenleving in de classis Delft en Delfland 1572–1621*, 2 vols. (Delft, 1994).

INTRODUCTION

Bayle, Pierre, *Dictionnaire Historique et Critique*, 4 vols., 6th ed. (Basel, 1741).
Bennassar, Bartolomé, "Modelos de la mentalidad inquisitorial: métodos de su 'pedagogia de miedo,'" in *Inquisición española y mentalidad inquisitorial*, Angel Alcalá ed. (Barecelona, 1984), 174–82.
Contreras, Jaime and Henningsen, Gustav, "Forty-Four Thousand Cases of the Spanish Inquisition (1540–1700): Analysis of a Historical Data Bank," in *The Inquisition in Early Modern Europe: Studies on Sources and Methods*, Gustav Hennigsen and John Tedeschi eds., in association with Charles Amiel (DeKalb, IL, 1986), 100–29.
Elias, Norbert, *The Civilizing Process*, Edmund Jephcott trans. (Cambridge, MA, 1994).
Gordon, Bruce, *Calvin* (New Haven, CT, 2009).
Mentzer, Raymond A., *Heresy Proceedings in Languedoc, 1500–1560* (Philadelphia, PA, 1984).
Monter, E. William, "Women and the Italian Inquisitions," in *Women in the Middle Ages and the Renaissance: Literary and Historical Perspectives*, Mary Beth Rose ed. (Syracuse, NY, 1986).
Monter, E. William and Tedeschi, John, "Toward a Statistical Profile of the Italian Inquisitions, Sixteenth to Eighteenth Centuries," in *The Inquisition in Early Modern Europe: Studies on Sources and Methods*, Gustav Hennigsen and John Tedeschi eds., in association with Charles Amiel (DeKalb, IL, 1986), 130–57.
Mout, M.E.H.N., "Limits and Debates: A Comparative View of Dutch Toleration in the Sixteenth and Early Seventeenth Centuries," in *The Emergence of*

Tolerance in the Dutch Republic, C. Berkvens-Stevelinck, J. Israel, and G.H. M. Posthumus Meyjes eds. (Leiden, 1997), 37–47.

Pomeau, René, *La Religion de Voltaire* (Paris, 1956).

Pullan, Brian, *The Jews of Europe and the Inquisition in Venice, 1550–1670* (Totowa, NJ, 1983).

Tailland, Michèle Janin-Thivos, *Inquisition et société: le cas du tribunal d'Evora, 1660–1821* (Paris, 2001).

Voltaire, *Philosophical Dictionary*, 2 vols., Peter Gay trans. and ed. (New York, 1962).

SECTION A: CHAPTERS 1 AND 2

Black, Christopher F., "Censorship and Indexes," in *Oxford Bibliographies: Renaissance and Reformation* (online resource).

Church, Religion and Society in Early Modern Italy (New York, 2004).

"Confraternities and the Italian Inquisitions," in *Brotherhood and Boundaries: Fraternità e barriere*, Stefania Pastore, Adriano Prosperi, and Nicholas Terpstra eds. (Pisa, 2011), 293–305.

Italian Confraternities in the Sixteenth Century (Cambridge, 1989).

"The Roman Inquisition," in *Oxford Bibliographies: Renaissance and Reformation* (online resource).

"The Trials and Tribulations of a Local Roman Inquisitor: Giacomo Tinti in Modena, 1626–1647," online, *Giornale di Storia* 12 (2012): www.giornale distoria.net.

Bruening, Michael, *Calvinism's First Battleground: Conflict and Reform in the Pays de Vaud, 1528–1559* (Dordrecht, 2005).

Burnett, Amy Nelson, *The Yoke of Christ: Martin Bucer and Christian Discipline* (Kirksville, MO, 1994).

Cameron, James K. ed., *The First Book of Discipline* (Edinburgh, 1972).

Cerrillo Cruz, Gonzalo, *Los Familiares de la Inquisición Española* (Valladolid, 2000).

Del Col, Andrea, *Domenico Scandella Known as Menocchio: His Trials before the Inquisition (1583–1599)*, John and Anne Tedeschi trans. (Binghamton, NY, 1996).

Denis, Philippe and Rott, Jean, *Jean Morély (ca. 1524 – ca. 1594) et l'utopie d'une démocratie dans l'Église* (Geneva, 1993).

Garrisson, Janine, *Protestants du Midi, 1559–1598* (Toulouse, 1980).

Ginzburg, Carlo, *The Cheese and the Worms. The Cosmos of a Sixteenth-Century Miller*, John and Anne Tedeschi trans. (Baltimore, MD, 1992).

Gorski, Philip S., *The Disciplinary Revolution. Calvinism and the Rise of the State in Early Modern Europe* (Chicago, 2003).

Greenleaf, Richard E., "Persistence of Native Values: The Inquisition and the Indians of Colonial Mexico," *The Americas* 50 3(1994): 351–76.

Greschat, Martin, *Martin Bucer: A Reformer and his Times* (Louisville, KY, 2004).

Havik, Philip J., "Walking the Tightrope: Female Agency, Religious Practice, and the Portuguese Inquisition on the Upper Guinea Coast (Seventeenth

Century)," in *Bridging the Early Modern Atlantic World: People, Products, and Practices on the Move*, Caroline A. Williams ed. (Farnham and Burlington, VT, 2009), 173–81.

Kingdon, Robert M., "La discipline ecclésiastique vue de Zurich et Genève au temps de la Réformation: l'usage de Matthieu 18, 15–17 par les réformateurs," *Revue de théologie et de philosophie* 133 (2001): 343–55.

"The Geneva Consistory in the Time of Calvin," in *Calvinism in Europe, 1540–1620*, Andrew Pettegree et al. eds. (Cambridge, 1994).

"Nostalgia for Catholic Rituals in Calvin's Geneva," in *Grenzgänge der Theologie Professor Alexandre Ganoczy zum 75. Geburtstag*, O. Meuffels ed. (Munster, 2004), 209–20.

Kingdon, Robert M. and Lambert, Thomas A., *Reforming Geneva: Discipline, Faith and Anger on Calvin's Geneva* (Geneva, 2012).

Kingdon, Robert M., Mentzer, Raymond A., and Reulos, Michel, "'Disciplines' réformées du XVIe siècle français: une découverte faite aux Etats-Unis," *Bulletin de la Société de l'Histoire du Protestantisme Français* 130 (1984): 69–86.

Kirk, James ed., *The Second Book of Discipline* (Edinburgh, 1980).

MacCulloch, Diarmaid, "Evil Just Is," review of *The Italian Inquisition*, by Christopher Black, *London Review of Books* 32 9(May 2010), 23–4.

Mayer, Thomas F., "The Roman Inquisition's Precept to Galileo (1616)," *The British Journal for the History of Science* 43 3(2010): 327–51.

Minchella, Giuseppina, "Alterità e Vicinanza: Cristiani, Turchi, Rinnegati, Ebrei a Venezia e nella Frontiera Orientale," *Giornale di Storia* 4 (2010): www.giornaledistoria.net.

Porre un soldato all'Inquisizione: L'intervento del Sant'Uffizio nella fortezza veneziana di Palmanova, 1595–1669 (Trieste, 2009).

Monter, E. William, *Calvin's Geneva* (New York, 1967).

Plakotos, Georgios, "Christian and Muslim Converts from the Balkans in Early Modern Venice: Patterns of Social and Cultural Mobility and Identities," in *Developing Cultural Identity in the Balkans: Convergence vs. Divergence*, Detrez Raymond and Plas Pieter eds. (Brussels, 2005), 125–45.

Reulos, Michel, "Police et discipline de l'Église de Saint-Lô (1563)," appended to "Les débuts des Communautés réformées dans l'actuel département de la Manche (Cotetin et Avranchin)," in *Réforme et Contre-réforme en Normandie*, special issue of *Revue du Département de la Manche* 24 (1982, fascicules 93-94-95), 31-57.

Rowland, Ingrid D., *Giordano Bruno: Philosopher/Heretic* (New York, 2008).

Valente, Michaela, *Contro L'Inquisizione. Il dibattito europeo secc. XVI-XVIII* (Turin, 2009).

Wagner, Christine, "Los luteranos ante la Inquisición de Toledo en el siglo XVI," *Hispania Sacra* 46 (1994): 473–510.

Wickersham, Jane K., *Rituals of Prosecution: The Roman Inquisition and the Prosecution of Philo-Protestants in Sixteenth-Century Italy* (Toronto, 2012).

SECTION B: CHAPTERS 3 THROUGH 7

Adorno, Rolena, *Guaman Poma: Writing and Resistance in Colonial Peru* (Austin, TX, 2000).

Ambrona, Antonio Gil, *Historia de la violencia contra las mujeres: misoginía y conflicto matrimonial en España* (Madrid, 2008).

Barbierato, Francesco, *The Inquisitor in the Hat Shop: Inquisition, Forbidden Books, and Unbelief in Early Modern Venice* (Farnham and Burlington, VT, 2012).

Bray, Gerald ed., *The Anglican Canons, 1529–1947* (Woodbridge, 1998).
   Tudor Church Reform: the Henrician Canons of 1535 and the Reformation Legum Ecclesiasticarum (Woodbridge, 2000).

Brodman, James William, *Charity and Welfare: Hospitals and the Poor in Medieval Catalonia* (Philadelphia, PA, 1998).

Brooks, Christopher W., *Law, Politics and Society in Early Modern England* (Cambridge, 2008).

Brucker, Gene A., "Ecclesiastical Courts in Fifteenth-Century Florence and Fiesole," *Mediaeval Studies* 53 1(1991): 229–57.

Brundage, James A., *Medieval Canon Law* (London, 1995).

Burns, Kathryn, "Nuns, Kurakas, and Credit: The Spiritual Economy of Seventeenth-Century Cuzco," *Colonial Latin American Review* 6 2 (1997): 185–204.

Calderwood, Alma ed., *Buik of the Kirk of the Canagait* (Edinburgh, 1961).

Candau Chacón, Maria Luisa, *Iglesia y sociedad en la campiña sevillana, la Vicaría de Ecija (1697–1723)* (Seville, 1986).

Carroll, Stuart, *Blood and Violence in Early Modern France* (Oxford, 2006).

Conner, Philip, *Huguenot Heartland: Montaubon and Southern French Calvinism During the Wars of Religion* (Aldershot, 2002), 31–87.

Coutts, W. and Forte, A.D.M., "Some Aspects of the Law of Marriage in Scotland: 1500–1700," in *Marriage and Property*, Elizabeth M. Craik ed. (Aberdeen, 1984), 104–18.

Crawford, David, "The Rule of Law? The Laity, English Archdeacons' Courts and the Reformation to 1558," *Parergon*, new series 4 (1986): 155–73.

Davies, Stephen J., "The Courts and the Scottish Legal System, 1600–1747: The Case of Stirlingshire," in *Crime and the Law: The Social History of Crime in Western Europe since 1500*, V.A.C. Gatrell, Bruce Lenman, and Geoffrey Parker eds. (London, 1980), 120–54.

De Klerk, Peter, *Renaissance, Reformation, Resurgence* (Grand Rapids, 1976).

Dougall, Alistair, *The Devil's Book: Charles I, the Book of Sports and Puritanism in Tudor and Early Stuart England* (Exeter, 2011).

Duffy, Eamon, *Fires of Faith: Catholic England under Mary Tudor* (New Haven, CT, 2009).

Edwards, John, *Christian Córdoba: The City and its Region in the Late Middle Ages* (Cambridge, 1982).

Elton, G. R., *Reform and Renewal: Thomas Cromwell and the Common Weal* (Cambridge, 1977).
   Encyclopedia of the Laws of Scotland (Edinburgh, 1927).

Fasolt, Constantin, "Visions of Order in the Canonists and Civilians," in *Handbook of European History, 1400–1600: Late Middle Ages, Renaissance and Reformation*, 2 vols., Thomas A. Brady, Heiko Oberman, and James Tracy eds. (Leiden, 1995), 2:31–59.

Fenster, Thelma and Smail, Daniel Lord eds., *Fama: The Politics of Talk and Reputation in Medieval Europe* (Ithaca, NY, 2003).

Ferreira dos Santos Silveira, Patricia, "A justiça eclesiástica e os mecanismos de busca de infratores: as queixas, as querelas e as denúncias no século XVIII," *Boletim do Arquivo da Universidade de Coimbra* 26 (2013): 137–60.

Fitzgerald, Monica D., "Drunkards, Fornicators, and a Great Hen Squabble: Censure Practices and the Gendering of Puritanism," *Church History* 80 (2011): 40–75.

Fragnito, Gigliola, "Introduction" and "The Central and Peripheral Organization of Censorship," in *Church, Censorship and Culture in Early Modern Italy*, Gigliola Fragnito ed., Adrian Belton trans. (Cambridge, 2001), 1–49.

Frere, Walter Howard and Douglas, C. E. eds., *Puritan Manifestoes: A Study of the Origin of the Puritan Revolt*, 2nd ed. (London, 1954).

García y García, Antonio, "La Canonísta Iberica (1150–1250)," *Bulletin of Medieval Canon Law* 11 (1981): 41–75.

Synodicon Hispanum, I–X vols. (Madrid, 1981).

Garnot, Benoît, "Justice, infrajustice, parajustice et extra justice dans la France d'Ancien Régime," *Crime, Histoire & Sociétés* 4 (2000): 103–20.

Gloag, W.M. and Henderson, R.C. eds., *Introduction to the Law of Scotland*, 7th ed. (Edinburgh, 1968).

González Rapariegos, de Cándido María Ajo ed., *Inventario general de los archivos de la Diócesis de Avila* (Madrid, 1969).

Grosse, Christian, "Les consistoires réformés et le pluralisme des instances de régulation des conflits (Genève, XVIe siècle)," in *Entre justice et justiciables: les auxiliaires de la justice du Moyen Âge au XXe siècle*, Claire Dolan ed. (Québec, 2005), 627–44.

L'excommunication de Philibert Berthelier: histoire d'un conflit d'identité aux premiers temps de la Réforme Genevoise, 1547–1555 (Geneva, 1995).

"'Il y avoit eu trop grande rigueur par cy-devant.' La discipline ecclésiastique à Genève à l'époque de Théodore de Bèze," in *Théodore de Bèze, 1519–1605: actes du colloque de Genève, septembre 2005*, Irena Backus ed. (Geneva, 2007), 55–68.

"'Obstinés et incorrigibles' L'impénitence devant le consistoire de l'église de Genève," in *Le criminel endurci: récidive et récidivistes du Moyen Age au XXe siècle*, Michel Porret and Françoise Briegel eds. (Geneva, 2006), 81–91.

Haigh, Christopher, *English Reformations: Religion, Politics and Society under the Tudors* (Oxford, 1993).

Hardwick, Julie, *Family Business: Litigation and the Political Economies of Daily Life in Early Modern France* (Oxford, 2009).

van der Heijden, Manon, "Punishment Versus Reconciliation: Marriage Control in Sixteenth- and Seventeenth-Century Holland," in *Social Control in Europe*, Herman Roodenburg and Pieter Spierenburg eds. (Columbus, 2004), 56–77.

Helmholz, R. H., *Marriage Litigation in Medieval England* (Cambridge, 2007).
  The Oxford History of the Laws of England. Volume I: The Canon Law and Ecclesiastical Jurisdiction from 597 to the 1640s (Oxford, 2004).
  Roman Canon Law in Reformation England (Cambridge, 1990).
Herlihy, David and Klapisch-Zuber, Christiane, *Les Toscans et leurs familles: Un etude du Castasto florentin de 1427* (Paris, 1978).
Hossain, Kimberly Lynn, "Was Adam the First Heretic? Luis de Páramo, Diego de Simancas, and the Origins of Inquisitorial Practice," *Archive for Reformation History* 97 (2006): 184–210.
Houlbrooke, Ralph, *Church Courts and the People during the English Reformation, 1520–1570* (Oxford, 1979).
  "The Decline of Ecclesiastical Jurisdiction under the Tudors," in *Continuity and Change: Personnel and Administration of the Church in England, 1500–1642*, Rosemary O'Day and Felicity Heal eds. (Leicester, 1976), 239–57.
Ingram, Martin, "From Reformation to Toleration: Popular Religious Cultures in England, 1540–1690," in *Popular Culture in England, c. 1500–1850*, Tim Harris ed. (Basingstoke, 1995), 101–18.
  "Puritans and the Church Courts," in *The Culture of English Puritanism, 1560–1700*, Christopher Durston and Jacqueline Eales eds. (Basingstoke, 1996).
  "Shame Punishments, Penance and Charivari in Early Modern England," in *Shame between Punishment and Penance: The Social Usages of Shame in the Middle Ages and Early Modern Times*, Bénédicte Sère and Jörg Wettlaufer eds. (Florence, 2013).
Kaden, Erich Hans, *Le juriconsulte Germain Colladon, ami de Jean Calvin et de Théodore de Bèze* (Geneva, 1974).
Kagan, Richard, *Lawsuits and Litigants in Castile, 1500–1700* (Chapel Hill, NC, 1981).
Kelly, Henry Ansgar, "Inquisition and the Prosecution of Heresy: Misconceptions and Abuses," *Church History*, 58 4 (Dec. 1989): 439–51.
  "Inquisition, Public Fame and Confession: General Rules and English Practice," in *The Culture of Inquisition in Medieval England*, Mary C. Flanner and Katie L. Walter eds. (Woodbridge, 2013).
  "The Right to Remain Silent: Before and After Joan of Arc," *Speculum* 68 4 (1993): 992–1026.
Kennedy, Chloë, "Criminal Law and Religion in Post-Reformation Scotland," *Edinburgh Law Review* 16 (2012): 178–97.
Kent, Joan, "Attitudes of Members of the House of Commons to the Regulation of 'Personal Life' in Late Elizabethan and Early Stuart England," *Bulletin of the Institute of Historical Research* 46 (1973): 41–71.
King, Walter J., "Punishment for Bastardy in Early Seventeenth-Century England," *Albion* 10 (1978): 130–51.
Kingdon, Robert M., "Calvin and the Establishment of Consistory Discipline in Geneva: The Institution and the Men Who Directed It," *Nederlands Archief voor Kerkgeschiedenis* 70 (1990): 158–72.
Kollmann, Nancy Shields, "Torture in Early Modern Russia," in *The New Muscovite Cultural History: A Collection in Honor of Daniel B. Rowland,*

Valerie Kivelson, Karen Petrone, Nancy Shields Kollmann, and Michael S. Flier eds. (Bloomington, IN, 2009), 159–70.

Kuttner, Stephen, "Raymond of Peñafort as Editor: The 'Decretales' and 'Constituciones' of Gregory IX," *Bulletin of Medieval Canon Law* 12 (1982): 65–80.

Lambert, Thomas A., "Cette loi durera guère: inertie religieuse et espoirs catholiques à Genève au temps de la Réforme," *Bulletin de la Société d'Histoire et d'Archéologie de Genève* 23 (1993): 5–24.

Lehfeldt, Elizabeth A., "Convents as Litigants: Dowry and Inheritance Disputes in Early-Modern Spain," *Journal of Social History* 33 3(2000): 645–64.

Lescaze, Bernard, "La confession de Nicolas Antoine (1632)," *Bulletin de la Société d'Histoire et d'Archéologie de Genève* 14 (1970): 277–323.

"Crime et criminels à Genève en 1572," in *Pour une histoire qualitative. Etudes offerts à Sven Stelling-Michaud*, Louis Binz ed. (Geneva, 1975), 45–71.

Levack, Brian P., "The Prosecution of Sexual Crimes in Early Eighteenth-Century Scotland," *Scottish Historical Review* 89 (2010): 172–93.

Loetz, Francisca, *Dealings with God from Blasphemers in Early Modern Zurich to a Cultural History of Religiousness* (Farnham, 2009).

Magdelaine, Michelle, "Le registre du consistoire de Francfort-sur-le-Main," *Bulletin de la Société de l'Histoire du Protestantisme Français* 153 (2007): 695–706.

Mantecón Movellan, Tomás A., "The Patterns of Violence in Early Modern Spain," *Journal of The Historical Society* 7 2 (2007): 229–64.

Marchant, Ronald A., *The Church under the Law: Justice, Administration and Discipline in the Diocese of York, 1560–1640* (Cambridge, 1969).

Mentzer, Raymond A., "Ecclesiastical Discipline and Communal Reorganization among the Protestants of Southern France," *European History Quarterly* 21 (1991): 163–83.

Monter, E. William, "Crime and Punishment in Calvin's Geneva, 1562," *Archiv für Reformationsgeschichte* 64 (1973): 281–7.

Murdock, Graeme, *Beyond Calvin: The Intellectual, Political and Cultural World of Europe's Reformed Churches, 1540–1620* (New York, 2004).

Naphy, William G., "Sodomy in Early Modern Geneva: Various Definitions, Diverse Verdicts," in *Sodomy in Early Modern Europe*, Tom Betteridge ed. (New York, 2002), 94–111.

Outhwaite, R. B., *The Rise and Fall of the English Ecclesiastical Courts, 1500–1860* (Cambridge, 2006).

Parker, Charles H., "Two Generations of Discipline: Moral Reform in Delft Before and After the Synod of Dort," *Archiv für Reformationsgeschichte* 92 (2001): 268–84.

Perry, Mary Elizabeth, *Crime and Society in Early Modern Seville* (Hannover, NH, 1980).

Peters, Edward, *Torture* (Philadelphia, PA, 1996).

Poncet, André-Luc, *Les châtelains et l'administration de la justice dans les mandements genevois sous l'Ancien Régime (1536–1792)* (Geneva, 1973).

Postles, Dave, "Penance and the Market Place: a Reformation Dialogue with the Medieval Church (c.1250–c.1600)," *Journal of Ecclesiastical History* 54 (2003): 441–68.

Price, F. Douglas, "Gloucester Diocese under Bishop Hooper, 1551–3," *Transactions of the Bristol and Gloucestershire Archaeological Society* 60 (1939 for 1938): 51–151.

Rappaz, Sonia Vernhes, "Criminalité réprimée, criminalité archivée au XVIe siècle à Genève (1555–72)," *Bulletin de la Société d'Histoire et d'Archéologie de Genève* 38 (2008): 33–44.

Rivera, Mariano Galván and Arrillaga, Basilio Manuel, *Concilio III Provincial mexicano: Celebrando en México el año de 1585, confirmado en Roma por el Papa Sixto V, y mandado observar por el Gobierno Español, en diversos reales ordenes* (Mexico City, 1859).

Robbins, Kevin C., *City on the Ocean Sea: La Rochelle, 1530–1650: Urban Society, Religion and Politics on the French Atlantic Frontier* (New York, 1997).

Ross, Richard J., "Puritan Godly Discipline in Comparative Perspective: Legal Pluralism and the Sources of Intensity," *American Historical Review* 113 (2008): 975–1002.

Safley, Thomas Max, *Let No Man Put Asunder: The Control of Marriage in the German Southwest: a Comparative Study, 1550–1600* (Kirksville, MO, 1984).

Sales Tirapu, José Luís, and Iigoyen, Isidro Ursúa, eds., *Catálogo del Archivo Diocesano de Pamplona*, 12 vols. (Pamplona, 1990).

Schwerhoff, Gerd, "Horror Crime or Bad Habit? Blasphemy in Premodern Europe, 1200–1650," *The Journal of Religious History* 32 (2008): 398–408.

Shagan, Ethan H., "The English Inquisition: Constitutional Conflict and Ecclesiastical Law in the 1590s," *Historical Journal* 47 (2004): 541–65.

Sharpe, James A., *Instruments of Darkness: Witchcraft in England, 1550–1750* (New York, 1996).

de Simancas, Diego, *Enchiridion Iudicum Violatae Religionis* (Venice, 1569).

Smail, Daniel Lord, *The Consumption of Justice: Emotions, Publicity, and Legal Culture in Marseille, 1264–1423* (Ithaca, NY, 2003).

Smith, Michael G., *The Church Courts, 1680–1840: From Canon to Ecclesiastical Law* (Lampeter, 2006).

Springer, Michael, *Restoring Christ's Church: John à Lasco and the Forma ac ratio* (Aldershot, 2007).

Testón Núñez, Isabel, *Amor, sexo y matrimonio en Extremadura* (Badajoz, 1985).

Thomas, Keith, "Puritans and Adultery: The Act of 1650 Reconsidered," in *Puritans and Revolutionaries: Essays in Seventeenth-Century History Presented to Christopher Hill*, Donald Pennington and Keith Thomas eds. (Oxford, 1978), 257–82.

Thompson, Roger, *Sex in Middlesex: Popular Mores in a Massachusetts County, 1649–1699* (Amherst, MA, 1986).

Todd, Margo, "Fairies, Egyptians and Elders: Multiple Cosmologies in Post-Reformation Scotland," in *The Impact of the European Reformation*, Bridget Heal and Ole Grell eds. (Aldershot, 2008), 189–208.

"Practicing the Books of Discipline: The Problem of Equality before the Law in Scottish Parish Consistories," in *Calvin and the Book: The Evolution of the Printed Word in Reformed Protestantism*, Karen E. Spierling ed. (Göttingen, 2014).

"Profane Pastimes and the Reformed Community: The Persistence of Popular Festivities in Early Modern Scotland," *Journal of British Studies* 39 (2000): 123–56.

ed., *The Perth Kirk Session Books, 1577–90* (Cambridge, 2012).

Trexler, Richard C., "Infanticide in Florence: New Sources and First Results," *History of Childhood Quarterly* 1 1 (1973): 98–116.

Synodal Law in Florence and Fiesole, 1306–1518 (Vatican City, 1971).

Usher, Roland G., *The Rise and Fall of the High Commission*, 2nd ed., introduction by Philip Tyler (Oxford, 1968).

Vázquez de Prada, Valentín, *Historia económica y social de España: Los siglos XVI y XVII* (Madrid, 1978).

Wachtel, Nathan, *La logique des bûchers* (Paris, 2009).

Walker, David M., *A Legal History of Scotland*, vol. 3 (Edinburgh, 1995).

Weisser, Mary, "Crime and Punishment in Early Modern Spain," in *Crime and the Law: The Social History of Crime in Western Europe since 1500*, V.A.C. Gatrell, Bruce Lenman, and Geoffrey Parker eds. (London, 1980), 76–96.

Wickham, Chris, *Courts and Conflict in Twelfth-century Tuscany* (Oxford, 2003).

Woodcock, Brian L., *Medieval Ecclesiastical Courts in the Diocese of Canterbury* (London, 1952).

Wunderli, Richard M., *London Church Courts and Society on the Eve of the Reformation* (Cambridge, MA, 1981).

SECTION C: CHAPTERS 8 AND 9

Barrio Conde, Maximiliano, "Burocracia inquisitorial y movilidad social. El Santo Oficio plantel de obispos (1556–1820)," in *Inquisición y Sociedad*, Ángel Prado Moura ed. (Valladolid, 1999), 107–38.

Caro Baroja, Julio, *El señor Inquisidor y otras vidas por oficio* (Madrid, 1968).

Davis, Natalie Z., *Protestantism and the Printing Workers of Lyons: A Study in the Problem of Religion and Social Class during the Reformation* (Ph.D. dissertation, University of Michigan, 1959).

Ditchfield, Simon, "Umberto Locati, O. P. (1503–1587): Inquisitore, Vescovo e Storico – un profilo bio-bibliografico," *Bollettino Storico Piacentino* 84 (1989): 205–21.

Dorward, Reinhold A., "Church Organization in Brandenburg-Prussia from the Reformation to 1740," *The Harvard Theological Review* 31 4 (1938): 275–90.

Edwards, John, "Trial of an Inquisitor: The Dismissal of Diego Rodríguez Lucero Inquisitor of Córdoba, in 1508," *Journal of Ecclesiastical History* 37 2 (1986): 240–57.

Feitler, Bruno, "A delegação de poderes inquisitoriais: o exemplo de Goa através da documentação da Biblioteca Nacional do Rio de Janeiro," *Tempo* 12 24 (2008): 127–48.

"Hierarquias e mobilidade na carreira inquisitorial portuguesa: a centralidade do tribunal de Lisboa," in *Raizes do privilegio: mobilidade social no mundo ibérico do Antigo Regime*, Rodrigo Bentes Monteiro, Bruno Feitler, Daniela Buono Calainho, and Jorge Flores eds. (Rio de Janeiro, 2011), 235–58.

"Teoria e Prática na Definição da Jurisdição e da Práxis Inquisitorial Portuguesa: da 'Prova' como Objeto de Análise," in *O Império por escrito. Formas de transmissão da cultura letrada no mundo ibérico. Séculos XVI-XIX*, Leila Mezan Algranti and Ana Paula Torres Megiani eds. (São Paulo, 2009), 73–93.

"Usos Políticos del Santo Oficio Portugués en el Atlántico (Brasil y África Occidental). El Período Filipino," *Hispania Sacra* 59 119 (2007): 269–91.

Galiffe, Jacques-Augustin, et al. eds., *Notices généalogiques sur les familles genevoises, depuis les premiers temps, jusqu'à nos jours*, 7 vols. (Geneva, 1829–95).

Kamen, Henry, "A Crisis of Conscience in Golden Age Spain: The Inquisition against Limpieza de Sangre," in *Crisis and Change in Early Modern Spain* (Aldershot, 1993), Article VII, 1–27.

Kevorkian, Tanya, *Baroque Piety: Religion, Society and Music in Leipzig, 1650–1750* (Aldershot, 2007).

Kingdon, Robert M., "The Deacons of the Reformed Church in Calvin's Geneva," in *Mélanges d'histoire du seizième siècle offerts à Henri Meylan* (Geneva, 1979), 81–90.

López-Salazar Codes, Ana Isabel, "'Che Si Riduca al Modo di Procedere di Castiglia.' El Debate Sobre el Procedimiento Inquisitorial Portugués en Tiempos de los Austrias," *Hispania Sacra* 59 119 (2007): 243–68.

Marcocci, Giuseppe, "Toward a History of the Portuguese Inquisition: Trends in Modern Historiography (1974–2009)," *Revue de l'histoire des religions* 227 3 (2010): 355–93.

Menchi, Silvana Seidel, "The Inquisitor as Mediator," in *Heresy, Culture, and Religion in Early Modern Italy: Contexts and Contestations*, Ronald K. Delph, Michelle M. Fontaine, and John Jeffries Martin eds. (Kirksville, MO, 2006), 173–92.

Mentzer, Raymond A., "Fasting, Piety, and Political Anxiety among French Reformed Protestants," *Church History* 76 2 (2007): 330–62.

Monter, William E., *Judging the French Reformation: Heresy Trials by Sixteenth-Century Parlements* (Cambridge, MA, 1999).

Moody, Michael E., "Trials and Travels of a Nonconformist Layman: The Spiritual Odyssey of Stephen Offwood," *Church History* 51 2 (1982): 157–71.

Nalle, Sara, "Inquisitors, Priests, and the People during the Catholic Reformation in Spain," *Sixteenth Century Journal* 18 (1987): 557–87.

Naphy, William G., *Plagues, Poison and Potions: Plague-Spreading Conspiracies in the Western Alps, c. 1530–1640* (Manchester, 2002).

Ogier, Darryl, "Night Revels and Werewolvery in Calvinist Guernsey," *Folklore* 109 (1998), 53–62.

Olival, Fernanda, "Quando o Santo Ofício Processava os seus Comissários (Portugal, 1600–1773)," in *Estudos em Homagem a Joaquim Romero Magalhães. Economia, Instituições e Império*, Álvaro Garrido, Leonor Freire Costa, and Luís Miguel Duarte eds. (Coimbra, 2012), 179–95.

de Paz, Amelia, *Góngora y el Señor Inquisidor. Un autógrafo inédito de Don Luis en edición facsímil* (Madrid, 2012).

van der Pol, Frank, "Religious Diversity and Everyday Ethics in the Seventeenth-Century Dutch City Kampen," *Church History* 71 1 (2002): 16–62.

de Prado Moura, Ángel, *Inquisición e Inquisidores en Castilla: El Tribunal de Valladolid Durante el Crisis de Antiguo Régimen* (Valladolid, 1995).

Prosperi, Adriano, *L'Inquisizione Romana: Letture e Richerche* (Rome, 2003).

Raath, Andries, "Covenant and the Christian Community: Bullinger and the Relationship between Church and Magistracy in Early Cape Settlement," *The Sixteenth Century Journal* 33 4 (2002): 999–1019.

Ramos, Gabriela, "La fortuna del inquisidor. Inquisición y poder en el Perú (1594–1611)," *Cuadernos para la historia de la evangelización en América Latina* 4 (1989): 89–122.

Renwick, John, "Voltaire and the Politics of Toleration," in *The Cambridge Companion to Voltaire*, Nicholas Cronk ed. (Cambridge, 2009).

Rieder, Philip, "Miracles and Heretics: Protestants and Catholic Healing Practices in and around Geneva 1530–1750," *Social History of Medicine* 23 2 (2010): 227–43.

Roget, Amédée, *Histoire du Peuple de Genève depuis la Réforme jusqu'à l'Escalade* (Geneva, 1870–7).

Santosuosso, Antonio, "The Moderate Inquisitor: Giovanni Della Casa's Venetian Nunciature, 1544–1549," *Studi veneziani* n.s. 2 (1978): 119–210.

Schutte, Anne Jacobson, "Un inquisitore al lavoro: Fra Marino da Venezia e l'Inquisizione veneziana," in *I Francescani in Europa tra riforma e controriforma* (Naples, 1987), 165–96.

Sprunger, Keith L., "Other Pilgrims in Leiden: Hugh Goodyear and the English Reformed Church," *Church History* 41 1 (1972): 46–60.

Sunshine, Glenn S., *Reforming French Protestantism: The Development of Huguenot Ecclesiastical Institutions, 1557–1572* (Kirksville, MO, 2003).

Tavárez, David, *The Invisible War: Indigenous Devotions, Discipline, and Dissent in Colonial Mexico* (Stanford, CA, 2011).

Tavuzzi, Michael M., *Renaissance Inquisitors: Dominican inquisitors and inquisitorial districts in Northern Italy, 1474–1527* (Leiden, 2007).

Tulchin, Allan, *That Men Would Praise the Lord: The Reformation in Nîmes, 1530–1570* (Oxford, 2010).

"The Michelade in Nîmes, 1567," *French Historical Studies*, 29 1 (2006): 1–35.

Wadsworth, James E., "Historiography of the Structure and Functioning of the Portuguese Inquisition in Colonial Brazil," *History Compass* 8 7 (2010): 636–52.

Watt, Jeffrey R., "Marriage Contract Disputes in Early Modern Neuchatel, 1547–1806," *Journal of Social History* 22 1 (1988): 129–47.

"The Reception of the Reformation in Valangin, Switzerland, 1547–1588," *The Sixteenth Century Journal* 20 1 (1989): 89–104.

Williams, Patrick, "A Jewish Councillor of Inquisition? Luis de Mercado, the Statutes of *limpieza de sangre* and the Politics of Vendetta (1598–1601)," *Bulletin of Hispanic Studies* 67 (1990): 253–64.

SECTION D: CHAPTERS 10 AND 11

Alpert, Michael, *Secret Judaism and the Spanish Inquisition* (Nottingham, 2008).

Arnaud, Eugène, *Documents protestants inédits du XVIe siècle* (Paris, 1872).

Baer, Fritz, *Die Juden im christlichen Spanien*, 2 vols. (Berlin, 1929–1936).

Baroni, Raphaël, *La tension narrative: suspense, curiosité et surprise* (Paris, 2007).

Barthes, Roland, "L'effet de réel," *Communications* 11 (1968): 84–9.

Bazeille, M., "Etude sur les registres paroissiaux antérieurs à l'établissement des registres d'état civil," *Bulletin Historique et Philologique* (1909): 327–59.

Beinart, Haim, *Conversos on Trial: The Inquisition in Ciudad Real* (Jerusalem, 1981).

Bennassar, Bartolomé, Bennassar, Lucile, *Les chrétiens d' Allah: l'histoire extraordinaire des renégats, XVIe et XVIIe siècles* (Paris, 1989).

Beretta, F., *Galilée devant le Tribunal de l'Inquisition: une relecture des sources* (Fribourg, 1998).

Bériou, Nicole et al. eds., *Prier au Moyen Age: pratiques et expériences (V^e-XVe siècles)* (Turnhout, 1991).

de Bèze, Théodore, *Histoire ecclésiastique des Eglises reformées au royaume de France*, 3 vols., G. Baum and Ed. Cunitz eds. (Paris, 1883–9).

Biondi, Grazia, "Le lettere della Sacra Congregazione romana del Santo Ufficio all'Inquisizione di Modena: note in margine a un regesto," *Schifanoia* 4 (1987): 93–108.

Boisson, Didier ed., *Actes des synodes provinciaux. Anjou-Touraine-Maine (1594–1683)* (Geneva, 2012).

Brambilla, E., *Alle origini del Sant'Uffizio: Penitenza, confessione e giustizia spiritual dal medioevo al XVI secolo* (Bologna, 2000).

Burn, John Southerden, *Registrum ecclesiae parochialis. The History of Parish Registers in England* (London, 1862).

Carbonnier-Burkard, Marianne, "'L'Histoire ecclésiastique des Eglises réformées...': la construction bézienne d'un 'corps d'histoire,'" in *Théodore de Bèze (1519–1605)* (Geneva, 2007), 145–61.

Chareyre, Philippe, "Le consistoire et l'advertisseur : étude croisée de deux séries de registres nîmois, XVIe-XVIIe siècles," *Bulletin de la Société de l'Histoire du Protestantisme* 153 (2007): 525–42.

Chevalier, F. ed., *Actes des synodes nationaux. Charenton (1644) – Loudun (1659)* (Geneva, 2012).

Courouau, Jean-François, "La Réforme et les langues de France," *Bulletin de la Société de l'Histoire du Protestantisme Français* 154 (2008): 509–29.

Crespin, Jean, *Histoire des martyrs*, 3 vols., Daniel Benoit ed. (Toulouse, 1885–9).

Daireaux, Luc, "Réflexions autour des registres consistoriaux des Eglises réformées normandes (XVIIe siècle)," *Bulletin de la Société de l'Histoire du Protestantisme Français* 153 (2007), 477–90.

Dall'Olio, Guido, "I rapporti tra la Congregazione del Sant'Officio e gli inquisitori locali nei categgi Bolognesi (1573 – 1594)," *Rivista storica italiana* 105 (1993): 246–86.

Davis, Natalie Z., *Fiction in the Archives: Pardon Tales and Their Tellers in Sixteenth-Century France* (Stanford, CA, 1987).

Del Col, Andrea, "I processi dell'Inquisizione come fonte: considerazioni diplomatiche e storiche," *Annuario dell'Istituto storico italiano per l'Età moderna e contemporanea 35–36* (1983–4): 29–49.

"Problemi e metodi attuali di storia istituzionale dell'Inquisizione romana," *Annali di storia moderna e contemporanea 6* (2000): 549–60.

Del Col, Andrea and Paolin, Giovanna eds., *L'inquisizione romana: metodologia delle fonti e storia istituzionale. Atti del seminario internazionale, Montereale Valcellina 23 e 24 settembre 1999* (Trieste, 2000).

Donati, Barbara, *Tra inquisizione e Granducato. Storie di Inglesi nella Livorno del primo Seicento* (Rome, 2010).

Dumur, Benjamin, "Notes extraites des registres de l'état civil de la paroisse de Pully," *Revue historique vaudoise 15* (1907): 329–42.

Edwards, John, "Was the Spanish Inquisition Truthful?," review essay, *The Jewish Quarterly Review 87* (1997): 351–66.

Faucher, Benjamin, "Les registres d'état civil protestant en France depuis le XVIe siècle jusqu'à nos jours," *Bibliothèque de l'Ecole des Chartes 84* (1923): 306–46.

Francillon, François ed., *Livre des délibérations de l'Eglise réformée de l'Albenc (1606–1682)* (Paris, 1998).

Furet, François, "L'histoire quantitative et la construction du fait historique," in *Faire de l'histoire*, Jacques Le Goff et Pierre Nora eds. (Paris, 1974), 67–91.

Garnot, Benoît ed., Histoire et criminalité de l'Antiquité au XXe siècle : nouvelles approches (Dijon, 1992).

L'infrajudiciaire du Moyen Âge à l'époque contemporaine (Dijon, 1996).

"Justice, Infrajustice, Parajustice et Extra Justice dans la France d'Ancien Régime," *Crime, Histoire & Sociétés*, 4 1(2000): 103–20.

Graizbord, David L., *Souls in Dispute: Converso Identities in Iberia and the Jewish Diaspora, 1580–1700* (Philadelphia, PA, 2003).

Greyerz, Kaspar von, "Portuguese Conversos on the Upper Rhine and the Converso Community of Sixteenth-Century Europe," *Social History 14* (1989): 59–82.

Grosclaude, Michel, "Registre du Consistoire de Montestrucq (1642–1663)," *Bulletin du Centre d'Etude du Protestantisme Béarnais 20* (1996): 6–9.

Grosse, Christian, "Des querelles 'dispendieuses et ruineuses'. Les limites de la régulation consistoriale des conflits comme instrument de lutte contre l'appauvrissement des familles," in *Richesse et pauvreté dans les républiques suisses au XVIIIe siècle*, André Holenstein et al. eds. (Genève, 2010), 51–63.

"Rationalité graphique et discipline ecclésiastique. Les registres du Consistoire de Genève à l'épreuve (XVIe – XVIIIe siècles)," *Bulletin de la Société de l'Histoire du Protestantisme Français 153* (2007): 543–60.

"Techniques de l'écrit et contrôle social à l'époque moderne. Les pratiques d'enregistrement des institutions genevoises (XVIe siècle)," in *Penser l'archive. Histoires d'archives – archives d'histoire*, Mauro Cerutti et al. eds. (Lausanne, 2006), 21–34.

Hsia, Ronnie Po-Chia, *Trent 1475: Stories of A Ritual Murder Trial* (New Haven, CT, 1992).

d'Huisseau, Isaac ed., *La Discipline ecclésiastique des Eglises réformées de France* (Amsterdam, 1710).

Klaniczay, Gábor and Kristóf, Ildikó, "Ecritures saintes et pactes diaboliques. Les usages religieux de l'écrit (Moyen Âge et Temps modernes)," *Annales HSS* 56 (2001): 947–80.

Marshall, Peter, *Belief and the Dead in Reformation England* (Oxford, 2002).

Matzinger-Pfister, Regula, *Les sources du droit du canton de Vaud, C. Epoque bernoise 1* (Basel, 2003).

Mentzer, Raymond A., "La mémoire d'une 'fausse religion': les registres de consistoires des Eglises réformées de France (XVIᵉ –XVIIᵉ siècle)," *Bulletin de la Société de l'Histoire du Protestantisme Français* 153 (2007): 461–75.

Messana, M. S., *Inquisitori, negromanti e streghe nella Sicilia moderna (1500–1782)* (Palermo, 2007).

Millioud, A. ed., *Le consistoire de Bex: 1659–1691* (Bex, 1914).

Mirto, Alfonso ed., "Un inedito del Seicento sull'Inquisizione," *Prattica per procedere nelle cause del S. Offizio, Nouvelles de la République des Lettres* 1 (1986): 99–138.

Moreil, Françoise, "Le consistoire de Courthézon au XVIIèmeᵉ siècle," Actes de colloque d'Avignon protestants du Vaucluse, *Mémoires de l'académie de Vaucluse*, 8 (1998): 69–86.

"Les Consistoires de la principauté d'Orange (XVIᵉ-XVIIᵉ siècles)," *Bulletin de la société de l'histoire du protestantisme Français* 153 (2007): 505–24.

Netanyahu, Benzion, *The Marranos of Spain: From the Late 14ᵗʰ to the Early 16ᵗʰ Century, According to Contemporary Hebrew Sources*, 3rd ed. (Ithaca, NY, 1999).

The Origins of the Inquisition in Fifteenth Century Spain (New York, 1995).

Prosperi, Adriano, "Vicari dell'Inquisizione fiorentina alla metà del Seicento. Note d'archivio," *Annali dell'Istituto storico italo-germanico in Trento* 8 (1982): 275–304.

Raemond, Florimond de, *L'histoire de la naissance, progrez et decadence de l'heresie de ce siecle* (Rouen, 1618).

Revaz, Françoise, *Introduction à la narratologie: action et narration* (Brussels, 2009).

Ricœur, Paul, *Temps et récit*, vol. 1 (Paris, 1983).

Romeo, Giovanni, *Esorcisti, confessori e sessualità femminile nell'Italia della controriforma* (Florence, 1998).

L'inquisizione nell'Italia moderna (Rome, 2002).

Roth, Cecil, *A History of the Marranos* (Philadelphia, PA, 1932).

Roth, Norman, *Conversos, Inquisition and the Expulsion of the Jews from Spain* (Madison, WI, 1995).

"Jewish Conversos in Medieval Spain: Some Misconceptions and New Information," in *Marginated Groups in Spanish and Portuguese History. Proceedings of the Seventeenth Annual Meeting of the Society for Spanish and Portuguese Historical Studies, University of Minnesota, Minneapolis, April 1986*, W. D. Phillips and C. Rahn Phillips eds. (Minneapolis, MN, 1989), 23–52.

Roth-Lochner, Barbara, *De la branche à l'étude: une histoire institutionnelle, professionnelle et sociale du notariat genevois sous l'Ancien Régime* (Geneva, 1997).

Sabean, David W., "Peasant Voices and Bureaucratic Texts: Narrative Structure in Early Modern German Protocols," in *Little Tools of Knowledge: Historical Essays on Academic and Bureaucratic Practices*, Peter Becker and William Clark eds. (Ann Arbor, MI, 2001).

Scaramella, Pierroberto, *Inquisizioni, eresie, etnie. Dissenso religioso e giustizia ecclesiastica in Italia (secc. XVI-XVIII)* (Bari, 2005).

Schwerhoff, G., *Aktenkundig und gerichtsnotorisch. Einführung in die Historische Kriminalitätsforschung* (Tübingen, 1999).

Siebenhüner, Kim, *Bigamie und Inquisition in Italien 1600 – 1750* (Paderborn, 2006).

   "Conversion, Mobility and the Roman Inquisition in Italy around 1600," *Past & Present* 200 (2008): 5–35.

Soman, Alfred, "Deviance and Criminal Justice in Western Europe, 1300–1800," *Criminal Justice History* 1 (1980): 3–28.

Staremberg Goy, Nicole, *Du buveur à l'ivrogne: le Consistoire de Lausanne face à l'abus d'alcool, 1754 à 1791* (Lausanne, 2006).

Tosato-Rigo, Danièle, "Registres consistoriaux et images de l'exil; un exemple lausannais," *Bulletin de la Société de l'Histoire du Protestantisme Français* 153 (2007): 649–70.

Viallet, Ludovic, "Le salaire de la plume: prières de notaires et de copistes à la fin du Moyen Âge (XIVᵉ-XVIᵉ siècles)," in *La prière en latin de l'Antiquité au XVIᵉ siècle*, Jean-François Cottier ed. (Turnhout, 2007), 291–307.

SECTION E: CHAPTERS 12 AND 13

Benedict, Philip and Fornerod, Nicolas eds., *L'organisation et l'action des Eglises réformées de France (1557–1563)* (Geneva, 2012).

Blanco White, J. M., *El Español*, 10 (1811).

Boeglin, M., "Disciplina religiosa y asentamiento de la doctrina: el delito de proposiciones ante la Inquisición sevillana (1560–1700)," *Historia, Instituciones, Documentos* 30 (2003): 121–44.

Boisson, Didier and Krumenacker, Yves eds., *La coexistence confessionnelle à l'épreuve. Etudes sur les relations entre protestants et catholiques dans la France Moderne* (Lyon, 2009).

Bossy, John, "The Counter-Reformation and the People of Catholic Europe," *Past and Present* 47 (1970), 51–70.

Burke, Peter, "How to Be a Counter Reformation Saint," in *Religion and Society in Early Modern Europe*, K. von Greyerz ed. (London, 1984), 45–56.

Chareyre, Philippe, "Le consistoire de Nîmes et l'Édit de Nantes," in *L'édit de Nantes, sa genèse, son application en Languedoc, Bulletin Historique de la Ville de Montpellier* 23 (1999): 117–28.

   "'La fleur de tous les anciens' ou le ministère des diacres à Nîmes XVIᵉ-XVIIᵉ siècles," in *Agir pour l'Eglise. Ministères et charges ecclésiastiques dans les Eglises réformées (XVIᵉ-XVIIᵉ)*, Didier Poton ed. (Paris, 2013), 91–110.

"Protestantisme et structuration de l'espace urbain: Nîmes 1561–1685," in *Le protestantisme et la cité*, Guy Astoul and Philippe Chareyre eds. (Montauban, 2013), 111–30.

Christian, William A., *Local Religion in Sixteenth Century Spain* (Princeton, NJ, 1981).

Cruz de Carlos Varona, María, "The Authority of Sacred Paintbrushes: Representing Medieval Sainthood in the Early Modern Period," in *Sacred Spain: Art and Belief in the Spanish World*, Ronda Kasl ed. (New Haven, CT, 2009), 101–20.

De Certeau, Michel, *El lugar del otro: Historia religiosa y mística* (Buenos Aires, 2007).

Ditchfield, Simon, "Il mondo della Riforma e della Controriforma," in *Storia della Santità nel cristianesimo occidentale*, Anna Benvenuti et al. eds. (Rome, 2005), 261–323.

De la Flor, Fernando R., *Emblemas: Lecturas de la imagen simbólica* (Madrid, 1995), 21–77.

Fragnito, Gigliola, "Aspetti e problemi della censura espurgatoria," in *L'Inquisizione e gli storici: un cantiere aperto: tavola rotonda nell'ambito della Conferenza annuale della ricerca, Roma, 24–25 giugno 1999* (Rome, 2000), 161–78.

"La censura eclesiástica en la Italia del Quinientos: órganos centrales y periféricos," *Cultura escrita & Sociedad* 7 (2008): 37–59.

Galende Díaz, Juan Carlos, "Una aproximación a la hermandad inquisitorial de San Pedro Mártir," *Cuadernos de investigación histórica* 14 (1991): 45–86.

García Cárcel, Ricardo and Doris Moreno, *Inquisición. Historia crítica* (Madrid, 2000).

García Cárcel, Ricardo and Orta, J. Palau, "Reforma y Contrarreforma Católicas," in *Historia del Cristianismo*, vol. 3, *El mundo moderno*, Antonio Luis Cortés Peña ed. (Granada, 2006), 187–226.

Gotor, Miguel, *I beati del papa: Santità, Inquisizione e obbedienza in età moderna* (Florence, 2002).

Greenleaf, Richard E., "The Inquisition Brotherhood, Cofradía de San Pedro," *The Americas* 40 (1983): 171–207.

Hsia, Ronnie Po-Chia, *The World of Catholic Renewal, 1540–1770* (Cambridge, 2005).

Labrousse, Elisabeth, "Les mariages bigarrés," in *Le couple interdit. Entretiens sur le racisme* (Paris, 1980), 159–76.

Lavenia, Vincenzo, *L'infamia e il perdono: Tributi, pene e confessione nella teologia morale della prima età moderna* (Bologna, 2004).

Lavrin, Asunción, "La Congregación de San Pedro: Una cofradía urbana del México Colonial, 1604–1730," *Historia Mexicana* 39 4 (1980): 562–601.

Le Goff, Jacques, ed. *Herejías y sociedades en la Europa preindustrial, ss. XI-XVIII* (Madrid, 1987).

Maravall, Juan Antonio, "Teatro, fiesta e ideología en el Barroco," in *Teatro y fiesta en el Barroco: España e Iberoamérica*, J. Mª Díez Borque ed. (Seville, 1986).

Marcocci, Giuseppe and Paiva, J. P., *História da Inquisicição portuguesa, 1536–1821* (Lisbon, 2013).

M'Crie, Thomas, *La Reforma en España en el siglo XVI* (Seville, 2008).

Mentzer, Raymond A. ed., *Les Registres des consistoires des Églises réformées de France — XVIe–XVIIe siècles: Un inventaire* (Geneva, 2014).

Monter, William E., "The Mediterranean Inquisitions of Early Modern Europe," in *Christianity. Reform and Expansion, 1500–1660*, Ronnie Po-Chia Hsia ed. (Cambridge, 2007), 283–301.

Nieto, J.C., "Two Spanish Mystics as Submissive Rebels," *Bibliotheque d'Humanisme et Renaissance* 33 (1971): 63–77.

Palomo, F., *A Contra-Reforma em Portugal 1540–1700* (Lisbon, 2006).

Pastore, Stefania, *Una herejía española. Conversos, alumbrados e Inquisición (1449–1559)* (Madrid, 2010).

Peña, M., "Leer con cautela: estrategias y nuevos modos de censurer en el siglo XVII," in *Historia y perspectivas de investigación: estudios en memoria del professor Angel Rodríguez Sánchez*, Miguel Rodríguez Cancho ed. (Mérida, 2002), 365–70.

"Normas y transgresiones. La cultura escrita en el Siglo de Oro," in *Grafías del imaginario: Representaciones culturales en España y América (siglos XVI-XVIII)*, Carlos Alberto González and Enriqueta Vila eds. (Mexico City, 2003), 120–39.

"Sobre expurgos y calificadores. Debates en torno a la censura inquisitorial (siglos XVI-XVII)," in *Edición y literatura en España (Siglos XVI y XVII)*, A. Cayuela and R. Chartier eds. (Zaragoza, 2012), 187–203.

Peyre, D., "La Inquisición o la política de la presencia," in *Inquisición española, poder político y control social*, Bartolomé Bennassar et al. eds. (Barcelona, 1984), 40–67.

Prudlo, Donald S., *The Martyred Inquisitor: The Life and Cult of Peter of Verona (†1252)* (Aldershot, 2008).

Pulido Serrano, Juan Ignacio, *Injurias a Cristo: Religión, político y antijudaísmo en el siglo XVII* (Alcalá de Henares, 2002).

Sarrión Mora, A., *Beatas y endemoniadas: mujeres heterodoxas ante la Inquisición, siglos XVI a XIX* (Madrid, 2003).

Tausiet, María, "Conciencias insumisas: la resistencia a la confesión en el arzobispado de Zaragoza a finales del siglo XVI," in *Felipe II y su tiempo*, J. L. Pereira Iglesias and J. M. González Beltrán eds. (Cádiz, 1999), 589–96.

"Gritos del más allá. La defensa del Purgatorio en la España de la Contrarreforma," *Hispania sacra* 57 (2005): 81–108.

SECTION F: CHAPTERS 14 AND 15

Ahlgren, Gillian T.W., *The Inquisition of Francisca: A Sixteenth-Century Visionary on Trial, The Other Voice in Early Modern Europe* (Chicago, 2005).

Beinart, Haim ed., *Records of the Trials of the Spanish Inquisition in Ciudad Real, 1483–1527*, 4 vols. (Jerusalem, 1974–85).

Bell, Rudolph, "Renaissance Sexuality and the Florentine Archives: An Exchange," *Renaissance Quarterly* 40 (1987): 485–511.

Fernández Majolero, Jesús, *Proceso inquisitorial a Rodrigo de Bivar, 'el mozo', clérigo de Santa María, 1553–1554* (Alcalá de Henares, 1989).

Firpo, Massimo, *Inquisizione romana e Controriforma: studi sul Giovanni Morone (1509–1580) e il suo processo d'eresia* (Bologna, 1992).

Firpo, Massimo and Marcatto, Dario, *Il proceso inquisitoriale del Cardinal Giovanni Morone, vol. III: I documenti difensivi* (Rome, 1985).

Homza, Lu Ann, "How to Harass an Inquisitor-General: The Polyphonic Law of Friar Francisco Ortiz," in *A Renaissance of Conflicts: Visions and Revisions of the Law and Society in Early Modern Italy and Spain*, John A. Marino and Thomas Kuehn eds. (Toronto, 2004), 299–336.

"The Merits of Disruption and Tumult: New Scholarship on Spain in the Reformation," *Archiv für Reformationsgeschichte* 100 (2009): 212–28.

Idígoras, Tellechea, *El Arzobispo Carranza y su tiempo* (Madrid, 1968).

Fray Bartolomé Carranza: documentos históricos, vol. 1 (Madrid, 1962).

Kuehn, Thomas, "Reading Microhistory: The Example of *Giovanni and Lusanna*," *Journal of Modern History* 61 (1989): 512–34.

Longhurst, John E., *Erasmus and the Spanish Inquisition: The Case of Juan de Valdés* (Albuquerque, NM, 1950).

Luther and the Spanish Inquisition: The Case of Diego de Uceda, 1528–1529 (Albuquerque, NM, 1953).

Ortega-Costa, Milagros, *Proceso de la inquisición contra María de Cazalla* (Madrid, 1978).

Perez Escohotado, Javier, *Proceso inquisitorial contra el Bachiller Antonio de Medrano (Logroño, 1526-Calahorra, 1527)* (Logroño, 1988).

de la Pinta Llorente, Miguel, *Procesos inquisitoriales contra los catedráticos hebraísticas de Salamanca, Gaspar de Grajal, Martínez de Cantalapiedra y Fray Luis de León* (Madrid, 1935).

Pullan, Brian, "A Ship with Two Rudders: 'Righetto Marrano' and the Inquisition in Venice," *The Historical Journal* 20 (1977): 25–58.

Schutte, Anne Jacobson ed., *Cecilia Ferrazzi: Autobiography of an Aspiring Saint, The Other Voice in Early Modern Europe* (Chicago, 2001).

Selke, Angela, *El Santo Oficio de la Inquisición: Proceso de Dr. Francisco Ortiz (1529–32)* (Madrid, 1968).

Los chuetas y la inquisicion: vida y muerte en el ghetto de Mallorca (Madrid, 1972).

"Vida y muerte de Juan López Celain, alumbrado vizcaíno," *Bulletin Hispanique* 62 (1960): 36–162.

Spohnholz, Jesse, *The Tactics of Toleration: A Refugee Community in the Age of Religious Wars* (Newark, DE, 2011).

Zagorin, Perez, *Ways of Lying: Dissimulation, Persecution and Conformity in Early Modern Europe* (Cambridge, MA, 1990).

Zito, Paola, *Giulia e l'inquisitore: simulazione di santita e misticismo nella Napoli di primo Seicento* (Naples, 2000).

SECTION G: CHAPTERS 16 AND 17

Bertheau, Solange, "Le Consistoire dans les Eglises Réformées du Moyen-Poitou au XVIIe siècle," *Bulletin de la Société de l'Histoire du Protestantisme Français* 116 (1970): 513–49.

Bethencourt, Francisco, "The Auto da Fé Ritual and Imagery," *Journal of the Warburg and Courtauld Institutes* 55 (1992): 155–68.

Borges Coelho, Antonio, *Inquisiçao de Evora* (Lisbon, 1987).

Burnett, Amy Nelson, "Church Discipline and Moral Reformation in the Thought of Martin Bucer," *The Sixteenth Century Journal* 22 (1991): 438–56.

Cañeque, Alejandro, "Theater of Power: Writing and Representing the Auto de Fe in Colonial Mexico," *The Americas* 52 3 (1996): 321–43.

Cavallero, Ricardo Juan, *Justicia inquisitorial: el Sistema de Justicia Criminal de la Inquisición española* (Buenos Aires, 2003).

Chareyre, Philippe, "Jeux interdits, jeux toléré. L'application de la discipline réformée dans la France méridionale," in *Le plaisir et la transgression en France et en Espagne aux XVIe et XVIIe siècles*, Maurice Daumas, Adrián Blázquez, Olivier Caporossi, and Philippe Chareyre eds. (Orthez, 2005), 385–414.

García Molina Riquelme, Antonio, *El Régimen de penas y penitencias en el tribunal de la inquisición de México* (Mexico City, 1999).

Greenleaf, Richard E., "The Great Visitas of the Mexican Holy Office 1645–1669," *The Americas* 44 4 (1988): 399–420.

Grosse, Christian, "Les Consistoires réformé et le pluralisme des instance de regulation des conflits (Genève, XVIe siècle)," in *Entre justice et justiciables: Les auxiliaires de la justice du Moyen Âge au XXe siècle*, Claire Dolan ed. (Québec, 2005), 627–44.

"'Pour bien de paix': La regulation des conflits par les consistoires en Suisse romand (XVIe – XVIIe siècles)," in *Figures de la mediation et lien social*, Jean-Luc Chabot, Stépahe Gal and Christophe Tournu eds. (Paris, 2006), 85–107.

Kingdon, Robert M., "Calvin and the Family: The Work of the Consistory in Geneva," *Pacific Theological Review* 17 (1984): 5–18.

Lewin, Boleslao, "'Las Confidencias' of Two Crypto-Jews in the Holy Office Prison of Mexico (1654–1655)," *Jewish Social Studies*, 30 1(1968): 3–22.

Maag, Karin ed., *The Reformation in Eastern and Central Europe* (Aldershot, 1997).

Parker, Charles H., "Pilgrims' Progress: Narratives of Penitence and Reconciliation in the Dutch Reformed Church," *Journal of Early Modern History* 5 (2001): 222–40.

Rawlings, Helen, "Representational Strategies of Inclusion and Exclusion in José Del Olmo's Narrative and Francisco Rizi's Visual Record of the Madrid Auto de Fe of 1680," *Romance Studies* 29 4 (2011): 223–41.

Saban, Mario J. ed., *Judíos Conversos*, 3 vols. (Buenos Aires, 1990–3).

Schmidt, Heinrich Richard, "Emden est partout; vers un modèle interactif de la confessionnalisation," *Francia: Revolution, Empire 1500–1815* 26 (1999): 23–45.

Spierling, Karen, "The Complexity of Community in Reformation Geneva," in *Defining Community in Early Modern Europe*, Michael J. Halvorson and Karen E. Spierling eds. (Aldershot, 2008), 81–101.

"Making Use of God's Remedies: Negotiating the Material Care of Children in Reformation Geneva," *The Sixteenth Century Journal* 36 (2005): 785–807.

Spinks, Bryan, "A Seventeenth-Century Reformed Liturgy of Penance and Reconciliation," *Scottish Journal of Theology* 42 (1989): 183–97.

Uchamany de la Peña, Eva Alexandra, "Simón Vaéz Sevilla," in *Estudios de Historia Novohispana*, vol. 4 (Mexico City, 1987), 67–93.

SECTION H: CHAPTERS 18 AND 19

Accati, Luisa, "The Spirit of Fornication: Virtue of the Soul and Virtue of the Body in Friuli, 1600–1800," in *Sex and Gender in Historical Perspective: Selections from Quaderni Storici*, Margaret A. Gallucci trans., Edward Muir and Guido Ruggiero eds. (Baltimore, MD, 1990).

Berco, Christian, *Sexual Hierarchies, Public Status: Men, Sodomy and Society in Spain's Golden Age* (Toronto, 2007).

Bethencourt, Francisco, *O imaginário da magia: feiticeiras, saludadores e nigromantes no seculo XVI* (Lisbon, 1987).

Blackmore, Josiah and Hutcheson, Gregory S. eds., *Queer Iberia: Sexualities, Cultures, and Crossings from the Middle Ages to the Renaissance* (Durham, NC, 1999).

Boeglin, Michel, *Inquisición y Contrarreforma: El Tribunal del Santo Oficio de Sevilla (1560 –1700)* (Seville, 2007).

Del Col, Andrea, "Alcune osservazioni sui processi inquisitoriali come fonti storiche," *Metodi e ricerche* 13 (1994): 85–105.

"I processi dell'Inquisizione come fonte: Considerazioni diplomatiche e storiche," *Annuario dell'Istituto storico italiano per l'età moderna e contemporanea* 35–6 (1983–4): 33–49.

Contreras, Jaime, *El Santo Oficio de la Inquisición en Galicia, 1560–1700: poder, sociedad y cultura* (Madrid, 1982).

Emerson, Mark Cooper, "Maria de Jesus: A Seventeenth-Century Trans-Atlantic Visionary," in "The Evolution of the Portuguese Altantic," Timothy Coates ed., special issue, *Portuguese Studies Review* 15 1–2 (2007): 307–19.

Esmein, A., *Le mariage en droit canonique*, 2 vols., 2nd ed. (Paris, 1929).

Gautier, Léon, *La médecine à Genève jusqu'à la fin du XVIIIᵉ siècle* (Geneva, 1906).

Gowing, Laura, "Language, Power, and the Law: Women's Slander Litigation in Early Modern London," in *Women, Crime and the Courts in Early Modern England*, Jennifer Kermode and Garthine Walker eds. (Chapel Hill, NC, 1994), 26–47.

Guilhem, Claire, "L'inquisition et la dévaluation des discours féminins," in *L'inquisition espagnole: XVe-XIXe siècle*, Bartolomé Bennassar ed. (Paris, 1979).

Haliczer, Stephen, *Sexuality in the Confessional: a Sacrament Profaned* (New York, 1996).

ed. and trans., *Inquisition and Society in Early Modern Europe* (Totowa, 1987).

Higgs, David, "Tales of Two Carmelites: Inquisitorial Narratives in Portugal and Brazil," in *Infamous Desire: Male Homosexuality in Colonial Latin America*, Pete Sigal ed. (Chicago, 2003).

Hossain, Kimberly Lynn, "Unraveling the Spanish Inquisition: Inquisitorial Studies in the Twenty-First Century," *History Compass* 5 4 (2007): 1280–93.

Johnson, Harold and Dutra, Francis A. eds., *Pelo vaso traseiro: Sodomy and Sodomites in Luso-Brazilian History* (Tucson, AZ, 2007).

Kallendorf, Hilaire ed., *A New Companion to Hispanic Mysticism* (Leiden, 2010).

Kamensky, Jane, "Words, Witches, and Woman Trouble: Witchcraft, Disorderly Speech, and Gender Boundaries in Puritan New England," in *New Perspectives on Witchcraft, Magic, and Demonology*, Brian P. Levack ed., vol. 4, *Gender and Witchcraft* (New York, 2001), 196–217.

Keitt, Andrew, *Inventing the Sacred: Imposture, Inquisition, and the Boundaries of the Supernatural in Golden Age Spain* (Leiden, 2005).

Kingdon, Robert M., with Lambert, Thomas A., *Reforming Geneva: Discipline, Faith, and Anger in Calvin's Geneva* (Geneva, 2012).

Köhler, Walther, *Zürcher Ehegericht und Genfer Konsistorium*, 2 vols. (Leipzig, 1932–42).

Lehfeldt, Elizabeth A., "Ideal Men: Masculinity and Decline in Seventeenth-Century Spain," *Renaissance Quarterly* 61 2 (2008): 463–94.

Martin, Ruth, *Witchcraft and the inquisition in Venice, 1550–1650* (Oxford, 1989).

Melammed, Renée Levine, *Heretics or Daughters of Israel?: The Crypto-Jewish Women of Castile* (Oxford, 1999).

Mentzer, Raymond A., "La Réforme calviniste des moeurs à Nîmes," in *La construction de l'identité réformée aux XVIe et XVIIe siècles: Le role des consistoires*, idem ed., (Paris, 2006), 19–48.

Mirrer, Louise, *Women, Jews, and Muslims in the Texts of Reconquest Castile* (Ann Arbor, MI, 1996).

Monter, William E., "Women in Calvinist Geneva (1550–1800)," *Signs* 6 (1980): 189–209.

Mott, Luiz, "Filhos de Abrãao e de Sodoma. Cristãos-novos homosexuais nos tempos da Inquisição," in *Ensaios sobra a intolerância. Inquisição, marranismo e anti-semitismo (homenagem a Anita Novinsky)*, Lina Gorenstein Ferreira da Silva and Maria Luiza Tucci Carneiro eds. (São Paulo, 2002), 23–63.

"*Justitia et Misericordia*: a Inquisição Portuguesa e a Repressão ao Nefando Pecado de Sodomia," in *Inquisição: Ensaios sobre a mentalidade, heresias e arte*, Anita Novinsky and Maria Luiza Tucci Carneiro eds. (São Paulo, 1992), 703–38.

Murdock, Graeme, "The Elders' Gaze: Women and Consistorial Discipline in Late Sixteenth-Century France," in *John Calvin, Myth and Reality: Images and Impact of Geneva's Reformer*, Amy Nelson Burnett ed. (Eugene, OR, 2011), 69–90.

Paiva, José Pedro, *Bruxaria e superstição num país sem "caça às bruxas": 1600–1774* (Lisbon, 1997).

Perry, Mary Elizabeth, *Gender and Disorder in Early Modern Seville* (Princeton, NJ, 1990).

The Handless Maiden: Moriscos and the Politics of Religion in Early Modern Spain (Princeton, NJ, 2005).

Pittard, Thérèse, *Femmes de Genève aux jours d'autrefois* (Geneva, 1946).

Poska, Allyson M., *Women and Authority in Early Modern Spain: The Peasants of Galicia* (Oxford, 2005).

Rieder, Philip, "Miracles and Heretics: Protestants and Catholic Healing Practices in and around Geneva 1530–1750," *Social History of Medicine* 23 (2010): 227–43.

Ruggiero, Guido, *Binding Passions: Tales of Magic, Marriage, and Power at the End of the Renaissance* (New York, 1993).

Safley, Thomas Max, *Let No Man Put Asunder: The Control of Marriage in the German Southwest: A Comparative Study, 1550–1600* (Kirksville, MO, 1984).

Sánchez Ortega, María Helena, "Sorcery and Eroticism in Love Magic," in *Cultural Encounters: the Impact of the Inquisition in Spain and the New World*, Mary Elizabeth Perry and Anne Cruz eds. (Berkeley, CA, 1991), 58–92.

"Woman as Source of 'Evil' in Counter-Reformation Spain," in *Culture and Control in Counter-Reformation Spain*, Anne J. Cruz and Mary Elizabeth Perry eds. (Minneapolis, MN, 1992), 196–215.

Sarrión Mora, Adelina, *Sexualidad y confesión. La solicitación ante el tribunal del Santo Oficio, siglos XVI-XIX* (Madrid, 1994).

Schlau, Stacey, *Gendered Crime and Punishment: Women and/in the Hispanic inquisitions* (Leiden, 2013).

Schmidt, Heinrich Richard, "Morals Courts in Rural Berne during the Early Modern Period," in *The Reformation in Eastern and Central Europe*, Karin Maag ed. (Aldershot, 1997), 155–81.

Schutte, Anne Jacobson, "Recent Research on the Roman inquisition: The Emergence of a New Paradigm," in *Politics and Reformations: History and Reformations*, Essays in Honour of Thomas A. Brady, Jr. Christopher Ocker, Michael Printy, Peter Starenko, and Peter Wallace eds. (Leiden, 2007), 91–11.

Seeger, Cornelia, *Nullité de mariage, divorce et séparation de corps à Genève au temps de Calvin: Fondements doctrinaux, loi et jurisprudence* (Lausanne, 1989).

Seitz, Jonathan, "'The Root is Hidden and the Material Uncertain': The Challenges of Prosecuting Witchcraft in Early Modern Venice," *Renaissance Quarterly* 62 (2009): 102–33.

Sluhovsky, Moshe, *Believe Not Every Spirit: Possession, Mysticism, and Discernment in Early Modern Catholicism* (Chicago, 2007).

Soyer, François, *Ambiguous Gender in Early Modern Spain and Portugal: Inquisitors, Doctors, and the Transgression of Gender Norms* (Leiden, 2012).

Twinam, Ann, "The Negotiation of Honor: Elites, Sexuality, and Illegitimacy in Eighteenth-Century Spanish America," in *The Faces of Honor: Sex, Shame and Violence in Colonial Latin America*, Sonya Lipsett-Rivera and Lyman Johnson eds. (Albuquerque, NM, 1998).

Velasco, Sherry, *Lesbians in Early Modern Spain* (Nashville, TN, 2011).

Vollendorf, Lisa, *The Lives of Women: A New History of inquisitional Spain* (Nashville, TN, 2005).

Vose, Robin, "Beyond Spain: Inquisition History in Global Context," *History Compass* 11 4(2013): 316–29.

Walker, Timothy D., *Doctors, Folk Medicine and the Inquisition: The Repression of Magical Healing in Portugal during the Enlightenment* (Leiden, 2005).

Watt, Jeffrey R., "Calvinism, Childhood, and Education: The Evidence from the Genevan Consistory," *Sixteenth Century Journal* 33 (2002): 439–56.

"Childhood and Youth in the Genevan Consistory Minutes," in *Calvinus Praeceptor Ecclesiae: Papers of the International Congress on Calvin Research*, Herman Selderhuis ed. (Geneva, 2004), 41–62.

"The Impact of the Reformation and Counter-Reformation," in *The History of the European Family, vol. 1: Family Life in Early Modern Times*, Marzio Barbagli and David I. Kertzer eds. (New Haven, CT, 2001), 123–51.

"Reconciliation and the Confession of Sins: The Evidence from the Consistory in Calvin's Geneva," in *Calvin and Luther: The Continuing Relationship*, Ward Holder ed. (Göttingen, 2013), 105–20.

Weber, Alison, *Teresa of Avila and the Rhetoric of Femininity* (Princeton, NJ, 1990).

SECTION I: CHAPTERS 20 AND 21

Antonio Gonsalves de Mello, José, Nederlanders in Brazilië (1624–1654). De invloed van de Hollandse bezetting op het leven en de cultuur in Noord-Brazilië, G. Visser trans., Ben Teensma eds. (Zutphen, 2001).

Behar, Ruth, "Sexual Witchcraft, Colonialism, and Women's Powers: Views from the Mexican Inquisition," in *Sexuality and Marriage in Colonial Latin America*, Asunción Lavrin ed. (Lincoln, NE, 1989), 178–206.

Bellini, Ligia, *A coisa obscura: mulher, sodomia e inquisição no Brasil colonial* (São Paulo, 1989).

Bennett, Herman L., *Africans in Colonial Mexico: Absolutism, Christianity, and Afro-Creole Consciousness, 1570–1640* (Bloomington, IN, 2003).

Bloch, Kristen, *Ordinary Lives in the Early Caribbean: Religion, Colonial Competition, and the Politics of Profit* (Athens, GA, 2012).

Bernardini, Paolo and Fiering, Norman eds., *The Jews and the Expansion of Europe to the West, 1450–1800* (New York, 2001).

van den Boogaart, Ernst, "De Nederlandse expansie in het Atlantische gebied, 1590–1674," in *Overzee. Nederlandse koloniale geschiedenis, 1590–1975*, idem et al. eds. (Haarlem, 1982), 113–44.

Boyer, Richard, *Lives of the Bigamists: Marriage, Family, and Community in Colonial Mexico* (Albuquerque, NM, 1995).

Bristol, Joan Cameron, *Christians, Blasphemers, and Witches: Afro-Mexican Ritual Practice in the Seventeenth Century* (Albuquerque, NM, 2007).

Buddingh, Hans, *Geschiedenis van Suriname* (Utrecht, 1999).

Cañeque, Alejandro, *The King's Living Image: The Culture and Politics of Viceregal Power in Colonial Mexico* (New York, 2004).

Clendinnen, Inga, *Ambivalent Conquests: Maya and Spaniard in Yucatan, 1517–1570* (Cambridge, 1987).

Cohen, Julie-Marthe ed., *Joden in de Cariben* (Zutphen, 2015).

Don, Patricia Lopes, *Bonfires of Culture: Franciscans, Indigenous Leaders and the Inquisition in Early Mexico, 1524–1540* (Norman, OK, 2010).

"The 1539 Inquisition and Trial of Don Carlos of Texcoco in Early Mexico," *Hispanic American Historical Review* 88 4(November 2008): 573–606.

Duviols, Pierre, *La lutte contre les religions autochtones dans le Péru colonial: "L'extirpationde l'idolâtrie," entre 1532 et 1660* (Toulouse, 2008).

Enthoven, Victor, "Suriname and Zeeland: Fifteen Years of Dutch Misery on the Wild Coast, 1667–1682," in *Proceedings of the International Conference on Shipping, Factories and Colonization*, J. Everaert and J. Parmentier eds. (Brussels, 1996), 249–60.

Escobar Quevedo, Ricardo, *Inquisición y judaizantes en América española, siglos XVI-XVII* (Bogotá, 2008).

Feitler, Bruno, *Nas malhas da consciência: Igreja e inquisição no Brasil* (São Paulo, 2007).

Few, Martha, *Women Who Live Evil Lives: Gender, Religion, and the Politics of Power in Colonial Guatemala* (Austin, TX, 2002).

Frijhoff, Willem, *Wegen van Evert Willemsz. Een Hollands weeskind op zoek naar zichzelf, 1607–1647* (Nijmegen, 1995).

"The West India Company and the Reformed Church: Neglect or Concern?" *De Halve Maen* 70 (1997): 59–68.

van Goor, J., "Predikanten in Brazilië," *Spiegel Historiael* 4 (1969): 651–8.

Greenleaf, Richard E., *The Mexican Inquisition of the Sixteenth Century* (Albuquerque, NM, 1969).

Zumárraga and the Mexican Inquisition, 1536–1543 (Washington, DC, 1961).

Haefeli, Evan, *New Netherland and the Dutch Origins of American Religious Liberty* (Philadelphia, PA, 2012).

Israel, Jonathan and Schwartz, Stuart B. eds., *The Expansion of Tolerance: Religion in Dutch Brazil (1624–1654)* (Amsterdam, 2007).

Jacobs, Jaap, *New Netherland: A Dutch Colony in Seventeenth-Century America* (Ithaca, NY, 2009).

Een zegenrijk gewest. Nieuw-Nederland in de zeventiende eeuw (Amsterdam, 1999).

Jaffary, Nora E., *False Mystics: Deviant Orthodoxy in Colonial Mexico* (Lincoln, NE, 2004).

Joosse, Leendert Jan, *Geloof in de Nieuwe Wereld. Ontmoeting met Afrikanen en Indianen (1600–1700)* (Kampen, 2008).

Klooster, Wim, "Jews in Suriname and Curacao," in *Jews and the Expansion of Europe to the West, 1450–1800*, Paolo Bernardini and Norman Fiering eds. (New York, 2001), 350–68.

Krabbendam, Hans, van Minnen, Cornelis A., and Scott-Smith, Giles eds., *Four Centuries of Dutch-American Relations, 1609–2009* (Albany, NY, 2009).

Lenders, Maria, *Strijders voor het Lam: Leven en werk van Herrnhutter broeders en –zusters in Suriname, 1735–1900* (Leiden, 1996).

Lewis, Laura, *Hall of Mirrors: Power, Witchcraft, and Caste in Colonial Mexico* (Durham, NC, 2003).

Lichtveld, U.M. and Voorhoeve, J. eds., *Suriname: Spiegel der vaderlandse kooplieden* (The Hague, 1980).

Liebman, Seymour B., *The Jews in New Spain. Faith, Flame, and the Inquisition* (Coral Gables FL, 1970).

van Lier, Rudolf, *Samenleving in een grensgebied: Een sociaal-historische studie van Suriname*, 3rd ed. (Amsterdam, 1977).

van der Linde, J.M., *Surinaamse Suikerheren en hun kerk. Plantagekolonie en handelskerk ten tijde van Johannes Basseliers, predikant en planter in Suriname, 1667–1689* (Wageningen, 1966).

McKnight, Kathryn Joy and Garofalo, Leo J. eds., *Afro-Latino Voices: Narratives from the Early Modern Ibero-Atlantic World, 1550–1812* (Indianapolis, IN, 2009).

Mello e Souza, Laura, *O diabo e a terra de Santa Cruz: Feitiçaria e religiosidade popular no Brasil colonial* (São Paulo, 1986).

Meuwese, Mark, "Dutch Calvinism and Native Americans: A Comparative Study of the Motivations for Protestant Conversion among the Tupis in Northeastern Brazil (1630–1654) and the Mohawks in Central New York (1690–1713)," in *The Spiritual Conversion of the Americas*, James Muldoon ed. (Gainesville, FL, 2004), 118–41.

Mott, Luiz, *Bahia: Inquisição e sociedade* (Salvador, 2010).

O sexo proibido: Virgens, gays e escravos nas garras da Inquisição (Campinus, 1988).

Novinsky, Anita, "Ser marrano em Minas colonial," *Revista Brasileira de História* 21 40(2001), http://dx.doi.org/10.1590/S0102-01882001000100008

Oort, J.W.C., *Surinaams verhaal: Vestiging van de Hervormde Kerk in Suriname, 1667–1800* (Zutphen, 2000).

O'Toole, Rachel Sarah, "Danger in the Convent: Colonial Demons, Idolatrous Indias, and Bewitching Negras in Santa Clara (Trujillo del Peru)," *Journal of Colonialism and Colonial History* 7 1 (Spring 2006).

Poole, Stafford, *Pedro Moya de Contreras: Catholic Reform and Royal Power in New Spain, 1571–1591* (Berkeley, CA, 1987).

Postma, Johannes, "Suriname and Its Atlantic Connections, 1667–1795," in *Riches from Atlantic Commerce: Dutch Transatlantic Trade and Shipping, 1585–1817*, Johannes Postma and Victor Enthoven eds. (Leiden, 2003), 287–322.

Schalkwijk, F.L., *The Reformed Church in Dutch Brazil, 1624–1654* (Zoetermeer, 1998).

Schwaller, Robert C, "Mulatos as Bilingual Intermediaries in Sixteenth-Century New Spain," *Ethnohistory* 59 4 (Fall 2012): 713–38.

Silverblatt, Irene, *Moon, Sun, and Witches: Gender Ideologies and Class in Inca and Colonial Peru* (Princeton, NJ, 1987).

Sweet, James H., *Domingos Álvares, African Healing, and the Intellectual History of the Atlantic World* (Chapel Hill, NC, 2011).

Tavárez, David, *The Invisible War: Indigenous Devotions, Discipline, and Dissent in Colonial Mexico* (Stanford, CA, 2011).

"Legally Indian: Inquisitorial Readings of Indigenous Identity in New Spain" in *Imperial Subjects: Race and Identity in Colonial Latin America*, Andrew B. Fisher and Matthew D. O'Hara eds. (Durham, NC, 2009), 81–100.

Teensma, B. N., "De Braziliaanse brieven van ds Vincent Joachim Soler," *Documentatieblad voor de Geschiedenis van de Nederlandse Zending en Overzeese Kerken* 4 (1997): 1–23.

Tortorici, Zeb, "Against Nature: Sodomy and Homosexuality in Colonial Latin America," *History Compass* 10 2 (2012): 161–78.

Vainfas, Ronaldo, *Trópico dos pecados: moral, sexualidade e Inquisição no Brasil* (Rio de Janeiro, 1989).

Venema, Janny, *Beverwijck: A Dutch Village on the American Frontier, 1652–1664* (Albany, NY, 2003).

Von Germeten, Nicole, *Violent Delights, Violent Ends: Sex, Race, and Honor in Colonial Cartagena de Indias* (Albuquerque, NM, 2013).

Wolbers, J., *Geschiedenis van Suriname* (Amsterdam, 1861).

SECTION J: CHAPTERS 22 AND 23

Amiel, Charles and Lima, Anne eds., *L'Inquisition de Goa; la relation de Charles Dellon (1687)* (Paris, 1997).

Aron-Beller, Katherine, *Jews on Trial. The Papal Inquisition in Modena, 1598–1638* (Manchester, 2011).

Biewenga, A., *De Kaap de Goede Hoop: Een Nederlandse vestigingskolonie, 1680–1730* (Amsterdam, 1999).

Blussé, L., *Strange Company: Chinese Settlers, Mestizo Women and the Dutch in VOC Batavia* (Leiden, 1988).

Cannas da Cunha, Ana, *A Inquisição no Estado da Índia. Origens (1539–1560)* (Lisbon, 1995).

Feitler, Bruno, "A delegação de poderes inquisitoriais: o exemplo de Goa através da documentação da Biblioteca Nacional do Rio de Janeiro," *Tempo* 12 24 (2008): 127–48.

    "A Sinagoga desenganada: um tratado antijudaico no Brasil do começo do século XVIII," *Revista de História* 148 (2003): 103–24.

Fernando, M. Radin, "The Lost Archives of Melaka: Are They Really Lost?" *Journal of the Malaysian Branch of the Royal Asiatic Society* 78 (2005): 1–36.

van Goor, J., *Jan Kompenie as Schoolmaster: Dutch Education in Ceylon 1690–1795* (Groningen, 1978).

Hsin-Hui, Chiu, *The Colonial "Civilizing Process" in Dutch Formosa: 1624–1662* (Leiden, 2008).

Kanumoyoso, B., *Beyond the City Wall: Society and Economic Development in the Ommelanden of Batavia, 1684–1740* (Ph.D. dissertation, Leiden University, 2011).

Marcocci, Giuseppe, *A Consciência de um império. Portugal e o seu mundo (sécs. XV-XVII)* (Coimbra, 2012).

    "A fé de um império: A Inquisição no mundo português de Quinhentos," *Revista de História* 164 (2011): 65–100.

Mooij, J. ed., *Bouwstoffen voor de Geschiedenis der Protestantsche Kerken in Nederlandsch-Indië*, 3 vols. (Batavia, 1931).

Niemeijer, Hendrik E., *Batavia. Een koloniale samenleving in de 17de eeuw* (Amsterdam, 2005).

Calvinisme en koloniale stadscultuur. Batavia 1619–1725 (Ph.D. dissertation, Vrije Universiteit van Amsterdam, 1996).

"Slavery, Ethnicity and the Economic Independence of Women in Seventeenth-Century Batavia," in *Other Pasts: Women, Gender and History in Early Modern Southeast Asia*, Barbara Watson-Andaya ed. (Honolulu, 2000), 174–95.

Niemeijer, Hendrik E. and van den End, Th., eds., *Bronnen betreffende de geschiedenis van Kerk en School in de gouvernementen Ambon, Ternate en Banda ten tijde van de Verenigde Oost-Indische Compagnie (VOC), 1605–1791* (The Hague, 2014).

Pagden, Anthony, *The Fall of Natural Man: The American Indian and the Origins of Comparative Ethnology* (Cambridge, 1982).

Plomp, J., *De kerkelijke tucht bij Calvijn* (Kampen, 1969).

Priolkar, Anant Kakba, *The Goa Inquisition. Being a Quatercentenary Commemoration Study of the Inquisition in India* (Bombay, 1961).

Reportorio geral de tres mil oito centos processos, que sam todos os despachados neste sancto Officio de Goa ... [1623]. Analyzed as www.i-m.co/reportorio/reportorio/home/html

Schutte, G. J. ed.,. *Het Indisch Sion. De Gereformeerde kerk onder de Verenigde Oost-Indische Compagnie* (Hilversum, 2002).

Singh, Anjana, *Fort Cochin in Kerala, 1750–1830: The Social Condition of a Dutch Community in an Indian Milieu* (Leiden, 2010).

Soleiman, Y., *The Dutch Reformed Church in Late Eighteenth-Century Java: An Eastern Adventure* (Zoetermeer, 2012).

Subrahmanyam, Sanjay, *Improvising Empire: Portuguese Trade and Settlement in the Bay of Bengal, 1500–1700* (Delhi, 1990).

The Portuguese Empire in Asia 1500–1700. A Political and Economic History, 2nd ed. (New York, 2012).

Thomaz, Luís Filipe F. R., *De Ceuta a Timor* (Lisbon, 1994).

Ward, Kerry, *Networks of Empire. Forced migration in the Dutch East India Company* (Cambridge, 2009).

Xavier, Ângela Barreto, *A Invenção de Goa. Poder imperial e conversões culturais nos séculos XVI e XVII* (Lisbon, 2008).

Zupanov, Ines, *Disputed Mission: Jesuit Experiment and Brahmanical Knowledge in Seventeenth-Century India* (Oxford, 1999).

SECTION K: CHAPTERS 24 AND 25

de Almeida, Fortunato, *História da Igreja em Portugal* (Porto, 1971).

de Azevedo, J. Lúcio, *História dos Cristãos-Novos Portugueses*, 3rd ed. (Lisbon, 1989).

Bachmann, Karl, *Geschichte der Kirchenzucht in Kurhessen von der Reformation bis zur Gegenwart. Ein Beitrag zur Kirchen- und Kulturgeschichte des Hessenlandes* (Marburg, 1912).

Barnard, T.C., "Reforming Irish Manners: The Religious Societies in Dublin during the 1690s," *The Historical Journal* 35 (1992): 805–38.

Bethencourt, Francisco, "Declínio e estinção do Santo Ofício," *Revista de História Económica e Social* (1987): 77–85.

"Inquisição e controle social," *História e critica* 14 (1987): 5–18.

Brecht, Martin, *Kirchenordnumg und Kirchenzucht in Württemberg vom 16. bis zum 18. Jahrhundert* [Quellen und Forschungen zur württembergischen Kirchengeschichte] (Stuttgart, 1967).

Burns, E. Bradford. "The Intellectuals as Agents of Change and the Independence of Brazil, 1724–1822," in *From Colony to Nation: Essays on the Independence of Brazil*, A.J.R. Russell-Wood ed. (Baltimore, MD, 1975).

Callahan, William J., *Church, Politics, and Society in Spain, 1750–1874* (Cambridge, 1984)

Dabhoiwala, Faramerz, *The Origins of Sex. A History of the First Sexual Revolution* (London, 2012).

van Deursen, A. Th., *Een dorp in de polder. Graft in de zeventiende eeuw* (Amsterdam, 1994).

van Eijnatten, Joris, *Liberty and Concord in the United Provinces. Religious Toleration and the Public in the Eighteenth-Century Netherlands* (Leiden, 2003).

de Freitas, Jordão, *O Marquez de Pombal e o Santo Officio da Inquisição: Memoria enriquecida com documentos inéditos e facsimiles de assignaturas do benemerito da cidade de Lisboa* (Lisbon, 1916).

Geudeke, Liesbeth, *De classis Edam, 1572–1650. Opbouw van een nieuwe kerk in een verdeelde samenleving* (Gouda, 2010).

Gorenstein Ferreira da Silva, Lina, Herético e impuros: A Inquisição e os cristãos-novos no Rio de Janeiro século XVIII (Rio de Janeiro, 1995).

Grünenfelder, Lukas, *Das Zürcher Ehegerecht. Eheschliessung, Ehescheidung und Ehetrennung nach der erneuerten Satzung von 1698* [Zürcher Studien zur Rechtsgeschichte 57] (Zürich, 2007).

Haliczer, Stephen, "Inquisition Myth and Inquisition History: The Abolition of the Holy Office and the Development of Spanish Political Ideology," in *The Spanish Inquisition and the Inquisitorial Mind*, Angel Alcalá ed. (Boulder, CO, 1987), 146–56.

Inquisition and Society in the Kingdom of Valencia, 1478–1834 (Berkeley, CA, 1990).

Hargreaves-Mawdsley, W. N. ed., *Spain under the Bourbons, 1700–1833. A Collection of Documents* (Columbia, 1973).

Hofer, Roland E., *"Üppiges, unzüchtiges Lebwesen." Schaffhauser Ehegerichtsbarkeit van der Reformation bis zum Ende des Ancien Régime (1529–1798)* (Bern, 1993).

Hurl-Eamon, Jennine, "Policing Male Heterosexuality: The Reformation of Manners Societies' Campaign against the Brothels in Westminster, 1690–1720," *Journal of Social History* 37 (2004), 1017–35.

Isaacs, Tina, "The Anglican Hierarchy and the Reformation of Manners 1688–1738," *Journal of Ecclesiastical History* 33 (1982): 391–411.

Israel, Jonathan I., *The Dutch Republic. Its Rise, Greatness and Fall 1477–1806* (Oxford, 2005).

Konersmann, Frank, *Kirchenregiment und Kirchenzucht im frühneuzeitlichen Kleinstaat. Studien zu den herrschaftlichen und gesellschaftlichen Grundlagen des Kirchenregiments der Herzöge von Pfalz-Zweibrücken 1410–1793* [Schriftenreihe des Vereins für Rheinische Kirchengeschichte] (Cologne, 1996).

Lea, Henry Charles, *The Inquisition in the Spanish Dependencies* (New York, 1908).

van Lieburg, Fred, *De Nadere Reformatie in Utrecht ten tijde van Voetius. Sporen in de gereformeerde kerkenraadsacta* (Rotterdam, 1989).

"Gerardus van Schuylenburg (1681–1770). Een piëtistisch predikantenleven," *Documentatieblad Nadere Reformatie* 16 (1992): 103–26.

Lipiner, Elias, *Terror e Linguagem: Um dicionário da Santa Inquisição* (1999).

Lüdicke, Martina, *Kirchenzucht und Alltagsleben. Untersuchungen in der reformierten hessischen Gemeinde Deisel 1781–1914* (Kassel, 2003).

Lustosa, Fernanda Mayer, *Raízes judaicas na Paraíba colonial: Séculos VXI-XVIII* (Master's Thesis, University of São Paulo, 2000).

Lynch, John, *Bourbon Spain, 1700–1808* (Cambridge, 1989).

Maxwell, Kenneth, *Pombal: Paradox of the Enlightenment* (Cambridge, 1995).

Mendes de Almeida, Candido ed., Ordenações Filipinas, Livro 5 (1870; reprint ed., Lisbon, 1985).

Mitchison, Rosalind and Leneman, Leah, "Acquiescence in and Defiance of Church Discipline in Early-Modern Scotland," *Records of the Scottish Church History Society* 25 (1993): 19–39.

Sexuality and Social Control. Scotland 1660–1780 (Oxford, 1989).

de Mooij, Charles, *Geloof kan Bergen verzetten. Reformatie en katholieke herleving te Bergen op Zoom 1577–1795* (Hilversum, 1998).

Muster, Michael, *Das Ende der Kirchenbuße. Dargestellt an der Verordnung über die Aufhebung der Kirchenbuße in den Braunschweig-Wolfenbüttelschen Landen vom 6. März 1775* (Hanover, 1983).

Nizza da Silva, Maria Beatriz, Cultura no Brasil Colônia (Petrópolis, 1981).

Quenet, Grégory, *Les tremblements de terre aux XIIe et XVIIIe siècles. La naissance d'un risque* (Seyssel, 2005).

Rawlings, Helen, *The Spanish Inquisition* (Malden, MA, 2006).

van Rooden, Peter, *Religieuze regimes. Over godsdienst en maatschappij in Nederland, 1570–1990* (Amsterdam, 1996).

Santos, Maria Helena Carvalho dos, "A abolição da Inquisição em Portugal: Um acto de poder," in *Inquisição*, 3 vols., idem ed. (Lisbon, 1989), 3: 1379–86.

Scharfe, Martin, "Subversive Frömmigkeit. Über die Distanz unterer Volksklassen zur offiziellen Religion. Beispiele aus dem württembergischen Protestantismus des 18. Jahrhunderts," in *Kultur zwischen Bürgertum und Volk* [Argument-Sonderband, AS 103], Jutta Held ed. (Berlin, 1983), 17–35.

Schilling, Heinz ed., *Kirchenzucht und Sozialdisziplinierung im frühneuzeitlichen Europa* [Zeitschrift für historische Forschung, Beiheft 16] (Berlin, 1994).

Schnabel-Schüle, Helga, "Der grosse Unterschied und seine kleinen Folgen. Zum Problem der Kirchenzucht als Unterscheidungskriterium zwischen lutherischer und reformierter Konfession," in *Krisenbewußtsein und*

Krisenbewältigung in der frühen Neuzeit – Crisis in Early Modern Europe.
Festschrift für Hans-Christoph Rublack, Monika Hagenmaier and Sabine
Holtz eds. (Frankfurt am Main, 1992), 197–214.

Shore, Heather, "'The Reckoning': disorderly women, informing constables and
the Westminster justices, 1727–33," *Social History* 34 (2009): 409–27.

Siqueira, Sonia A., "Os Regimentos da Inquisição," *Revista do Instituto Histórico
e Geográfico Brasileiro* 157 392(July–Sept. 1996): 495–1020.

Spaans, Joke, *Armenzorg in Friesland. Publieke zorg en particuliere liefdadigheid
in zes Friese steden: Leeuwarden, Bolsward, Franeker, Sneek, Dokkum en
Harlingen* (Hilversum, 1997),

Taylor, Stephen, "Whigs, Tories and Anticlericalism: Ecclesiastical Courts Legislation in 1733," *Parliamentary History* 19 (2000): 329–55.

Thomson, Andrew, "Church Discipline: The Operation of the Winchester Consistory Court in the Seventeenth Century," *History* 91 (2006): 337–59.

Torres, José Veiga, "Uma longa guerra social: Os rítmos da repressão inquisitorial
em Portugal," *RHES* 1 (Jan-June, 1978): 55–68.

"Da repressão religiosa para a promoção social: A Inquisição como instância
legitimadora da promoção social da burguesia mercantile," *Revista Crítica de
Ciências Sociais* 4 (October 1994): 109–35.

Villalta, Luiz Carlos, "As licenças para posse e leitura de livros proibidos," in *De
Cabral a Pedro I: Aspectos da colonização portuguesa no Brasil*, Maria
Beatriz Nizza da Silva ed. (Porto, 2001), 235–46.

Wadsworth, James E., "Celebrating St. Peter Martyr: The Inquisitional Brotherhood
in Colonial Brazil," *Colonial Latin American Historical Review* 12 2 (2003):
173–227.

*In Defence of the Faith: Joaquim Marques de Araújo, a Comissário in the Age
of Inquisitional Decline* (Montreal & Kingston, 2013).

CONCLUSION

Borromeo, Agostino ed., *L'Inquisizione. Atti del Simposio internazionale, Città
del Vaticano, 29–31 ottobre 1998* (Vatican City, 2005).

Clasen, Claus-Peter, *Anabaptism: A Social History* (Ithaca, NY, 1972).

Kamen, Henry, *Inquisition and Society in Spain in the Sixteenth and Seventeenth
Centuries* (Bloomington, IN, 1985).

The Spanish Inquisition: An Historical Revision (London, 1997).

Monter, William E., "The Inquisition," in *A Companion to the Reformation
World*, Ronnie Po-Chia Hsia ed. (Oxford, 2004), 255–71.

"The Mediterranean Inquisitions of Early Modern Europe," in *The Cambridge
History of Christianity, vol. 6, Reform and Expansion, 1500–1660*, Ronnie
Po-Chia Hsia ed. (Cambridge, 2007), 283–301.

O'Malley, John, *Trent: What Really Happened at the Council* (Cambridge, 2012).

Robinson, Marilynne, *The Death of Adam* (New York, 2005).

Rupp, E.G. and Drewery, Benjamin eds., *Martin Luther* (New York, 1970).

Tolley, Bruce, *Pastors and Parishioners in Wurttemberg during the Late Reformation, 1581–1621* (Stanford, CA, 1995).

Index

abonos, 58
abortion, 80–1
absolutism, 321–2
abstention, 314
Academy of Geneva, 17
Accati, Luisa, 244
Act of Disobedient Persons, 46
Acts of Uniformity, 98–9
Adam, Guillaume, 211–12
Admonition to the Parliament (Field and
      Wilcox), 93–4
adultery, 68–9, 71, 74–5, 96, 231, 236–7
Adventura de Morsier, Jacques, 210
Afonso, María, 241–2
African slaves, 257–62, 275
Afro-Mexicans, 277
agency, 181–2, 234–5, 314
Albert, Arnau, 125
Alberti, Leandro, 125
Alberto (cardinal), 296–7
Alexander III (pope), 85–6
Alfar, Gaspar de, 221–2
Algonquian groups, 260–1
Almeida, Jorge de, 296, 298–9
Almeida, Mencia de, 57–8
Alonso, Hernando, 266–7
alumbradismo, 169–70, 202–3, 245–6,
      275–6
alumbrados, 36–7
Álvares, Domingos, 275–6
Ambon, 280–1
amende honorable, 160–1
American tribunals, 273–8

Ames, Christine Caldwell, 54
Anabaptism, 6, 181, 187, 189, 335
ancien régime, 137
Andreae, Johann Valentin, 333
Anglicans, 314–15
Anglo-Spanish wars (1796–1802), 324
Angola, 123–4, 260–1
annulments, 273–4
Antecamotim, 301–2
anthropologists, 143–4
anti-Trinitarian theology, 70
Antoine, Nicolas, 71–2
appeals, 82–3
Aragon, 196–7
archbishops, Neapolitan, 33–4
archdiocesan courts, 82. *See also* diocesan
      courts
Arias de Ugarte, Hernando, 270
aristocracy, 319–20
articles of inquiry, 94
artisans, 79
atonement, 96
attestatie, 281–2
attorneys, defense, 56–8
audience chamber, 220–2
audiencia, 266–7
Augustine (saint), 30–1, 339–40
auto de fe, 37, 172–4, 220–2, 225, 298–300
      general, 172
      Iberia and, 63
Avignon, 31–2, 38–9
Azores, 37, 123–4
Aztec empire, 266

bad repute (*mala fama*), 197
Baer, Fritz, 145
Bahia, 268, 272
bailies, 44–5
Baltics, 6–7
Banda, 280–1
baptism, 188–9
baroque religious feasts, 171–2
Barros, Antonio de, 297
Basoche, 72–3
Basques, witchcraft hysteria of, 216–17
Basseliers, Johannes, 262
bastardy, 98–9. *See also* illegitimacy
Batavia, 280–2, 287
 church districts in, 283–5
 consistorial discipline in, 282–3
Beam, Sara, 7–8, 64, 104–5, 129–30
Behrend-Martinez, Edward, 7–8
Beinart, Haim, 145–6
Belgic Confession, 187
Benandanti, 143–4
Benella, Marguerite, 187
Beney, Bertin, 232–3
Bennassar, Bartolomé, 8–9, 145–6, 167–8,
 225–6
Bennassar, Lucile, 145–6
Bernard, Louis, 112–13
Bertheau, Solange, 205–6
Betanzos, Domingo de, 266–7
Beteta, Luis de, 199–200
Bethencourt, Francisco, 7–8, 56, 63–4,
 117–18, 322, 338
Beza, Theodore, 19, 104, 135–6
bigamy, 37, 68, 98–9, 273–4, 288,
 324–5
bishops, 33–4, 77, 79–80, 86, 90–1
Bivar the Elder, Rodrigo, 199–200
Bivar the Younger, Rodrigo, 199–200
Black, Christopher, 7, 61–2, 217
Black Legend, 28–9
Blanca, María, 275
Blandin, Mermet, 110–11
blasphemy, 70–2, 200–1, 237, 246–7
 civil authorities and, 69–70
 slaves and, 275
 Small Council and, 68–9
Bogardus, Everardus, 259–60
Bolsec, Jerome, 229
bondage (debt relations), 287
Bonivard, François, 187–90
Bonivard, Michel, 235

Bonna, Pierre, 112–13
Book of Sports, 101–2
books of votes (*libros de votos*), 224–5
Borromeo, Carlo, 32–3, 174–5
Borsatti, Nicolas, 69–70
Bourbon monarchy, 319–21
Braekcer, Andries de, 186–7
Brans, Margeriete, 189–90
Brasichel, Juan Maria, 169–70
Brazil, 31–2, 123–4, 253–5, 268, 272–3,
 322–3
 Classis of, 256–8, 264
 Dutch, 255–9
 indigenous Brazilians, 257–8
breach of faith, 90–1
bridal pregnancy, 99–100
Britillion, Pierre, 110–11
Brotherhood of Saint Peter Martyr, 174,
 324–5
brouillard (fog), 130–1
Brown, Barbara, 48–9
Brucker, Gene, 81–2
Bruno, Giordano, 29–30, 37
Bucer, Martin, 16–17, 30–1, 207–8
bureaucratic culture, 129–30
Burmod, Nicolas, 67–8
buytenarmen, 285
byconsistories, 137

caciques, 269–70
Calvin, John, 17–18, 104, 109–10, 131–2,
 206–7, 233–4, 332–5
 ecclesiastical institutions and, 15
 ecclesiastical structure of, 19
 excommunication and, 21–2
 Farel and, 16–17
 lay personnel and, 108–9
Calvinism, 1–5, 10–12, 35–6, 38–9, 41,
 113–14, 215–16
 first-generation, 40
 jurisdiction and, 43–4
 local reception of, 2–3
Campeggi, Camillo, 125
Campomanes, Count of, 320–1
canon law, 56–7, 63–4, 77–9, 119–20
Capuchins, 35–7
Carafa, Gian Pietro (Paul IV), 30–1, 123,
 170–1
Carib Indians, 261–3
Carnesecchi, Pietro, 29–30, 37
Caro Baroja, Julio, 116–17

Carranza, Bartolomé de, 55–6, 124–5, 193–5, 197–8
Cartagena de Indias, 272–3
Carvajal, Luis de, 271–2
Carvalho e Melo, Sebastião José de, 321–2
Castain, Claude, 208–10
Castile, 31–2
Castilho, Pedro de, 297
Catalonia, 31–2
Catechism (Calvin), 206–7
catechism, social control and, 289–90
Cathars, 30
Catherine of Siena (saint), 198
caute lege, 169–70
cautioners, 48
Cazalla, Maria de, 198–200, 202
censorship, 169–70, 176–7, 323–4, 327
Central America, 10, 267–8
Certeau, Michel de, 167–8
Cesasie, Francesco, 140
Cespedes, Elena/Eleno, 244–5
Ceylon, 280–1
Champrenaux, Jeanne Elizabeth, 75–6
Chapelaz, Jacques, 70
Chappeaurouge, Etienna, 210
Chappuis, Jean, 110–11
Chareyre, Philippe, 8–9, 47–8, 112–13, 130, 210–11
charitable admonition, 95
charity, moral reformation through, 157–8
Charles I (king), 98–9
Charles II (king), 102
Charles III (king), 320–1
Charles IV (king), 321
Charles V (king), 266–9
Charvier, Jacques, 182
Chasteaunef, Amédée, 111–12
Christelijcke Republiek, 290
Christendom, 1, 335–6, 339–40
Christian, William, 176
Christian republics, 279
Christians of the land (*cristãos da terra*), 293–5
Chuchiak, John, 8–10, 58–9
church courts. *See* English church courts
church law, 78–9
Church of Castres, 21–2
Church of Nîmes, 20–2
Church of Scotland, 308–9
churchwardens, 94
Ciudad Real, 196–7

civil authorities, 63–4, 73–4
civil courts, 66–7, 74–5
civil honesty, 164
civil law, 119–20
civil registers, 135
Civil Wars, 89–90, 102
civilizing process, 3, 286
class, 246
Classis of Amsterdam, 254–5, 257–8
Classis of Walcheren, 254–5, 262–3
Clement VIII (pope), 174
clerical crimes, 81
clerical power, 53–4
clerics, 79–80
Coen, Jan Pieterszoon, 282–3
Coimbra, 293–4
collective enterprise, 132
College of Cardinals, 1–2
colloquies, 25
colonial litigation, 86–7
colonial social context, 287–8
comisario, 84, 171–2
common bruit, 44–5
communal bonds, 63
communal harmony, negotiation of, 211–12
communalism, 310
communion, 185–6
Companhia dos Familiares, 323–4
Company of Pastors, 42–3, 109, 114
"competents," 289–90
concubines, 287–8
confession, 1–2, 57–8, 170
    extortion of, 217–20
    false, 59
    inducing, 217–20
    resistance to, 178
    spontaneous, 54
confessional identity, 6–7
confessionalization, 6–7, 128, 167, 333
Congo, 260–1
congregational discipline, 95
conscience, 170, 314
Consejo Superior (Supreme Council), 174–5
Conselho Geral (General Council), 16–17, 34–5, 60, 326–7
consistorial secretaries, 134
consistorial studies, 336–40
consistorial-synodal system, 23–4
consistory records (*notulen*), 285
Constitution of 1812, 325–6
consultants, 223–7

consultations of the faith (*consultas de fe*), 223
convents, 81–2
conversos, 145–6, 200–1, 241–4
corporal punishment, 5, 40–1, 48–9, 70–1
Corro, Antonio del, 217–18
Cortés, Hernán, 266–7
Council of Sixty, 18–19
Council of the Indies, 269–70
Council of Trent, 78–9, 122–3, 167–8, 331–4
Council of Two Hundred, 18–19, 109
Councilors of Inquisition, 118–19
counseling, compulsory, 19–20
Counter Remonstrant, 255, 259–61
Counter-Reformation, 172, 176–7, 229, 308
court records, 140–1
Courthézon, 130–1
Coutinho, Azeredo, 323–4
Cranmer, Thomas, 91–2
Crespin, Jean, 135–6
criminal
    behavior, 140–1
    cases, 80–1, 84–5
    courts, secular, 66
    executions, 64
    sentences, 66–8
    trials, 70–1
criminalization of sin, 205–6
cristãos da terra (Christians of the land), 293–5
crypto-Hinduism, 292
crypto-Judaism, 145, 221–2, 292
Cudbert, Elspet, 44–5
Cuels, Jan, 186–7
cursing, 236–7

da Fonseca, Bartolomeu, 296–7
da Gama, Vasco, 292–3
da Silva, Gonçalo, 298
dance, 165
Dancet, Claude, 69–70
d'Arlod, Domaine, 111–12
Davidson, Nicholas, 35
Davis, Natalie Zemon, 132, 140–1
day of the censures, 160–1
de la Cruz, Isabel, 202–3
de la Maisonneuve, Jean, 112–13
deacons, 18–22, 25–6, 42, 157
debt relations (*bondage*), 287
Dechallon, Claudaz, 188–9

Declaration of Sports, 101
Dedieu, Jean-Pierre, 145–6, 176–7
defense attorneys, 56–8
Del Col, Andrea, 29–30, 142–4
del Corro, Antonio (Reginaldus Montanus), 28–9
Dentand, Dominique, 112–13
denunciation, 32
detective services, 46–7
Dias Falcão, Aleixo, 296
Díaz, Catalina, 196–7
Dincklagen, Lubbert, 259–60
diocesan courts, 77, 82, 84. *See also* archdiocesan courts
Directorium Inquisitorum (Eymeric), 35
discipline, 89, 306–7
    congregational, 95
    consistorial, in Batavia, 282–3
    medicinal, 307–8
    national, 22–3
    procedures of, 158
    secular, 311–12
    social, 309–10, 333
    spiritual, 311–12
    women and, 234–5
Discipline de l'Église de Saint-Lô, 22–3
Discipline of the Reformed Churches of France, 19–22, 159–60, 163–5
diseases, epidemic, 50
districts, 44
divorce, 231–2, 273–4
dizeniers, 130
doctors, 19
doctrine, received, 17
domestic violence, 231–3
Dominicans, 30, 119–21, 217, 266–7, 281
Donaldson, Margaret, 45–6
donec corrigatur, 169–70
Donzel, Jean-Philibert, 110–11
Dorsieres, Bartholomee, 68
d'Orsières, Pierre, 110–12
drunkenness, 98–9
Du Frêney, Claudine, 189–90
Du Frêney, François, 189–90
Du Jusse, Marquet, 186–8
Duchy of Modena, 318–19
Duchy of Württemberg, 310
Dufour, Claude, 204–5, 208
Dutch Brazil, 255–9
Dutch East India Company (VOC), 10, 279–82

Dutch Reformed Church, 23–4, 312–13
Dutch Republic, 71–3, 253–4, 279–80

Eastern Europe, 6–7
ecclesiastical districts, 156–7
ecclesiastical justice, 83–4
Ecclesiastical Ordinances, 16–17, 19–20,
    44, 112–13, 155–6
ecclesiastical space, 155–7
ecclesiastical tribunals, 1
Edict of Faith, 240–2, 320–1, 323–4
Edict of Nantes, 129–30
Edict of Silence, 216–17
edification, 134
education, moral, 157–8, 162–5
Edward VI (king), 91–2, 96
effect of reality, 136–7
efficacy, of inquisitorial action, 175–8
Eguiluz, Paula de, 276–7
elders, 17–18, 20–6, 40–9, 67, 69, 71,
    104–14, 121–2, 129–33, 156,
    161–5, 186, 256, 294, 308
Elias, Norbert, 3, 128, 286
Elizabeth (queen), 92–3, 95–9, 101–2
Elizabethan England, 49, 89–90
Emden, 180–1, 184, 189–90
Emden Articles, 23–4
emigrants, 271–2
emplotment, 136–7
England, 6–7
    Anglo-Spanish wars, 324
    Elizabethan, 49, 89–90
    episcopal court system of, 7–8
    Jacobean, 89–90, 99–101
    New England, 253–5
English church courts, 8, 89–90
    around 1500, 90–1
    congregational discipline and, 95
    crisis and collapse of, 101–2
    in eighteenth century, 102
    Inquisition and, 92–3
    Jacobean, 99–101
    penance and, 95–8
    Reformation and, 91–2
    secular courts and, 98–9
    visitations and, 93–4
Enlightenment, 10–11, 319, 327–8, 333–4
epidemic diseases, 50
episcopal courts, 7–8, 77–8
Erasmians, 36–7
Erasmus, Desiderius, 202

Errol, Earl of, 45–6
Estado da Índia, 292–4, 296, 302–3
evangelism, 93–4
evidentiary standards, 52
ex officio proceedings, 91
excommunication, 21–2, 24–5, 49, 97–8,
    109, 210–11
execution, 37–9, 49–50, 63–4
exemplarity, 171–5
exile, 63
Exponi Nobis, 266
Expurgatory Index, 169–70
Extirpation, 270
extramarital affairs, 79–80. *See also* adultery
Eymeric, Nicholas, 35, 56–7

Fabri, Suor Maria Deodata, 242
Falquet, Etienne, 68
false confessions, 59
false sanctity, 37
fama, 52–3, 55–6. *See also mala fama*
familiars (*familiari*), 35, 171–2
family, 163–4, 208–9, 274–5
Farel, Guillaume, 16–17
Farinacci, Prospero, 35
Fassoret, Jeanne, 235–8
Favre, François, 112–13
fear, resistance to, 216–17
Fehler, Timothy, 8–9
feitiçero (sorcerer), 275–6
Feitler, Bruno, 9–10, 61–2
female slaves, 287–8
femininity, 235–6, 241–2
Ferdinand (king), 30, 266–7
Ferdinand VI (king), 320–1
Ferdinand VII (king), 325–6
Fernandes, Manoel, 272–3
Ferreira, Jorge, 298–9
Field, John, 93–4
Final Judgment, 1
final sentence, negotiation of, 223–7
fines, 40–1, 47–8
fintados, 322
First Book of Discipline, 22–3, 49
first consistory, 108–9
first-generation Calvinism, 40
fiscal general, 81
fiscale (prosecutor), 34
fog (*brouillard*), 130–1
forged testimonials, 47
fornication (*paillardise*), 68–9

Foucault, Michel, 128
France, 2–3, 6–7, 15, 19–20, 22–5, 72–3, 128, 157
  consistories in, 15–18
  deacons in, 20–2
  excommunication in, 21–2
  Franco-Spanish conflict, 324
  local church in, 20
  mixed marriages in, 162–3
  New France, 254–5
  Religious Wars of, 35–6, 73, 211–12, 308
  Revolution of, 321–2, 325
Franciscans, 120–1, 217, 266, 268–9, 281
Franco, Francisco, 193, 337–8
Franco Tavares, Rodrigo, 224–5
Franco-Spanish conflict (1793–1795), 324
Franguerio Cabras, Bautista, 220–1
Freemasons, 317–18
Friulian Inquisition, 244
Furtado de Mendonça, Heitor, 268

Galileo, 29–30, 62–3
games, 165
gaoling, 46
Garayzabal, Antonio de, 81
García de Trasmiera, Diego, 125
garrucha (strappado), 61
gender, 9–10, 241–2, 273–8. *See also* women
  analysis of, 229–30, 240
  bending of, 244–5
  norms of, 275–6
  orthodoxy and, 240
General Assembly, 23–4
General Council (*Conselho Geral*), 16–17, 34–5, 60, 326–7
Geneva, 7–8, 19–20, 24–5, 42, 72–3, 104–5, 113–14, 131–2, 136, 155–6, 159, 165, 181–2, 185–90, 204, 207–12, 229–37, 335–8
  civic polity of, 113
  corporal punishment in, 48–9
  criminal sentences and, 66–8
  excommunication in, 21–2
  jurisdiction in, 43–4
  Kingdon and, 15–16
  moral purity and, 71
  political constitution of, 18–19
Geneva Consistory, 137–8
Genod, Jehanton, 110–11
gentilism, 298–303

geography, 336
Germany, 1–2, 17–18, 21–2, 128, 181–2, 259–60, 333
Gil Frazão, Marcos, 297
Giles, Mary, 242
Ginzburg, Carlo, 2–3, 143–4
Goa, 31–2, 37, 61–2, 120, 292–5, 302–3, 326
Godoy, Manuel, 321
Gómez, Antonio, 215–16
Gonçalves, Manuel, 302
Góngora, Luis de, 126
González, Juana, 61
González, Marina, 197–8
good neighborhood, 40–1
gossip networks, 45–6
Granada, 266–9
Grand Duchy of Tuscany, 317–18
Gratian, 78–9
Gray, David, 49–50
Great Conspiracy, 272
Gregory IX (pope), 30
Gregory XIII (pope), 56–7, 124–5
Gros, Ami, 236–7
Gros, Guillauma, 236–7
Grosse, Christian, 8, 151, 164–5, 180, 207–8, 211–12, 284–5
Guilhem, Claire, 240
Gutiérrez de Ulloa, Antonio, 267–8
Gutiérrez Flores, Juan, 124–5

Habsburgs, 37
Haliczer, Stephen, 246–7, 323–4
Hampton Court Conference, 93
handelskerk (trade-church), 262
Harmony of the Gospels (Calvin), 17–18
hearsay evidence, 58
Heidelberg Catechism, 289–90
Henningsen, Gustav, 142–3, 145–6, 245–6, 337–8
Henrique (cardinal), 120–1, 301–2
Henry VIII (king), 91–2, 332–3
heresy, 36–7, 52–5, 167–8, 218
  confession and, 170
  minor, 243–4
  recidivism and, 294–5
  secret, 55–6
  sentencing of, 223
Herlihy, David, 85–6
heterodoxy, 163–4
High Commission, 92–3, 96, 102

High Court of Judiciary, 73–4
Hindus, 293–4, 298–9, 301–3
Histoire ecclésiastique des Eglises réformées au royaume de France (Beza), 135–6
Holland, 128, 159–60
Holy Office, 30, 116, 142–3, 146–7, 167–8, 215–16, 293–4, 329
   archive of, 32–3
   censorship and, 176–7
   comisario and, 84
   notaries and, 83–4
   torture and, 59
homosexuality, 277
Homza, Lu Ann, 8–9, 60
honor, 201–2, 208–10, 308–11
Hooper, John, 91–2
Hormuz, 292–3
Hospital-General, 19, 112–13
House of Savoy, 317–18
household servants, 210
Hsia, R. Po-Chia, 140–1, 333
Hugoccio, 78–9
Hugoz, Denys, 182–4
Hulsebos, A., 282–3
human culture, 315
human nature, 315
Hungary, 17–18, 24, 42, 72–3
Hunne, Richard, 90–1

Iberia, 7–8, 31–2, 36–9, 60–2, 85–6, 145
   auto de fe and, 63
   Inquisitions of, 319–22
   institutions of, 322–5
identity, confessional, 6–7
Idiaquez Velez Yqueziara, Don Antonio Francisco de, 82
idolatry, 56, 162
illegitimacy, 99–100, 231, 308–9
illuminism, 202–3
Index of 1612, 169–70
Index of the Master of the Holy Palace, 169–70
India, 280–1, 296–7. *See also* Goa
indigenous Brazilians, 257–8
indirectas, 58
individualism, 310
infanticide, 80–1
infidels, 300–1
information distortions, 130–3
infrajustice, 75, 128–30

Ingram, Martin, 7–8, 206, 335–6
Innocent III (pope), 77–9, 85–6
inquisitio (inquiry), 28, 52–3
inquisitorial executions, 64
inquisitorial studies, 336–40
Inquisitors, 118–26, 143–4
Inquisitors General, 116–17
inspector generals (*visitadores*), 81–2
Institutes (Calvin), 207–8
institutional sociability, 235
insubordination, 159–60
intention, 200–1
Inter Caetera, 266–7
Interregnum, 89–90, 102
interrogation minutes, 142–3
interrogative torture, 52
Ireland, 6–7
Isabella (queen), 30, 58, 266–7
Isabella II (queen), 326
Islam, 28–9, 243–4, 268–9, 296, 298–9
Italian Inquisitions, 317–19
Italian Wars, 30–1
Italy, 1–3, 6–8, 29–30, 32–3
   censorship in, 169
   Judaizers and, 37
   urban courts in, 85–6

Jaccon, Pierre, 70–1
Jacobean England, 89–90, 99–101
Jacobin movement, 319–20
Jaffary, Nora, 275–6
Jakarta. *See* Batavia
James I (king), 101–2
James II (king), 102
James VI (king), 49, 93, 98–9
Jansenism, 6–7
Japan, 281
Jeronimus, Anne, 189–90
Jesuits, 6–7, 35–7, 92–3, 119–20, 257–8, 281, 302
Jewish converts, 28–30
Jiménez Monteserín, Miguel, 176
João VI (king), 326–7
John of the Cross, 178
José I (king), 321–2
Judaism, 243–4, 260–1, 324
Judaizers, 28–30, 38–9, 58, 60, 145, 147–8
   Italy and, 37
   women and, 245–6
judges, 122–3, 147
   lay, 42–3

judicial tribunals, 8, 64
judicial violence, 52
judicializing procedure, 137–8
juezes de commission (provisional judges), 82
Juntas of Faith, 326
jurisdiction, 43–4, 55–6, 312–14
Justiznutzung (utilization of justice), 147

Kagan, Richard, 242–3
Kals, Jan Willem, 262–4
Kamen, Henry, 29–30, 37, 176–7, 337–8
Kelly, Henry Ansgar, 56–7
Kingdon, Robert M., 2–3, 15–16, 19, 205–6, 336–7
Kirchenbuße, 311–12, 315–16
Kirchenconvente, 310
kirk sessions, 73–4, 96–7, 155, 209–10, 308–9
Klapisch-Zuber, Christiane, 85–6
Knox, John, 22–3
Konsistorien, 311
Kriner, Lucas, 109

La Rochelle, 72–3
labradores (small farmers), 79
laity, 25–6, 40, 54
    agency of, 181–2
    elders, 24–6, 41–2
    judges, 42–3
    personnel, 108–9
    prosecution, 44–7
    representatives, 32
    vigilantes, 315–16
Landa, Diego de, 269–70
Langley, Chris, 113–14
language differences, 3–4
Lasco, John à, 49
Latin America, 7–8, 86
law
    canon, 56–7, 63–4, 77–9, 119–20
    church, 78–9
    civil, 119–20
    Mosaic, 200–1
    Roman, 5, 28, 52, 56–8, 77
    secular, 56
    statute, 49–50
Le Chapuis, Philiberte, 182–3
Lea, Henry Charles, 28–9, 195, 199–200, 336–7
legal culture, 54–5
legal training, 121

Leiden magistracy, 24–5
León, Lucrecia de, 242–3
Leopold, Peter, 317–18
letters, 142
liberalism, 10–11
libraries, 125–6
libros de votos (books of votes), 224–5
Licet ab initio (Paul III), 30
Lichtenberg, Julius Philips, 262–3
limpieza de sangre (purity of blood), 271–2, 321–3
Lipscomb, Suzannah, 211–12
Lithuania, 1–2
Livre des martyrs (Crespin), 135–6
Llorente, Juan Antonio, 28–9, 321–2
Lobo Guerrero, Bartolomé, 270
local church, 20
local knowledge, substantial, 111
localism, 52
Locati, Umberto, 125
Lollard heretics, 90
Lombard, Peter, 78–9
López Rivas, Simón, 222
Lord's Supper, 21–2, 24, 158–60
Loup, Françoise, 184–6
Low Countries, 259–60
Lower Guinea Coast, 261
Luna, Mencía de, 60–1
Lusitanianizing, 300–1
Luther, Martin, 30–1, 331–2
Lutheranism, 1–2, 6–7, 36–7, 202, 260, 263–4, 270–1, 310
Lynn, Kimberly, 7–8, 34–5, 45–6, 110–11

Macanaz, Melchor Rafael de, 320–1
Macao, 292–3
MacGregor, Christen, 49–50
Madeira, 123–4
magic, 166, 236–7, 244–5
magistrates, 71–2, 108
Makchanse, George, 44–5
mala fama (bad repute), 197. *See also fama*
Malabar rites controversy, 302
Mallorca, 124–5
Malta, 31–2, 120–1
Manetsch Scott, 15–16
Mantuan Inquisition, 217
Manuel, Bernarda, 242–3
Maravall, J. A., 172
Marcellus II (pope), 123
Mardijkers, 283–4, 286–7, 289

Maria Teresa, 318–19
marital difficulties, 68
marketplace penance, 95–8
marriage, 91, 100, 229–31, 273–5. *See also*
    bigamy
  broken promises in, 79
  concubines and, 287–8
  courts, 309–10
  divorce and, 231–2
  extramarital affairs, 79–80
  family and, 163–4
  Hindus and, 302–3
  mixed, 162–4
  poverty and, 286
  premarital sex, 99–100
Marriage Law of 1622, 288
Marti, Guillem, 221–2
martyrdom, 174–5
Mary (queen), 92–3
masculinity, 235–6, 246–8
Masini, Eliseo, 35, 218–19
Matellin, Thivent, 110–11
Matos Noronha, Antonio, 124–5
Matthew (saint), 95
Mayans, 269–70
Mayer, Thomas, 53–4, 56–7
M'Crie, Thomas, 176
media, print, 162
Medici Grand Dukes, 32–3
medicinal discipline, 307–8
Medina Rico, Pedro de, 219–20
Medrano, Antonio de, 197–8
Megapolensis, Johannes, 260–1
Melaka, 292–3
Melanchthon, Philip, 30–1
*Mémoire de l'ordre qu'on tient au
    consistoire de Nîmes*, 22–3
Mendes, Maria, 220–1
Méndez de Rivera, Blanca, 272
Menéndez y Pelayo, Marcelino, 193
Mentzer, Raymond, 7, 47–8, 66–7, 105, 107,
    111, 159, 164, 181–2, 204–5, 285
méreau, 161–2
Merlin, Jean, 211–12
Mermod, Clauda, 68–9
Mesa da Consciência e Ordens, 301
Messeler, Peter de, 184–5
mèstèr keliling, 289–90
mestizos, 286–7
Mestrazat, Pierre, 182–3
Meuwese, Mark, 9–10

Mexican Inquisition, 215, 219–22
Mexico, 59, 266–8, 270, 276–7
Michielssen, Jan, 190–1
microhistory, 193–4
Minas Gerais, 272–3
minor heresies, 243–4
mixed marriages, 162–4
Modena, Duchy of, 318–19
Modernism, 327
Moluccas, 280–1
Mombasa, 292–3
Montanus, Reginaldus (Antonio del Corro),
    28–9
Monter, William, 11–12, 205–6
Morales, Gonzalo de, 266–7
morality, 313–14
  education, 157–8, 162–5
  personal, 91
  public, 306, 313
  purity, 71, 73–4
  reform, 8–9, 19
    through charity, 157–8
    of church, 158–62
Moravians, 263–4
Morcante, Giovanni Domenico, 147–9
Morcante, Mariana, 147–50
Morel, Jean François, 71, 111
Morel, Michel, 110–11
Morel, Petramande, 71
Morellet, Jacques, 209–10
Morély, Jean, 24
Moreno, Doris, 8–9, 31–2, 37, 63
Moriscos, 29–30, 36–9
Morone, Giovanni, 29–30, 193–5
Mosaic Law, 200–1
Mott, Luiz, 246
Mouri, Jehan, 183–4, 189
Moya de Contreras, Pedro, 245–6, 267–8,
    270–1
Mozambique, 292–3
Muslims. *See* Islam
mysticism, 36–7

Nagasaki, 292–3
Nalle, Sara, 123–4, 176
Name of God (Nome di Dio), 36–7
Naphy, William, 8, 18–19, 66–7, 121, 335–6
narrative experience, 132
nascent state, 52–4
Nassau, 24
national boundaries, 3–4

national discipline, 22–3
nationalism, 3–4
Navetta, Jehan, 210
Neapolitan archbishops and bishops, 33–4
negotiation, 204–6
  with church members, 208–11
  of communal harmony, 211–12
  of final sentence, 223–7
  of penance, 206–8, 220–2
nell'Emilia, Reggio, 318–19
Neri, Philip, 174–5
Netanyahu, Benzion, 145–6
Netherlands, 4–7, 15, 20–1, 24–5, 113, 155, 181–2
  consistorial-synodal system of, 23–4
  New Netherlands, 253–5, 259–61
  women in, 45–6
Neuchâtel, 104–5
New Christians, 257, 272, 293–5, 299, 319, 322, 324–5
New England, 253–5
New France, 254–5
new institutional history, 7
New Jerusalem, 334–5
New Netherlands, 253–5, 259–61
New Spain, 37, 86, 254–5
New Testament, 5
New World, 86–7
nicodemism, 178
Niemeijer, Hendrik, 9–10, 73
Nieto, José C., 178
Nome di Dio (Name of God), 36–7
nonconformity, religious, 237–8
North Africa, 296
Northern Rising, 92–3
notarial contracts, 287
notarial records, 113
notaries, 35–6, 144–5
notulen (consistory records), 285

oaths, 46–7
Oestreich, Gerhard, 128
Olivares, Count-Duke of, 272
Olivi, Giovanni Battista de Freschi, 57–8
O'Malley, John, 333–4
Ometochtli, Don Carlos, 269–70
Omnímoda, 266
On the Libertines (Calvin), 206–7
Ordinance of 1624, 282–3
ordinary, 224
original sin, 339–40

orthodoxy, 37, 163–4, 240, 253
Ortiz, Francisco, 178, 198–9, 202
Ortiz, Tomás, 266–7
Ovalle y Pizarro, Isabel de, 57–8

Padroado, 268
paganism, 39, 300–1
paillardise (fornication), 68–9
Palatinate, 24
Papa, Pierre, 237
Papal Bull of Excommunication, 92–3
Papal State, 28–31, 53–4, 85–6
Pape, Jacques, 185–6
Páramo, Luis de, 116–17, 122–3, 125
parish presbyteries, 42
Parker, Charles, 159–60
partially proven, 61–2
party-and-party litigation, 90–1, 98
pastoral care, 180–1
pastoral renewal, 92–3
pastorate, 15–16
patriarchal family, 274–5
Patronato, 266–8
Paul (saint), 30–1
Paul III (pope), 30
Paul IV (pope), 30–1, 123, 170–1
Paul V (pope), 123–5, 174, 327
Pays de Vaud, 130–2, 159–60
Peace of Westphalia, 311
Peña, Francisco, 35, 56–7, 218–19, 225–6
penalties, 47–50, 61–4
penance, 95–8, 308–11, 331–6
  negotiation of, 206–8, 220–2
penitence, 1–2
  public, 311–12
Pentecostal churches, 316
Peralta, Alonso de, 224–5
Pereira, Antonia, 82–4
Pereira, Diego, 146–7
Pereira, Luis, 298
perjury, 109
perpetual incarceration, 62–3
Perrin, Ami, 24–5, 112–13
Perrinist party, 24–5
Perry, Mary Elizabeth, 240, 245–6
personal morality, 91
personnel, 41–3
  Inquisitions and, 117–18
  lay, 108–9
Perth, Scotland, 41–3, 46, 48–50
Peru, 37, 86, 267–8, 270, 276–7

Peter of Arbués, 174–5
Peter of Verona, 118–19, 174
Peters, Edward, 56–7
Pettegree, Andrew, 205–6
Philip II (king), 30–2, 197–8, 267–8, 272
Philip IV (king), 272
Philip V (king), 320–1
Philippines, 267–8
Philosophical Dictionary (Voltaire), 116
Pieterszoon, Lenaert, 189–90
Pius V (pope), 123, 170
plague, 49–50
plantation colony, 261–2
pluralism, religious, 263–4
Police de l'Église réformée de Bayeux, 22
politico-religious unity, 167
Pollmann, Judith, 106, 129, 133, 235
Poma de Ayala, Guaman, 86
Pombal, Marquis de, 292, 321–2
poor tax, 157–8
popular culture, 134
popular superstitions, 169
Portugal, 1–3, 10–11, 28, 31–2
    censorship in, 169
    execution rates in, 38–9
    Inquisition of, 53–5, 218
    Inquisitors of, 118–22
Portuguese Binnenkerk, 283–4
Portuguese Buitenkerk, 283–4
Poska, Allyson, 9–10, 229
possession, 34–5
potro (rack), 61
poverty, 79, 99–100, 286
premarital sex, 99–100
Presbyterians, 93, 98, 334
presence, politics of, 171–5
print media, 162
private plantations, 261–2
private sin, 25–6, 207–8, 307–8
processi (processes), 32
proofs of guilt, 221–2
property
    rights, 288
    seizure of, 61–2
Proposiciones, 320–1
prosecution
    lay, 44–7
    protocols of, 52
prosecutor (*fiscale*), 34
Prosperi, Adriano, 29–30, 334
prostitutes, 49

provincial synods, 25
provisional judges (*juezes de commission*), 82
psychological force, 60–1
public humiliation, 48
public morality, 306, 313
public penitence, 311–12
public records, 135
public scandal, 25–6, 207–8
public sin, 25–6, 207–8, 306–8
Pulido, Juan Ignacio, 174
Pullan, Brian, 145–6
punishment, 308–11
Puritans, 93–4, 98, 101–2, 253
purity of blood (*limpieza de sangre*), 271–2,
    321–3

Quakers, 260–1
queen of proofs, 57–8
Quemada, Licenciado, 199–200
Quiroga, Gaspar de, 124–5

race, 246, 273–8
rack (*potro*), 61
Raemond, Florimond de, 134–5
rationalism, 10–11
Real Mesa Censória, 322
received doctrine, 17
recidivism, 294–7
reconciliation, 164–5, 311–12
Reformatio legum ecclesiasticarum, 91–2
Reformed worship, 134–5
refugees, 24–5
regalism, 321–2
regimento, 322
registration procedures, 130–3
Reinhard, Wolfgang, 5–6, 128
relaciones de causas, 142, 150–1
religion. *See also specific religions*
    culture of, 155–6
    feasts, 171–2
    nonconformity and, 237–8
    observance of, 91
    pluralism of, 263–4
Renaissance inquisitors, 125
reparation of honor, 137
repentance, 160–1
    performance of, 308–9
    resistance to, 216–17
    seat of, 48
    tokens of, 96–7
Reportorio of processos, 301–2

Representación a Carlos IV sobre lo que era el Tribunal de la Inquisición, 321
res mixtae, 306–7, 309–11, 313, 315
resistance, silent, 178
reversed sins, 334
Revista de Archivos, Bibliotecas, y Museos, 193
Richecourt, Count of, 317–18
Rieder, Philip, 104–5
Riego, Rafael de, 325–6
Righetto, Abraham, 198–9
righteous correction, 53–4
Ripoll, Cayetano, 326
ritual actors, 134–5
rivalries, 189
Rivilliod, Aimé, 189
Rivit, Jacques, 68–9
Robinson, Marilynne, 339–40
Rojas, Francisco, 274–5
Rojas, Juan de, 125
Roldan, Juan Francisco, 81
Roman Congregation of Inquisition, 118
Roman Inquisition, 30–4, 36–7, 53–4, 140, 327
Roman Inquisitors, 118–22
Roman law, 5, 28, 52, 56–8, 77
Roodenburg, Herman, 209–10, 312–13
Rota, 56–7
Roth, Cecil, 145
Roth, Norman, 145–6
Rulman, Anne, 165
rumor, 44–5

Sabean, David, 137
Sacraments of the Gospel, 332–3
Sacred Congregation, 60–2, 327
sacred justice, 64
sacred sites, 155–6
Sacro Arsenale (Masini), 35, 218–19
Salazar Frías, Alonso de, 193–4, 216–17
Salgado, James, 28–9
San Juan de Huaylla, Ambrosío Martínezin, 86
San Miguel, Marina de, 275–6
Sánchez Ortega, María Helena, 240, 244
sanctification, 134–8
Sanhedrin, 17–18
Santo Domingo, 86, 266–7
Saraiva, António José, 145–6
Sardinia, 34, 317–18
Scandella, Menocchio, 32–3
Scandinavia, 6–7, 259–60

Schilling, Heinz, 3, 5–6, 128, 205–6, 286
Schlau, Stacey, 241–2
Schutte, Anne Jacobson, 240, 247
Schwartz, Stuart, 273–4
Scotland, 8–9, 15, 38, 41–3, 49, 72–3, 93, 106–7, 113–14, 128, 131, 159, 164, 166, 209–10, 315, 333, 336, 338
  civil authorities in, 73–4
  consistorial model in, 23–4
  districts in, 44
  illegitimacy in, 308–9
  jurisdiction in, 43–4
  kirk sessions in, 73–4, 96–7, 155, 209–10, 308–9
  national discipline and, 22–3
  Perth, 41–3, 46, 48–50
seat of repentance. *See* stool of repentance
Second Anglo-Dutch War (1665–1667), 261–2
Second Book of Discipline, 23–4
second consistory, 108–11
secret heresies, 55–6
secretaries, 18–19
secular courts, 84–5
  criminal, 66
  English church courts and, 98–9
secular discipline, 311–12
secular justice, 64
secular law, 56
secular power, 53–4
Seghizzi, Michele, 32–3
seigneurie, 309–10
self-denunciation, 32
Selijns, Henricus, 261
Senate, 108–9
sentences
  criminal, 66–8
  final, 223–7
Sephardim, 271–2
Servand, François, 110–11
servants, 104–5
  household, 210
  women as, 25
Servetus, Michael, 70, 229, 334–5
Severina (saint), 218–19
sexuality, 74–5, 229–30, 234–5, 273–4, 286
  homosexuality, 277
  offenses of, 68–9, 71–2, 91, 99–100
  premarital sex, 99–100
  scandals and, 87
Siam, 281

Siebenhüner, Kim, 8, 54, 170
silent resistance, 178
Simancas, Diego de, 122–3
Simões Margiocchi, Francisco, 326–7
simulated drowning (*toca*), 61
Sixtus IV (pope), 30
Sixtus V (pope), 120–1, 123
slaves, 257–64
  blasphemy and, 275
  female, 287–8
  maltreatment of, 284–5
  trade of, 272–3
Smail, Daniel, 54
Small Council, 18–19, 66–9, 71–2, 186, 235
small farmers (*labradores*), 79
Smyth, Thomas, 48–9
social conflict, 164, 286
social context, colonial, 287–8
social control, 104, 108, 191, 225–6,
  289–90, 315, 328
social differences, 166
social discipline, 309–10, 333
social norms, 140–1
social power, 209–10
Society of Surinam, 261–2, 264–5
sodomy, 55–6, 80–1, 196–7, 246–8, 277,
  324–5
Sodrinho de Mesquita, Rui, 296
Soler, Vincent, 256–7, 259
"Soli Deo Gloria," 134–5
Soman, Alfred, 136–7
sorcerer (*feitiçero*), 275–6
Sousa, Fray Antonio de, 218
South America, 10
Soutier, Claude, 231–2
Spaans, Joke, 10–11, 238
Spain, 1–3, 10–11, 28–30, 33–4, 82–3.
  See also Suprema
  Anglo-Spanish wars, 324
  censorship in, 169–70
  execution rates in, 38–9
  Franco-Spanish conflict, 324
  Inquisition of, 28–9, 53–6, 217
    church courts and, 84–5
    jurisdiction and, 56
  Inquisitors of, 118–22
  New Spain, 37, 86, 254–5
  Succession of, 317–20
Spierling, Karen, 8–9, 104–5, 180–1,
  216–18, 224–6
spiritual discipline, 311–12

spiritual jurisdiction, 312–14
spontaneous appearance, 35–6, 170–1
spontaneous confessions, 54
sponte comparentes, 140, 146–7, 150–1
stadskerk, 285
Starr-LeBeau, Gretchen, 7–8, 45–6
state courts, 3–4
state power, 5
status animarum (state-of-souls), 36–7
statute law, 49–50
statutory penalties, 47–8
stool of repentance, 48, 160–1
strappado (*garrucha*), 61
Stuyvesant, Petrus, 260
Suárez, Francisco, 170–1
sub-judicial justice, 164–5
subjustice, 75
substantial local knowledge, 111
Sufism, 36–7
sugar production, 264
superstitions, 34–5
  popular, 169
Suprema, 31–5, 118–20, 122–3, 125–6,
  146–7, 217
  administrative resources of, 3
  Sardinia and, 34
  sodomy and, 246
  torture and, 60
Supreme Council (*Consejo Superior*), 174–5
Surinam, 254–5, 261–5
suspicion, 168–71
Swenton, John, 46
Swiss Confederacy, 309–10
Switzerland, 2–3, 6–7, 21–2, 128, 137–8
Synod of Dordrecht, 23–4, 282–3, 338–9
synods, 25, 78–9, 256–7

Tacet, Estienne, 190–1
tachas, 58
Taiwan, 281
Tavuzzi, Michael, 123–5
Tedeschi, John, 29–30
Ten Commandments, 229–30
Teresa of Avila, 229, 238, 242
Ternate, 280–1
Thirty Years War, 310, 333
Tissot, Pierre, 112–13
toca (simulated drowning), 61
Todd, Margo, 7–8, 70–1, 106–7, 113,
  160–1, 164–5, 308
tokens of repentance, 96–7

tolerance, 328
Toleration Act, 102
Toral, Francisco de, 269–70
Torquemada (Inquisitor General), 34
Torres, Cristóbal de, 172–4
torture, 40–1, 59–61, 146–7, 218–20
  Holy Office and, 59
  interrogative, 52
  Suprema and, 60
  of women, 242
town watch, 44–5
Tractatus de haeresi (Farinacci), 35
trade-church (*handelskerk*), 262
trading ports, 279
translations, 144–5
translators, 35–6
Transylvania, 24, 42
treasurer of the poor fund, 157
Treaty of Breda, 261–2
Treaty of Cateau-Cambrésis, 30–1
Trexler, Richard, 78–81
trial summaries, 142, 150–1
Tribunal of Jurisdiction, 318–19
Tribunal of Pisa, 224
Truffet, Pierre, 187–8
truth, 46–7, 146–7, 149
Tully, Effie, 44–5
Tupis, 258
Tuscany, Grand Duchy of, 317–18
Twinam, Ann, 246–7
Tymmermann, Hermann, 189

University of Bologna, 86
University of Coimbra, 120
University of Salamanca, 202
unmarried women, 68
Unzaga, Diego de, 81–2
urban boundaries, 3–4
urban courts, 85–6, 98
urban tribunals, 42–3
utilization of justice (*Justiznutzung*), 147
Uytenbogaert, Johannes, 4–5

Valangin, 104–5
Valdés, Juan, 30–1, 170–1
Valencia, Martín de, 266
van Aetdael, Rogier, 184
van der Vinct, Oliver, 188–9
van Limborch, Philipp, 28–9, 336–7
van Vijven, Lieven, 184
Varro, Michel, 111–12

Vatican, 338–9
Velasco, Sherry, 244–5
Vellut, Guillaume, 111–12
Venetian State, 32
Venitt, Beti de, 81–2
Vergara, Juan de, 198
via por fuerza, 84–5
Viana, Manuel João, 299–300
vicar general, 81
vicars, 34–5
viceroys, 32
vices, 25–6
Vietnam, 281
Villagómez, Pedro de, 270
Villegas, Pedro de, 196–7
Viret, Pierre, 159–60
Virgin Mary, 233–4
visitadores (inspector generals), 81–2
visitations, 93–4
VOC. *See* Dutch East India Company
Voltaire, 28–9, 116–17
votos, 223–7
Vuarin, Claude, 188–9
Vulliermoz, Claude, 69–70

Wadsworth, James, 10–11, 238
Waldensians, 36–7
Ward, Kerry, 279–80
Wars of Religion, 35–6, 73, 211–12, 308
Watson, Helen, 49–50
Watt, Jeffrey, 9–10, 70–1, 104–5
Weber, Alison, 240, 242
West India Company (WIC), 253–7,
  259–60, 264
White, Blanco, 176–7
white population, 277
WIC. *See* West India Company
Wilcox, Thomas, 93–4
witchcraft, 85–6, 216–17, 276–7, 324–5
witch-hunts, 38–9
witnesses, 140
  secrecy of, 58
  testimony of, 145–6, 151
women, 9–10, 24–5, 198, 200–1, 230–1
  agency of, 234–5
  alumbradismo and, 275–6
  discipline and, 234–5
  dress of, 165
  false sanctity of, 37
  gossip networks of, 45–6
  institutional sociability and, 235

Judaizing of, 245–6
magic and, 244
oaths and, 46–7
servant, 25
as slaves, 287–8
testimony of, 46–7, 82
torture of, 242
unmarried, 68
work of, 235–6
Württemberg, Duchy of, 310

Ximenéz de Reynoso, Alonso, 223

Yucatán, 269–70

Zapata Cisneros y Mendoza, Antonio,
    124–5
Zaragoza tribunal, 324
Zeeland, 261–5
Zumárraga, Juan de, 266–7, 269–70
Zwingli, Huldrych, 30–1, 159–60

Lightning Source UK Ltd.
Milton Keynes UK
UKHW020637290620
365657UK00015BA/186

9 781316 505861